A PRACTICAL GUIDE
TO FAMILY PROCEEDINGS

A PRACTICAL GUIDE
TO FAMILY PROCEEDINGS

District Judge Robert Blomfield TD

Helen Brooks

The Training Officer of the
Principal Registry of the
Family Division

𝑓 Family Law

2002

Published by Family Law
a publishing imprint of
Jordan Publishing Limited
21 St Thomas Street
Bristol BS1 6JS

British Library Cataloguing-in-Publication Data
A catalogue record for this book is available from the British Library.

ISBN 0 85308 763 6

Photoset by Mendip Communications Ltd, Frome, Somerset
Printed and bound in Great Britain by Bell & Bain Ltd, Glasgow

FOREWORD

Courts at all levels are concerned that delay is caused and costs wasted when practitioners make errors in documentation and in preparation for court hearings. It is not always easy to identify the correct procedure and therefore this practical guide, based on extensive experience, is to be welcomed as a useful and helpful addition to the library of family law publications.

The Honourable Mrs Justice Bracewell
Family Division

PREFACE TO THE FIRST EDITION

This book is intended to be, as the title implies, a practical guide and aid, and is not a substitute for major published texts such as *The Family Court Practice* (Family Law) (the 'Red Book') and *Rayden and Jackson on Divorce and Family Matters* (Butterworths). The text principally deals with commonplace aspects of family law work, together with some areas which are rather more unusual. However, it is by no means exhaustive and there are some matters which the authors felt were inappropriate for inclusion in a work of this length. Similarly, procedures to be adopted have in many cases been abbreviated in order to simplify the presentation and with the intention of making it more readily understood.

It is often said that the break-up of a family is one of the most, if not in many ways *the* most, traumatic experience which can affect an individual. That being so, it is perhaps up to all of us who are involved in the process of resolving the resultant problems to do our best to ensure that those involved can return to a life of normality with the minimum of delay. Perhaps this is more likely to be achieved if practitioners are able to persuade clients to be realistic and adopt a sensible and conciliatory attitude. Of course, there will inevitably be cases which defy all the best attempts to engender such an approach but at least practitioners can create the appropriate environment, by pointing their clients in the right direction, making it clear what orders are likely to be made and above all else by getting the simple things right.

The origins of this book lie in the frustration which the authors have frequently experienced as a result of, what are often quite elementary, errors made by practitioners in procedure and in the preparation of documents for presentation to the court. These errors cause not only a considerable amount of unnecessary work for the court office but also for hard-pressed solicitors, with the attendant wasted costs and sense of frustration. It also creates a great deal of unnecessary and avoidable delay in matters being successfully concluded.

The authors hope that, in using this book, practitioners will be able to avoid the vast majority of the most common pitfalls.

District Judge Robert Blomfield TD

Helen Brooks
The Training Officer of the
Principal Registry of the Family Division

PREFACE TO THE SECOND EDITION

In this second edition we have reviewed and revised the book generally and, where necessary, have amended and updated the text. In addition, we have included a completely new chapter on reciprocal enforcement of maintenance orders, an area of practice in which solicitors often have considerable difficulty. As a result of recommendations made to us by practitioners, we have also persuaded our publishers to include the complete Family Proceedings Rules. At Appendix C, there is a comprehensive list of organisations which may be able to assist disabled litigants.

If any of our readers think that they have found an error, anywhere in the book, we would welcome being told, even if that error is thought to be insignificant or unimportant. We would also welcome any constructive comment on possible improvements, or as to any additional material which might be included in the next edition.

Finally, we have to say that we have been very pleasantly surprised by all the interest which has been shown in our book and flattered by all the generous praise. It is our hope that this second edition will prove to be equally well received.

District Judge Robert Blomfield TD

Helen Brooks
The Training Officer of the Principal
Registry of the Family Division

ACKNOWLEDGEMENT

The authors wish to thank District Judge Graham Maple of the Principal Registry of the Family Division for his thoughts on a number of amendments which have been incorporated in this second edition and, in particular, with regard to his contribution to the new chapter on Reciprocal Enforcement of Maintenance Orders.

ACKNOWLEDGEMENT

The author owes a debt to...

CONTENTS

. . . .

Special procedure documentation

Requests for directions for trial otherwise than under the special procedure provisions

Matrimonial applications and orders

Sundry documentation

TABLE OF CASES AND PRACTICE DIRECTIONS

References are to paragraph numbers.

TABLE OF STATUTES

References are to paragraph numbers and to checklists and Appendix documents.

TABLE OF STATUTORY INSTRUMENTS

References are to paragraph numbers and to checklists and Appendix documents.

TABLE OF ABBREVIATIONS

LEGISLATION

AA 1955	Army Act 1955
AD(E)O 1996	Attachment of Debts (Expenses) Order 1996, SI 1996/3098
AEA 1971	Attachment of Earnings Act 1971
AFA 1955	Air Force Act 1955
CA 1989	Children Act 1989
CACA 1985	Child Abduction and Custody Act 1985
CAFCASS	Children and Family Court Advisory and Support Service
C(AP)O 1991	Children (Allocation of Proceedings) Order 1991, SI 1991/1677
CCA 1981	County Courts Act 1981
CCR	County Court Rules 1981, SI 1981/1687
CLA(Gen)Regs 1989	Civil Legal Aid (General) Regulations 1989, SI 1989/339
CLA(Gen)A Regs 2000	Civil Legal Aid (General) Amendment Regulations 2000, SI 2000/451
CLS(F)Regs 2000	Community Legal Services (Financial) Regulations 2000, SI 2000/516
CPR 1998	Civil Procedure Rules 1998, SI 1998/3132
CSA 1991	Child Support Act 1991
DMPA 1973	Domicile and Matrimonial Proceedings Act 1973
D(P) Regs 2000	Divorce etc (Pensions) Regulations 2000, SI 2000/1123
FLA 1986	Family Law Act 1986
FLA 1996	Family Law Act 1996
FLA 1996(Pt IV)(AP)O 1997	Family Law Act 1996 (Part IV) (Allocation of Proceedings) Order 1997, SI 1997/1896
FLRA 1969	Family Law Reform Act 1969
FPR 1991	Family Proceedings Rules 1991, SI 1991/1247
HCCCJO 1991	High Court and County Courts Jurisdiction Order 1991, SI 1991/724
I(PFD)A 1975	Inheritance (Provision for Family and Dependants) Act 1975
LAA 1988	Legal Aid Act 1988
MCA 1973	Matrimonial Causes Act 1973
MC(REMO)R 1974	Magistrates' Courts (Reciprocal Enforcement of Maintenance Orders) Rules 1974, SI 1974/668

MFPA 1984	Matrimonial and Family Proceedings Act 1984
MOA 1950/1958	Maintenance Orders Act 1950/1958
MO(RE)A 1972	Maintenance Orders (Reciprocal Enforcement) Act 1972
MWPA 1882	Married Women's Property Act 1882
NDA 1957	Naval Discipline Act 1957
NF(EML)A 1947	Naval Forces (Enforcement of Maintenance Liabilities) Act 1947
PA 1995	Pensions Act 1995
PD(C) Regs 2000	Pensions on Divorce etc (Charging) Regulations 2000, SI 2000/1049
PHA 1997	Protection from Harassment Act 1997
RSC	Rules of the Supreme Court 1965, SI 1965/1776
TLATA 1996	Trusts of Land and Appointment of Trustees Act 1996
WRPA 1999	Welfare Reform and Pensions Act 1999

PRACTICE DIRECTIONS

PD of 3 June 1958	Registrar's Direction (Proceeding on Answer)
PD of 15 December 1960	Practice Direction (Charge of Adultery against Girl under 16 Years) [1960] 1 All ER 129
PD of 19 December 1964	Practice Direction (Divorce: Application to Expedite Decree Absolute) [1964] 1 WLR 1473, [1964] 3 All ER 775
PD of 17 February 1972	Practice Direction (Blood Tests) [1972] 1 WLR 353, [1972] 1 All ER 640
PD of 7 May 1974	Practice Direction of 7 May 1974
PD of 8 May 1975	Practice Direction (Omission of Petitioner's Address) [1975] 1 WLR 787, [1975] 2 All ER 223
PD(N) of 10 February 1976	Practice Note of 10 February 1976
PD of 15 June 1977	Practice Direction (Expedition of Decree Absolute: Special Procedure Cases) [1977] 1 WLR 1123, [1978] 2 All ER 714
PD of 19 December 1978	Practice Direction (Divorce: Directions for Trial) [1979] 1 WLR 2
PD of 10 March 1980	Practice Direction (Maintenance Orders: Registration in Magistrates' Court) [19080] 1 WLR 354, [1980] 1 All ER 1007
PD of 8 December 1981	Practice Direction (Joinder as Parties) [1982] 1 WLR 118, [1982] 1 All ER 319
PD of 15 October 1987	Practice Direction (Removal from Jurisdiction)
PD of 13 February 1989	Practice Direction (Disclosure of Addresses by Government Departments) [1989] 1 WLR 219, [1989] 1 All ER 765, [1989] 1 FLR 307
PD of 18 October 1991	Practice Direction (Children: Conciliation)

PD of 5 June 1992 — Practice Direction (Family Division: Distribution of Business) [1992] 1 WLR 586, [1992] 3 All ER 151, [1992] 2 FLR 87

PD of 22 February 1993 — Practice Direction (Children Act 1989: Applications by Children) [1993] 1 WLR 313, [1993] 1 All ER 820, [1993] 1 FLR 668

PD of 10 July 1995 — Practice Direction (Consolidation)

PD of 16 June 1997 — Practice Direction (Ancillary Relief Procedure: Pilot Scheme) [1997] 2 FLR 304

PD of 22 April 1999 — Practice Direction (Civil Procedure Rules 1998: Allocation of Cases: Costs) [1999] 1 FLR 1295

PD of 9 December 1999 — President's Direction (Family Law Act 1996: Attendance of Arresting Officer) [2000] 1 FLR 270

PD of 10 March 2000 — President's Direction (Court Bundles) [2000] 1 WLR 737, [2000] 2 All ER 287, [2000] 1 FLR 537

PD of 25 May 2000 — President's Direction (Ancillary Relief Procedure) [2000] 1 WLR 1480, [2000] 3 All ER 379, [2000] 1 FLR 997

PD of 16 March 2001 — President's Direction: Committal Applications

OTHER

BFPO — British Forces Post Office

Rayden — *Rayden and Jackson on Divorce and Family Matters* (Butterworths), 17th edition

Part I

PROCEEDINGS FOR:

DIVORCE
JUDICIAL SEPARATION
NULLITY
PRESUMPTION OF DEATH AND DISSOLUTION
DECLARATION OF MARITAL STATUS
DECLARATION OF PARENTAGE, LEGITIMACY
AND LEGITIMATION

CHAPTER 1

THE DIVORCE PETITION

1.1 INTRODUCTION

FPR 1991, r 2.2(1)

Divorce proceedings are initiated by a petition.

The proceedings are sometimes referred to as a divorce suit. The party to the marriage who issues the petition is referred to as the petitioner; the party against whom it is issued is referred to as the respondent.

All matters relating to the issue of a petition and the way in which it is conducted are determined by the provisions of the Matrimonial Causes Act 1973 (MCA 1973) (as amended) and the Family Proceedings Rules 1991 (FPR 1991) (as amended). Both the Act and the Rules, together with annotations, are set out in *The Family Court Practice* (Family Law, annual) and *Rayden and Jackson on Divorce and Family Matters* (Butterworths) 17th edn (referred to throughout this book as '*Rayden*'). The Rules are also to be found at Appendix D of this book.

1.2 QUALIFYING CRITERIA

In order to issue a petition for divorce it is necessary to satisfy the following criteria:

MCA 1973, s 3(1)

(a) the parties must have been married for more than one year immediately preceding the presentation of the petition;

(b) as from 1 March 2001, where it is alleged that the court has jurisdiction under the Council Regulation, the grounds of jurisdiction under Article 2(1) must be stated:

    (i) the petitioner and respondent are both habitually resident in England and Wales;

    (ii) the petitioner and respondent were last habitually resident in England and Wales and the petitioner (or respondent) still resides there;

    (iii) the respondent is habitually resident in England and Wales;

    (iv) the petitioner is habitually resident in England and Wales and has resided there for at least one year immediately prior to the presentation of the petition (in which case relevant addresses should be given, with the length of time lived at each address);

(v)   the petitioner is domiciled and habitually resident in England and Wales and has resided there for at least six months immediately prior to the presentation of the petition;

(vi) the petitioner and the respondent are both domiciled in England and Wales;

Art 2(1) of Council Regulation (EC) No 1347/2000

or, if the court has jurisdiction other than under the Council Regulation, this should be stated and either of the parties must:

(i)   be domiciled in England and Wales (by either birth or choice) at the date of the presentation of the petition; or

FPR 1991, App 2, para 1(c)

(ii) have been habitually resident in England and Wales for a period of not less than one year immediately preceding the presentation of the petition.

FPR 1991, App 2, para 1(d) and DMPA 1973, s 5(2)

It should be noted that the Council Regulation is binding in all member States of the European Union with the exception of Denmark.

(c)   the marriage must have irretrievably broken down by reason of one of the five facts detailed in MCA 1973, s 1(2).

Note: For an example of the wording to be used where one of the parties has been habitually resident in England and Wales for a period of not less than one year immediately preceding the presentation of the petition, see para 3 of the petition at Appendix A(3). For examples of jurisdiction being stated under the Council Regulation, see para 3 of the petitions at Appendix A(1) and (2).

1.3   GROUND FOR DIVORCE

Under the MCA 1973, irretrievable breakdown is the sole ground for a divorce and must be recited on the face of the petition.

FPR 1991, App 2, para 1(l)

The five facts which constitute reasons for irretrievable breakdown are as follows:

(a)   the respondent has committed adultery and the petitioner finds it intolerable to live with the respondent;

(b)   the respondent has behaved in such a way that the petitioner cannot reasonably be expected to live with the respondent (unreasonable behaviour);

(c)   the respondent has deserted the petitioner for a continuous period of at least two years immediately preceding the presentation of the petition;

(d) the parties to the marriage have lived apart for a continuous period of at least two years immediately preceding the presentation of the petition and the respondent consents to a decree being granted;

(e) the parties to the marriage have lived apart for a continuous period of at least five years immediately preceding the presentation of the petition.

MCA 1973, s 1(2)(a)–(e)

1.3.1 Adultery

FPR 1991, r 2.7(1)

If adultery is alleged against an identified person, he/she is referred to as the co-respondent. However, there is no requirement for the petitioner to name a co-respondent even if his/her identity is known.

Even when the identity of the co-respondent is known, it is usually better not to name that person. Leaving the co-respondent unidentified will avoid potential problems with regard to service and the possibility of an answer being filed. Dealing with the matter in this way will invariably ensure that the proceedings are not unnecessarily delayed and that areas of friction are minimised. It is also likely to keep costs to a minimum. Whilst a petitioner may feel particularly vindictive and/or deeply hurt and therefore may wish to name a co-respondent, it is sensible to try to dissuade him/her from taking such a course.

FPR 1991, r 2.7(2)

If the petitioner makes an allegation that the respondent has raped another person, under no circumstances should that person be named as a co-respondent, unless otherwise ordered by a judge.

MCA 1973, s 2(1)

Once a spouse has knowledge of adultery but chooses to continue to reside with the other spouse for a period exceeding six months, it will no longer be possible to rely on that particular act of adultery. However, if the adultery is continuing, each further act will have the effect of recommencing the six-month period.

FPR 1991, App 2, para 1(m)

In the case of an adultery petition, brief particulars of the allegation or allegations should be recited and, where possible, the relevant date(s) and place(s).

1.3.2 Unreasonable behaviour

Where a petition is based upon unreasonable behaviour, whilst it is possible to rely upon a single very serious allegation, usually it will be a course of conduct which has eventually resulted in the breakdown of the marriage. However, it is not necessary to set out a long rambling history of the marriage. Generally, details of the first, last

and most serious incidents will suffice. In short, the
petition should be kept as succinct as possible – avoid
being too verbose.

FPR 1991, App 2,
para 1(m)

1.3.3 Agreement prior to proceedings

Where possible, it is sensible to invite the respondent to
agree, in advance of the petition being filed, the proposed
details of the allegations to be made by the petitioner. This
simple expedient will reduce the areas of possible conflict
and provide an indication of the general approach to be
adopted. It is likely to assist in reaching agreement on
other matters and lead to an early conclusion of the
proceedings. It will also keep costs to a minimum.

1.3.4 Desertion, two years' separation with consent or five years' separation

In a petition based upon desertion, two years' separation
with consent or five years' separation, it is important to
provide details of the date upon which the parties
separated, together with brief details of the circumstances
bringing about the separation.

FPR 1991, App 2,
para 1(m)

Where a party is unable to recall the precise date of
separation, the pleading will refer to the date as being, for
example, 'in or about April 1995'. In these circumstances,
the relevant time for a petition based on MCA 1973, s 1(2)
(c), (d) or (e) will start to run from the last day of that
particular month.

With regard to a petition based on two years' separation
with consent or five years' separation, the husband and
wife will be treated as living apart even though they are
under the same roof, provided that the judge is satisfied
that they are living separate lives.

MCA 1973, s 2(6)

The test which is applied is a high one and the court will
require full details of the parties' living arrangements,
including those which relate to sleeping, eating and
domestic duties.

In the case of a petition based on two years' separation
with consent, details of how the consent is provided will
be found in Chapter 3.

No consent is required in order to obtain a decree nisi after
five years' separation and, accordingly, if the fact of the
five-year separation is not in dispute a decree cannot be
opposed. However, the respondent to the petition may be
able to prevent a divorce on the basis that the dissolution
of the marriage will result in grave financial or other

MCA 1973, s 5(1)

hardship and that it would be wrong in all the circumstances to dissolve the marriage.

Note: For fuller details of the procedure, see **4.1**.

FPR 1991, App 2,
para 1(k)

A petition based on five years' separation must also state whether or not any agreement or arrangement has been made or is proposed to be made between the parties for the support of the petitioner or respondent and any dependent child of the family.

1.4   ATTEMPTS AT RECONCILIATION

Under the provisions of MCA 1973, s 2, the parties are permitted to attempt a period or periods of reconciliation, not exceeding in total six months, without it affecting their entitlement to file a petition on any of the facts set out in s 1(2). In the case of a petition based upon desertion, two years' separation with consent, or five years' separation, the period or periods during which the parties have attempted reconciliation must be added to the relevant period. For example, if the parties make two attempts at reconciliation, one lasting two months and one three months, a total of five years and five months will have to elapse from the date of separation to the date of presentation, in respect of a petition based on five years' separation.

Bradley v Bradley [1973]
3 All ER 750

The fact that the parties have continued to live in the same household for a period in excess of six months will not necessarily be a bar to a petition based upon unreasonable behaviour in circumstances where there is no or no realistic alternative accommodation.

1.5   PLEADING MORE THAN ONE FACT

It is possible to plead more than one fact within a petition, either in tandem or in the alternative.

Note: Examples of both forms of pleading are to be found in the petitions at Appendix A(1) and (2).

1.6   CONTENTS OF THE PETITION

All the matters which must be included within the formal parts of the petition are set out in Appendix 2 to the FPR 1991, which has now been amended to comply with Art 2(1) of Council Regulation (EC) No 1347/2000 of 29 May 2000.

Note: See the various petitions included at Appendix A. The contents of the petition are also dealt with in detail in the checklist at the end of Chapter 2.

1.7 PRAYER

The petition must conclude with a prayer in which the petitioner sets out details of the decree and other orders which he/she is seeking.

FPR 1991, App 2, para 4(a)

1.8 SIGNATURE

The petition should be signed by the petitioner in person or by solicitors if they are intending to place themselves on the court record.

FPR 1991, r 2.5

1.9 ADDRESS FOR SERVICE

The petition must give an address for service in England and Wales, to which documents for the petitioner may be delivered or sent. If a solicitor is acting, this should be the solicitor's address. The solicitor's address may also be shown in a 'care of' capacity if the petitioner is receiving advice under the Legal Help Scheme.

FPR 1991, App 2, para 4(c)

An address for service should also be provided for the respondent and any named co-respondent.

FPR 1991, App 2, para 4(b)

1.10 FURTHER PETITIONS

It is important to note that, other than with leave of the court, a petitioner may not issue a second petition for divorce until the first petition has been dismissed or otherwise disposed of.

FPR 1991, r 2.6(4)

Note: For circumstances in which leave may be granted for the filing of a second or further petition, see **5.2**.

1.11 EXAMPLES OF PETITIONS

There are four examples of petitions to be found at Appendix A(1)–(4). These are for:

(1) divorce based upon desertion and adultery (in tandem);

(2) divorce based upon unreasonable behaviour and two years' separation with the respondent's consent (in the alternative);

(3) divorce based upon five years' separation, where:

    (i) neither party is domiciled in England and Wales but where one party has been habitually resident in the jurisdiction for a period of at least six months; and

    (ii) the whereabouts of the respondent is not known to the petitioner;

(4) judicial separation based upon unreasonable behaviour and which incorporates an allegation of an improper association.

Note: Proceedings for a decree of judicial separation are dealt with in Chapter 8.

CHAPTER 2

REQUIREMENTS ON ISSUE OF PETITION

2.1 WHICH COURT?

A petition can be issued in the Principal Registry of the Family Division or any county court in England and Wales which has divorce jurisdiction. Neither party is required to reside within the jurisdiction of a particular court.

MFPA 1984, s 33

2.2 DOCUMENTS TO BE FILED

The following should be filed in order to issue proceedings:

(a) the petition;

(b) a copy petition for service on the respondent and every named co-respondent;

FPR 1991, r 2.6(5)
MCA 1973, s 6(1)

(c) a certificate of reconciliation in Form M3.
Note that a certificate of reconciliation is required only where solicitors are acting for the petitioner and intending to place themselves on the court record. It should not be filed where solicitors are merely advising the client under the Legal Help Scheme created by the Access to Justice Act 1999, which came into force on 1 April 2000;

FPR 1991, r 2.6(2)

(d) the marriage certificate.
Note that:

(i) if not in English, a certified translation of the certificate will also be required;

(ii) in exceptional circumstances, most usually where proceedings need to be commenced urgently, a district judge can give leave for the petition to be filed without a marriage certificate but will generally require it to be filed by a specified

FPR 1991, r 2.6(2)

date. For marriages which took place in England and Wales, a certified copy certificate can be obtained from the Family Records Centre, 1 Myddelton Street, London EC1R 1UW. The telephone enquiry number is 0151 471 4800;

(iii) there may be some cases in which there is no marriage certificate, for example where the parties have been married in accordance with tribal custom or where, in a war-torn country, the certificate has been lost and a copy cannot be obtained. In such an event, directions should be sought from a district judge;

(iv) if there is a discrepancy between the parties' current names and the names which appear on the marriage certificate, an explanation must be set out in paragraph 1 of the petition;

Note: An example of the appropriate wording is to be found in the petition at Appendix A(2).

(e) a statement of arrangements in Form M4 in respect of any minor child of the family who is:

(i) under the age of 16 years; or

(ii) between the age of 16 and 18 years and receiving instruction at an educational establishment or undergoing training for a trade, profession or vocation, whether or not he/she is also in gainful employment.

The statement must always be signed by the petitioner personally and not by solicitors on his/her behalf;

FPR 1991, r 2.2(2)

Note: See **14.2** for more comprehensive details regarding a statement of arrangements.

(f) a copy statement for service on the respondent;

FPR 1991, r 2.6(5)

(g) copies of all orders relating to previous proceedings and referred to within the petition which concerns either the marriage or the children of the family.

2.3 OTHER CONSIDERATIONS

2.3.1 Persons under disability

Special rules apply to a party to the proceedings who is under a disability, by reason of either being under the age of majority (at present 18 years) or mental incapacity. These rules are complex and should be carefully considered prior to the filing of a petition or answer. If there is any doubt as to the appropriate steps to be taken, an application for directions should be made to a district judge so that appropriate guidance can be obtained.

FPR 1991, r 9

2.3.2 Court fee

At the time of issue, the appropriate court fee must be paid. If the person concerned is being advised under the Legal Help Scheme or is otherwise in receipt of State benefit, an application for exemption of court fee, signed by the petitioner in person, will be required. The application will be referred to an executive officer of the issuing court for authorisation.

Note: A comprehensive checklist for issuing a petition is to be found at the end of this chapter which, if followed, should eradicate most if not all of the most commonly made errors.

2.3.3 Omitting petitioner's address

If a petitioner wishes to omit his/her address from the petition, the leave of a district judge will be required. The rules provide for the court to order that the requirements of FPR 1991, Appendix 2 be waived.

FPR 1991, r 2.3 and PD
of 8 May 1975

The application is made ex parte (ie without notice being given to the respondent) at the time the petition is issued and is supported by an affidavit or signed statement setting out the reasons why the application is being made. It is advisable to check with the court in which the petition is to be issued as to whether an affidavit or a statement is required. The application attracts a court fee, unless the petitioner is exempt from fees.

If leave is granted, the court will lodge and retain the petitioner's address on the court file in a sealed envelope. The envelope is not to be opened without leave of a judge and is endorsed accordingly.

Note: An example of a petition in which the petitioner's address is omitted is to be found in the judicial separation petition at Appendix A(4); an example of an application, by way of affidavit, to omit is to be found at Appendix A(18); and an example of the resultant order is to be found at Appendix A(19).

Where leave has been granted, care should be taken to ensure that the details of the petitioner's address are not inadvertently provided in the statement of arrangements. Similarly, details of a child's school should not be disclosed, where that child resides with the petitioner.

CHECKLIST FOR ISSUING PETITION

Parties' names

1. The petitioner's name must appear both in the title and in paragraph 1 of the petition.

2. The names in paragraph 1 of the petition will be those which the petitioner and respondent currently use. If they are not as recorded in the marriage certificate, an explanation must be included in paragraph 1. For example, there may simply be an error on the face of the marriage certificate or one of the parties may have changed a forename or surname by deed or statutory declaration. A copy of the relevant document detailing the change of name may be required by the court.

Note: The appropriate wording where there is an error in a name on the marriage certificate can be found in paragraph 1 of Appendix A(2).

Date and place of marriage

3. The date and place of marriage must be recited in the petition precisely as recorded in the marriage certificate.

Foreign marriages

4. If the marriage certificate is not in English, a translation certified by a notary public or authenticated by affidavit must be filed.

Duration of marriage

5. More than one year must have elapsed since the date of the marriage.

6. If it has not, the petition can only be for:

    (a) judicial separation, or
    (b) nullity.

Cohabitation as husband and wife

7. The words 'as husband and wife' should appear in paragraph 2 of the petition after the words 'last lived together'.

Jurisdiction

8. The petition must be specific as to whether jurisdiction is claimed by reason of domicile or habitual residence for a period of not less than 12 months, or if under Council Regulation (EC) No 1347/2000 by reason of one of the grounds set out at **1.2** (b)(i)–(v).

Addresses of the parties

9. Residential addresses must be given in paragraph 3 of the petition. In particular, it is not appropriate to give either the work address of a party or that of a solicitor.

10. However, it is self-evident that no address will be given where a judge has given leave to omit.

Children's details

11. The full names and dates of birth of all children of the family under the age of 18 years or otherwise under a disability must be given in paragraph 4 of the petition.

Children no longer in full-time education

12. If a child is between the ages of 16 and 18 and is employed or undergoing training for a trade, profession or vocation, the relevant details should be set out in paragraph 4 of the petition.

Children under a disability

13. If a child is over the age of 18 years but under a disability either mental and/or physical, the relevant circumstances must be confirmed in paragraph 4 of the petition.

Previous proceedings

14. If there have been previous matrimonial proceedings the petition must state whether the parties have resumed cohabitation.

Proforma petitions

15. Where a proforma petition has been used and there:
    (a) is no child of the family now living; or
    (b) is no other child now living who has been born to the wife during the marriage; or
    (c) have been no other proceedings with reference to the marriage or between the petitioner and respondent with reference to any property of either or both of them; or
    (d) is or has been no application to the Child Support Agency in respect of a minor child of the family; or
    (e) are no proceedings continuing in any country outside England and Wales in respect of the marriage which are capable of affecting its validity or subsistence; or
    (f) is no agreement or arrangement which has been made or is proposed to be made between the parties with regard to maintenance

    ensure that the word 'except' is deleted from each paragraph.

Facts evidencing irretrievable breakdown

16. The petition must set out the facts in accordance with s 1(2) of the MCA 1973 together with sufficient particulars.

    Note that the petition must state that the marriage has irretrievably broken down if the petition is one for divorce.

Details of separation

17. Check that the particulars are properly given, specifically the date of separation in cases under MCA 1973, s 1(2)(c), (d) or (e).

    Note that if the particulars extend to a separate sheet this must be attached to the petition. *Loose sheets will not be acceptable.*

18. The relevant period of time must have elapsed before the date of issue of the petition in cases under MCA 1973, s 1(2)(c), (d) or (e).

Prayer

19. Ensure that there is a prayer for dissolution of the marriage, or for judicial separation or annulment.

Costs

20. If the petitioner wishes to claim costs, ensure such claim is included in the prayer of the petition.

Signature of petitioner

21. If solicitors are intending to place themselves on the record, the petition must be signed by them, otherwise it must be signed by the petitioner in person.

Address for service

22. Where solicitors have signed the petition, their address must be given as the address for service of all documents relating to the proceedings.

23. Where the petitioner, although acting in person, is receiving advice from a solicitor under the Legal Help Scheme, the solicitor's firm and address may be given as a 'care of' address for service.

Parties under disability

24. If one of the parties is a person under disability, the requirements of FPR 1991, r 9 must be complied with.

Solicitors for the petitioner

25. Where solicitors are intending to go on the record and the petition is for divorce, a certificate of reconciliation must be filed.

Previous orders

26. Copies of any previous orders referred to in the petition must be lodged.

Statement of arrangements for children

27. A statement of arrangements signed by the petitioner in person and a copy for service must be provided in respect of each child of the family who is:
    (a) under 16 years; or
    (b) between the ages of 16 and 18 years and still in full-time education; or
    (c) over 18 years and either mentally or physically incapacitated.

28. If the statement refers to a child or children suffering from a serious illness, a medical report is almost always required.

Court fees

29. Ensure that the correct court fee is tendered or that an application for exemption of fees signed by the petitioner in person is prepared and ready for filing.

CHAPTER 3

PROCEDURE – FROM ISSUE OF PETITION TO DIRECTIONS FOR TRIAL UNDER SPECIAL PROCEDURE PROVISIONS

3.1 SERVICE

3.1.1 Service generally

After the court issues the divorce petition, it will send a sealed copy with supporting documentation (if any) to the respondent unless the solicitors request that they effect service themselves.

Where it has been indicated that solicitors will accept service on behalf of a respondent or co-respondent, service will be effected by sending the petition to those solicitors:

(a) by first-class post; or
(b) through the document exchange; or
(c) by fax in accordance with the limited provisions of RSC Ord 65, r 5(2B).

The petition is served together with a notice of proceedings to which an acknowledgement of service is attached.

Note: See the special procedure checklist, paragraph 1(a), which is to be found at the end of Chapter 6.

If the petition is based on adultery, the petition will also be served on any named co-respondent.

3.1.2 Service where improper association is alleged

If a petition, based upon unreasonable behaviour, alleges an improper association with a person/persons of the opposite sex or of the same sex, who has/have been specifically named, a district judge may direct that such person/persons be made party to the suit (as a co-respondent(s)) and be served with a copy of the petition.

It is expedient at the outset of proceedings to draw the attention of the court to the reference to an improper association with a named person and request that a district judge consider at that stage whether or not the person

FPR 1991, r 2.9(4)

FPR 1991, r 10.2

FPR 1991, r 2.6(6)

FPR 1991, r 2.9(1)

FPR 1991, r 2.7(3)

named should be joined as a co-respondent. The district judge may decide that it is a matter which is best considered with both the petitioner and the respondent present and accordingly order that a directions hearing be fixed.

FPR 1991, r 2.7(3)

The main purpose of a decision to make such a person a co-respondent is to inform him/her of the proceedings and, provide an opportunity, if appropriate, to defend the allegation.

Note: An example of an application for a direction as to whether a named person against whom there is an allegation of an improper association should be joined in the suit as a co-respondent is to be found at Appendix A(20).

3.1.3   Service on a regular member of the armed forces

A regular member of the armed forces can be traced through the appropriate Service Department. If he/she is serving overseas, service can be effected by sending a sealed copy of the petition and all related documents to the appropriate British Forces Post Office (BFPO). Details of all BFPO numbers can be obtained from the Defence Mail and Courier Services. As much information as possible should be provided and, in particular, the service number, rank and last known unit of the person concerned.

PD of 13 February 1989 and Annex to CPR 1998, Part 6, PD 6

Note: The address of the Defence Mail and Courier Services is to be found at Appendix C(1).

3.1.4   Service on a prisoner

Where a respondent is serving a term of imprisonment in a civilian prison within the United Kingdom, service may be effected either by:

(a)   post, c/o the prison governor; or
(b)   personal service, by making a formal request to the governor for a face-to-face meeting with the respondent, so that the petition and the related documents can be handed directly to the respondent. However, serving a prisoner in this way, because of prison bureaucracy, can be a very time-consuming exercise.

3.1.5   Service by court bailiff or process server

Personal service may also be effected, most commonly by a county court bailiff or a process server instructed by solicitors.

FPR 1991, r 2.9(1) and (4)

If bailiff service is required, a formal request (in Form D89 in a county court or Form D379 in the Principal Registry) must be made to the court, together with, if possible, a recent photograph of the person to be served. The request must be signed by the petitioner in person unless solicitors are on the court record. The request, which should be accompanied by copies of the petition and all other documents to be served, attracts a court fee unless the petitioner is exempt from fees.

Whenever possible, the bailiff will obtain the signature of the person being served, which can be identified in the special procedure affidavit in exactly the same way as an acknowledgement of service which has been personally signed by the respondent. Whether or not a signature is obtained, the bailiff will complete an indorsement of service. If service cannot be effected, the bailiff will complete an indorsement of non-service.

CCR Ord 7, r 6

It should be noted that an application for bailiff service may be refused by the court where the application is made by a party who has solicitors on the record as acting. If bailiff service is refused then service will need to be attempted by a process server. This will not apply where the solicitors are advising under the Legal Help Scheme.

If service is effected by a process server, such service will be proved by filing an affidavit of service which must state how identification has been established.

In circumstances where the current home address of the person to be served is not known, an application can be made to a district judge for an order enabling service to be attempted by an alternative mode or at an alternative address, for example his/her place of work. This process is referred to as substituted service.

It is not appropriate to seek bailiff service upon either a regular member of the armed forces or a prisoner who is in a United Kingdom civilian prison. See **3.1.3** and **3.1.4**.

3.1.6 Service by a petitioner

FPR 1991, r 2.9(3)

Under no circumstances can a petition be properly served by a petitioner.

3.1.7 Respondent or co-respondent outside the jurisdiction

Where either the respondent or co-respondent is to be served outside England and Wales, the appropriate time within which the acknowledgement of service is to be returned is provided for in FPR 1991, r 10.6(4). However, leave to serve a petition out of the jurisdiction is not required.   FPR 1991, r 10.6

Note: See **3.3.1** with regard to completing the acknowledgement of service where a respondent or co-respondent is within the jurisdiction.

3.2   CIRCUMSTANCES AFFECTING SERVICE ON CO-RESPONDENT

3.2.1   Removing name of co-respondent from suit

Although the co-respondent may be named in the petition, there may be circumstances in which it is subsequently appropriate to dismiss him/her from the suit, for example where he/she denies the allegation and adultery cannot otherwise be proved.

3.2.2   Action following death of a co-respondent

If a named co-respondent dies after the issue of a petition but prior to the pronouncement of the decree nisi, it will be appropriate to apply to the court to dispense with making that person a co-respondent and for the name of the deceased to be removed from the title of the suit. The application will be made on two clear days' notice and will attract a court fee unless the petitioner is exempt from fees.

If the person with whom the respondent is alleged to have committed adultery dies before the presentation of the petition, it is not necessary to make that person a co-respondent but reference to his/her death should be given in the particulars.   FPR 1991, r 2.7(5)

3.2.3   Co-respondent under a disability

If a named co-respondent is a person under a disability, directions from a district judge should be sought:

(a) as to whether that person should be made a co-respondent and served; and
(b) generally with regard to the conduct of the   FPR 1991, rr 2.7(1)(b) proceedings.   and 9.3 and PD of 15 December 1960

3.3   ACKNOWLEDGEMENT OF SERVICE

3.3.1   Completing the acknowledgement

The respondent (and co-respondent where applicable) should within eight days (or such longer period as stipulated by the court where the party is living outside the jurisdiction of the court) return the acknowledgement of service to the court and indicate whether or not he/she wishes to defend the proceedings.   FPR 1991, r 10.8(2)

The form also includes provision for:

(a) the respondent to give information regarding any pending proceedings in any country outside England and Wales which relate to the marriage;

(b) the respondent to give information regarding domicile, habitual residence or nationality as required by Art 2(1) of Council Regulation (EC) No 1347/2000 of 29 May 2000;

Note: If, on receipt of the acknowledgement of service, it appears that the court may not have jurisdiction, the proceedings will be stayed pending a hearing to determine the issue.

FPR 1991,
r 2.27A(2)

(c) the respondent/co-respondent, in the case of an adultery petition, to admit the alleged adultery. However, it should be noted that there is no obligation to provide an answer to this question;

(d) the respondent, in the case of a two years' separation with consent petition, formally to provide that consent;

(e) the respondent, in the case of a two years' separation with consent or five years' separation petition, to indicate whether or not there is a wish to have the financial position, as it will be after the divorce, considered prior to the issue of the decree absolute;

Note: For further details on this subject, see **11.3.14**.

(f) the respondent, in the case of a five years' separation petition, to indicate whether he/she intends to defend the proceedings on the grounds of grave financial or other hardship;

Note: For further details on this subject, see **4.1**.

(g) the respondent to indicate whether or not there is an issue concerning the arrangements for any children of the family; and

(h) the respondent/co-respondent to indicate whether or not he/she objects to any claim for costs which has been made in the petition and, if so, on what grounds.

3.3.2 Signature on acknowledgement

The acknowledgement can be signed by either a respondent/co-respondent in person or, where solicitors have been instructed to act, by them on their client's behalf. However, it should be noted that where solicitors do sign:

(a) in the case of an adultery petition, where that adultery is admitted on the face of the acknowledgement, the respondent/co-respondent must also sign;

(b) in the case of a two years' separation with consent
     petition, where that consent is to be provided within
     the acknowledgement, the respondent must also sign.

3.3.3 Procedure where acknowledgement of service not filed

If an acknowledgement of service is not returned to the
court, other steps will have to be taken to prove that the
petition has been served or to seek an order from the court
for leave to proceed notwithstanding that no
acknowledgement has been filed.

In some circumstances, a district judge may:

(a) dispense with service, where it is likely to prove
     impossible to effect service upon the respondent or
     where, at best, it is improbable that service can be
     effected; or   FPR 1991, r 2.9(11)
(b) deem that service has been effected, where it is likely
     from facts that have come to the notice of the
     petitioner and/or solicitors (who are either on the
     record or merely advising) that service has taken
     place, for example where it can be inferred from
     correspondence or a conversation that the respondent
     has in fact received the petition; or   FPR 1991, r 2.9(6)
(c) order substituted service upon the respondent/co-
     respondent. This may be done either:
     (i) by post at an address at which it is believed that
          the person receives mail; or
     (ii) by way of an advertisement in a newspaper.   FPR 1991, r 2.9(9)

Note: (i) If the order is one which requires postal service, it is the
responsibility of the petitioner or his/her solicitors (if they are on the
court record) to effect such service. This should be done by way of
first class recorded delivery. Once effected, the recorded delivery
slip should be exhibited to an affidavit of service.

(ii) Although the rules provide for a district judge to settle the
wording of a newspaper advertisement, practitioners may find it
helpful to submit a draft in the form set out in Appendix A(25). Before
giving directions, the judge may also be assisted by receiving
guidance from solicitors as to suitable newspapers in which the
advertisement could appear in order to bring the proceedings to the
attention of the party to be served. The judge in giving his direction
will determine the number of times the advertisement is to appear.

Applications either to dispense with service, to deem that it
has taken place or for substituted service, which, by their
very nature, are made ex parte, must be supported by an
affidavit which fully sets out the basis upon which such   FPR 1991, r 2.9(9) and
application is made.   (11)

Note: In some limited circumstances, an order for deemed service
may be made without the need to file an affidavit.   FPR 1991, r 2.9(6)

In the case of an application to dispense with service, there is a standard form of affidavit (Form D13B) which contains all the relevant questions and which, once answered, will enable the district judge to consider making an order. All such applications attract a court fee unless the petitioner is exempt from fees.

Before ordering that service of the petition be dispensed with, a district judge will often direct that enquiries be made of the Department of Social Security and/or the National Health Service Central Register in an effort to trace the respondent. In accordance with a directive of the Data Protection Registrar, an order of a district judge is required before either department is prepared to effect a search for the respondent's address or, in the case of the National Health Service, the address of the health authority where the person sought is registered with a National Health Service doctor.

The district judge may also direct that a search be made in the national index of decrees absolute held at the Principal Registry of the Family Division. For each period of ten years which is searched, a court fee is payable, unless the petitioner is exempt from fees.

FPR 1991, r 2.9(6A)

An order dispensing with service or for deemed service will not be made in respect of a petition based solely upon two years' separation with consent unless a separate document can be filed containing the consent of the respondent to a decree being granted. However, as previously explained, the consent will most usually be provided within an acknowledgement of service.

Note: A draft letter of consent for the purposes of MCA 1973, s 1(2)(d) is to be found at Appendix A(15).

Similarly, an order dispensing with service, or one for deemed service, should not be made in respect of a petition based solely upon adultery, unless the petitioner is able to adduce independent evidence of the alleged adultery. However, in most cases, the acknowledgement of service will provide that evidence.

3.4 DISPOSAL OF SUIT

FPR 1991, r 2.8

The petitioner can file a notice of discontinuance and ask the court to dismiss the petition, provided that the petition has not yet been served.

There is no provision in the FPR 1991 for a petition to be merely withdrawn.

There are some circumstances, for example if the parties are attempting a reconciliation, where the court can order a stay of the proceedings. It is stressed that this is not a final disposal of the petition.

MCA 1973, s 6(2)

Once a petition has been served, an application by either the petitioner or the respondent to dismiss must be made on not less than two clear days' notice to a district judge. A petition can be disposed of only by the granting of a decree or by dismissal. The application attracts a court fee unless the applicant is exempt from fees.

3.5   DOMICILE OR HABITUAL RESIDENCE CHALLENGED

If there is an issue with regard to either domicile or habitual residence as set out in the petition and the respondent is asserting that neither party conforms to the requirement of Part II, s 5(2) of the Domicile and Matrimonial Proceedings Act 1973 (DMPA 1973), an application must be issued for a hearing inter partes, on not less than two clear days' notice, for this preliminary issue to be determined.

Note: See **1.2** at (b).

The application will be heard by a High Court judge or, if it is considered more appropriate, a circuit judge, either of whom will sit in chambers and, accordingly, counsel, a solicitor or a legal executive will have the right of audience.

PD of 5 June 1992

The application attracts a court fee unless the applicant is exempt from fees.

If it is found that the requirement of s 5(2) has not been fulfilled, the petition must be dismissed and no further steps can be taken, other than with regard to the costs of the proceedings.

It should be noted that an application for an order under Art 11 of the Council Regulation is to be made to a district judge, who may determine the application or refer it to a High Court or circuit judge for determination.

FPR 1991, r 2.27A(1)

3.6   SPECIAL PROCEDURE (UNDER FPR 1991, r 2.24(3))

If an acknowledgement of service is filed in the court office, a copy is sent to the petitioner or to his/her solicitors if they are on the court record. Where a petitioner is acting in person, an explanatory leaflet is also

FPR 1991, r 2.9(8)

sent, together with a form to request directions for trial under the Special Procedure provisions and a supporting pro forma affidavit.

If the respondent does not oppose the petition or if, having indicated that he/she intends to defend, does not file a defence (known as an answer) within the prescribed time limit (normally 28 days), the petitioner can then apply to the court for a decree nisi of divorce under the special procedure provisions (see below).

The 28-day period referred to above is calculated by adding the seven days allowed for filing the acknowledgement of service/notice of intention to defend to the 21 days allowed thereafter for the filing of an answer. If service has been effected outside the jurisdiction, the seven-day period will have been extended

FPR 1991, r 2.12(1)

and will thus extend the 28 days.

Where no acknowledgement of service is filed but the petitioner is otherwise able to prove service, the application may be made after eight days have elapsed from the date of service.

If a district judge has dispensed with service or has deemed that service has taken place and the time for giving notice of intention to defend is deemed to have expired, the application may be made immediately after the order has been made.

The application is made by way of a request for directions for trial (Form D84) under the special procedure provisions and must be signed by the petitioner in person, unless solicitors are on the court record. This means that where a solicitor is merely advising under the Legal Help Scheme the request must be signed by the client.

The request for directions for trial must be supported by an affidavit sworn by the petitioner. Care should be taken to ensure that the correct form of affidavit is used: it should be noted that there is a different form for each of the five

FPR 1991, r 2.24(3)

individual facts set out in s 1(2) of the MCA 1973.

If, exceptionally, more than one fact is pleaded, suitable amendments will have to be made to ensure that all relevant information is given to the court. In such a case, the appropriate questions from the relevant forms should be amalgamated in one specially prepared affidavit and answered accordingly. Alternatively, it is acceptable for two affidavits to be sworn, one in respect of each of the facts pleaded.

Note: For further information on this subject, see the special procedure checklist at the end of Chapter 6.

Where this is required by FPR 1991, the affidavit should
exhibit the acknowledgement of service and identify the
respondent's signature.

FPR 1991, r 2.24(3)(a)

Note: See **3.6.1** and **3.6.2** for circumstances in which this is essential.

3.6.1 Proceedings based upon the respondent's adultery

In the case of a petition based upon adultery, an admission
within the acknowledgement of service is usually the only
or principal evidence that such adultery has taken place.
Accordingly, if it is the only evidence, it is essential that:

(a) the acknowledgement of service is personally signed
     by the respondent;
(b) the respondent's signature is identified by the
     petitioner.

FPR 1991, r 2.24(3)(a)

3.6.2 Proceedings based upon two years' separation with the respondent's consent

In the case of a petition based on two years' separation
with consent:

(a) there is an absolute requirement for the respondent
     personally to consent, in writing, to a divorce;
(b) the consent may be within the acknowledgement of
     service or otherwise; however, it must be given in
     writing;

FPR 1991, r 2.10(1)

Note: See Appendix A(15) for an example of acceptable wording
giving such consent.

(c) in whatever form the consent is given, the
     respondent's signature must be identified by the
     petitioner in the special procedure affidavit;

FPR 1991, r 2.24(3)(a)

(d) the respondent can withdraw consent at any time prior
     to the pronouncement of the decree nisi. If consent is
     withdrawn, the petition cannot succeed on this fact
     and will be stayed pending amendment or dismissal.

FPR 1991, r 2.10(2)

Note: See Chapter 5 with regard to the amendment of a petition.

3.7 SPECIAL PROCEDURE AFFIDAVIT IN JUDICIAL SEPARATION PROCEEDINGS

As will be seen later, in Chapter 8, petitions for a decree of
judicial separation proceed in much the same way as for
divorce. However, care must be taken to ensure that the
special procedure affidavit is amended so that it refers
throughout to judicial separation and not divorce and also
that there is no reference to the marriage having broken
down irretrievably.

Note: A comprehensive special procedure checklist is to be found at
the end of Chapter 6. This sets out in considerable detail all aspects
of the procedure and, if followed, should eradicate most if not all of
the most commonly made errors.

CHAPTER 4

ANSWER AND SUBSEQUENT PLEADINGS

4.1 ANSWER

FPR 1991, r 2.12(4)

An answer (which is in effect a defence) filed by a respondent may simply be a denial of the facts in the petition, together with a prayer that the petition be dismissed and that the respondent's costs be paid by the petitioner.

MCA 1973, s 5(1)

In the case of a petition based on five years' separation pursuant to s 5(1) of the MCA 1973, the repondent may be able to oppose the granting of a decree on one of the two statutory bases. The statutory bases are that the dissolution of the marriage will result in either grave financial or other hardship and that it would be wrong in all the circumstances to dissolve the marriage.

Note: See **1.3.3**.

MCA 1973, s 5(2)

If the court concludes that the dissolution of the marriage would result in grave financial or other hardship to the respondent and that it would be wrong in all the circumstances to dissolve the marriage, it must dismiss the petition. The court is required, in reaching such a decision, to consider all the circumstances, including:

(a)   the conduct of the parties;
(b)   their intentions;
(c)   the interests of any minor child of the family and/or any other person who may be affected.

This, of course, assumes that the petitioner has not relied on any other s 1(2) fact, on which he/she may be able to proceed to a decree nisi.

MCA 1973, s 5(3)

For the purposes of s 5, hardship includes the loss of the chance of acquiring any benefit to which the respondent would be entitled if the marriage were not dissolved.

Precise details of the alleged financial or other hardship should be specifically pleaded and also, if it be the case, that the petitioner has not made any, or any satisfactory, proposal(s) to provide the respondent with some acceptable form of recompense.

As previously explained in Chapter 1, if the assertion that the parties have been apart for a period of five years is not disputed, a divorce cannot be opposed except as explained in this section.

4.2   ANSWER AND CROSS-PETITION

An answer may also include a cross-petition for divorce, which will be based on one or more of the five facts set out at **1.3**.

FPR 1991, r 2.15(1)

In cases under the provisions of MCA 1973, s 1(2)(c), (d) or (e), the relevant period of time must have elapsed prior to the date upon which the answer is filed (that is, presented).

FPR 1991, r 2.12(1)(b)

Note: An example of an answer containing a cross-petition for divorce is to be found at Appendix A(9).

As an alternative to divorce, a cross-petition can include a prayer for nullity or judicial separation.

Note: For information on nullity and judicial separation, see Chapter 9.

Although the formal parts of the petition, that is to say paragraphs 1 to 8 inclusive, can simply be admitted in the answer, in the manner set out in the example provided at Appendix A(9), it is better practice to recite the relevant paragraphs in full. This is because, if agreement is subsequently reached with the petitioner for the proceedings to continue undefended under the special procedure rules (see **4.7** below) on the prayer contained in the answer, rather than that contained in the petition, subsequent mistakes may well be avoided in completing the special procedure affidavit.

Note: See Chapter 3 and the special procedure checklist at the end of Chapter 6 for more details on the special procedure affidavit.

If adultery is alleged against an identified person, he/she is referred to as the party cited.

FPR 1991, r 2.16

The answer should be signed by the respondent in person or otherwise by solicitors if they are on the court record.

FPR 1991, rr 2.15(6) and 2.5

A copy of the answer should be provided for service upon the petitioner and any named party cited.

FPR 1991, r 2.17

Irrespective of whether the answer includes a cross-petition or is merely a denial, a filing fee (currently £50 less than that payable on the filing of a petition) will be payable unless the respondent is being advised under the Legal Help Scheme or is otherwise in receipt of State benefit and is therefore making an application for exemption of court fees.

4.3 ANSWER OF CO-RESPONDENT

A co-respondent who wishes to defend may file an answer denying the allegations in exactly the same way as a respondent, and ask the court, in the form of a prayer, to be dismissed from the suit and for a consequential order for costs.

FPR 1991, r 2.12(1)(a)

The answer should be signed by the co-respondent in person or otherwise by solicitors, if they are on the court record.

FPR 1991, r 2.5

In addition, the co-respondent must provide:

FPR 1991, r 2.12

(a) a copy of the answer for service on all other interested parties; and
(b) a filing fee unless the co-respondent is being advised under the Legal Help Scheme or is otherwise exempt from fees.

4.4 FILING AN ANSWER OUT OF TIME

Even where the acknowledgement of service, filed by either the respondent or co-respondent, does not include an intention to defend, neither is precluded from filing an answer.

FPR 1991, r 2.12(2)

Provided that the answer is received in the court office within 28 days of the date of service of the petition (or such other period as may be specified in the notice of proceedings, where the person to be served is outside the jurisdiction) and provided that directions for trial have not been given, it may be filed without leave.

FPR 1991, r 10.6
FPR 1991, r 2.12(1)

If the mandatory period provided by FPR 1991, r 2.12(1) for the filing of an answer has expired, it will be necessary to apply to the court for leave to file the answer out of time. If the district judge has granted his certificate under the special procedure rules, it will also be necessary, within the same application, to apply to set aside the certificate. The application is made on two clear days' notice and attracts a court fee unless the applicant is exempt from fees.

The application for leave to file the answer out of time may need to be supported by an affidavit or statement setting out the basis upon which the application is made and explaining the reasons for the delay. It is also good practice to attach a draft of the proposed answer.

4.5   SERVICE OF THE ANSWER

A sealed copy of the answer is served upon the petitioner.
A party cited is similarly served with a sealed copy of the
answer, together with notice of proceedings and
acknowledgement of service.   FPR 1991, r 2.17

If there is an allegation of improper association with a
named person contained within the answer, it is advisable
to draw the attention of the court to the allegation and
request that a district judge consider whether the person
named be made a party cited and served.   FPR 1991, r 2.16

The provisions set out in Chapter 3, with regard to service,
apply in much the same way to an answer and cross-
petition.   FPR 1991, r 2.9

4.6   ANSWER OF PARTY CITED

If a party cited wishes to defend, he/she should within
eight days of service (or such longer period as stipulated
by the court) file an acknowledgement of service and give
notice of intention to defend. Thereafter, an answer should
be filed denying the allegations in exactly the same way as
a respondent or co-respondent. There should be a request,
in the form of a prayer, for the party cited to be dismissed
from the suit with a consequential order for costs against
the respondent. The answer must be signed by the party
cited in person or by a solicitor, if on the record as acting.
A copy of the answer should be provided for service upon   FPR 1991, rr 2.12 and
the respondent, and a fee is payable on the filing of an   2.16(2)
answer by a party cited, unless he/she is making an
application for exemption of fees, using the same criteria
as explained at **4.2**.

A sealed copy of the answer will be served upon the
respondent.   FPR 1991, r 2.17

4.7   PETITIONER'S REPLY

Where a petitioner wishes to take issue with all or any of
the allegations contained within a respondent's answer,
he/she may file a reply which must be done within 14 days
of receipt of the answer.   FPR 1991, r 2.13(1)

Such reply should set out the denial in detail, in the form
of a formal pleading and should be signed by the petitioner   FPR 1991, rr 2.5 and
in person or by solicitors if on the record as acting.   2.15(6)

Whilst a copy of the reply should be provided for service,
exceptionally no fee is payable on filing.   FPR 1991, r 2.17

FPR 1991, r 2.13(1)

If the reply is not filed within the prescribed period of 14 days provided by the rules, leave of a judge to file it is required.

The application must be made on not less than two clear days' notice and attracts a court fee, unless the petitioner is exempt from paying fees.

FPR 1991, r 2.13(2)

If no reply is filed, the petitioner is deemed to have made a blanket denial of all the allegations contained in the answer.

Note: An example of a reply is to be found at Appendix A(10).

4.8 SUBSEQUENT PLEADINGS

FPR 1991, r 2.13(3)

Leave is required in all circumstances to file a rejoinder or any subsequent pleading.

The application must be made on not less than two clear days' notice and attracts a court fee, unless the applicant is exempt from fees. However, it is now most unusual for pleadings to extend beyond a reply.

4.9 COMPROMISING A SUIT

4.9.1 Proceeding on the cross-prayer in the answer

It is possible for the petitioner to agree to the divorce proceeding undefended on the cross-prayer contained in the answer, rather than on the prayer of the petition itself. In such a case, a consent application should be made to a district judge who will consider the application without the attendance of the parties, or their solicitors, before the request for special procedure directions for trial is lodged. The application attracts a court fee and is payable by the party issuing the application, unless that party is exempt from fees. The resultant order will normally:

(a) stay the prayer for dissolution contained in the petition;

(b) dismiss that prayer on pronouncement of decree nisi; and

(c) provide for the cause to proceed undefended on the prayer of the respondent's answer.

Note: An example of this type of order is to be found at Appendix A(21).

PD of 3 June 1958

The order is for a stay and subsequent dismissal of the prayer for dissolution only. This is because there is invariably a further prayer for ancillary relief which may well be required in any related financial proceedings.

The title of the suit will remain unaltered.

4.9.2 Proceeding on the prayer in an amended petition

Similarly, where an answer has been filed it is possible for the respondent to agree to the matter proceeding undefended on the prayer contained in an amended petition. This may happen in circumstances where allegations in the original petition have been disputed and, by agreement, these are deleted or made more palatable in an amended petition. The application will be made to a district judge on two clear days' notice (unless by consent) and will attract a court fee unless the person making the application is exempt from fees. The resultant order will normally:

(a) stay the prayer for dissolution contained in the answer;

(b) dismiss that prayer on pronouncement of decree nisi; and

(c) provide for the cause to proceed undefended on the prayer of the amended petition.

Note: See Chapter 5 with regard to an amended petition.

4.9.3 Respondent's request for directions for trial under the special procedure rules

If the answer is proceeding under the special procedure provisions, the request for directions for trial must be supported by an affidavit in exactly the same way as would be the case if the matter were proceeding on the prayer in the petition itself.

FPR 1991, r 2.24(3)

Note: For the procedure to be followed, see **3.6**.

The request for directions for trial must be amended to show that it is the respondent who is applying. It is also important to note that the affidavit must be likewise amended, so that if the answer has merely adopted the formal parts of the petition, reference is made to both the petition and the answer, and where the answer recites the formal parts, reference is made solely to the answer. In either case, references to the petitioner and respondent will have to be reversed.

Note: An example of an amended special procedure request for directions for trial, of an amended special procedure affidavit, where the formal parts of the petition have been adopted, and of an amended special procedure affidavit, where the formal parts of the petition have not been adopted, are to be found at Appendix A(11), (12) and (13) respectively.

4.9.4 Proceeding on prayers in both petition and answer

It is also possible for agreement to be reached to enable both the prayer in the petition and that contained in the answer to proceed side by side to pronouncement of cross-decrees (in which case, both the petitioner and the respondent will obtain a decree nisi of divorce). This agreement may be reached at a pre-trial review. Otherwise, an application may be made to a district judge who will consider it without the attendance of the parties or solicitors on the court record. The application attracts a court fee unless the party issuing it is exempt from fees.

Note: For pre-trial review, see **6.2**.

If leave is granted for the pronouncement of cross-decrees, both the petitioner and the respondent will be required to file a request for directions for trial under the special procedure provisions, and each will be required to swear an affidavit in support. The respondent's affidavit must be amended in exactly the same way as set out at **4.9.3**. One of the parties should accept responsibility for lodging the requests and affidavits together, so that they can be considered at the same time by a district judge. It should be noted that both decrees will be contained in a single document, an example of which is to be found at Appendix A(22).

In these circumstances either party is entitled, as of right, to apply for the decree nisi to be made absolute.

Note: For the procedure to be followed, see **7.1**.

4.9.5 Consolidation of petitions

If both the husband and wife have issued a petition for divorce, it is possible for the suits to be consolidated and then proceed similarly to cross-decrees. If the petitions are to be dealt with in this way, no later than when a request for directions for trial is lodged in either suit, application must be made to the court for:

RSC Ord 4, r 9, and PD of 10 July 1995

(a) a direction as to consolidation; or

(b) the stay or dismissal of one of the petitions.

Note: To assist practitioners to focus on the procedural steps which need to be taken and the form of application to be issued, examples of the resultant orders consolidating two petitions have been included at Appendix A(22) and (23).

If the suits are consolidated:

(a) the parties are referred to throughout as husband and wife;

(b) one of the two petitions should be nominated by a district judge as the lead suit. The purpose of this is to ensure that all documents are filed on one file and that both decrees nisi are incorporated into one document. However, only one decree absolute is issued;

(c) the procedure for requesting directions for trial is identical to that explained and set out at **4.9.4**.

If the suits have been previously consolidated, both requests for directions for trial under the special procedure provisions and the supporting affidavits will require amendment so that the parties are referred to throughout as husband and wife.

Note: An example of an amended affidavit under the special procedure provisions referring throughout to husband and wife is to be found at Appendix A(14).

4.10   STRIKING OUT A CROSS-PETITION

If a respondent is not prosecuting (pursuing) a cross-petition properly, or at all, that cross-petition can be struck out by an order of the court.

CHAPTER 5

AMENDED, FURTHER AND SUPPLEMENTAL PETITIONS

After a petition has been issued, there may be a need either to amend it or add supplementary information. This is done by filing either an amended, supplemental or further petition.

5.1 AMENDED PETITION

An amended petition can be used by the petitioner to:

(a) provide information erroneously omitted from the original petition;

(b) correct errors on the face of the original petition;

(c) pray for divorce rather than judicial separation, provided that the parties have been married for more than one year prior to the date of issue of the original petition;

Note: See **9.1** for circumstances in which leave is not required.

(d) base the petition on a different or alternative fact;

(e) delete allegations which have been made in the original petition upon which it is no longer intended to rely.

This often happens in circumstances where a respondent will agree to a petition proceeding undefended, provided certain allegations are withdrawn by the petitioner.

An amended petition is based upon a precise copy of the original petition, with the amendments shown in red. The following must be legibly written or typed in red:

(a) the heading 'AMENDED PETITION';

(b) all amendments (including deletions);

(c) the date the amendment was effected;

(d) the re-signature of the petitioner or solicitor, depending upon who is on the court record at the time the amended petition is presented.

Note that it is possible to make further amendments, with each subsequent amendment being shown in a different colour. The sequence of such colours is green, purple, yellow and brown. All re-amended petitions must be re-signed and re-dated in the appropriate colour.

A petition may be amended without leave at any time before an answer is filed but thereafter only with leave.

FPR 1991, r 2.11(1)(b)

Even where an answer has not been filed, the petition cannot be amended without leave after directions for trial have been given.

FPR 1991, r 2.14

The district judge may, if he/she thinks fit, require the application to be supported by an affidavit.

FPR 1991, r 2.11(3)

However, it is advisable to check with the relevant court as to local practice. A copy of the proposed amended petition should be attached to the application.

Application for leave under FPR 1991, r 2.11 may be considered ex parte if it is by consent, otherwise the application will have to be made on two clear days' notice to all other parties.

FPR 1991, r 2.11(1)(b), (2)(a) and (b)

Whether the application is considered ex parte or on notice, it attracts a court fee unless the petitioner is exempt from fees.

Unless otherwise directed, the amended petition will have to be served in accordance with FPR 1991, rr 2.6(6) and 2.9.

Note: See **5.5** with regard to service. For the requirements on filing an amended petition, see **5.4**.

5.2 FURTHER PETITION

It is particularly important to note that it is not possible to file an amended petition in circumstances where it is proposed to proceed on desertion, two years' separation with the consent of the respondent or five years' separation, where the relevant period of time prior to the date upon which the original petition was presented has not elapsed. In these circumstances, it would be necessary to apply either to have the original petition stayed and dismissed upon pronouncement of the decree in subsequent proceedings, or for it to be dismissed forthwith. Either way, leave to file an entirely new petition (referred to as a further petition) must be sought. A fee is payable on the application for leave to file this further petition unless the applicant is exempt from fees. If leave is given, there is a reduced fee payable on the filing of the further petition, unless the petitioner is exempt from fees.

There is also some debate as to whether or not it is possible to file an amended petition where it is proposed to allege adultery, but where such adultery has taken place after the date the original petition was presented, and practice does vary from court to court. Accordingly, it is advisable to have the original petition dismissed and to file an entirely new one (also referred to as a further petition). This likewise attracts a reduced fee, unless the petitioner is exempt from fees.

5.3 SUPPLEMENTAL PETITION

A supplemental petition can be used by a petitioner to:

(a) update the original petition, for example by adding further allegations of unreasonable behaviour or adultery which have taken place since the date of the original petition. This is frequently required where, following the issue of a petition, there has been a long delay before requesting directions for trial;

(b) add the details of a child who has been born to the wife (whether she is the petitioner or the respondent) subsequent to the date of the original petition.

Note: In this connection, see **5.4**.

It is not possible to change the nature of a petition by means of a supplemental petition.

FPR 1991, r 2.11(1)(a)

A supplemental petition can be filed without leave at any time before an answer is filed but thereafter only with leave.

FPR 1991, r 2.14

Even where an answer has not been filed, a supplemental petition cannot be filed without leave after directions for trial have been given.

FPR 1991, r 2.11(3)

The district judge may, if he/she thinks fit, require the application for leave to be supported by an affidavit. However, it is sensible to check with the relevant court as to local practice.

A draft of the proposed supplemental petition should be attached to the application.

FPR 1991, r 2.11(1)(a),
(2)(a) and (b)

An application for leave under FPR 1991, r 2.11 may be considered ex parte if it is by consent, otherwise the application will have to be made on two clear days' notice to all other parties. Whether the application is considered ex parte or on notice, it attracts a court fee unless the petitioner is exempt from fees.

Unless otherwise directed, the supplemental petition will have to be served in accordance with FPR 1991, rr 2.6(6) and 2.9.

Note: See **5.5** with regard to service.

There may be circumstances in which it is necessary to file or seek to file an amended supplemental petition.

5.4 REQUIREMENTS ON FILING AN AMENDED OR SUPPLEMENTAL PETITION

When filing an amended or supplemental petition, sufficient copies for service should be lodged with the court. Where an amended or a supplemental petition is in respect of a child, a statement of arrangements must also be filed, together with a copy for service upon the respondent.

A fee is payable on the filing of an amended petition, unless the petitioner is exempt from fees; but exceptionally there is no fee on the filing of a supplemental petition.

5.5 SERVICE OF AN AMENDED OR SUPPLEMENTAL PETITION

In addition to a sealed copy of the amended or supplemental petition, a notice of proceedings and acknowledgement of service must also be served, for completion and return to the court in the usual way.

It is important to ensure that the notice of proceedings and acknowledgement of service are amended throughout so that they refer to either the amended or supplemental petition (as appropriate).

Service upon the respondent (and where appropriate the co-respondent) of either an amended or supplemental petition must be effected unless a judge has made an order:

(a) dispensing with such service;
(b) deeming service to have been effected; or
(c) that there be substituted service.

Note: For fuller details of these processes and service generally, see **3.3.3.**

If service is not deemed or dispensed with, copies of the amended or supplemental petition will be required for service.

The procedures set out above apply equally to the filing of an amended or supplemental answer.

FPR 1991, r 2.18

CHAPTER 6

JUDICIAL INVOLVEMENT LEADING TO DECREE NISI

6.1 DIRECTIONS FOR TRIAL IN AN UNDEFENDED CAUSE

The request for directions for trial in an undefended cause does not attract a court fee and is considered by a district judge in the absence of the parties. If he/she is satisfied that the petitioner has fulfilled the requirements for a divorce by establishing a case both in the petition and the supporting affidavit, he/she will complete and sign a certificate authorising the pronouncement of the decree nisi under the special procedure provisions.

FPR 1991, r 2.36(1)

Note: See **6.1.5** for action to be taken in circumstances where the district judge is not satisfied.

The certificate also deals with the costs of the divorce suit itself.

FPR 1991, r 2.36(3)

Once the district judge's certificate has been signed, the court office will fix a date and time for the pronouncement of the decree by a district judge and inform all parties.

FPR 1991, r 2.36(2)

There is no necessity for any party to attend unless the granting of a decree is to be opposed or there is an issue as to costs.

6.1.1 Dispute as to costs

If there is an issue with regard to costs, a hearing will be fixed before a district judge when the matter will be determined. Generally, it will take place on the same date and time as pronouncement of the decree nisi. At the hearing, representations can be made by or on behalf of the parties to the judge as to why an order for payment of costs should not be made in favour of the petitioner.

FPR 1991, r 2.37(1) and (2)

This is so irrespective of whether or not there has been a previous indication that the petitioner's claim for costs is disputed. In such circumstances, the judge may decide to adjourn the matter to enable notice of the application to be given to the petitioner.

Since the arrival of the Civil Procedure Rules 1998 (CPR 1998), courts now deal with costs by way of summary assessment. However, whilst the principle of which party (if either) is to pay the costs can be determined, it may be that costs cannot be summarily assessed on the date the decree is granted because the relevant information is not available. In these circumstances, the hearing can be adjourned at the request of either party or otherwise as directed by the district judge.

6.1.2 Minor children

The district judge will certify whether or not there is a minor child of the family and, if there is, will either:

(a) issue a certificate of satisfaction regarding the arrangements made for that child; or

(b) give specific directions, for example, requiring further written evidence to be filed; or

(c) require the parties to attend before a district judge to give further evidence.   FPR 1991, r 2.39

In exceptional circumstances, the district judge may also direct that the decree nisi is not to be made absolute until he/she is satisfied as to the arrangements for the children.   MCA 1973, s 41(2)

The court is also given power by the Children Act 1989, ss 7 and 37 to order a welfare report, where there is particular concern in respect of a child.

Note: The provisions of these two sections are dealt with in some detail at **15.4**. For a more detailed account of the requirements of MCA 1973, s 41, see Chapter 14.

6.1.3 Dispensing with procedural formalities

If at any time, either before or after a petition is issued, it is considered expedient, and with the agreement of both the petitioner and the respondent, a judge can dispense with the formalities set out in this book and pronounce the decree nisi immediately. This is an exceptional step and will be taken only in circumstances where:

(a) either an order which the judge considers to be of particular importance cannot be made prior to the pronouncement of the decree, or

(b) there is an urgent need to reduce friction and/or resolve issues as between the parties.

If the decree is pronounced prior to a further petition being issued, an undertaking will have to be given by counsel or solicitors on behalf of the proposed petitioner to:

(a) file a petition within a specified period of time, which is unlikely to be more than 48 hours; and

(b) pay the court fee or lodge an application for exemption of fees at the time of issue.

The circumstances in which a decree nisi might be expedited in this manner are:

(a) as the result of a compromise being reached immediately before or during the trial of a defended suit; or

(b) where the respondent is in the process of dissipating or disposing of family assets which need to be protected by the granting of an injunction pursuant to MCA 1973, s 37 and where all or a part of those assets are urgently required by the petitioner. A hypothetical example might be where the parties, without the benefit of legal advice, have reached agreement to separate and sell the matrimonial home, which is in the respondent's sole name. The parties having also agreed to a division of the proceeds to enable both to purchase an alternative property, for the respondent subsequently to renege on the agreement immediately prior to the completion of the sale of the matrimonial home. In this example, it is likely that there would be an additional requirement for the petitioner to be granted an expedited decree absolute, so that a final ancillary relief order could be put into immediate effect.

Note: Injunctions granted under the MCA 1973 are considered in Chapter 12. Procedure for expediting the granting of a decree absolute is discussed at **7.2**.

Formalities can also be dispensed with where a party is terminally ill and there is a wish to finalise divorce and/or ancillary relief proceedings prior to death.

Note: See also **7.2**.

6.1.4 Requirement to provide further evidence

Occasionally, the district judge will not grant a certificate under the special procedure provisions because he/she is not satisfied by the evidence which has been disclosed. In these circumstances, an order will be made that the matter be set down for hearing in open court, before a circuit judge, so that further evidence can be given orally under oath. Alternatively, a district judge may give a petitioner the opportunity of filing further evidence.

FPR 1991, r 2.36(1)(b)

6.1.5 Action to be taken where a petition is ordered to be heard in open court

If the district judge decides that the petition is not suitable to be dealt with under the special procedure provisions and orders it to be listed before a circuit judge in open court, the petitioner should apply for directions for trial, using the form set out at Appendix A(16). There is no fee payable.

6.2 DIRECTIONS FOR TRIAL IN A DEFENDED CAUSE

If the suit is defended, either the petitioner or the respondent, having first complied with FPR 1991, r 2.25, can request directions for trial in the prescribed Form D21 in the county court (Form D266 in the Principal Registry of the Family Division) for a defended cause. Form D266 is to be found at Appendix A(17). It must be signed by the party in person unless solicitors are on the court record. The request attracts a court fee, unless the applicant is exempt from paying fees.

FPR 1991, r 2.24(1)

Upon receipt of the request for directions for trial, a pre-trial review is usually fixed before a district judge.

FPR 1991, r 2.24(4) and PD of 19 December 1978

At the pre-trial review, the parties are encouraged to reach some agreement as to the progress of the suit, possibly with a view to cross-decrees.

Note: See 4.9.1. An example of a decree nisi reciting cross-decrees is to be found at Appendix A(24).

If the parties cannot be persuaded to compromise, the district judge will give directions for trial and the petition and/or cross-petition will be set down for trial in open court, usually before a circuit judge or exceptionally before a High Court judge.

FPR 1991, r 2.24(5)

If the trial has a time estimate of a half-day or more or, irrespective of the time estimate, it is in the High Court or in the Royal Courts of Justice at county court level, court bundles must be prepared and lodged in accordance with the relevant President's Direction.

PD of 10 March 2000

At the trial, oral evidence will be given under oath with that evidence being subject to cross-examination in the usual way. At the conclusion of the trial, the judge may:

(a) pronounce a decree or, if there is a finding for both parties, cross-decrees;
(b) dismiss the petition and/or strike out the answer and cross-petition;
(c) make any consequential orders.

Counsel or a solicitor has the right of audience before a circuit judge and counsel or a solicitor with higher court rights of audience may appear before a High Court judge.

Even when a decree is pronounced on a cross-petition (which means that the decree is pronounced in favour of the respondent and not the petitioner), the title of the suit remains unaltered.

6.3 AVOIDANCE OF BRITISH IMMIGRATION LAWS

Where after the issue of a petition it appears to the court that the parties have married for the purpose of avoiding British immigration law, there is a requirement for the court to notify the Home Office. If notification has not been given by the court office of its own volition, the judge can be expected to give a direction in this regard when considering directions for trial or subsequently.

SPECIAL PROCEDURE CHECKLIST

1 Service of the petition

(a) Have all parties been properly served and the appropriate acknowledgements of service filed? Although there is an obligation on the part of the court to ensure that the correct form of notice of proceedings with acknowledgement of service attached is served on the recipient, solicitors are advised to check that this has been done. This is because the various forms contain questions which are specific to the fact upon which the petition is based. The forms are:

D8(1)   adultery/unreasonable behaviour/desertion
D8(2)   co-respondent
D8(3)   two years' separation with consent
D8(4)   five years' separation
D8(5)   a combination of 1, 3 and 4 above.

(b) Has an affidavit of service been filed, including details as to how the server identified the respondent/co-respondent?

(c) If service has been effected by court bailiff, has he/she lodged an endorsement of service or has the respondent/co-respondent signed to confirm service?

(d) If none of the above applies, has the district judge made an order dispensing with or deeming service?

Note: an order dispensing with service or for deemed service will not be made in respect of a petition based upon two years' separation by consent unless a separate document is filed containing the consent of the respondent to a decree being granted.

2 Expiry of time-limit

Has the time for filing an answer elapsed where the acknowledgement states an intention to defend?

3 Signing request for directions for trial

The request for directions for trial in Form D84 must be signed by solicitors, if on record as acting, otherwise by the petitioner in person.

4 The special procedure affidavit

(a) Is it on the correct D80 form?

Note: Forms D80(a), (b), (c), (d) and (e) correspond to the five facts set out in MCA 1973, s 1(2).

(b) Has it been properly completed?
(c) Have all questions been answered?
(d) Have all amendments been initialled?
(e) If an amended or supplemental petition has been filed or the suit is proceeding on the answer (incorporating a cross-prayer), has the affidavit been amended to reflect this? In the case of a supplemental petition, the affidavit must also refer to the petition.

(f) If the parties are still living together more than six months after the date of the final allegation relied on to establish breakdown, have full details of and reasons for their living arrangements been given?

(g) Do the places of residence specified cover the whole of the separation period in MCA 1973, s 1(2)(c), (d) or (e) cases?

(h) Does the affidavit ask, in the case of a divorce petition, that the marriage be dissolved or, in the case of a judicial separation petition, that the petitioner may be granted a decree of judicial separation?

(i) Has one of the alternatives 'husband/wife' been deleted as appropriate?

(j) Is the signature on the acknowledgement of service (or other appropriate document) correctly identified?

Note: (i) This is particularly important in MCA 1973, s 1(2)(a) and (d) cases.

   (ii) It will seldom, if ever, be appropriate to purport to identify the signature of a co-respondent.

(k) If the petition has been personally served and identification is established by photograph, the petitioner may be required to verify the photograph as being that of the respondent.

(l) Costs can be claimed only in circumstances where they have been included in the prayer of the petition; otherwise, reference to costs in the affidavit is inappropriate.

(m) The affidavit and exhibits must be properly sworn or affirmed before an appointed officer of the court or a solicitor of the Supreme Court.

5   Previous court orders

Have any previous court orders referred to within the petition been filed?

6   Children of the family

Does the petition mention any children of the family? If so:

(a) if any children of the family have reached the age of 16 years since the petition was issued, is there any updating statement of arrangements or a letter stating whether the children are continuing in education or are undergoing training for a trade, profession or vocation?

(b) does the respondent agree with the petitioner's proposals? If so, and the acknowledgement of service has been signed by the respondent, has the signature been identified by the petitioner?

(c) has the respondent filed a statement containing views on the present arrangements or the proposed arrangements for the children?

(d) if the petitioner takes issue with any statement of the respondent, have those views been set out in that part of the special procedure affidavit which is devoted to a child of the family?

(e) have any orders been made under the Children Act 1989 or are any applications pending?

(f) has either party indicated an intention to apply for such an order?

CHAPTER 7

DECREE ABSOLUTE

7.1 APPLICATION IN FORM M8

Once six weeks have elapsed from the date of the decree nisi and provided that a district judge has certified that he/she is satisfied as to the arrangements with regard to any minor child of the family, the petitioner can apply, as of right, for a decree absolute of divorce.

MCA 1973, s 1(5)

If the decree nisi has been pronounced in favour of the respondent, on the prayer of the cross-petition, the respondent can similarly apply for a decree absolute of divorce.

In circumstances where cross-decrees have been pronounced, either party has an equal right to apply for the decree absolute; there is no purpose in both parties applying, because as soon as a decree absolute is granted the marriage is dissolved.

FPR 1991, r 2.49(1)

The application for the decree absolute is made ex parte on a standard form (M8) and attracts a court fee unless the person making the application is exempt from fees. The application must be signed by the party in person unless solicitors are on record.

There is no provision in the rules for the respondent to object to the issuing of a decree absolute after the period of six weeks has elapsed, save as provided by the provisions of MCA 1973, s 10(2).

Note: See **11.3.14**.

7.2 ABRIDGING TIME

The period of six weeks can be abridged (shortened) by a district judge. Such application may be made only by the party who obtained the decree nisi and must be made on notice to the other party or parties. The application attracts a court fee, unless the applicant is exempt from fees. Evidence in support is required, by way of either affidavit or statement and can be provided by either party. It is advisable to check with the court in which the suit is proceeding as to its precise requirements.

There is a general reluctance to abridge time for the granting of a decree absolute unless there are genuinely exceptional circumstances. Judges are, however, usually more willing to expedite the pronouncement of a decree nisi. Either way, an application should be supported by affidavit or evidence in writing, setting out why the matter should be viewed as urgent. In particular, if the application is being made because of the impending birth of a child, medical evidence of the expected date of confinement should be provided. Practitioners are advised to enquire at the court where the suit is proceeding, as to whether or not an affidavit is required. This topic has been the subject of two Practice Directions issued by the President of the Family Division which should be taken into account prior to any application being made.

PD of 19 November 1964 and PD of 15 June 1977

7.3   APPLICATION ON NOTICE

If the petitioner does not apply for the decree absolute after the six-week period, then the respondent may apply once a further three months have elapsed. Similarly, if the decree nisi has been pronounced on an answer and the respondent does not apply for the decree absolute, the petitioner may apply in this way.

MCA 1973, s 9(2)

Such application must be made to a district judge on notice, who may require an affidavit in support. Accordingly, applicants are advised to check with the relevant court as to local practice. Unusually, four clear days' notice is required.

FPR 1991, r 2.50(2)

Note: Applications generally require only two days' notice. See FPR 1991, r 10.9(1)(b) which adopts RSC Ord 32, r 3 and, for proceedings in the county court, CCR Ord 13, r 1(2).

The application attracts a court fee, unless the applicant is exempt from fees.

There is no provision in the rules for the respondent (or petitioner if the decree nisi was pronounced in favour of the respondent) to apply for the statutory period to be abridged.

A decree absolute which has been erroneously obtained before the statutory period provided by MCA 1973, s 9(2) has elapsed is null and void and, once that fact has been brought to the attention of the court, must be set aside. This is so even though either one or both of the parties have remarried.

Manchanda v Manchanda [1995] 2 FLR 590, CA

Dennis v Dennis
[2000] 3 WLR 1443

Exactly the same principle will apply in circumstances where notice of a respondent's application under FPR 1991, r 2.50(2) has not been served upon the petitioner.

7.4 APPLICATION AFTER 12 MONTHS FROM DECREE NISI

After 12 months have elapsed from the date of the decree nisi, the application for decree absolute by either the petitioner or the respondent must be referred to a district judge who must ensure that the following statutory information is provided:

(a) the reason for the delay in making the application;
(b) whether or not the parties have lived together since the date of the decree nisi and, if so, between what dates;
(c) whether the applicant:
   (i) being the wife has given birth to a child since the pronouncement of the decree nisi; or
   (ii) being the husband has reason to believe that his wife has given birth to a child since the pronouncement of the decree nisi;
(d) if a child has been born, the applicant must set out the relevant facts and state whether or not it is alleged that the child is or may be a child of the family.

FPR 1991, r 2.49

The information required by FPR 1991, r 2.49 will usually be provided in the form of a written statement, either by the applicant or by solicitors who are on the court record. The judge has complete discretion although it should be noted that some will require an affidavit to verify the information. Accordingly, applicants are advised to check with the relevant court as to local practice.

An application made by the party in whose favour the decree was pronounced will be considered by a district judge without giving notice to the other party; otherwise the application will be listed for hearing on notice (see **7.3**).

7.5 STAY ON DECREE ABSOLUTE UNDER SECTION 41 OF THE MATRIMONIAL CAUSES ACT 1973

There will be exceptional cases where a judge has ordered, pursuant to MCA 1973, s 41, that there be a stay on the issuing of a decree absolute as a result of concern as to the arrangements for a child or children of the family.

MCA 1973, s 41(2)

In such circumstances, an application will have to be made
for the stay to be lifted. The application does not attract a
court fee.

7.6   ISSUE OF THE DECREE

Once the various steps set out above have been complied
with, and subject to the requirements of FPR 1991,
r 2.49(2), the decree absolute will be issued.

FPR 1991, r 2.51(2)

Practitioners should ensure that their client's copy of the
decree is endorsed with an original court seal.

A certificate of decree absolute which has been issued in
error can be set aside. This can be done on application by
either party or of the court's own motion. However, the
court will exercise caution before taking such a step
because of the potentially far-reaching consequences, for
example, either one or both of the parties may have
remarried.

A decree absolute which contains an error or errors on the
face of the certificate can be rectified.

CCR Ord 15, r 5; RSC
Ord 20, r 11

A decree absolute, which has been inadvertently granted
ignoring the requirements of MCA 1973, s 10(3), is
voidable.

MCA 1973, s 10(4)

A decree absolute which has been made after a petitioner
or respondent has died is a nullity and therefore of no
effect. In these circumstances, the suit may be abated. This
could potentially be of importance where the surviving
spouse is entitled to pension benefits, payable upon the
death of the other spouse.

Note: For further details of abatement, see **8.3**.

It is the decree absolute, and not the decree nisi, which
formally ends the marriage. The date and precise time at
which the decree is made absolute is endorsed on the court
copy of the decree nisi.

FPR 1991, r 2.51(1)

This endorsement on the decree nisi provides evidence
should there be a subsequent issue with regard to matters
arising out of the provisions of the Inheritance (Provision
for Family and Dependants) Act 1975 or, possibly, an
allegation of a bigamous marriage.

CHAPTER 8

DISPOSAL OF SUIT OTHER THAN BY DECREE

8.1 DISMISSAL

In some circumstances, for example where the petitioner has failed to prosecute (pursue) the petition to a conclusion or where the parties have become reconciled, the petition can be dismissed.

Where the parties have become reconciled, the application will be made by consent and will be considered, by a district judge, without the attendance of either party.

If the application is opposed, it will be heard by a district judge on not less than two clear days' notice to the other party. The hearing will be in chambers and, accordingly, counsel, a solicitor or a legal executive will have the right of audience. For circumstances where the application will be heard in open court, see **8.4**.

Whether by consent or heard inter partes, the application attracts a court fee unless the applicant is exempt from fees.

Once a petition has been dismissed, no further steps can be taken in connection with the suit, other than outstanding issues relating to costs. The effect is to make it impossible for a respondent to pursue the prayer for divorce contained in an answer. If it is the parties' intention to conclude the divorce on the cross-prayer, the appropriate procedure to follow is fully set out at **4.9.1**.

8.2 WITHDRAWAL

There is no provision in the rules for a petition to be merely withdrawn. However, provided a petition has not been served, the petitioner can file a notice of discontinuance and thereby ask the court to dismiss the petition.

8.3 NOTICE OF ABATEMENT UPON THE DEATH OF EITHER A PETITIONER OR A RESPONDENT

Prior to decree absolute, notice of abatement may be filed on the death of either the petitioner or the respondent in order to dispose of the suit. The district judge may require a copy of the death certificate to be filed.

For circumstances where the application will be heard in open court, see **8.4**.

Before filing a notice of abatement, great care should be taken to ensure that the benefit of any outstanding financial claims to which the surviving spouse and any child of the family may be entitled are not lost.

Note: Full details of the various issues which this subject raises are set out in *Rayden*, 17th edn, Chapter 13, Section 1.

There will undoubtedly be circumstances in which it is not appropriate to file a notice of abatement.

No fee is payable on the filing of the notice.

It should be noted that, once the decree absolute has been made, the death of either party will not affect the suit, the decree absolute remaining in force for all purposes.

Note: A form of notice of abatement is to be found at Appendix A(26).

8.4   RESCISSION OF DECREE NISI

There are circumstances in which a decree nisi of divorce or a decree of judicial separation may be rescinded, for example where the respondent was misled, whether intentionally or unintentionally, into consenting to a decree which was based on two years' separation with consent or where the parties have reconciled.

MCA 1973, s 10(1)
FPR 1991, rr 2.44 and 2.48

The decree nisi must not be made absolute whilst an application to rescind is pending.

Unless the decree nisi is to be rescinded by consent, the application will be heard in open court before the same category of judge as the one who pronounced the decree.

FPR 1991, r 2.44(1)

If opposed, the notice of application must be served on the party in whose favour the decree was pronounced not less than 14 days before the date fixed for the hearing of the application.

FPR 1991, r 2.44(3)

The application must be supported by an affidavit setting out the facts upon which the applicant relies. A copy of the affidavit will be served together with the notice of application.

FPR 1991, r 2.44(4)

The application, whether by consent or on notice, attracts a court fee unless the applicant is exempt from fees.

Whilst rescission will usually lead to the ultimate dismissal of the petition, this may not always be so. An example of circumstances where the petition may not be dismissed might be where service upon a respondent has been dispensed with and that respondent subsequently makes contact with the court, with a view to defending the petition. The proceedings will then be determined in accordance with the procedures set out in the preceding chapters.

CHAPTER 9

OTHER MATRIMONIAL DECREES

9.1 JUDICIAL SEPARATION

As with divorce proceedings, all matters relating to the issue of a judicial separation petition and the way it is conducted are determined by the provisions of the MCA 1973 (as amended) and the FPR 1991 (as amended).

The petition can be issued in the Principal Registry of the Family Division or any county court with divorce jurisdiction.

MFPA 1984, s 33

A petition for a decree of judicial separation is dealt with in much the same way as set out in Chapters 1 to 8 with regard to the prosecution of a divorce petition. It will be based on one of the five facts set out at **1.2**.

MCA 1973, s 17(1)

Note: An example of a judicial separation petition is to be found at Appendix A(4).

The principal differences are as follows:

(a) a petition may be presented within 12 months of the marriage. This is so because the bar contained in MCA 1973, s 3 relates only to petitions for divorce;

(b) the marriage may not necessarily have irretrievably broken down and reference to this will not be included in the petition;

MCA 1973, s 17(2)

(c) the prayer will seek a judicial separation;

(d) although the petition is served in exactly the same way as a divorce petition, the notice of proceedings and acknowledgement of service are amended throughout to refer to judicial separation;

(e) with regard to a petition based on five years' separation, the respondent is not able to prevent a decree on the grounds that it will result in either grave financial or other hardship;

MCA 1973, s 5(1)

(f) the decree of judicial separation is the only and final decree. Accordingly, a certificate for the purposes of MCA 1973, s 41 must be granted prior to the pronouncement of the decree;

MCA 1973, s 41(2)

(g) the parties remain married after the decree.

There are perhaps four reasons why a party to a marriage might file a petition for judicial separation rather than for divorce:

(a)   the parties have not been married for more than 12 months;

(b)   a petitioner (for religious reasons) is not prepared to divorce the respondent;

(c)   the petitioner wishes to prevent the respondent from remarrying but at the same time is concerned to have other matrimonial matters resolved, for example, maintenance or the ownership of matrimonial property. However, in this connection, as has been seen at **4.1**, once five years have elapsed from the date that the parties separated, it becomes very difficult to oppose the granting of a decree of divorce;

(d)   where a petitioner is concerned to preserve pension rights, which would accrue on the death of the respondent but would be lost as a result of a divorce.

If a petition for a judicial separation has been presented within 12 months of the date of the marriage, it cannot, even by consent, be amended to pray for a decree of divorce. Accordingly, once the period of 12 months has elapsed, a further petition for a decree of divorce should be presented. Provided it is based upon the same fact as the original judicial separation petition, exceptionally, leave of a district judge is not required. The issuing of the divorce petition will have the effect of superseding that for judicial separation.

FPR 1991, r 2.6(4)

A decree of divorce which has been erroneously obtained as a result of a petition, filed within the 12-month period, being incorrectly amended to pray for divorce must be set aside because it contravenes the mandatory statutory requirement. The court has no discretion in this regard.

Manchanda v Manchanda [1995] 2 FLR 590, CA

Conversely, where the judicial separation petition has been presented after the 12-month period, it is possible to amend that petition to one for divorce. Provided directions for trial have not been given or an answer filed, the amendment can be made without the leave of a district judge. However, care should be taken to ensure that, in cases of desertion, two years' separation with the respondent's consent and five years' separation, the relevant period of time has elapsed prior to the date upon which the original judicial separation petition was filed.

MCA 1973, s 1(2)(c), (d) and (e)

If the relevant period has not elapsed, a further petition will have to be filed, in which case the leave of a district judge will be required. The application for leave must be made on not less than two clear days' notice and attracts a court fee, unless the petitioner is exempt from fees.

MCA 1973, s 4(2)

At any time after the pronouncement of a decree of judicial separation, a petition for divorce can be presented. If it is based on the same fact and on the same, or substantially the same, evidence as that previously provided, it may not be necessary to prove the evidence again, to which end there is merit in making reference, in the particulars contained in the divorce petition, to the fact that the decree of judicial separation was founded on the same or similar evidence. In other words, the existing decree of judicial separation may be sufficient proof.

MCA 1973, s 18(2)

Practitioners' attention is also drawn to the fact that if, whilst a decree of judicial separation is in force and the separation is continuing, either of the parties dies intestate, all his/her real or personal property will devolve as if the other party to the marriage had then been dead.

9.2 NULLITY

As with divorce proceedings, all matters relating to the issue of a nullity petition and the way it is conducted are determined by the provisions of the MCA 1973 (as amended) and the FPR 1991 (as amended).

MFPA 1984, s 33

The petition can be issued in the Principal Registry of the Family Division or any county court with divorce jurisdiction.

The petition is dealt with in much the same way as set out in Chapters 1 to 8 with regard to the prosecution of a divorce petition, except as explained below:

(a) it may be presented within 12 months of marriage. This is because the bar contained in MCA 1973, s 3 relates only to a petition for divorce;

(b) the content will not include reference to the marriage having irretrievably broken down;

(c) the prayer will seek the annulment of the marriage;

(d) although the petition is served in exactly the same way as a divorce petition, the notice of proceedings and acknowledgement of service are amended throughout to refer to nullity;

(e) it is particularly important to note that the special procedure provisions do not apply, and directions for trial should be sought in accordance with FPR 1991, rr 2.24 and 2.25, whether the suit is defended or undefended.

Note: (i) If the petition is defended, see **6.2** for the required procedure.
(ii) If the petition is undefended, the petitioner should apply to the court for directions for trial (general procedure), in the form set out at Appendix A(16) – Form D21 in the county court and Form D267 in the Principal Registry of the Family Division. There is no fee payable.

Generally, all evidence relating to a petition is given orally under oath and is heard in open court before either a High Court judge or circuit judge. This means that only counsel or a solicitor can appear in the county court, and counsel or a solicitor with higher court rights of audience in the High Court. However, evidence as to incapacity to consummate a marriage may be given in chambers or in open court in camera.

Irrespective of whether or not a petition is undefended, a district judge has absolutely no discretion to try the case.   FPR 1991, r 2.32

If the trial has a time estimate of a half-day or more or, irrespective of the time estimate, it is in the High Court or the Royal Courts of Justice at county court level, court bundles must be prepared and lodged in accordance with the relevant President's Direction.   PD of 10 March 2000

As with divorce proceedings, a decree nisi will be pronounced and, after the expiration of the statutory period (presently six weeks), an application can be made for decree absolute. The application attracts a court fee, unless the applicant is exempt from fees.

Note: For full details of how either a petitioner or a respondent can apply for decree absolute, see Chapter 7.

A marriage may be annulled on the grounds that it is void or voidable.

9.2.1 Void marriage   MCA 1973, s 11

A void marriage is one which in law never existed and therefore a decree pronounced on this basis means that the parties were never married.

The grounds for presenting such a petition are:

(a) the marriage was celebrated between persons who are related within the prohibited degrees (for example, brother and sister). For full details, see the First

Schedule to the Marriage Act 1949 (as amended by the Marriage (Prohibited Degrees of Relationship) Act 1986);

(b) the marriage was celebrated when one of the parties was under the age of 16 years (the age of consent);

(c) one or more of the formalities required by law were not complied with, of which the following are more likely to arise:

    (i) a minor between the ages of 16 and 18 years married without the consent of his/her parent or guardian;

    (ii) marriage banns were not published or not published correctly;

    (iii) the marriage ceremony took place after the expiration of three months from the banns being published;

    (iv) the place of celebration of the marriage was not licensed;

    (v) the person celebrating the marriage was not properly licensed;

    (vi) a party to the marriage married using a false name;

(d) the parties were not respectively male and female;

(e) a party to the marriage was already lawfully married (bigamy);

(f) a polygamous marriage was entered into outside England and Wales when either party was domiciled in England and Wales at the time of the marriage.

MCA 1973, s 11(a)–(d)

Note: An example of a nullity petition (void) is to be found at Appendix A(5).

MCA 1973, s 12

9.2.2 Voidable marriage

A voidable marriage is one which is valid unless annulled by decree.

The grounds for presenting such a petition are:

(a) the incapacity of either party to consummate the marriage. Note that an impotent man or woman can petition on the grounds of his/her own incapacity to consummate the marriage;

(b) the wilful refusal of the respondent to consummate the marriage;

(c) that either party to the marriage did not give a valid consent to the marriage as a consequence of duress or mistaken identity, or whilst suffering unsoundness of mind (want of consent). Note that a person of unsound mind may file his/her own petition, where necessary presenting it through a next friend;

FPR 1991, r 9.2

(d) that, at the time of the marriage, either party, although
     capable of giving a valid consent, was suffering from
     a mental disorder within the meaning of the Mental
     Health Acts;
(e) that the respondent was suffering from venereal
     disease, in a communicable form, at the time of the
     marriage; or
(f) the respondent was pregnant by another man at the
     time of the marriage.   MCA 1973, s 12(a)–(f)

Petitions under s 12(e) or (f) above must state whether the
petitioner was, at the time of the marriage, ignorant of the
facts alleged.

Where a respondent is suffering from a mental disorder,
irrespective of whether or not notice of an intention to
defend has been given, the leave of a district judge is
required before the cause can proceed.   FPR 1991, r 9.4(1)

In permitting the cause to continue, the district judge may
order that a guardian ad litem be appointed.   FPR 1991, r 9.4(2)

Proceedings under MCA 1973, s 12(c), (d), (e) or (f) as set
out above must be instituted within three years of the
marriage unless a district judge gives leave to issue a
petition out of time in circumstances where the petitioner
has at some time during that period suffered from a mental
disorder within the meaning of the Mental Health Acts and   MCA 1973, s 13(2)
it is just to grant leave.   and (4)

A decree will not be granted under s 12(e) or (f) above
unless the court is satisfied that, at the date of the marriage,
the petitioner was ignorant of the facts alleged.   MCA 1973, s 13(3)

The court must not grant a decree of nullity on the ground
that a marriage is voidable if the respondent satisfies the
court that:

(a) the petitioner, knowing that the marriage could be
     avoided, continued the relationship with the
     respondent in such a manner as to lead the respondent
     to reasonably believe that no such step would be
     taken; and
(b) it would be unjust to the respondent to grant the
     decree.   MCA 1973, s 13(1)

With a nullity petition on the ground of incapacity, the
petitioner must apply before directions for trial are granted
for a district judge to determine whether a medical
inspector (ie a medical practitioner) should be appointed to
examine either or both of the parties and for any
consequential directions. Where an inspection is ordered it

will generally be appropriate for joint instructions to be given to a single inspector but in any event a report for filing at court will be required.

FPR 1991, r 2.22(1)–(5)

If the petition is defended, the application must be made on not less than two clear days' notice. If the respondent has not given notice of an intention to defend within the statutory period or otherwise has not filed an answer within the further statutory period, the application may be considered ex parte by a district judge. In either case, a court fee is payable unless the petitioner is exempt from fees.

Where the petition is undefended and the petitioner is not petitioning on the grounds of his/her own incapacity, it will often not be necessary for an inspection to be conducted.

FPR 1991, r 2.22(2)

The rules with regard to a nullity petition on the ground of non-consummation owing to the wilful refusal of the respondent are similar to those on the ground of incapacity set out above, although in these circumstances either party may apply to the court for the appointment of a medical inspector.

FPR 1991, r 2.22(6)

Note: An example of a nullity petition (voidable) is to be found at Appendix A(6).

9.3 PRESUMPTION OF DEATH AND DISSOLUTION OF MARRIAGE

A married person who believes that reasonable grounds exist for presuming the death of their spouse may present a petition to the court for the marriage to be dissolved on such grounds.

MCA 1973, s 19(1)

All matters relating to the issue of a petition for presumption of death and the way it is conducted are governed by MCA 1973, s 19 and FPR 1991.

The petition may be issued in the Principal Registry of the Family Division (exercising its county court jurisdiction) or any county court in England and Wales which has divorce jurisdiction.

MFPA 1984, s 33

The petitioner must be either domiciled in England and Wales or have been habitually resident in England and Wales for a period of at least one year prior to the date of the presentation of the petition.

DMPA 1973, s 5(4)

The petition must state:

(a) the last place at which the parties to the marriage cohabited;

(b) the circumstances in which the parties ceased to cohabit;
(c) the date when and the place where the respondent was last seen or heard of;
(d) the steps which have been taken to trace the respondent.

FPR 1991, App 2, para 3(a)–(d)

At the same time as the petition is issued, an affidavit should be filed, dealing with (d) above. This will enable the district judge to decide whether or not an order should be made formally dispensing with service.

The district judge may, however, direct further enquiries to be carried out in an attempt to trace the respondent, for example by contacting:

(a) the Department of Social Security; or
(b) the National Health Service Central Register via the Office for National Statistics; or
(c) one of the various military pensions offices.

Note: See Appendix C(1) for the relevant military addresses.

The district judge may also require a search to be made of the central register of decrees absolute held at the Principal Registry of the Family Division, in order to ensure that the respondent has not already divorced the petitioner.

If the respondent is traced, the petition cannot succeed and must be dismissed.

The special procedure provisions do not apply and, on application, directions for trial will be given by a district judge, leading to a final hearing before a High Court or circuit judge in open court. The form, D21 in the county court, or D267 in the Principal Registry of the Family Division, request for directions for trial, is set out at Appendix A(16) and does not attract a court fee.

Whilst issued as a suit in the county court, the petition may proceed in the High Court and be heard by a High Court judge. This, of course, means that only counsel or a solicitor with higher court rights of audience can appear.

If the trial is in the High Court or the Royal Courts of Justice, at county court level, court bundles must be prepared and lodged in accordance with the relevant President's Direction.

PD of 10 March 2000

If the person has been continually absent for a period of at least seven years and the petitioner has no reason to believe that the respondent is alive, such evidence will normally be accepted as sufficient for the death of the respondent to be presumed.

It is possible to file a petition within the seven-year period where, although no body has been found, there is a significant likelihood of death having taken place, for example, where there has been an air crash or where a serviceman has been lost in action.

If the petition is successful, the judge will pronounce a decree nisi. The petitioner can then apply for a decree absolute after the statutory period has elapsed (presently six weeks). There is a fee payable on the application unless the petitioner is exempt from fees.

Following the pronouncement of the decree nisi but before the decree absolute, should it become known that the respondent is alive, the decree nisi must be rescinded and the petition dismissed. The application to rescind will normally be made to the judge who pronounced the decree and will be made on not less than two clear days' notice. There is a fee payable on the application unless the applicant is exempt from fees.

If, after the decree absolute, the respondent is traced, either party will be able to apply for ancillary relief in exactly the same way as would be the case in divorce proceedings.

Note: For ancillary relief, see Chapter 11. An example of a presumption of death and dissolution of marriage petition is to be found at Appendix A(7).

CHAPTER 10

DECLARATORY DECREES

10.1 MARITAL STATUS

A declaration may be sought as to:

(a) the validity of a marriage at its inception;
(b) whether on a specified date the marriage subsisted;
(c) whether on a specified date the marriage did not subsist;
(d) whether a decree pronounced outside the jurisdiction should be recognised in England and Wales;
(e) whether a decree pronounced outside the jurisdiction should not be recognised in England and Wales.

FLA 1986, s 55

All matters relating to the issue of a petition for declaration as to marital status and the way that it is conducted are governed by Part III of the Family Law Act 1986 (FLA 1986) and the FPR 1991.

The application is commenced by petition, the content of which must comply with FPR 1991, r 3.12.

A copy of any relevant marriage certificate or decree of divorce must be annexed to the petition.

FPR 1991, r 3.12(3)

It is possible for a third party to apply for a declaration as to marital status, but the court may refuse to hear the application if it considers that the applicant does not have a sufficient interest in the determination thereof.

FLA 1986, s 55(3)

If the petition is issued by a third party, both parties to the marriage will be respondents.

FPR 1991, r 3.12(5)

The petition may be issued in either the High Court, which includes the Principal Registry of the Family Division, or any county court but, in respect of declarations of marriage, may not be issued in a divorce county court (which includes the Principal Registry of the Family Division exercising its county court jurisdiction).

FLA 1986, s 63

The court has jurisdiction to consider an application for a declaration as to marital status if either party to the marriage to which the petition relates:

(a) is domiciled in England and Wales at the date of presentation of the petition;

(b)   has been habitually resident in England and Wales
      throughout the period of one year ending with that
      date; or

(c)   died before that date and was at death domiciled in
      England and Wales or had been habitually resident in
      England and Wales throughout the period of one year   FLA 1986, s 55(2),
      ending with the date of death.   FPR 1991, r 3.12(1)(e)

The procedure for prosecuting the petition is not dissimilar
to the procedure for divorce proceedings, although there
are some significant differences. These include a
requirement to file an affidavit with the petition setting out
the circumstances and full details of all those who may be
affected by the proceedings.   FPR 1991, r 3.16(1)

There is also a requirement for the Treasury Solicitor,
acting on behalf of the Attorney General, to be given not
less than one month's notice of the intention to commence
proceedings relating to marital status.   FPR 1991, r 3.16(4)

Note: Full details of the procedure to be followed are set out in
Rayden, 17th edn, Chapter 18.11, p 550.

A court fee is payable on the issue of the petition unless
the petitioner is fees exempt.

The petition and affidavit are served on all respondents,
together with a notice of proceedings, with an
acknowledgement of service attached.   FPR 1991, r 2.6(6)

Once the respondent has indicated his/her intentions with
regard to the future conduct of the proceedings, the
Treasury Solicitor is in a position to obtain instructions
from the Attorney General as to whether or not it is his
intention to intervene.

It is open to the Attorney General to intervene in any
event, and reference should be made to FPR 1991, r 3.16
(5), (7), (9) and (10) in this regard.

In circumstances where what is being sought is a
declaration that a foreign decree is not valid, coupled with
a prayer for a decree of divorce, exceptionally the petition
must be presented at a divorce county court or the
Principal Registry of the Family Division (exercising its
county court jurisdiction).

A respondent wishing to defend the proceedings should file
an answer, the procedure for which is much the same as is
set out in Chapter 4.

It should be noted that, whether defended or not, the
special procedure provisions do not apply and directions

for trial will be given by a district judge, normally at a pre-trial review, leading to a final hearing before a High Court or circuit judge in open court. If the petition is undefended, the request for directions for trial does not attract a court fee but does so if the petition is defended. See Appendix A(16) and (17) for the relevant forms.

FLA 1986, s 60(4)

The court may direct that the application be heard in camera.

Counsel or a solicitor may appear if the petition is proceeding in the county court but only counsel or a solicitor with higher court rights of audience may appear in the High Court.

If the trial has a time estimate of a half-day or more or, irrespective of the time estimate, is in the High Court or the Royal Courts of Justice at county court level, court bundles must be prepared and lodged in accordance with

PD of 10 March 2000

the relevant President's Direction.

At the conclusion of the hearing, the judge will make a declaration as to whether or not there is a valid and subsisting marriage or divorce. The declaration is made in the form of a decree which is the only and final decree.

10.2 PARENTAGE

Any person may apply for a declaration that the person named in the application is or was the parent of another

FLA 1986, s 55A(1)

person so named.

All matters relating to the issue of an application for a declaration of parentage and the way it is conducted are governed by Part III of the FLA 1986 and the FPR 1991.

The application is commenced by petition, the content of which must comply with FPR 1991, r 3.13(1).

FPR 1991, r 3.13(2)

A copy of the relevant birth certificate must be annexed to the petition unless the court directs otherwise.

The respondents to the petition will be:

(a) the person whose parentage is in issue; and
(b) any person who is, or who is alleged to be, the mother or father of the person whose parentage is in issue;

FPR 1991, r 3.13(3)

excluding the petitioner.

As with a declaration for marital status, the petition may be issued in either the High Court or any county court. The procedure to be followed is as set out at **10.1**.

The court has jurisdiction to consider an application for a declaration as to parentage if the person whose parentage is in issue or the person whose parenthood is in issue:

(a) is domiciled in England and Wales on the date of the presentation of the petition;
(b) has been habitually resident in England and Wales throughout the period of one year ending with that date; or
(c) died before that date and either was at death domiciled in England and Wales, or had been habitually resident in England and Wales throughout the period of one year ending with the date of death.

FLA 1986, s 55A(2), FPR 1991, r 3.13(1)(h)

An affidavit in support must be filed in accordance with FPR 1991, r 3.16(1).

Frequently, the petition will be issued on behalf of a child and thus the proceedings will have to be commenced by his/her next friend.

FPR 1991, r 9.2(1)

Where the mother is a respondent, an alternative next friend may be necessary, and accordingly, consideration will need to be given as to the appointment of another close relative, such as a grandparent, aunt or uncle.

A written consent to act must be filed by the next friend. If the petition is presented through a next friend, the affidavit in support will be sworn by the next friend.

FPR 1991, r 9.2(2) and (7)

FPR 1991, r 3.16(1)

There is no longer a requirement for the Treasury Solicitor, acting on behalf of the Attorney General, to be given notice of the intention to commence proceedings.

FPR 1991, r 3.16(4)

Directions for trial are applied for in exactly the same way as set out at **10.1**.

The court is required, within 21 days of the declaration being made, to notify the Registrar General by forwarding to him a copy of the declaration together with a copy of the petition.

FPR 1991, r 3.13(5)

However, it is prudent to ensure that the appropriate steps have been taken by the court.

Note: An example of a declaration of parentage petition is to be found at Appendix A(8).

10.3 LEGITIMACY OR LEGITIMATION

A declaration may be sought that a person:

(a) is a legitimate child of his/her parents;
(b) has become a legitimated person;
(c) has not become a legitimated person.

FLA 1986, s 56(1)(b)

FLA 1986, s 56(2)

For the definition of 'legitimacy', see Legitimacy Acts of 1926 and 1976.

All matters relating to the issue of a petition for a declaration of legitimacy or legitimation and the way it is conducted are governed by Part III of the FLA 1986 and the FPR 1991.

The application is commenced by petition, the content of which must comply with FPR 1991, r 3.14(1).

FPR 1991, r 3.14(2)

A copy of the petitioner's birth certificate must be annexed to the petition unless the court directs otherwise.

FPR 1991, r 3.14(3)

The respondents to the petition will be the petitioner's father and mother or the survivor of them.

Where a parent is dead this may mean that the grandparents will be respondents.

The petition may be issued in the High Court or any county court. The procedure to be followed is as set out at **10.1**. The court has jurisdiction to consider an application for a declaration as to legitimacy or legitimation if the petitioner:

(a) is domiciled in England and Wales on the date of the presentation of the petition; or

FLA 1986, s 56(3), FPR 1991, r 3.14(1)(e)

(b) has been habitually resident in England and Wales throughout the period of one year ending with that date.

An affidavit in support must be filed in accordance with FPR 1991, r 3.16(1).

FPR 1991, r 3.16(4)

There is a requirement for the Treasury Solicitor, acting on behalf of the Attorney General, to be given not less than one month's notice of the intention to commence proceedings. As described at **10.2**, it may be necessary for a next friend to act for the petitioner.

Directions for trial are applied for in exactly the same way as set out in **10.1**.

Part II
FINANCIAL APPLICATIONS

CHAPTER 11

FINANCIAL APPLICATIONS WITHIN PROCEEDINGS UNDER THE MATRIMONIAL CAUSES ACT 1973

11.1 INTRODUCTION

11.1.1 Definition of ancillary relief

This chapter is concerned with claims pursuant to ss 10(2), 23, 24, 24A, 24B, 25B and 25C of the MCA 1973 – collectively referred to as 'ancillary relief'.

An application for ancillary relief or, perhaps more accurately, financial ancillary relief is the process whereby a petitioner and/or a respondent in a suit for divorce, judicial separation or annulment who has included a prayer for such relief in the petition or answer (as the case may be) applies to the court for an order with regard to the financial aspect of the parties' separation.

FPR 1991, r 2.53(1)

Note: MCA 1973, s 10(2) is dealt with as a separate topic at **11.3.17**.

11.1.2 Points to note

Curiously, whilst FPR 1991, r 2.53(1) is mandatory, para (2) provides that, where a prayer for ancillary relief has been omitted from the petition or answer, the parties are nevertheless subsequently able to apply by leave of the court or at the trial.

FPR 1991, r 2.53(2)(a)

Prior to decree nisi, the petition can be amended to pray for the relief sought.

Note: For the procedure with regard to amending a petition, see **5.1**.

Even though at the time the petition is issued it is not anticipated that there will be any requirement for the petitioner to apply for lump sum or property adjustment orders, practitioners are nevertheless urged to include such a prayer. This is because, if the court is not seised of an application and, following a decree absolute, the petitioner remarries, that remarriage will operate as a bar to the court entertaining an application for such relief and there will then be no means by which an application for ancillary relief can be issued under the provisions of the MCA 1973. This could ultimately lead to the possibility of solicitors facing a negligence claim.

MCA 1973, s 28(3)

Provided that there is a prayer for ancillary relief in the petition or answer (as the case may be) the court may assume jurisdiction after the remarriage of an applicant.

Jackson v Jackson
[1973] Fam 99

11.2 SCOPE OF THE COURT'S JURISDICTION

An ancillary relief order can potentially deal with:

(a) the matrimonial home;
(b) all other matrimonial assets including, by way of example, land, contents of the matrimonial home, life policies, stocks and shares and motor vehicles;
(c) accrued pension benefits;
(d) maintenance for either party (also referred to as periodical payments);
(e) in limited circumstances, maintenance for a child of the family. The majority of such cases now come under the jurisdiction of the Child Support Agency. Details of how the Child Support Act 1991 (CSA 1991) operates and the circumstances in which the court is empowered to make orders are set out in Chapter 11 of the *Ancillary Relief Handbook* by District Judge Roger Bird (3rd edn, Family Law, 2002).

Maintenance can potentially include provision for the payment of school or college fees.

The district judge has very wide powers to order:

(a) a transfer of property from one party to the other or of joint property into the sole name of one party;
(b) a transfer of a tenancy from one party to the other or a joint tenancy to the sole name of one party;
(c) a sale of property owned by one or both of the parties and a related distribution of the proceeds to either one or both of the parties;
(d) a payment of a lump sum from one party to the other or to a relevant child of the family;
(e) a future payment of a lump sum or maintenance to one party out of monies which are due to be received by the other party upon retirement or death in service. These are referred to as 'pension attachment' or sometimes as 'pension ear-marking orders'. In the event of an anticipated application for such an order, the trustees of the pension fund should be served with notice of the application as explained in **11.3.1**. The

reason for this is that the court will need to be satisfied by the fund manager that the proposed order is capable of being made. Full details on the subject of ear-marking orders are set out at **10.18** et seq of District Judge Roger Bird's *Ancillary Relief Handbook*;

PA 1995 and MCA 1973, ss 25B–25D

(f) a variation of a party's pension provision for the benefit of the other. This is referred to as a pension-sharing order. Such an order can only be made where the petition was filed on or after 1 December 2000;

D(P) Regs 2000

(g) a variation of any financial agreement made before or after the marriage;

(h) a charge in favour of one party over the assets of the other;

(i) secured provision in respect of maintenance.

The orders listed at (a), (c) and (d) above may be deferred until the remarriage, or long-term cohabitation, of a party, a minor child/children of the marriage reaching a specific age or ceasing full-time tertiary or higher education, or other pre-determined event.

11.2.1 Lump sum order

A lump sum referred to at (d) above can be payable by instalments and could include, for example, a payment to be made out of capital which is due to the other party upon retirement or upon a life policy maturing.

Although the total amount of a lump sum order once made is incapable of being varied, where it is payable by instalments, the court may, in exceptional circumstances, consider a variation as to the amount of the instalments

MCA 1973, s 31(2)(d)

and/or the dates upon which they are due to be paid.

11.2.2 Secured provision in respect of maintenance

The order at (i) above provides for the paying party to transfer, at the direction of the court, an income-bearing asset, for example shares or premises which have been let, such transfer to be for a specified period of time in order to secure maintenance payments.

11.2.3 Maintenance orders

Maintenance payments must always have a commencement date, and the order must be clear as to the duration and as to the rate and frequency of payments.

Where maintenance payments are in respect of a child of the family, they will be expressed to be payable until that child reaches the age of 17 years or ceases full-time

education, whichever is the later, or until further order. It
is important, in order to avoid future uncertainty and the
possibility of a further application to the court, to make it
clear whether the payments will come to an end once the
child finishes either secondary or tertiary education.

The specified duration of the order for a spouse will be for
such term as the court thinks fit, subject to the following
limitations:

(a)   the term cannot begin earlier than the date of the
      application for the order. An application for this
      purpose is either a prayer, in a petition or answer,
      which includes ancillary relief or an application in
      Form A;

(b)   the term cannot extend beyond the death of either
      party or the remarriage of the party in whose favour
      the order was made.   MCA 1973, s 28(1)(a)

The court also has power to direct that, upon the expiry of
a maintenance order, which is limited in duration, the
receiving party shall not be entitled to apply under s 31 of
the MCA 1973 for an extension of the term which is
specified in that order.   MCA 1973, s 28(1A)

11.2.4   Interim maintenance

Maintenance prior to the final decree is referred to as
maintenance pending suit for a spouse and as interim
periodical payments for a child. After the final decree, both
are referred to as interim periodical payments until the
final ancillary relief order has been made, after which they
are simply referred to as periodical payments.

Once a notice of application for interim maintenance has
been issued, a date will be fixed for a hearing which must
be not less than 14 days after the date of issue.   FPR 1991, r 2.69F(2)

The applicant is required to serve the respondent forthwith
with a copy of the notice of application.   FPR 1991, r 2.69F(3)

Where an application is made before a party has filed
Form E (see **11.3.2** with regard to Form E), that party must
file with the application and serve on the other party a draft
of the order requested and a short sworn statement
explaining why an order is necessary and providing
information as to his/her means.   FPR 1991, r 2.69F(4)

Not less than seven days before the date fixed for the
hearing, the respondent must file with the court and serve
on the applicant a short sworn statement with regard to
means, unless a Form E has already been filed by him/her.   FPR 1991, r 2.69F(5)

No fee is payable on an application for maintenance pending suit or interim periodical payments as this will have been covered by the fee already paid on the issue of the substantive application.

A party who has an order in his/her favour for maintenance pending suit may request, in Form I, that a periodical payments order may be made at the same rate.

FPR 1991, r 2.67

In this regard there is a court fee payable unless the applicant is exempt from fees.

11.2.5   Child Support Agency

See **18.3.1** for information with regard to the position concerning a child who falls within the ambit of the CSA 1991.

11.2.6   Application by a child

A child of the family may be able to apply to a district judge, on his/her own behalf, for leave to intervene in the ancillary relief proceedings for the purpose of asking the court to make an order, against either or both parents, for the various forms of ancillary relief set out above. The court has jurisdiction to make both periodical payments and lump sum order or orders. Where the child is a minor, he/she will apply by way of a next friend, in accordance with the rules.

FPR 1991, r 2.54(f)

FPR 1991, r 9.2

11.2.7   Application by a bigamist

A person who knowingly enters into a bigamous marriage is unlikely to obtain a financial order although there is no bar to making an application.

Whiston v Whiston [1995] Fam 198

11.2.8   Limitation on final orders

The court has no power to make final orders for ancillary relief until after the decree nisi has been pronounced in the case of a divorce or nullity suit, or after the pronouncement of the decree in the case of judicial separation.

Munks v Munks [1985] FLR 576

11.2.9   Members of the armed forces

Where the respondent to an application for maintenance is a regular member of the armed forces, being male or female, it is possible to apply to his/her unit commander for a compulsory allotment of the respondent's pay. This will be simpler and quicker than proceeding through the Child Support Agency for an assessment or through the court for an order.

Note: For further information concerning maintenance from a member of the armed forces, see Chapter 21.

11.3 ANCILLARY RELIEF PROCEDURE

Since 5 June 2000, the pilot scheme provisions, which had been in operation after 1 October 1996 in selected courts, have had general application, in their amended form, throughout all courts in England and Wales. The provisions now govern the issue and conduct of all ancillary relief proceedings commenced pursuant to ss 10(2), 23, 24 and 25 of the MCA 1973 (as amended).

These provisions contain the procedural code which enables the court to deal with cases justly.

A comprehensive definition of the meaning of 'dealing with a case justly' is set out in FPR 1991, r 2.51B(2)–(6).

In short, the underlying philosophy of the new procedure is to enable the court to take an active part in the management of a case, thereby reducing delay and the tension which inevitably arises in matrimonial disputes, encouraging settlements and keeping costs within reasonable bounds.

11.3.1 Issuing and serving an application

In order to commence proceedings, a party must issue an application in Form A, which is filed with the court together with a copy for service and the appropriate court fee unless the applicant is exempt from fees. An applicant with the benefit of a legal aid or Community Legal Services funding certificate must pay the full court fee.

FPR 1991, r 2.61A(1)

Note: See also **11.1.2** for further information regarding commencement of proceedings.

The application should set out all forms of ancillary relief which are being sought by the applicant and/or on behalf of a relevant child of the family and should include specific details of any order sought pursuant to s 24B, s 25B or s 25C.

Where an application for ancillary relief is filed, in respect of a petition which has been issued on or after 1 December 2000, seeking a pension sharing order, the provisions of FPR 1991, r 2.70 apply.

FPR 1991, r 1.2(2)

An application for a pension sharing order must be specifically applied for and the terms of the order sought included in Form A.

FPR 1991, r 2.53(1)

FPR 1991, r 2.59(2)

Where an application is for a property adjustment or an avoidance of disposition order, relating to land, the notice in Form A must identify the land by description and, where appropriate, the Land Registry registration number and give particulars of any known mortgage.

Note: For information concerning an avoidance of disposition order, see **12.2**.

Form A must be signed by solicitors if they are on the record for the purposes of ancillary relief, whether or not the applicant is legally aided. Otherwise the form must be signed by the litigant in person.

FPR 1991, r 2.61A(4)(a)

Upon issue the court will allocate a date for a first appointment not less than 12 weeks and not more than 16 weeks after the filing of the notice of application. The details will appear in the Notice of First Appointment in Form C.

FPR 1991, r 2.61A(5)

The date fixed for the first appointment and any subsequent hearing date cannot be adjourned other than by order of a judge and only to a further fixed date.

FPR 1991, r 2.61A(4)(b)

The copy of Form A, sealed by the court, and the related Form C must be served upon the respondent to the application within four days of the date upon which the notice was filed. It should be noted that the rules now stipulate that the court must effect service. This is so even in circumstances where solicitors intend themselves to effect service.

FPR 1991, r 2.61B

Accordingly, the court is required to issue the application on the date it is filed. The court will also provide two copies of Form E (financial statement) for completion, one for the applicant and the other to be sent to the respondent at the same time the Form A is served.

FPR 1991, r 2.9(9)

If the whereabouts of the respondent to the application is not known it will be necessary to apply to the court for an order for leave to substitute some other form of service or, exceptionally, to dispense with service altogether. For full details see **3.3.3**. The application attracts a court fee unless the applicant is exempt from fees.

If the respondent to the application is residing overseas at the time the application is issued and does not have a solicitor in England and Wales on the record as acting, or otherwise does not have an address for service within the jurisdiction, the time for service of the application may be extended in accordance with the provisions of FPR 1991, r 10.6.

If the respondent to the application is a regular member of the armed forces, currently serving overseas, and does not have a solicitor in England and Wales who is on the record, he/she may be served by posting the application and all related documents to the relevant British Forces Post Office address. Details of BFPO addresses can be obtained from the manning office of the various services.

Note: For details see Appendix C(1).

Where the application is specifically for a maintenance order, service upon a regular member of the armed forces may be effected by registered post upon his/her commanding officer and is deemed good service.

NDA 1957, s 101, AA 1955, s 153 and AFA 1955, s 153

A copy of Form A and Form E completed by the applicant must be served upon any person who has the potential to be affected by the application.

FPR 1991, r 2.59(3) and (4)

Where an order for ancillary relief is sought which includes provision to be made pursuant to MCA 1973, s 25B or s 25C, the applicant should also file with the court written confirmation that the trustees or managers of the pension scheme have been served with a copy of Form A and provided with the information required in accordance with FPR 1991, r 2.70(4).

If at any stage a matrimonial or other caution is registered, at either the Land Registry or the Land Charges Registry, which relates to a family asset, early disclosure should be provided to the other side. Failure to disclose is liable to create distrust and resultant judicial displeasure.

11.3.2 Preliminary aspects leading to the first appointment

Not less than 35 days before the date of the first appointment, the parties must simultaneously exchange their completed statements in Form E, which they have sworn to be true.

FPR 1991, r 2.61B(1)(b) and (2)

Once sworn, the statement should be filed at court without delay. Practitioners should draw to their clients' attention the warnings set out on the front of the form with regard to failure to give full and accurate disclosure and to being deliberately untruthful.

The statement should be kept succinct and to the point and the inclusion of irrelevant historical matters should be avoided.

An application based on the alleged behaviour of the other party is possible; however, such behaviour will have to be serious and relevant to the financial issues for the court to take it into account. Examples of relevant conduct are:

(a) an assault on the part of the respondent which results in the applicant being unable to work or left with an impaired ability to work;

(b) the respondent having dissipated all or most of the available family assets.

Where there are medical problems of a type referred to in (a) above, a supporting medical report should be filed and served at an early stage.

If a form or other document filed with the court contains an allegation of adultery or an improper association with a named person, the court may direct that the party who filed the relevant form or documents serve a copy of part or all of the form or document on the named person, together with Form F.

FPR 1991, r 2.60(1)

If the court makes a direction as to service in accordance with r 2.60(1), the named person may file a statement in answer to the allegation.

FPR 1991, r 2.60(2)

Form E must have attached to it:

FPR 1991, r 2.61B(1)(c)

(a) any document required by that form;

(b) such other document as may be necessary to explain or clarify any of the information set out in the form. This should include a medical report where it is claimed that gainful employment is impossible or the ability to work impaired.

FPR 1991, r 2.61B(3)(a) and (b)

No other documents should be attached to it.

FPR 1991, r 2.61B(4)

Where a party is unavoidably delayed or prevented from sending any document required by Form E, that party must at the earliest opportunity:

(a) serve copies on the other party; and

(b) file a copy with the court together with an explanation for the delay.

FPR 1991, r 2.61B(5)(a) and (b)

The comprehensive disclosure required by Form E should make it possible for practitioners to start negotiations, without delay, with a view to reaching an early settlement.

No disclosure should be sought or given between the issue of Form A and the first appointment, except:

(a) for copy documents sent with Form E; or

(b) in accordance with the questionnaire referred to below.

FPR 1991, r 2.61B(6)

If discosure has not already been provided, practitioners should ensure that a matrimonial or other caution, which a

party has registered at the Land Registry, is disclosed to
the other side when Form E is served.

At least 14 days before the date of the first appointment
each party shall file and serve on the other:

(a) a concise statement of issues;
(b) a chronology;
(c) a questionnaire setting out details of any information
     sought from the other party and a schedule of the
     documents sought from the other party;
(d) notice in Form G which requires each party to state
     whether or not the first directions appointment can be
     used as a financial dispute resolution appointment and
     confirmation of service pursuant to FPR 1991,
     r 2.59(3) and (4) or r 2.70(4).   FPR 1991, r 2.61B(7)(d)

Note: See **11.3.4** with regard to a financial dispute resolution
appointment.

Failure to comply with the requirement set out above may
result in a costs penalty being imposed at the first
appointment.   FPR 1991, r 2.61D(2)(e)

Immediately prior to the first appointment, each party
should prepare a costs estimate in Form H for production
to the court. In addition, it may be appropriate to prepare a   FPR 1991, r 2.61F(1)
separate schedule to deal with discreet issues.

Practitioners should be aware that no first directions
appointment can be adjourned other than with leave of the
court and this is so even where the parties are in agreement
that the appointment can be vacated. In any event, the
appointment cannot be adjourned generally, but must be
adjourned to a further fixed date.   FPR 1991, r 2.61A(5)

11.3.3   The first appointment

The first appointment is governed by FPR 1991, r 2.61D.
The main purpose of this appointment, at which both
parties are expected to attend, is to enable a district judge   FPR 1991, r 2.61D(1) and
to define the issues, with a view to saving costs.   (5)

At the first appointment, the district judge will make
consequential directions and in particular will be
concerned with:

(a) determining the extent to which the questionnaire
     from each party shall be answered, which documents
     are required to be produced and giving directions as
     to the production of future and updating
     documentation;   FPR 1991, r 2.61D(2)(a)

FPR 1991, r 2.61D(2)(b)(i) and (ii) and (f)(iii)

(b) giving directions as to valuations of all assets, of whatever nature, owned jointly or by either party and the obtaining of any necessary expert evidence;

FPR 1991, r 2.61D(2)(b) (iii)

(c) giving directions as to any other evidence sought, which might include a narrative affidavit where specific issues have been raised;

(d) giving directions as to any chronologies or schedules which are likely to be required;

(e) giving directions leading to the financial dispute resolution appointment unless, exceptionally, he/she decides that such an appointment is inappropriate in the circumstances.

FPR 1991, r 2.61D(2)(c)

Note: See **11.3.4** with regard to a financial dispute resolution appointment.

With regard to (b) above:

(i) wherever possible it is desirable, in the interest of saving costs and minimising the issues between the parties, for a joint valuer to be instructed by or on behalf of the parties. This is particularly important in view of the fact that CPR 1998, Part 35, which deals with expert evidence, is incorporated into ancillary relief proceedings.

PD of 25 May 2000

Practitioners may find it least contentious to agree a joint letter of instruction, written on plain paper. If the content of the letter cannot be agreed, it should be possible to request a district judge to settle the form of words to be used.

Similarly, if there is a disagreement as to which expert is to be appointed, the court should give a direction in this regard.

(ii) Where the asset is a business and a party is either self-employed or a director of a closed company, it may be appropriate to request several years' accounts so that trends can be established. Bearing in mind the increasing need for proportionality, practitioners should consider whether a forensic accountant is really necessary. If needed, it may be possible to provide a focus by posing structured questions.

If the district judge decides that a financial dispute resolution appointment is not appropriate, he/she will:

(a) fix a further directions appointment;

(b) fix an appointment with a view to an interim order being made;

(c) fix a final hearing and at the same time give a direction as to the category of judge who is to hear the matter;

(d) adjourn for out-of-court mediation;

(e) exceptionally, adjourn the application generally.

FPR 1991,
r 2.61D(2)(d)(i)–(iv)

Although the first appointment is primarily intended as a hearing for directions, the district judge may, having regard to the completed Form G, indicate that the appointment is to be used as a financial dispute resolution appointment (see **11.3.4**). This will provide an early opportunity for the parties to settle the differences between them with the assistance of their legal advisers and/or the district judge. Using the appointment in this way may be of particular assistance where the matrimonial assets are modest and the issues are straightforward.

FPR 1991, r 2.61D(2)(f)(ii)

At the first appointment, consideration can also be given to the making of an interim order where an application has been made in accordance with FPR 1991, r 2.69F.

FPR 1991, r 2.61D(2)(f)(i)

Note: For fuller details see the section on interim maintenance at **11.2.4**.

Where either party, a cohabitee of either party or any other person fails to produce a document which is relevant to the proceedings, an application can be made to a district judge for an order requiring that person to attend court and produce the document for inspection.

FPR 1991, r 2.62(7)

This is potentially a powerful weapon which is significantly under-used. It might also be invoked against a bank or similar institution which is failing to co-operate.

A fee is payable on the application unless the applicant is exempt from fees.

Failure to comply with a directions order may result in a costs penalty being imposed at the financial dispute resolution appointment.

Notice in Form D, setting out the place, date and time of the appointment for the financial dispute resolution, is served by the court on both parties together with the directions order made at the first appointment.

Immediately prior to the financial dispute resolution appointment each party should prepare a costs estimate in Form H for production to the court. In addition, it may be appropriate to prepare a separate schedule to deal with discreet issues.

FPR 1991, r 2.61F(1)

Practitioners should be aware that no financial dispute resolution appointment can be adjourned other than with leave of the court and this is so even where the parties are in agreement that the appointment can be vacated. In any event, the appointment cannot be adjourned generally, but must be adjourned to a further fixed date.

FPR 1991, r 2.61A(5)

11.3.4 The financial dispute resolution appointment

The financial dispute resolution appointment is governed by FPR 1991, r 2.61E. The meeting is arranged for the purpose of discussion and exploring the possibilities of a negotiated settlement.

FPR 1991, r 2.61E(1)

The parties' representatives are encouraged to mediate and, where appropriate, the district judge conducting the hearing may be prepared to intervene in an effort to break any deadlock.

FPR 1991, r 2.61E(1)

The extent to which a district judge is prepared to intervene will vary, although it can be anticipated that in some cases he/she will be prepared to express robust views.

In all events, as Sir Stephen Brown made clear when he was President of the Family Division, an environment must be created in which the parties feel able to approach the mediation process openly and without reserve.

PD of 16 June 1997

The Form D is endorsed with a notice which directs that not later than seven days before the appointment the applicant must provide the court with details of all offers, proposals and responses concerning the application.

FPR 1991, r 2.61E(3) and (4)

However, if a settlement is not reached, any privileged documents must not be retained on the court file. Accordingly, the parties' legal representatives should ensure that they are returned by the district judge at the conclusion of the appointment.

FPR 1991, r 2.61E(5)

It is an essential aspect of the procedure that both parties attend the appointment together with their legal representative, who is required to have a thorough knowledge of the case and the issues between the parties. That person can be either a legal executive, solicitor or counsel.

FPR 1991, r 2.61E(9)

Even if not specifically ordered at the first appointment, the parties and their legal representatives should attend court at least one hour prior to the hearing, in order to carry out preliminary discussions and hopefully to narrow the issues.

The hearing usually commences with the case being
outlined to the district judge and the parties' respective
positions stated. Thereafter the district judge can adjourn
the matter as many times as he/she considers expedient, to
enable the parties to consider their respective positions. In
any event, both parties will be expected to put forward
realistic offers, which thereafter are to be given proper
consideration by the other side.

If the parties reach agreement, the legal representatives are
encouraged to settle the minutes of agreement and consent
order for approval by the district judge. If agreement
cannot be achieved but where it is likely that, upon further
reflection, a settlement can potentially be reached, the
district judge can fix a further financial dispute resolution
appointment. If, on the other hand, it is clear that a
settlement is not going to be possible the district judge will
fix a date for the final hearing.

FPR 1991, r 2.61E(8)

Practitioners should take great care to ensure that before
finalising a draft consent order they have the clear and
unequivocal approval of their client. This is because it is
possible for the court to impose the terms of a draft order
in circumstances where a party withdraws at the last
moment.

Xydhias v Xydhias
[1999] 1 FLR 683

It should be noted that:

(a) a judge who has been involved in a financial dispute
     resolution appointment will not be the tribunal judge
     for a final contested hearing.

FPR 1991, r 2.61E(2)

(b) any views, as to settlement, expressed by a judge
     during the financial dispute resolution appointment
     are not, in any circumstances, binding on the trial
     judge.

11.3.5 Preparation for the final hearing

Not less than 14 days before the date fixed for the final
hearing of the application, the applicant must (unless the
court directs otherwise) file with the court an open
statement which sets out concise details, including the
amounts involved, of the orders which are sought. At the
same time a copy must be served on the other side.

FPR 1991, r 2.69E(1)

Not more than seven days after service of the statement
referred to above, the respondent must file with the court
an open statement which sets out concise details, including
the amounts involved, of the orders which he/she proposes
to ask the court to make. At the same time a copy must be
served on the other side.

FPR 1991, r 2.69E(2)

FPR 1991, r 2.61F(1)

Immediately prior to the final hearing each party should prepare a costs estimate in Form H for production to the court. In addition, it may be appropriate to prepare a separate schedule to deal with discreet issues.

PD of 10 March 2000

If practicable, not less than two clear days prior to the commencement of the final hearing, the applicant must lodge with the court an agreed bundle of documents which has been indexed and paginated. An additional bundle will be required for use by witnesses.

In preparing the bundle, the inclusion of endless material, such as bank statements, which is unlikely to be referred to at the hearing should be avoided. Packing out the bundle with superfluous material is not only likely to incur judicial displeasure but also unnecessary costs. However, do ensure that any particulars of property, which either party intends to draw to the attention of the court, are included. It is also helpful to include a map of the relevant area(s).

The judge will be greatly assisted by an agreed chronology, schedule of issues, schedule of assets (identifying liquid assets) and a schedule of *Calderbank* offers (for production at the conclusion of the hearing).

FPR 1991, r 2.61A(5)

Practitioners shoud be aware that no final hearing can be adjourned other than with leave of the court and this is so even where the parties are in agreement that the hearing can be vacated. In any event, the hearing cannot be adjourned generally, but must be adjourned to a further fixed date.

11.3.6 The final hearing

FPR 1991, r 2.61E(2)

The final hearing will not be before a district judge who has already conducted a financial dispute resolution appointment in the matter, because what is said during such an appointment is privileged and, in the absence of the parties' consent, should not be referred to during the final hearing.

Unless otherwise ordered by the court, both the applicant and the respondent should attend the court for the purpose of cross-examination.

Advocates should adopt a realistic approach and arguments in their respective openings to the trial judge, for example, with regard to alternative accommodation for the parties. Lengthy cross-examination on matters of a historical nature should be avoided except, for example, in a case where it is alleged that a party has dissipated significant matrimonial assets.

The judge is likely to be concentrating on what is now available to distribute between the parties and how best to achieve a fair division, based on the needs of both parties. The judge will take into account a number of important factors including the future ability of the parties to provide for themselves, their respective pension provisions (if any) and any significant medical problems. Generally judges do not want the parties to dwell on the past but are anxious to concentrate on what can be constructively achieved to secure the future of both parties and any relevant child of the family.

As with the financial dispute resolution appointment, a party may be represented by counsel, a solicitor or a legal executive, and preferably by the same person who appeared at the earlier hearing(s).

11.3.7   Offers to settle (*Calderbank* offers)

Either party may at any time make a written offer to the other party which is expressed to be 'without prejudice except as to costs' and which relates to any issue in the proceedings relating to the application. Indeed, the court will expect both parties to have made sensible offers to settle.

FPR 1991, r 2.69(1)

Where an offer to settle is made that fact is not to be communicated to the court, except in accordance with r 2.61E(3), until the question of costs falls to be decided.

FPR 1991, r 2.69(2)

Where an order made in favour of a party is more advantageous than an offer made by the other party under FPR 1991, r 2.69(1), the court must, unless it considers it unjust to do so, order that other party to pay any costs incurred after the date beginning 28 days after the offer was made.

FPR 1991, r 2.69B(1) and (2)

11.3.8   Interest

Where an order in favour of a party is more advantageous than an offer made by the other party under FPR 1991, r 2.69(1), the court may, where it considers it just, order the unsuccessful party to pay:

(a)   interest on the whole or any part of any capital sum awarded, at a rate not exceeding 10% above base rate, for some or all of the period beginning 28 days after the offer was made;

FPR 1991, r 2.69C(1)–(3)

(b)   indemnity costs from the period beginning 28 days after the offer was made and interest on those costs at a rate not exceeding 10% above base rate.

FPR 1991, r 2.69C(4)(a) and (b)

However, such penalties are less likely to be imposed in a case where there are modest assets to be divided on a needs basis.

11.3.9   Consent orders

Financial aspects of a suit are often agreed between the parties. Once the form of the agreement and consent order have been approved by both parties, the draft should be lodged at court for a district judge to consider making the order.

The draft must be:

(a)   signed by solicitors if on the court record or otherwise by the parties in person. In any event, where either or both of the parties have given undertakings, that party or both parties should preferably sign even though solicitors are on the record and accordingly have themselves signed in the usual way. This is particularly so where the proposed order includes provision for child maintenance because the CSA 1991 specifically requires such an order to have arisen out of an agreement between the parties;

CSA 1991, s 9

(b)   accompanied by a financial statement in Form M1 completed by both parties;

FPR 1991, r 2.61(1)

(c)   accompanied by a Form A completed by or on behalf of the respondent to the application (even if only for dismissal purposes) unless he/she has previously filed an application for full ancillary relief. It is acknowledged that not all courts insist upon Form A being filed solely for the purposes of dismissal.

FPR 1991, r 2.53(2)(b)

Where a pension sharing order is made by consent, confirmation must be given that no objection has been:

(a)   made by the person responsible for the pension arrangement, or

FPR 1991, r 2.70(15)(k)

(b)   received and considered by the court.

Practitioners should ensure that the order itself contains only provisions which, if not complied with, are capable of being enforced by the court. If incapable of enforcement in this way, such provisions should be made the subject of recitals or undertakings.

Note: A very useful and comprehensive booklet of precedent agreements and consent orders has been produced by the Solicitors Family Law Association. Copies of the booklet can be obtained through the Association Secretary, PO Box 302, Orpington, Kent, BR6 8QX or DX 86853 Locksbottom.

It is important to ensure that the following matters are
dealt with when lodging a draft minute of agreement and
consent order for approval:

(a)   where there is an apparent inequality in the terms of
      the settlement, that the reason(s) is/are fully explained
      in the Form M1 or in a covering letter;
(b)   where a party who is not working is to provide for the
      payment of a lump sum, that an explanation is given
      as to the source of such moneys;
(c)   that all assets which are referred to in the draft are
      detailed in the Form M1, in particular, the value of
      collateral life policies, which are frequently omitted.

11.3.10   Final order after decree

Although the substantive order cannot be made until after
the decree nisi or decree of judicial separation has been
pronounced, it is not unusual for the application to be filed   MCA 1973, ss 23(1) and
and directions orders made before the decree.   24(1)

A substantive order inadvertently made before
pronouncement of the decree must be set aside by a judge.   *Munks v Munks* [1985]
It cannot be amended under the provisions of the slip rule.   FLR 576

Accordingly, therefore, it may be considered advisable not
to lodge a draft consent order for approval until after the
decree has been pronounced. It should also be noted that
the information which must be provided to the court
pursuant to FPR 1991, r 2.61(1) should be current as at the
date when the draft order is submitted. It follows that if
there is any inordinate delay between lodging the draft and
the pronouncement of the decree, the court may require
confirmation that the parties' circumstances are unchanged.
This will inevitably lead to unnecessary work and further
delay.

Whilst the substantive order can be made after decree nisi
and before decree absolute it cannot take effect until, at the
earliest, the date of the decree absolute. Exceptionally, a
judge may expedite the decree nisi and/or decree absolute
where there is an urgent need to conclude all outstanding
ancillary relief matters. See **6.1.3** for dispensing with
formalities.

11.3.11   Pension sharing or attachment orders

When the court fixes a first appointment as required by
r 2.61A(4)(a), the party with pension rights shall, within
seven days after receiving notification of the date of that

appointment, request the person responsible for each pension arrangement under which he has or is likely to have benefits to furnish the information referred to in reg 2(2) and (3)(b) to (f) of the Pensions on Divorce etc (Provision of Information) Regulations 2000.

FPR 1991, r 2.70(2)

Within seven days of receiving the above information, the party with pension rights shall send a copy of it to the other party, together with the name and address of the person responsible for each pension arrangement.

FPR 1991, r 2.70(3)

A request under r 2.70(2) above need not be made where the party with pension rights is in possession of, or has requested, a relevant valuation of the pension rights or benefits accrued under the pension arrangement in question.

FPR 1991, r 2.70(4)

Upon making or giving notice of intention to proceed with an application for ancillary relief, including provision to be made under s 24B (pension sharing) of the Act of 1973, or upon adding a request for such provision to an existing application for ancillary relief, the applicant shall send to the person responsible for the pension arrangement concerned a copy of Form A.

FPR 1991, r 2.70(6)

Upon making or giving notice of intention to proceed with an application for ancillary relief, including provision to be made under s 24B or 25C (pension attachment) of the Act of 1973, or upon adding a request for such provision to an existing application for ancillary relief, the applicant shall send to the person responsible for the pension arrangement concerned:

(a) a copy of Form A;
(b) an address to which any notice which the person responsible is required to serve on the applicant under the Divorce etc (Pensions) Regulations 2000 (D(P) Regs 2000) is to be sent;
(c) an address to which any payment which the person responsible is required to make to the applicant is to be sent; and
(d) where the address in sub-paragraph (c) is that of a bank, a building society or the Department of National Savings, sufficient details to enable payment to be made into the account of the applicant.

FPR 1991, r 2.70(7)

A person responsible for a pension arrangement on whom a copy of a notice under r 2.70(7) is served may, within 21 days after service, require the applicant to provide him with a copy of section 2.16 of the statement in Form E supporting his/her application. The applicant must then

provide that person with the copy of that section of the
statement within the time specified by r 2.61B(2), or 21
days after being required to do so, whichever is the later. FPR 1991, r 2.70(8)

A person responsible for a pension arrangement who
receives a copy of section 2.16 of Form E as required
pursuant to r 2.70(8) may within 21 days after receipt send
to the court, the applicant and the respondent a statement
in answer. FPR 1991, r 2.70(9)

A person responsible for a pension arrangement who files a
statement in answer pursuant to r 2.70(9) shall be entitled
to be represented at the first appointment, and the court
must, within 4 days of the date of filing of the statement in
answer, give the person notice of the date of the first
appointment. FPR 1991, r 2.70(10)

Where the parties have agreed on the terms of an order
including provision under s 25B or 25C (pension
attachment) of the Act of 1973, then unless service has
already been effected under r 2.70(7), they shall serve on
the person responsible for the pension arrangement
concerned:

(a) the notice of application for a consent order under
     r 2.61(1);
(b) a draft of the proposed order under r 2.61(1),
     complying with r 2.70(13); and
(c) the particulars set out in sub-paragraphs (b), (c) and
     (d) of r 2.70(7) above. FPR 1991, r 2.70(11)

No consent order under r 2.70(11) shall be made unless
either:

(a) the person responsible has not made any objection
     within 21 days after the service on him of such notice;
     or
(b) the court has considered any such objection,

and for the purpose of considering any objection the court
may make such direction as it sees fit for the person
responsible to attend before it or to furnish written details
of his objection. FPR 1991, r 2.70(12)

(a) Pension sharing order
A **pension sharing order** creates a separate pension fund
for the applicant and reduces the respondent's fund by the
same amount. Orders for pension sharing can be made
within applications for ancillary relief in divorce or nullity
but not in judicial separation proceedings. The petition
must be one issued on or after 1 December 2000.

When an order is made, varied or discharged which contains pension sharing provision, it must comply with r 2.70(13)(a) and must be accompanied by an annex in Form P1 containing the information set out in r 2.70(14) of the FPR 1991. A copy of Form P1 is to be found at Appendix C. When the application is lodged as a consent order, this annex, completed by the solicitors acting, should be lodged with the application for the order. If the order is the result of a contested hearing, the annex should, at the end of the hearing, be completed by the solicitors for the applicant.

The order takes effect no earlier than 21 days from the making of the order or from decree absolute, whichever is the later. Page 2 of the annex needs to have that date inserted in the box marked 'THIS ORDER TAKES EFFECT FROM'. Practitioners need to check that the correct date has been entered.

FPR 1991, r 2.70(13)(b)

Practitioners should note that a separate annex is required for each pension referred to in the order.

Once there is a decree absolute, practitioners should check that the pension provider has been served with:

(a)   a copy of the ancillary relief order;
(b)   a copy of the annex;
(c)   a copy of the decree of divorce or nullity; and

FPR 1991, r 2.70(16)

(d)   a copy of the decree absolute certificate.

It is for the court to serve these documents in accordance with FPR 1991, r 2.70(17).

(b) Pension attachment order
A **pension attachment order** requires a payment or payments to be made to the applicant directly from the pension fund manager. It is a form of security for payment. These can be made within applications for ancillary relief in divorce, nullity and judicial separation proceedings and may appear in cases filed prior to 1 December 2000, provided that the petition was issued on or after 1 July 1996.

The order, which must comply with r 2.70(13)(a), must be accompanied by an annex in Form P2, containing the information set out in r 2.70(15) of the FPR 1991. A copy of Form P2 is to be found at Appendix C. When the application is lodged as a consent order, the solicitors acting should lodge the annex with the application for the order. In consent cases, confirmation that notice of the application for the order has been given to the pension provider is required on the back of Form P2 and must be completed by the court. This information should be in Form M1, which accompanies the draft consent order. If the order is the result of a contested hearing, the annex should, at the end of the hearing, be completed by the solicitors for the applicant.

Practitioners should note that a separate annex is required for each pension referred to in the order.

FPR 1991, r 2.70(13)(b)

Practitioners should check that once there is a decree absolute, or if it is a judicial separation case, the pension provider is served with:

(a) a copy of the ancillary relief order;
(b) a copy of the annex;
(c) a copy of the decree of divorce, nullity or judicial separation; and
(d) a copy of the decree absolute certificate (not applicable in judicial separation).

FPR 1991, r 2.70(16)

It is for the court to serve these documents in accordance with FPR 1991, r 2.70(17).

It should be noted that the person responsible for the pension arrangement may recover prescribed charges in respect of complying with a pension attachment order.

WRPA 1999, s 29, PD(C) Regs 2000

11.3.12   Legal Aid or Community Legal Services statutory charge

In circumstances where a party to ancillary relief proceedings has the benefit of a legal aid certificate or Community Legal Services funding certificate, any monies or property which have been recovered or preserved by that party, as a result of an order made in the proceedings, will be the subject of the statutory charge.

LAA 1988, s 16, CLA (Gen) Regs 1989, Part XI and CLS(F) Regs 2000, Part III

For a detailed account of the operation of the statutory charge, practitioners should refer to the extensive Notes for Guidance contained in the *Legal Aid Handbook*, in respect of certificates granted prior to 1 April 2000, and in the *Legal Services Commission Manual*, in respect of certificates granted on or after 1 April 2000, both of which are Sweet & Maxwell publications. The *Legal Services Commission Manual* will be published annually.

Practitioners must, as a matter of course, ensure that a client who has a certificate granted by the Legal Aid Board or Legal Services Commission fully understands the operation of the statutory charge and that he/she is periodically reminded, particularly with regard to a situation where litigation costs are escalating as a result of intransigence or an unreasonable approach on the part of the client. Indeed, it may be appropriate, in an extreme case and where a practitioner is concerned, to refer the matter to the Area Office of the Legal Services Commission.

11.3.13   Postponement of statutory charge

It will usually be possible to postpone the operation of the statutory charge in circumstances where:

(a)   a lump sum is to be paid to a spouse who has the benefit of either a legal aid or Community Legal Services funding certificate to enable him/her to purchase a house for the benefit of himself/herself and/or a dependant; or

(b)   a house has been preserved for the benefit of a spouse who has such a certificate and/or his/her dependant; or

CLA (Gen) Regs 1989, regs 96 and 97 and CLS(F) Regs 2000, reg 52(1)(a)

(c)   a house is to be transferred to a spouse who has such a certificate, for the benefit of that spouse and/or a dependant.

CLS(F) Regs 2000, reg 52(1)(b)

The postponement of the charge is subject to the Commission being satisfied that the property in question will provide such security as it considers appropriate.

Where it is sought to postpone the charge, the order must be endorsed with a declaration to that effect.

CLA (Gen) Regs 1989, reg 99 and CLS(F) Regs 2000, regs 52(3) and 53

Practitioners should be aware that the operation of the relevant regulations attracts interest on the amount outstanding under the charge, until it is redeemed.

Note: The appropriate wording required by the regulations to be included on the face of the order in these circumstances is as follows:

–   It is certified pursuant to [*insert appropriate regulation*] and solely for the purposes of the [*insert the title of the relevant authority*] that the lump sum hereby ordered to be paid is to be used for the purpose of purchasing a home for the Petitioner and her dependants.

and/or

–   It is hereby certified pursuant to [*insert appropriate regulation*] and solely for the purposes of the [*insert the title of the relevant authority*] that the property at .... aforesaid hereby ordered to be transferred is to be used for the purpose of providing a home for the Petitioner and her dependants.

It should be noted that the first £2,500 which has been recovered or preserved is exempt from the operation of the statutory charge. This exemption also applies to orders made pursuant to ss 2 and 6 of the Inheritance (Provision for Family and Dependants) Act 1975 (I(PFD)A 1975) and s 17 of the Married Women's Property Act 1882 (MWPA 1882).

CLA (Gen) Regs 1989, reg 94 and CLS(F) Regs 2000, reg 44(1)(d) and (2)

11.3.14   Application to set aside final order

Although the court will only rarely entertain an application to set aside an order imposed by the court or made by consent, an application may be considered in circumstances where there has been:

(a) a material non-disclosure or misrepresentation;
(b) fraud or undue influence;
(c) an event which post-dates the order and which has the effect of undermining the basis upon which the order was made.

Note: A full and helpful analysis of this subject is to be found in the *Ancillary Relief Handbook* by District Judge Roger Bird (2nd edn, Family Law, 2000) at **9.16** et seq.

11.3.15   Application to vary or discharge a maintenance order

Once a final maintenance order has been made, any application to the court of origin to vary or discharge it is treated as an application for ancillary relief and accordingly must be made in Form A and the procedure set out at **11.3.1** followed in all respects.

If the application to vary is being made as a matter of some urgency, for example where a paying party's financial circumstances have taken a dramatic turn for the worse, it may be appropriate to apply to the court for an interim order, when the procedure set out at **11.2.4** should be followed.

Practitioners should be aware that it is essential that an application to vary periodical payments be issued prior to the expiration of the existing order.

G v G (Periodical Payments) [1997] 1 All ER 272, CA

If the parties are able to reach agreement, then the procedure for consent orders set out at **11.3.9** should be followed. However, it should be noted that in some courts it is likely that there will be no requirement to file a Form A, where the minute of agreement and consent order are lodged for approval prior to a formal application being issued. Accordingly, practitioners should check with the relevant court as to local practice.

11.3.16 Application to vary a lump sum order which is payable by instalments

Once a lump sum order, which is payable by two or more instalments, has been made, any application to the court to vary the amount of any instalment or the due date for payment is treated as an application for ancillary relief. Accordingly, the application must be made in Form A and the procedure set out at **11.3.1** followed in all respects.

If the parties are able to reach agreement, then the procedure for consent orders set out at **11.3.9** should be followed. However, it should be noted that in some courts it is likely that there will be no requirement to file a Form A, where the minute of agreement and consent order are lodged for approval prior to a formal application being issued. Accordingly, practitioners should check with the relevant court as to local practice.

11.3.17 Matrimonial Causes Act 1973, section 10(2)

The provision of MCA 1973, s 10(2) enables the respondent in divorce proceedings commenced under the provisions of s 1(2)(d) and (e) to apply to the court for it to consider his/her financial position as it will be after the divorce. The application can be made either before or after the decree nisi but cannot be made after the decree absolute has been granted.

FPR 1991, r 2.45(1)

With the general application of the ancillary relief pilot scheme, an application pursuant to s 10(2) is issued by way of Form B. The procedure thereafter is identical to that which is set out in the earlier parts of this chapter.

Wherever possible the application should be heard together with any substantive application for ancillary relief because the issues to be considered by the court are invariably identical. It will be evident that, dealt with in this way, there will be a significant saving of costs.

The application may be transferred to the High Court, although the suit itself may continue in the county court.

A decree absolute, which has been inadvertently granted, ignoring the requirements of s 10(2), is voidable.

The provision of s 10(2) should not be confused with that of s 5 of the MCA 1973. The operation of s 10(2) in the first instance merely acts as a stay upon the decree absolute, whereas s 5 provides a basis for a defence to a divorce petition itself.

Proceedings under s 10(2) are conducted in chambers before a district judge, whereas a s 5 defence is heard in exactly the same way as an answer to a petition, in open court, before a circuit judge or High Court judge.

Note: See **4.1** for a fuller explanation of the provisions of s 5 of the MCA 1973.

CHAPTER 12

OTHER FINANCIAL APPLICATIONS GOVERNED BY THE FAMILY PROCEEDINGS RULES 1991

12.1 FAILURE TO PROVIDE REASONABLE MAINTENANCE

The provisions of MCA 1973, s 27 provide the mechanism for a spouse to apply to the court for a maintenance order in circumstances where no other matrimonial proceedings have been issued.

12.1.1 The nature of the relief

Either husband or wife (and this includes parties who are judicially separated) can apply, by originating application, for maintenance from the other on the ground that he/she has failed to provide reasonable maintenance for the applicant or failed to make a proper contribution towards the maintenance of any child of the family.

The range of the orders which the court is empowered to make are set out in MCA 1973, s 27(6)(a)–(f).

Unlike s 23 of the MCA 1973, under the provisions of s 27 a child of the family cannot apply on his/her own behalf and consequently is reliant upon a parent to make the application.

MCA 1973, s 27(1)

Where there is an urgent need for immediate assistance, it is possible to apply to the court for an interim order.

All matters relating to the issue and conduct of these proceedings are governed by the provisions of the FPR 1991.

FPR 1991, r 3.1

As with other proceedings under the MCA 1973, one of the parties must be domiciled or habitually resident in England and Wales for a period of at least one year prior to the date upon which the application is issued.

Note: See **3.6** for the procedure to be followed in circumstances where the respondent alleges that neither party conforms with the provisions of s 5(2) of the DMPA 1973.

12.1.2 Procedure

The originating application (in Form M19) can be issued in a divorce county court or the Principal Registry of the Family Division (exercising its county court jurisdiction). A copy must be provided for service upon the respondent. A court fee is payable unless the applicant is exempt from fees.

FPR 1991, r 3.1(1)

An affidavit in support of the application, providing the information required by FPR 1991, r 3.1, must be filed at the time of issue and a copy provided for service.

FPR 1991, r 3.1(2) and (3)(a)–(c)

Sealed copies of the originating application and supporting affidavit must be served upon the respondent, together with the notice of proceedings in Form M20 and acknowledgement of service in Form M6, suitably amended to refer to an originating application.

FPR 1991, r 3.1(4)

The notice of proceedings is endorsed with the date and time of the first hearing, which will normally be for directions only.

Once served the respondent should return the acknowledgement of service to the court within eight days, unless the time has been extended to take account of service having been effected outside the jurisdiction.

FPR 1991, r 10.6

Thereafter, the respondent is required to file an affidavit in reply within 14 days after the period of time allowed for the filing of the acknowledgement of service.

FPR 1991, r 3.1(5)

The affidavit of the respondent must contain the information required by FPR 1991, r 3.1(5)(a)–(c).

Where the respondent makes an allegation of adultery or improper association against a named person the court may direct service of all or part of the respondent's affidavit upon that named person.

FPR 1991, r 3.1(7)

All hearings are listed in accordance with FPR 1991, r 2.66 and are heard before a district judge sitting in chambers. Accordingly, counsel, a solicitor or a legal executive has the right of audience.

If the final hearing has a time estimate of a half-day or more, court bundles must be prepared and lodged in accordance with the relevant President's Direction.

PD of 10 March 2000

12.2   INJUNCTIONS UNDER SECTION 37 OF THE MATRIMONIAL CAUSES ACT 1973

12.2.1   The nature of the relief

Section 37 of the MCA 1973 provides the means for a party to matrimonial proceedings, who has issued an application for ancillary relief, to apply to the court for an order (injunction) restraining the other spouse from attempting to defeat a claim for ancillary relief.

The application is usually made:

(a)   with a view to freezing assets; or
(b)   to set aside a transfer, which has already taken place.

An order made under this section will often remain in effect until the conclusion of the ancillary relief proceedings.

In a case of extreme urgency, a judge may make an immediate order even though no application for ancillary relief has been issued. However, in such circumstances, there will be a requirement to provide an undertaking to issue the application by a specified date (usually not more than seven days ahead).

Note: For the meaning and scope of ancillary relief see Chapter 11.

12.2.2   Procedure

The procedure to be followed in the case of an emergency application is set out in greater detail in Chapter 21.

The application may be made using a general form of application or the standard county court Form N16A, suitably adapted, in either way supported by an affidavit setting out full details of why the relief is sought. Copies of both documents must be provided for service and a court fee is payable unless the applicant is exempt from fees.

The application can be made:

(a)   in an urgent situation to a judge (usually a district judge) without giving notice to the other party (ex parte). In the Principal Registry of the Family Division this will be to the district judge of the day; or
(b)   where the element of surprise is not required, on notice (inter partes).

Unlike civil proceedings, an applicant for a s 37 order may not be required to give security for costs. Further information on this topic can be found in *Rayden*, 17th edn, para 32.71.

If the matter is considered ex parte, the district judge can be expected to make either:

(a) an interim order and fix an early return date, on notice; or
(b) no order but fix a return date.

The return date is fixed so that the application can be fully considered on its merits.

By the very nature of the relief granted, and the fact that a penal notice will be endorsed on the order, virtually every order which is made will need to be personally served upon the respondent to the application.

Where the subject matter is money, in an account, or an assurance policy, it is essential to serve the organisation which holds the funds or policy so as to ensure that the asset is properly protected.

Rather than dealing with a s 37 application in isolation, it may be appropriate for arrangements to be made for the final ancillary relief hearing to be expedited, so that all issues can be resolved at the one hearing. FPR 1991, r 2.62(2)

This has the obvious merit of minimising overall costs. However, in order to make a final ancillary relief order and to bring it into effect, it may also be necessary for the decree nisi and decree absolute to be expedited.

Note: See **6.1.3** for procedure relating to dispensing with formalities.

Where property has already been transferred to a third party, that person or organisation may need to be made a party to the s 37 application. If not made a party that person or organisation may wish to apply to the court to be made a party, in order to make representations.

Notice of the initial appointment must be given to every party to the application. FPR 1991, r 2.62(3)

The application will be heard in chambers, usually before a district judge, and therefore counsel, a solicitor or a legal executive has the right of audience. FPR 1991, r 2.68(1)

If the application is to freeze assets worldwide the application is made to a High Court judge of the Family Division and, if made, the resultant order is known as a freezing injunction (previously a *Mareva* injunction).

If a hearing has a time estimate of a half-day or more or, irrespective of the time estimate is before a High Court

PD of 10 March 2000

judge, court bundles must be prepared and lodged in accordance with the relevant President's Direction.

Where the application is being heard as a matter of urgency, the President's Direction of 10 March 2000 does not apply.

Note: For the procedure to follow where there has been a breach of an injunction or undertaking, see **23.2**.

12.2.3   Undertakings

As an alternative to the court granting an injunction, it may be appropriate in some circumstances for the respondent to the application to give an undertaking, preferably in Form N117 (county court) or Form D787 (PRFD), in respect of a part or all of the assets in issue. However, it can be anticipated that a penal notice will attach in much the same way as it would have done to an order.

12.3   SECTION 17 OF THE MARRIED WOMEN'S PROPERTY ACT 1882

12.3.1   The nature of the relief

The application can be filed by either party to a marriage, at any time during the marriage or within three years of the date of decree absolute for:

(a)   a declaration as to their respective equitable interest in any land or other property which they jointly own; and

(b)   an order for sale or, in the case of chattels, a distribution as between the parties.

By virtue of the Matrimonial Causes (Property and Maintenance) Act 1958, s 7, these remedies are also available to those who have been engaged, provided proceedings are instituted within three years of the termination of the agreement to marry. This may present potential difficulties in determining whether or not the parties were actually engaged and, subsequently, the date upon which the engagement came to an end.

12.3.2   Procedure

An application under s 17 of the MWPA 1882 may be issued as:

FPR 1991, r 3.6(1)(a)

(a)   an originating summons in Form M23 in the High Court;

FPR 1991, r 3.6(1)(b)

(b)   an originating application in the county court but not the Principal Registry of the Family Division exercising its county court jurisdiction;

(c)   an application in Form D11 within any ancillary relief
       proceedings.   FPR 1991, r 3.6(2)

The procedure generally is set out in FPR 1991, r 3.6. Note
in particular:

(a)   the application must be supported by an affidavit and
       a court fee is payable unless the applicant is exempt
       from fees;
(b)   a sealed copy of the application and affidavit are
       served on the respondent together with an
       acknowledgement of service, in Form M28 in the
       High Court and Form M6 in the county court. No
       acknowledgement of service is provided in
       circumstances where the application is commenced
       within ancillary relief proceedings;
(c)   where the property concerned is subject to a
       mortgage, a copy of the application must be served on
       the mortgagee.   FPR 1991, r 3.6(6)

The application form will be endorsed with the date and
time of the first hearing, when a district judge will usually
give directions as to the conduct of the proceedings.

If the respondent intends to defend, he/she must, within 14
days after the time allowed for the filing of the
acknowledgement of service, file and serve an affidavit in
answer to the application.   FPR 1991, r 3.6(7)

The acknowledgement should be returned to the court
within eight days of service, unless the address for service
is outside England and Wales and the time for filing the
acknowledgement has been extended.   FPR 1991, r 10.6

The final hearing will usually be before a district judge
sitting in chambers and accordingly counsel, a solicitor or
a legal executive has the right of audience.

If the final hearing has a time estimate of a half-day or
more, court bundles must be prepared and lodged in
accordance with the relevant President's Direction.   PD of 10 March 2000

If the parties have been married, wherever possible the
applicant for financial and property orders will use the
provisions of ss 24 and 24A of the MCA 1973, rather than
those provided by s 17 of the MWPA 1882. This is
because under the MCA 1973 the court:

(a)   has the very much wider powers set out in **11.2**; and
(b)   can make an order or orders under ss 24 and 24A
       even though a previous order or orders have been
       made under s 17 of the MWPA 1882.

CHAPTER 13

FINANCIAL APPLICATIONS GOVERNED BY THE CIVIL PROCEDURE RULES 1998

13.1 TYPES OF APPLICATION

Unlike all other financial proceedings set out in this book, applications pursuant to s 14 of the Trusts of Land and Appointment of Trustees Act 1996 (TLATA 1996) and s 2 of the I(PFD)A 1975 are governed by the provisions of the CPR 1998 rather than by the FPR 1991.

PD of 22 April 1999

13.2 PROCEDURE

13.2.1 Requirements on issue

An application should be commenced as a Part 8 action in Form N208 and attracts a civil procedure court fee unless the claimant is exempt from fees. The claim form, together with a signed statement of truth, should be supported by a witness statement or an affidavit of the claimant.

CPR 1998, PD 8, 2.1

CPR 1998, r 22.1

Where the claimant is a minor or otherwise under a disability, the claim must be made through a litigation friend acting on behalf of the claimant and a certificate in Form N235, signed by the litigation friend, must be filed.

CPR 1998, r 21.2

Sufficient copies of the claim form and statement or affidavit should be filed for service on every defendant.

13.2.2 Service

Each defendant must be served with:

CPR 1998, r 8.5(2)
CPR 1998, r 8.5(2)
CPR 1998, r 8.5(2)

(a) a copy of the claim form;
(b) a copy of the claimant's statement or affidavit;
(c) an acknowledgement of service in Form N210;
(d) notes for guidance for the defendant in Form N208C;
(e) notice of the place, date and time of the first directions hearing, if fixed by the court at this stage.

A defendant will be served by the court by first-class post unless solicitors have indicated that they wish to effect service otherwise in accordance with CPR 1998, r 6.2.

A claim form must be served within four months of issue.

CPR 1998, r 7.5(2)

This period is extended to six months where the claim form is to be served out of the jurisdiction.

CPR 1998, r 7.5(3)

The claimant may apply for an order extending the period within which the claim form may be served.

CPR 1998, r 7.6(1)

The general rule is that an application to extend the time for service must be made:

(a) within the period for serving the claim form specified by r 7.5; or
(b) where an order has been made under r 7.6, within the period for service specified by that order.

CPR 1998, r 7.6(2)

If the claimant applies for an order to extend the time for service of the claim form after the end of the period specified by r 7.5 or r 7.6, the court may make such an order only if:

(a) the court has been unable to serve the claim form; or
(b) the claimant has taken all reasonable steps to serve the claim form but has been unable to do so; and
(c) in either case the claimant has acted promptly in making the application.

CPR 1998, r 7.6(4)

An application, preferably in Form N244, for an order extending the time for service:

(a) must be supported by evidence; and
(b) may be made without notice.

CPR 1998, r 7.6(4)

A court fee is payable unless a claimant is exempt from fees.

Once served, a defendant is required to file at court within 14 days of service, a completed and signed acknowledgement of service.

CPR 1998, r 10.3(1)

On receipt of the acknowledgement of service, the court must notify the claimant in writing.

CPR 1998, r 10.4

Practitioners should note that although a defendant has a 14-day period within which to file an acknowledgement of service, the rules give authority to the court to bring forward a hearing. This enables a judge to direct that a date be fixed within the 14-day period in an urgent case or where there is a perceived need for the matter to be listed on the same day and at the same time as a hearing in prior related proceedings.

CPR 1998, r 10.3(2)(a)

Where service is to be effected out of the jurisdiction, the period of time for filing an acknowledgement of service is calculated by reference to RSC Ord 11.

For procedure concerning an application for service out of the jurisdiction, reference should be made to RSC Ord 11, r 4 and CPR r 6.17 et seq.

Where the claim is being brought in the county court it may only be started in the county court for the district in which:

CPR 1998, PD 8B, para B.6

(a)   the defendant or one of the defendants lives; or

(b)   the subject matter of the claim is situated.

13.2.3   Rights of audience

Substantive hearings will, unless otherwise directed, be in open court before a district judge but may, if there are complex or other significant issues, be before a circuit or High Court judge. Practitioners may therefore wish to check with the court as to the level of judge before making a decision as to who is to appear.

13.3   SECTION 14 OF THE TRUSTS OF LAND AND APPOINTMENT OF TRUSTEES ACT 1996

The procedure for issuing a claim under s 14 of TLATA 1996 is set out in **13.2**. The claim can be commenced in a county court (but not the Principal Registry of the Family Division exercising its county court jurisdiction) or the High Court by a joint owner of land (including buildings on the land) for:

(a)   a declaration as to his/her equitable interest in that land; and/or

(b)   a consequential order/orders, for example an order for sale.

HCCCJO 1991, art 2(1)(p)

A county court has jurisdiction whatever the amount involved in the proceedings and whatever the value of any fund or asset connected with the proceedings.

TLATA 1996, s 15

Practitioners should make a careful note of the various matters to which the court must have regard in determining an application under s 14.

There is no requirement for the joint owners to have been married or engaged.

If the parties have been married, wherever possible the applicant for financial and property orders will use the provisions of ss 24 and 24A of the MCA 1973, rather than

the provisions of s 14 of the TLATA 1996. This is because
under the MCA 1973 the court:

(a) has the very much wider powers set out in Chapter
     11; and
(b) can make an order or orders under ss 24 and 24A
     even though a previous order or orders have been
     made under s 14 of the TLATA 1996.

The provisions of TLATA 1996, s 14 are also used to
enforce a charging order by sale. Full details of the
procedure in this respect are set out at **21.4.2**.

13.4   SECTION 2 OF THE INHERITANCE (PROVISION FOR FAMILY AND DEPENDANTS) ACT 1975

The procedure for issuing a claim under s 2 of the
I(PFD)A 1975 is set out in **13.2**. The claim can be
commenced in a county court or the High Court for
reasonable financial provision to be provided from the
estate of the deceased for:

(a) a surviving or former spouse who has not remarried;
     or
(b) a child of the deceased;
(c) a person who, whilst not a child of the deceased, was
     treated at any time as a child of the family in relation
     to a marriage to which the deceased was a party;   I(PFD)A 1975, s 1
(d) a person who, at the date of death of the deceased,
     was dependent upon him/her.

If the value of the claim is more than £50,000, the
application must be issued in the High Court. If it is less
than £25,000, it must be commenced in a county court and
if it is between £25,000 and £50,000, it can be commenced
in either.   HCCCJO 1991, art 7

The application can be made for both maintenance and/or
capital.

In a case of need, the court may be prepared to entertain an
application for interim maintenance.   I(PFD)A 1975, s 5

The application must be made within six months of either
grant of probate or taking out letters of administration.   I(PFD)A 1975, s 4

A separate application, in Form N244, may be made to a
district judge for leave to issue an application even though
the six-month period has expired. The application must be
made on notice supported by a witness statement or
affidavit setting out the reasons for the delay.   I(PFD)A 1975, s 4

RSC Ord 99, r 3(6)

The application must be supported by a witness statement or affidavit by the claimant, exhibiting an office copy of the grant of representation to the deceased's estate and of every testamentary document admitted to proof.

Action to be taken by a defendant who is a personal representative and any other defendant is set out at RSC Ord 99, r 5.

The various matters to which the court is to have regard in exercising its powers under the provisions of s 2 are set out in s 3 of the I(PFD)A 1975.

I(PFD)A 1975, s 19(3)

A copy of every substantive order which is made by the court must be sent to the Probate Department of the Principal Registry, together with the original grant. This is to enable a memorandum of the order to be endorsed on the probate or letters of administration under which the estate is being administered.

MCA 1973, s 18(2)

Practitioners' attention is drawn to the fact that if, whilst a decree of judicial separation is in force and the separation is continuing, either of the parties dies intestate all his/her real or personal property will devolve as if the other party to the marriage had then been dead.

Part III
CHILDREN

CHAPTER 14

SECTION 41 OF THE MATRIMONIAL CAUSES ACT 1973

14.1   THE DUTY OF THE COURT

Section 41 requires the court in any proceedings for a decree of divorce, nullity of marriage or judicial separation to certify whether or not there is a child of the family and, if there is, to consider the arrangements which have been, or are proposed to be, made for the upbringing and welfare of that child.

MCA 1973, s 41(1)(a) and (b)

A child of the family is a child of one party or both parties to the marriage (and this includes an adopted child) either:

MCA 1973, s 41(3)(a)

MCA 1973, s 41(3)(b)

(a) who is under 16 years of age; or
(b) whom the court directs shall be made the subject of an order under the provisions of this section.

Examples of a child who is likely to fall within the scope of (b) above are:

(a) one who is over the age of 16 but receiving education or training by way of an apprenticeship or training for a profession or vocation, irrespective of whether that child is also in gainful employment; or
(b) one who is over the age of 16 but severely mentally or physically impaired.

14.2   STATEMENT OF ARRANGEMENTS

When the petition is filed, it must be accompanied by a statement of arrangements in Form M4. This form requires the petitioner to provide comprehensive information relating to all aspects of a child's welfare.

FPR 1991, r 2.2(2)

It is particularly important to ensure that where the court makes an order granting the petitioner leave to omit his/her address from the face of the petition, the address is not inadvertently disclosed in the statement of arrangements. Similarly, the details of the school which the child attends should be omitted in order to avoid the possibility of the respondent being able to trace the petitioner's address from the information provided.

If a child is the subject of a care or supervision order or is on a local authority 'at risk' register, a copy of the relevant order or notification of registration should accompany the statement of arrangements. Where a local authority is involved, it is advisable to provide the court with a letter from the social services department, dealing with the present and anticipated future positions. The court may also require a letter or report from any other person involved with the child's welfare, for example a hospital psychiatrist.

The statement of arrangements can, and where possible should, be agreed by the respondent prior to filing at court, and there is provision on the form for the respondent to indicate such agreement. As with the content of a petition, prior agreement will reduce the scope for possible conflict or perhaps eliminate it altogether.

FPR 1991, r 2.2(2)

Even where the content of the statement has been agreed and signed by the respondent, it is still necessary for the respondent to be formally served with a sealed copy at the same time as the sealed copy of the petition and notice of proceedings with acknowledgement of service attached.

FPR 1991, r 2.6(5)

Even if the arrangements are not previously agreed, the respondent can nevertheless indicate his agreement to them on the acknowledgement of service form, which is served together with the petition. If the arrangements are not agreed, the respondent can file an alternative statement and, in any event, can subsequently apply to the court with regard to any matter of particular concern.

FPR 1991, r 2.38

It may be necessary to file a subsequent, updated or supplemental statement of arrangements, for example, after the parties have unsuccessfully attempted a reconciliation.

14.3 REQUIREMENT FOR A JUDGE TO BE SATISFIED AS TO THE ARRANGEMENTS FOR A CHILD

A judge must certify that the arrangements for a child are satisfactory before the final decree is granted. Since with a judicial separation petition there is only one decree, the arrangements must be declared to be satisfactory prior to the pronouncement of that decree.

If the petition is proceeding under the special procedure provisions, a district judge will consider the arrangements, as a paper exercise, at the same time as dealing with the divorce itself. If there is any reason for concern, the judge may:

(a) require further written evidence to be filed, for example a statement from a parent or social worker; and/or

(b) order a hearing to take place so that the court can receive oral evidence from either one or both of the parents.

FPR 1991, r 2.39(3)

In exceptional circumstances, the judge may order a stay on the issuing of the decree absolute of divorce or nullity or decree of judicial separation until the court orders otherwise. In practice, this means that until such time as the court is satisfied as to the arrangements or accepts that whilst not being entirely satisfactory they are the best which can be devised in the circumstances, the suit cannot be concluded.

MCA 1973, s 41(2)

With regard to (b) above, if the court orders a hearing, it will take place before a district judge in chambers.

If a petition for divorce or judicial separation was filed prior to 14 October 1991, or after that date is a defended suit, and in the case of all nullity petitions irrespective of the date of filing, the s 41 hearing should be listed before a circuit judge sitting in chambers.

At a s 41 hearing, the judge will either:

(a) certify that he is satisfied as to the arrangements for each child; or

(b) adjourn the hearing, giving such directions as may be necessary, with a view to further evidence being presented to the court.

MCA 1973, s 41(2)

In an exceptional case, a judge may order that there be a stay on the issuing of the decree absolute of divorce or nullity or the decree of judicial separation (see above).

Irrespective of whether the hearing takes place before a district judge or a circuit judge it will be in chambers. This means that counsel, a solicitor or a legal executive will have the right of audience. It also means that, other than with leave of the court, only the parties and their legal representatives will be permitted to be present.

CA 1989, s 10(1)

When considering the arrangements for a child of the family, the court may make orders with regard to residence and contact. The jurisdiction conferred by the Children Act 1989 is explained at **15.8**.

CHAPTER 15

CHILDREN – PRIVATE LAW ISSUES

15.1 PARTS I AND II OF THE CHILDREN ACT 1989

The Children Act 1989 (CA 1989) is concerned with all aspects of the welfare and general upbringing of a child. Parts I and II of the CA 1989 relate to private law matters, that is to say proceedings brought by one individual against another individual or individuals. Parts III to XI concern public law matters, that is to say proceedings brought by a local authority against an individual or individuals. Part XII deals with both private and public law matters. The public law aspects of the CA 1989 are outside the scope of this book and accordingly are not further considered.

In making an order under the various provisions of Parts I and II, the court must have regard to the provisions of s 1(3). These provisions are commonly referred to as the welfare checklist. However, it should be noted that it is a basic principle of the CA 1989 that no order should be made unless it would be in the best interest of a child to make one. This is generally referred to as the 'non-intervention principle'.

CA 1989, s 1(5)

15.2 PROCEDURE

15.2.1 Jurisdiction

Proceedings can be issued in the High Court, in the Principal Registry of the Family Division (exercising its county court jurisdiction) and any divorce county court. Proceedings can similarly be issued in a magistrates' court exercising family jurisdiction (a family proceedings court). Save as referred to in **15.2.2**, with regard to transfer, proceedings in the magistrates' court are outside the scope of this book.

C(AP)O 1991, art 20, as amended by SI 1997/1897

The Lambeth, Shoreditch and Woolwich County Courts have all been granted special limited jurisdiction to hear applications pursuant to ss 4 and 8 of the CA 1989.

15.2.2 Transfer of proceedings

With regard to all proceedings referred to in this chapter, the rules provide for the unrestricted transfer between different types of court and between courts of the same tier, although the ability to transfer from a county court to a family proceedings court is infrequently exercised. Where there is an issue with regard to the appropriate tier of court, it generally falls to be determined by a district judge.

FPR 1991, r 4.6

Whenever proceedings are transferred, whether vertically or laterally, the court from which the matter is being transferred should ensure that the next hearing date is fixed with the receiving court. This date should then be incorporated within the order for transfer.

FPR 1991, r 4.15(2)

15.2.3 Hearings

Practitioners should refer to the Family Proceedings (Allocation to Judiciary) Directions 1999 [1999] 2 FLR 799 for full details of the allocation of CA 1989 hearings as between the various categories of judges. In any event, it should be noted that all proceedings relating to children are heard in chambers and accordingly counsel, a solicitor or a legal executive will have the right of audience. Other than with leave of the court, only the parties and their legal advisers will be permitted to be present.

FPR 1991, r 4.16(7)

It is generally accepted that cases which include a substantial foreign element are usually more suitable for determination by a High Court judge.

15.2.4 Commencement of proceedings

Proceedings will be commenced by issuing a free-standing application unless there are any pending proceedings, in which case there is a requirement for the application to be issued within those existing proceedings.

FPR 1991, r 2.40(1)

Where the application is free-standing it must be commenced using Form C1. If the application is made in existing family proceedings it must be commenced using Form C2. In either case, sufficient copies of the application must be sent to the court, for service on any respondent, together with the court fee, unless the applicant is exempt from fees. See **15.2.5** with regard to service.

For the purposes of r 2.40(1) of the FPR 1991, the proceedings shall be treated as pending for a period of one year after the last hearing or judicial intervention within those proceedings. However, an application for a variation order, even though it may be made after a period of one year, is normally made within those proceedings, by way of Form C2.

FPR 1991, r 2.40(3)

If the applicant does not wish to reveal his/her address or that of a relevant child, a Form C8 must be completed. Once filed at court, the address should not be disclosed to any person other than by order of the court. The form will be placed, in a sealed envelope, on the court file which will be marked accordingly.

FPR 1991, r 10.21

Application Forms C1 or C2 should be confined to relevant factual information and should avoid unnecessary inflammatory allegations. Once issued, every respondent must be served with:

(a) a copy of the Form C1 or C2;
(b) Form C6 (notice of proceedings);
(c) Form C7 (acknowledgement).

FPR 1991, r 4.4(1)(b)

If there is a requirement to serve a person who is not a party to the proceedings, for example a relative with whom a child resides, the notice will be in Form C6A and not C6.

The Form C6 or C6A will be endorsed with the time and date of the first hearing or directions appointment.

15.2.5   Service

The first hearing or directions appointment date will be fixed sufficiently far ahead to allow time for the respondent to be served in accordance with the rules (see below).

FPR 1991, r 4.4(2)(a)

Unlike most other applications in family proceedings, unless otherwise stated, the applications referred to in this chapter will require service on any respondent on not less than 14 clear days' notice.

FPR 1991, App 3, col (ii)

Appendix 3 to the FPR 1991 provides full details of the minimum number of days' notice required prior to a hearing or directions appointment in respect of all CA 1989 applications.

If a respondent to the application is residing overseas at the time of the application, the time for service will be extended by reference to the provisions of FPR 1991, r 10.6, taking account of the fact that the time for service within the jurisdiction is 14 days. In some circumstances, service may be effected through the foreign process section of the Master's Secretary's Department, Room E219 in the Royal Courts of Justice.

If the respondent is a member of the armed forces and is currently serving overseas, he/she may be served by posting the application and all related documents to the relevant British Forces Post Office address. A BFPO address can be obtained from the armed forces postal and courier service, details of which can be found in Appendix C(1).

Unless otherwise directed, service should be effected either by first-class post upon the respondent or, where a solicitor is acting, by first-class post, document exchange or facsimile transmission.

FPR 1991, r 4.8(1)(a) and (b)

Wherever possible, a further application, by any party, relating to the same child or a sibling of that child will be listed on the same day and at the same time as the original application. This will invariably mean that the time for service on any respondent will need to be abridged (shortened). The applicant will need to apply ex parte, by way of Form C2, to a district judge for such an order. The application attracts a court fee unless the applicant is exempt from fees.

Where the time for service has been abridged, in practice solicitors will almost certainly wish to arrange for personal service by process server.

15.2.6   Proceedings commenced by or on behalf of a person under disability

Proceedings commenced by or on behalf of a person under disability are governed by FPR 1991, rr 9.2 and 9.2A.

The rules relating to a person under disability commencing or defending proceedings under the provisions of the CA 1989 are complex and if there is any doubt in the mind of a practitioner as to the requirements, the rules should be carefully checked. However, the more important aspects are set out below.

Normally an application made by a child pursuant to s 8 of the CA 1989 will be commenced on behalf of that child by a next friend, in any of the courts referred to in **15.2.1**. It will often be appropriate for one solicitor to accept instructions from both the next friend, on behalf of the child, as well as a parent of that child.

If the application is issued by a next friend, he/she should sign and lodge a formal consent to act on behalf of the child. However, it is also possible for a child to apply, by way of Form C2, to be separately represented by his/her own solicitor. If the application is made to a court other than the High Court it should be transferred to that court, without delay, initially for a High Court judge to determine the issue as to representation. This does not necessarily mean that the application will be transferred to the Royal Courts of Justice, since in many cases, it will be more appropriate to list the matter in a nearby district registry, where there is a High Court judge sitting.

Practitioners should be clear that an application by a child for separate representation is not an automatic process and that it will be critically viewed, particularly in circumstances where the parent with whom the child resides is not in receipt of Community Legal Services funding. In other words, the application will not succeed where it is seen as a naked attempt to circumvent the constraints of the Community Legal Services provisions.

Where the High Court judge has given leave for the child to be separately represented but he/she does not have the benefit of a next friend, it is open to the judge to find that there are exceptional circumstances which make it desirable, in the interests of his/her welfare, for a member of the Children and Family Court Advisory and Support Service (CAFCASS) or the Official Solicitor to be appointed as next friend. In March 2001, the Director of CAFCASS Legal Services issued a comprehensive practice note on the subject, followed on 2 April 2001 by an equally comprehensive practice note from the Official Solicitor. Copies of the relevant extracts from both notes are to be found at Appendix C(6).

In any event, a child may proceed without having a next friend where:

(a) leave of the court has been granted; or
(b) a solicitor is of the opinion that the child is of sufficient understanding to give instructions in relation to the proceedings and that solicitor has accepted instructions.

The child can apply for the leave of the court, without a next friend, by either:

(a) filing a written request setting out the reasons for the application; or
(b) making an oral request at any hearing in the proceedings.

Similar provisions to those set out above, concerning the appointment of a guardian ad litem or a member of CAFCASS, apply with regard to a respondent who is a

Margin notes:

PD of 22 February 1993

FPR 1991, r 9.2A(1)(a) and (b)

FPR 1991, r 9.2A(2)(a) and (b)

minor child and who wishes to defend the proceedings.
However, the Court of Appeal has emphasised that in the
great majority of cases it is unnecessary to join the child as
a party and that should only be done in exceptional
circumstances.   PD of 8 December 1981

Where a party is an adult under mental disability, the
principles with regard to the appointment of a next friend,
guardian ad litem or Official Solicitor apply in much the
same way as they do to a minor.   FPR 1991, r 9.2(3) and (4)

Separate legal representation is likely to be appropriate in
most cases where a party is under a mental disability.

15.2.7   Protecting the interests of a child

In circumstances where it becomes clear that there is the
possibility of a conflict between the interests of a child and
the person with whom that child resides, it may be
appropriate for the court to invite the Official Solicitor to
act on behalf of the child.

15.2.8   Emergency applications

This topic is covered in Chapter 20.

15.2.9   Action following service upon a respondent

Within 14 days of service of the application or, where the
respondent is outside the jurisdiction, such additional
period as has been allowed by the court, the respondent is
required to file a completed acknowledgement of service
(Form C7) and serve a copy on all other parties.   FPR 1991, r 4.9(1)

If any respondent does not wish to disclose his/her address,
a Form C8 should be completed and lodged at court by or
on behalf of that party. Once filed at court the Form C8   FPR 1991, r 10.21
will be placed in a sealed envelope on the court file, which
will be marked accordingly. Similarly, if the address of a
child who is the subject of the proceedings is to remain
confidential a Form C8 should be completed on behalf of
that child.

Once a Form C8 has been lodged with the court, the
address of the person concerned must not be disclosed
other than by order of the court.

In order to comply with the rules, the applicant is required
to file a statement of service, in Form C9, prior to the first
hearing or directions appointment confirming the details of
service upon each respondent.   FPR 1991, r 4.8

15.2.10 Preparation and filing of statements

Careful note should be taken of the provisions of FPR 1991, r 4.17 with regard to the filing of documentary evidence and statements. In particular, in proceedings for an order under CA 1989, s 8, no document or statement beyond that which is set out in Form C1 or C2 should be filed or served without the specific leave of the court.

FPR 1991, r 4.17(4) and (5)

Most courts are particularly rigorous in insisting upon compliance with r 4.17 and accordingly, great care should be exercised to ensure that it is strictly adhered to.

All statements should be prepared in such a way as to avoid inflammatory allegations or generally referring to past conduct as between the parties, unless they are serious and likely to be considered relevant by the court. It is far better to concentrate on current issues and the view of each party with regard to the arrangements which are proposed for the future welfare of a child.

15.2.11 Directions

The FPR 1991 provide the court with wide powers to give, vary or revoke directions for the conduct of the proceedings. However, in all cases the court must give the parties an opportunity to be heard.

FPR 1991, r 4.14(2)

The directions hearing can arise either:

(a) of the court's own motion; or

FPR 1991, r 4.14(3)(a) and (b)

(b) as the result of a written request of a party made in Form C2.

FPR 1991, r 4.14(5)

On receipt of a written request, in Form C2, the court will fix a hearing date on not less than two clear days' notice.

FPR 1991, r 4.14(3)(c)

Directions orders may also be made by the court as a result of a consent application being filed by the parties in Form C2. It can be anticipated that most such applications will be considered in the absence of the parties.

All applications referred to in this section attract a court fee unless the applicant is exempt from fees.

15.2.12 Interim orders

In circumstances where the final hearing is some time ahead, it may be appropriate to ask the court to consider making an interim order so that, for example, contact with a parent with whom the child does not live is maintained.

If the application is in the High Court or the Royal Courts of Justice, at county court level, court bundles must be prepared in accordance with the relevant President's Direction.

PD of 10 March 2000

An interim order is unlikely to remain in force beyond the date fixed for the final hearing. This is because the court will be concerned to ensure that there is no appearance of the final outcome being predetermined.

15.2.13   Where a party is in prison

If the presence of a party who is in prison is reasonably required at a hearing, it may be necessary to apply to the court for an order directing the governor of the relevant prison to produce the prisoner at that hearing (this is referred to as a production order).

An application for a production order is normally made on notice to the prison governor, to enable objections to be made to the court in circumstances where, for example, the prisoner is violent or would otherwise pose a threat. The application should be made on Form C2, in respect of which a fee is payable unless the applicant is exempt from fees.

Care should be taken to ensure that the production order specifies a particular hearing and is not couched in general terms.

15.2.14   Application to adjourn a final hearing

Once a final hearing has been fixed, it will only be in the most exceptional circumstances that the court will be persuaded to agree to the date being adjourned. In this connection, the court will be highly reluctant to allow further time for the filing of any additional evidence if it would result in an adjournment.

Any such application will almost certainly have to be made on Form C2, with a very full explanation as to the reason why that application is being made. If it is on medical grounds, a medical certificate will undoubtedly be required. A court fee will be payable unless the applicant is exempt from fees.

No CA 1989 application should be adjourned generally but should always be adjourned to another fixed date.

FPR 1991, r 4.15(2)

The only means of disposing of an application prior to a final hearing is for it to be withdrawn. This will be achieved either by consent or following an application. Either way the leave of the court will be required. If the application is made on notice, all respondents will require not less than seven clear days' notice.

FPR 1991, r 4.5(1), (2) and (4)

It is also possible for the applicant to make an oral application to the court for leave to withdraw, in circumstances where all relevant parties are present.

FPR 1991, r 4.5(3)

15.2.15   Preparation for the final hearing

If the hearing has a time estimate of a half-day or more or, irrespective of the time estimate, is in the High Court or the Royal Courts of Justice at county court level, court bundles must be prepared and lodged in accordance with the relevant President's Direction.

PD of 10 March 2000

15.2.16   Final order

As has previously been explained, although the underlying ethos of the CA 1989 is, wherever possible, not to make an order, in some cases there will be no alternative. Often the order will be expressed to be final. However, no order relating to a child is ever truly final since it is always subject to variation, where necessary to reflect changing circumstances.

15.2.17   Penal notice

Most judges are unwilling to attach a penal notice to any order relating to a child and one is unlikely to be granted, other than as a last resort. This is because there is a general reluctance subsequently to make a committal order and particularly against a person with whom the child resides. However, where, despite warnings, there has been a flagrant disregard of court orders there may be, in a very few extreme cases, no alternative but to commit that person to prison.

C v C [1990] 1 FLR 462, CA

Where there is a contact order in place and the person with whom a child resides is refusing to comply with that order, an alternative to an application for a penal notice might be to apply for a residence order.

In any event, it should be noted that attaching a penal notice to a s 8 order requires a specific application to be made, either at the time of the substantive order or subsequently.

FPR 1991, r 4.21A

Note: See Chapter 23 generally with regard to penal notices and committal applications.

15.3   CONCILIATION OR MEDIATION

Many courts now operate some form of in-court
conciliation or mediation. It usually takes place on the first
occasion that the matter comes before a district judge,
when the parties will be expected to be present, and
invariably takes place with the assistance of a Family
Court Adviser.

In some cases, a court may require a meeting to take place
between a child who is the subject of an application and a
Family Court Adviser of the Children and Family Court
Advisory and Support Service (CAFCASS), formerly a
court welfare officer. In particular, the Principal Registry
of the Family Division will expect a child over the age of
nine years to be available at court for this purpose. Other
courts may make arrangements for the child to see the
Family Court Adviser from CAFCASS on a later occasion
and at a venue away from the court environment.   PD of 18 October 1991

Because of the many different systems which operate, a
practitioner who is attending an unfamiliar court is advised
to check with the court office as to the details of local
practice.

The Family Court Adviser and/or the district judge may
ultimately adopt a firm approach if one of the parties is
being unreasonably intransigent and may, in an obvious
case, make it clear as to the likely outcome if the matter
were to go to a fully contested final hearing.

It may be that more than one conciliation or mediation
meeting is necessary before a satisfactory conclusion is
finally achieved.

By the very nature of these meetings, where an order is
required to be made, it will be by agreement. The court
will not impose orders, save perhaps by way of resolving
minor issues where the parties are generally close to
agreement, for example if there is merely a difference of
opinion as to the time of collection and or return of a child
for the purpose of contact.

Other than where discussions take place in the presence of
a judge, what the parties say to a Family Court Adviser
during the course of a conciliation or mediation meeting is
privileged and will not be disclosed to the court on that or
any subsequent occasion. However, where allegations of
abuse against a child who is the subject of the application
are raised, there is a requirement for the court to be
informed, so that consideration can be given as to whether

or not a report should be ordered pursuant to s 37 of the CA 1989. For information concerning this point see **15.4**.

It can be anticipated that all relevant parties to the application will be required to attend every conciliation or mediation meeting. Accordingly, if it is known that a party is unable to attend, an early application must be made to a district judge for an adjournment. The application, in Form C2, should set out details of the circumstances which prevent that party from being present. The application attracts a court fee unless the person making the application is exempt from fees.

If the conciliation or mediation proves unsuccessful at the first meeting or on any subsequent occasion, a district judge will give directions and timetabling leading to a final contested hearing. However, this is a last resort and, in the interests of the child, every effort will be made to try and persuade those responsible for the upbringing of a child to settle their differences and reach a compromise.

Unless there are wholly exceptional circumstances, a judge who has been involved in the conciliation or mediation process will automatically be disqualified from presiding over the final hearing.

15.4 WELFARE REPORTS

Where conciliation or mediation has not been successful and directions are then required for the conduct of the application leading to a final hearing, such directions may well include provision for the preparation of a welfare report. If that report is to be prepared by a Family Court Adviser from CAFCASS, it must be by one who has not participated in conciliation or mediation between the parties. The court will specify the date by which the report is to be filed, usually being a period of between 10 and 12 weeks from the date of the order.

CA 1989, s 7

If a local authority social services department has been involved with a child, it will usually be appropriate for the s 7 report to be prepared by a social worker from that local authority, rather than by a Family Court Adviser.

If, when the order for a s 7 report from social services is made, it is known that a particular social worker has been closely involved with one party to the dispute, consideration should be given to inviting the court to make a direction that a different person should be responsible for the preparation of the report.

In preparing the report, the Family Court Adviser or social worker should have regard to the s 1(3) welfare checklist.

The court will specify the scope of the report, for example whether it is to embrace a number of issues relating to a child or be limited to one particular aspect. Some courts may even limit the investigation of the reporting officer or social worker to the views of the child in question, where that child is of such an age and understanding as to be capable of expressing clear and unequivocal opinions.

For the purpose of a s 7 report, the court may order that there be such interim contact between a party, with whom the child in question does not reside, and the child, as the reporting officer shall reasonably require for the purpose of preparing the report.

Where another agency has been involved with the relevant child or with the family in general, there may be a requirement for the reporting officer or social worker to liaise with that agency. It may be necessary to interview, for example, the child's general medical practitioner, hospital consultant, health visitor, school head or class teacher, education welfare officer, guardian ad litem or the Official Solicitor. Where the report is to be prepared by a Family Court Adviser, it may also be necessary to consult with social services where they have previously been called upon to assist or are still assisting the family.

It is advisable to request the court to authorise specifically the release of copies of such documents from the court file as the reporting officer or social worker might require to assist in the preparation of the report. It is also advisable to request the court to authorise the release of a copy of any medical report which is to be generated subsequent to the directions hearing.

In circumstances where there is sufficient concern on the part of the court to raise the possibility of a care or supervision order being made in respect of a child, the local authority in whose area the child resides may be ordered to prepare a report in respect of this particular issue. The CA 1989 requires such a report to be filed within a period of eight weeks of the date of the order, unless the court directs otherwise. CA 1989, s 37

It should be noted that the CA 1989 makes it clear that a s 37 report, unlike a s 7 report, must be prepared by a social worker and it therefore follows that it cannot be prepared by a Family Court Adviser.

At the time of making the order for a s 37 report, the judge should specify on the face of the order which copy documents are to be served on the local authority and by whom they are to be provided. Copies of any documents which are on the court file should be served together with a copy of the relevant order.

FPR 1991, r 4.26(4)

If care or supervision order criteria are unlikely to be met, the court will order the local authority to prepare a report under the provisions of CA 1989, s 7 (see above). A report pursuant to s 37 will not be ordered as an alternative to s 7, and most emphatically not as a means of expediting the matter.

All s 7 and s 37 reports are confidential and accordingly practitioners should take great care that they are not disclosed to anyone other than the client or a person authorised by the court. Once the report is released by the court it is often preferable to require a client to read and consider it in a solicitor's office or counsel's chambers, rather than sending a copy by post. This will ensure that there is no possibility of the report being read by an unauthorised person.

15.5 BLOOD OR DNA TESTS

If the mother or the father of a child challenges or wishes to establish paternity, the most obvious means of resolving the issue is by way of blood or DNA tests. Blood tests were once the only way of determining paternity. However, they have become much less frequent as a result of the greater accuracy of DNA profiling.

Having taken account of any representations made on behalf of the parents, the court will order the manner in which the samples are to be given. The most common methods now used for obtaining a DNA sample are either by way of a buccal swab, which simply involves taking saliva from inside the mouth, or by removing a hair.

A sample will need to be taken from each of the mother, putative father and the child.

The ability of the court to order scientific tests is conferred by the provisions of s 20(1) of the Family Law Reform Act 1969 (FLRA 1969), as amended.

Note: An example of the relevant order is included at Appendix B(2).

Once ordered, the court is able to provide the direction forms (Scientific Test 1). A form must be completed and signed by or on behalf of each person who is to be tested.

PD of 17 February 1972

Note: An example of the direction form is to be found at Appendix B(1).

Arrangements for the taking and testing of samples will be made by the solicitor for the party on whose application the direction was given.

PD of 17 February 1972

Note: A list of laboratories approved by the Lord Chancellor to test samples in cases of disputed parentage is to be found at Appendix B(3).

Provided that the arrangements made for the testing are satisfactory, each form should also be signed by a judge, preferably the one who made the order.

PD 17 February 1972

In the case of a child under the age of 16, the formal consent of the person with whom the child resides will be required. Accordingly, details of that person will need to be specifically included in the order which authorises the testing.

FLRA 1969, s 21(3)

There are circumstances in which the court can order a sample to be taken even though the person with care and control of the child does not consent. For further details, see the Noter-up to *Rayden*, 17th edn, Chapter 35.22.

It should be noted that once a child is over the age of 16 years the consent of only that child is required.

FLRA 1969, s 21(2)

Where the person to be tested is a Mental Health Act patient, a sample may be taken, provided that there is the agreement of the person who has care and control of that patient and the consent of his/her medical practitioner.

FLRA 1969, s 21(4)

If a mother or putative father refuses to provide a sample, the court will inevitably draw such conclusions as may appear appropriate in the circumstances.

Whilst the process is not intrusive, as the law presently stands, the person with whom a child resides can refuse to allow a sample to be taken from that child. This is so even though such refusal may have the effect of denying a child the right to have paternity established.

Re O and J (Paternity: Blood Tests) [2000] 1 FLR 418, Wall J

15.6   FAMILY ASSISTANCE ORDER

In any family proceedings, the court has power to make an order requiring either a member of CAFCASS or a social worker to advise, assist and (where appropriate) befriend any parent, guardian, any person with whom a child is

CA 1989, s 16(1) and (2)

living, any person in whose favour a contact order is in force or the child concerned.

A court is not empowered to make a family assistance order unless:

(a) it is satisfied that the circumstances of the case are exceptional; and

(b) every person to be named in the order, other than the child in question, consents to the order being made.

CA 1989, s 16(3)

Unless a shorter period is specified, a family assistance order will remain in force for six months.

CA 1989, s 16(5)

Before an order is made requiring a social worker to become involved, a court must be satisfied that:

(a) the local authority agrees; and

(b) the child concerned lives within the area of that social worker.

CA 1989, s 16(7)

15.7 PARENTAL RESPONSIBILITY

Section 3 of the CA 1989 defines parental responsibility as being all the rights, duties, powers, responsibilities and authority which by law a parent of a child has in relation to the child and his property. Where the mother and father of a child were married to each other at the date of the birth, both parents have automatic parental responsibility.

CA 1989, s 2(1)

Where the mother and father of a child were not married to each other at the date of the birth only the mother will have parental responsibility and the father will have no such responsibility, other than as may be acquired in accordance with the CA 1989.

CA 1989, s 2(2)

If the father of a child who was not married to the mother at the date of birth wishes to assume parental responsibility he may:

(a) apply to the court for a parental responsibility order;

(b) enter into an agreement with the mother (referred to as a parental responsibility agreement). Unlike an application to the court, no fee is payable.

CA 1989, s 4(1) and (2)

The courts have recently shown a much greater willingness to grant a parental responsibility order, particularly where the father has demonstrated a commitment to the child and a reasonable degree of co-operation with the mother.

The requirements and form of a parental responsibility agreement are contained in the Parental Responsibility Agreement Regulations 1991. A copy of the blank form of agreement is to be found at Appendix A(27). Particular note should be taken of the fact that the signature of the mother and the father can be witnessed only by a Justice of the Peace, a justice's clerk or an authorised officer of the court. Accordingly, a solicitor is not empowered to sign as a witness.

Where more than one child is involved, a separate form of agreement is required in respect of each child.

Once executed, a parental responsibility agreement should be lodged with the Principal Registry of the Family Division who will then record it in the national register which is maintained at that court. No fee is payable. The register may be searched upon the payment of a fee unless the applicant is exempt from fees.

A parental responsibility agreement may be brought to an end if either the person with parental responsibility or the child in question makes application to the court.

CA 1989, s 4(3)

The procedure to be followed is set out at **15.2.4**.

Where the court makes a residence order in favour of the father of a child it shall, if the father would not otherwise have parental responsibility for the child, also make an order under s 4 giving him that responsibility.

CA 1989, s 12(1)

Where the court makes a residence order in favour of any person who is not the parent or guardian of the child concerned that person shall have paternal responsibility for the child while the residence order remains in force.

CA 1989, s 12(2)

Where a person has parental responsibility for a child as a result of subs (2), he/she shall not have the right:

(a) to consent, or refuse to consent, to the making of an application with respect to the child under s 18 of the Adoption Act 1976;

(b) to agree or refuse to agree to the making of a an adoption order or an order under s 55 of the Adoption Act 1976, with respect to the child; or

(c) to appoint a guardian for the child.

CA 1989, s 12(3)(a) to (c)

By reason of s 12(2), a person who is not a parent of the child, who subsequently ceases to have a residence order in his/her favour, will also cease to have parental responsibility.

15.8 ORDERS UNDER SECTION 8 OF THE CHILDREN ACT 1989

Subsections (4) and (5) of s 10 of the CA 1989 set out lists of the persons who are entitled to make an application for an order under s 8. Careful note should be made of the fact that subs (4) deals with s 8 applications in general, whereas subs (5) is more restrictive and deals only with residence or contact. Save as set out in these two subsections, all other persons who seek an order must apply in the first instance for the leave of the court to make the application.

CA 1989, s 10(1)(a)(ii)

This will invariably include a grandparent and other members of the wider family.

An application for leave to seek a s 8 order must be made in Form C2, setting out the reasons for the application together with a draft of the substantive application. In the first instance, the application will be considered, ex parte, by a district judge. If leave is not immediately granted, a hearing will be fixed to enable the matter to be considered

FPR 1991, r 4.3

in greater detail.

Section 10(1) makes it clear that a s 8 order can be made, without a specific application having been made, in any family proceedings in which a question arises with respect to the welfare of a child. Family proceedings are defined by s 8 as any proceedings under:

(a) inherent jurisdiction of the High Court in relation to children; or

(b) any of the enactments (as amended) set out in the

CA 1989, s 8(4)

section.

However, it should be noted that an opposed application, for a s 8 order, commenced in a divorce county court which is not also a family hearing centre must be

C(AP)O 1991, art 16(c)

transferred to one that is.

A list of family hearing centres is set out in Sch 1 to the Children (Allocation of Proceedings) Order 1991 (C(AP)O 1991).

Section 8 enables an application to be made for any one or more of the following orders:

(a) residence;

(b) contact;

(c) prohibited steps;

(d) specific issue.

Each type of order will be considered in detail below.

A court is not empowered to make a s 8 order which is to have effect after a child has reached the age of 16, unless it

CA 1989, s 9(6)

is satisfied that there are exceptional circumstances.

15.8.1   Residence

A residence order is defined in the CA 1989 as one which settles the arrangements to be made as to the person with whom a child is to live.

CA 1989, s 8(1)

It is possible for a residence order to be made in favour of two people (referred to as a joint residence order). However, such orders are still relatively unusual and are unlikely to be made in circumstances where both parties are not in full agreement.

The historical reluctance on the part of the court to make a joint residence order is based upon the perceived need for a child to have a clearly defined base. Although it is conceded that in the modern environment, where both parents might be working and taking an active part in the child's upbringing from an early age, a joint residence order may be a more obvious solution than it has been in the past. *D v D* [2001] 1 FLR 495 should provide helpful guidance on the subject.

Where a parent and a grandparent are each seeking residence and the competing applications have equal merit, generally the court will prefer that of the parent.

Re N [2001] 1 FLR 1028

A residence order confers on the person in whose favour it is made the right and duty to provide for the day-to-day care of a child and, by reason of parental responsibility, the right and duty to deal with all other aspects of a child's upbringing including, for example, education, religion and major medical treatment.

CA 1989, s 12(2)

Note: See **15.7** for the limitation of the power conferred by CA 1989, s 12(3)(a)–(c) and generally on the subject of parental responsibility.

If, however, a parent with whom a child does not reside enjoys parental responsibility, either by agreement or court order, that parent will also have a right to be consulted with regard to all matters of significance which cannot reasonably be regarded as day-to-day arrangements, and to be a part of the decision-making process.

All residence orders are endorsed with a warning which makes it clear, that throughout the period an order is in force:

(a)   no person may cause a child to be known by a new surname without the leave of the court; and

(b)   unless specific authority, in the form of a court order, has been granted, no person may remove a child from the United Kingdom without the written consent of every person with parental responsibility for that child or without the leave of the court. However, this provision does not prevent the removal of a child from the jurisdiction:

(i)   for a period of less than one month, by the person in whose favour the residence order has been made; or

CA 1989, s 13(2)

(ii)   generally to other parts of the United Kingdom.

If there is concern that the child may be removed from the jurisdiction, the court has the power to require any person to surrender any United Kingdom passport which has been issued to, or contains particulars of, the child in question.

FLA 1986, s 37

Since 5 October 1998, it has not been possible to apply for a child to be included in an adult's passport. Instead, applications have to be made for children to be issued with their own passports, although adults' passports which already include their children remain valid for the time being.

To remove a child from the United Kingdom other than with written consent or with leave of the court may be a criminal offence under the Child Abduction Act 1984 (see **16.2** with regard to child abduction).

A residence order may itself permit the child to reside outside the United Kingdom, either generally or for specified purposes.

CA 1989, s 13(3)

Where the court has given leave for a child to reside permanently outside the United Kingdom, it may be appropriate to ask the court to consider either:

(a)   inviting the parent who is taking the child abroad to provide an undertaking to return him/her to the jurisdiction if called upon to do so; or

(b)   making an order in such terms.

Such an undertaking or order may well facilitate enforcement in circumstances where a parent subsequently refuses to return a child from a foreign jurisdiction.

Re E (Minors)
(Residence Orders)
[1997] 2 FLR 638

Where a person has been granted a residence order, the Court of Appeal has made it clear that a court will not fetter the right of a carer to choose where to live within the United Kingdom or with whom.

Note: See Chapter 23 with regard to the consequences of failing to comply with the warnings endorsed on a residence order.

For information on making an application to the court for an order granting leave:

(a)   to change the surname of a child, see **15.9.1**; and
(b)   to remove a child from the United Kingdom, see **15.9.2**.

15.8.2   Contact

A contact order is defined in the CA 1989 as an order
which requires the person with whom a child lives, or is to
live, to allow that child to visit or stay with the person
named in the order, or for the person named in the order to
have some other form of contact with the child.   CA 1989, s 8(1)

In the context of the definition referred to above, some
other form of contact means telephone calls or indirect
contact, for example by letters, cards or e-mails.

Contact issues can properly be divided into:

(a)   the principle of whether or not contact should take
      place at all; and
(b)   if it is to take place, how such contact is to be defined.

With direct contact, the arrangements will often need to
include specific dates, times and venues for each period of
contact and for the collection from and the return to a
child's home or other specified place, for example the local
railway station.

Where there is concern as to the possible impact which
contact will have on a child, it may be necessary to make
arrangements for contact to be supervised. The supervision
may be conducted by a relative, a trusted friend of the
family or, in exceptional circumstances, by a person in
authority, for example a social worker or Family Court
Adviser. However, if a person in authority is to assist it
will only be for a limited period of time and then only with
the consent of that person.

There is now a much greater judicial understanding and
acceptance of the adverse effect of domestic violence in
general upon the mind of a child and, in particular, the fact
that sometimes he/she does not wish to see or otherwise
maintain contact with the perpetrator of that violence.
Practitioners should be aware of the guidelines for good
practice on parental contact in cases where there is
domestic violence produced in a report by the Children Act
sub-committee to the Lord Chancellor in April 2000. The
guidelines, a copy of which is to be found at Appendix
C(7), were referred to by the Court of Appeal in the
judgment in *Re L (a child) and others*, which was handed
down on 19 June 2000.

In some cases, the person with whom the child resides may
need to be present during contact; this may be particularly
so in cases where a child has not had recent contact with
the party in whose favour the order has been granted.

However, it should be anticipated that such an arrangement will be an interim measure and designed to last for a limited period.

It may also be necessary for a mother to be present during contact where a child is very young and in particular is being breast-fed.

A number of charitable agencies operate contact centres, which can be especially useful in a case where contact has to be supervised. A contact centre may also be used where there is no, or no suitable, intermediary readily available or no one who is acceptable to both sides.

A contact centre will be of considerable assistance where the level of mistrust is such as otherwise to make direct contact impossible. A particularly good example would be where a parent has been convicted of a serious sexual offence involving a minor. Judges and magistrates have been asked to take account of a protocol for referrals to contact centres which has been produced by the National Association of Child Contact Centres and endorsed by the President of the Family Division, who is also the patron of the Association. Practitioners should note in particular the fact that most Child Contact Centres do *not* offer supervised contact. The provision which most offer is supported contact. This is described as:

(a) low vigilance;
(b) several families at a time in one or a number of rooms;
(c) volunteers and staff keeping a watchful eye;
(d) conversations not being monitored.

If the court is considering making an order for contact in a case where domestic violence is an issue, it is asked to ensure that it has addressed that issue and, in particular:

(a) the effect on the resident parent and the child concerned of any domestic violence which has been found or which is alleged and that;
(b) notwithstanding these matters the court is satisfied that supported contact is appropriate. If supported contact is not appropriate, the court should consider supervised contact where it is available.

The court is also asked to check that:

1. The Child Contact Centre Co-ordinator has been contacted and has confirmed that:
   (a) the referral appears to be suitable for that particular Centre;

Note: Child Contact Centres can refuse to accept families if the circumstances appear inappropriate for the Centre.

    (b) the intended day and times are available at the particular Centre concerned;

    (c) a vacancy is available or a place on a waiting list has been allocated.

2.   It has directed a copy of the order to be provided to the Centre by one or other of the parties, within a specified time, together with any other injunctive or relevant orders on the court file.

3.   It has been agreed who will have responsibility for completing and returning the Centre's referral form.

Note: Solicitors for both parties should agree the contents and it should be forwarded to the Child Contact Centre within 24 hours of the court hearing.

4.   If contact is to be observed at the Child Contact Centre by a Family Court Adviser or other third party, it is a facility offered by that Centre and that the Centre has agreed to this course of action.

Note: Many do not permit such attendance.

5.   The parties understand whether the Centre offers supported or supervised contact and appreciate the difference.

6.   It is agreed who is going to tell the children where and when they will see their non-resident parent.

7.   The order clearly defines whether or not any other family members are to be a part of the contact visit.

8.   It has been agreed who will be responsible for informing the Centre when the place is no longer required.

9.   A date has been set for a review of the contact and any other steps parties have been ordered to take, or have undertaken to perform, which are relevant to the contact issue and for further directions if necessary.

Note: Only in the most exceptional circumstances should the use of a Centre be open-ended.

Practitioners should note that:

1.   It is a requirement of some centres that parents and children attend a pre-contact meeting (parents are seen separately) so that they can follow their own risk assessment procedure. Others will either welcome or insist on a pre-contact visit by the resident parent to acclimatise the child(ren). Non-resident parents are also welcome.

2.   The order may need to be worded 'Subject to the parties' attendance at a pre-contact meeting (if

applicable), the availability of a place and the parties abiding by the rules of the centre ...'.

Family Court Advisers attending conciliation or mediation appointments should be able to provide details of contact centres in their areas. If a centre is required outside their area, they will usually have the means of obtaining the relevant information. Otherwise, practitioners can contact the National Association of Child Contact Centres (NACCC) at Minerva House, Spaniel Row, Nottingham NG1 6EP; telephone number 0115 948 4557.

If a contact centre is to be used, it will be important to check the days and times it is open, the availability and any limitations which may be imposed. Some centres will not accept a person who has been convicted of a violent offence.

Even when supervised contact is ordered, it may be appropriate for the court to allow the person with residence to remain on the premises during the early stages of the process. This is to enable that person to witness contact when there is concern as to the way in which a child may react, to be readily available if there are problems or simply to provide reassurance.

In many cases, it will be appropriate for the court to make provision for a child to stay overnight with the parent with whom that child does not reside or with another close relative. Such arrangements may be for a single night, a weekend or for a longer period during school holidays.

Where a child has not recently stayed with the person concerned, it may be necessary to make a stepped order, that is to say one which gradually increases the contact over a period of time. This may entail an arrangement which starts with short periods of visiting contact, which are gradually increased in duration and which, if successful, will eventually culminate in staying contact.

Whatever form the contact takes, the court will strive to create a regular pattern, for example alternate weekends or one day each weekend.

As a child grows up, his/her views will inevitably become increasingly important and there will accordingly need to be a much greater need for flexibility and common sense.

However, whereas the courts in England and Wales have historically taken the view that it is the right of a child to see a parent rather than the other way round, subject to the important provisions at para (2), it is clear that para (1) of Article 8 in Sch 1 to the Human Rights Act 1998 now provides a parent who does not have residence with the same right.

In any event, it is important that a person who receives the benefit of a court order understands the importance of ensuring that contact periods run smoothly, that a child is collected and returned promptly and strictly in accordance with the order.

Practitioners should also instil in a client the need to ensure that if a problem arises which will affect contact, for example illness or an unavoidable obligation to work, the person with whom the child resides is informed at the earliest opportunity.

Where there has been a flagrant disregard of a contact order, see **15.2.17** for guidance.

15.8.3 Holiday contact

Contact during holiday periods can be ill-thought out and not infrequently leads to unnecessary last-minute applications being made to the court which, with a little anticipation and an early exchange of proposed dates, could so often be avoided.

Practitioners should be aware that not less than 14 days' notice is normally required for an application of this nature and that the court is unlikely to be well disposed towards dealing with a matter as an emergency, simply because of lack of forethought on the part of the parties and/or their legal advisers.

Easter and, particularly, Christmas contact can be problematic and should be addressed as early as possible. So often, courts find themselves inundated with applications shortly before holidays are due to commence and with little or no available time for them to be heard.

Invariably as a result of negotiation, the parties are eventually persuaded to agree to or the court imposes an arrangement whereby Easter and Christmas contact takes place on an alternating annual basis. Accordingly, practitioners are urged to encourage a settlement with this in mind.

School holidays in general can also be a potential cause of friction, there being two particular sources of conflict:

(a) on the one hand, a parent with whom the child resides may be in full-time employment and be concerned to ensure that the other parent takes what he/she views as a fair share of the holiday burden; or

(b) on the other hand, a party who does not have residence may wish to play a significant part in the upbringing of a child and wish to maximise the holiday period.

This is an aspect of contact which can usefully be resolved as a broad principle, in order to avoid the necessity of making a succession of applications.

Courts are likely to be sympathetic towards an application for leave to remove a child from the United Kingdom for a reasonably short period of time during a school holiday, where, for example, the purpose is to enable the child to visit relatives or for an educational visit.

Where the court has given leave for a child to leave the United Kingdom for the purpose of a holiday, it may be appropriate to ask the court to consider either:

(a) requiring the person who is taking the child abroad to provide an undertaking, perferably in Form N117 (county court) or Form D707 (PRFD), to return him/her to the jurisdiction at the end of the holiday period; or

(b) making an order in such terms.

Note: For further information, see the Noter-up to *Rayden*, 17th edn, at 48.16.

15.8.4 Prohibited steps and specific issues

A prohibited steps order is defined in the CA 1989 as one preventing any step which could be taken by a parent in meeting his/her parental responsibility for a child being taken by any person without the consent of the court.

CA 1989, s 8(1)

A specific issue order is defined by the CA 1989 as an order giving directions for the purpose of determining a specific question which has arisen, or which may arise, in connection with any aspect of parental responsibility for a child.

CA 1989, s 8(1)

The CA 1989 goes on to say that no court shall exercise its powers to make a specific issue order or a prohibited steps order with a view to achieving a result which could be achieved by making a residence or contact order.

CA 1989, s 9(5)(a)

The court has a wide discretion, through these two types of order, to exercise powers over a broad range of issues. They include:

(a) education;
(b) religion;
(c) a course of medical treatment;
(d) blood transfusions;
(e) surgery.

In some circumstances, a prohibited steps order can be made against a person who neither has parental responsibility nor is a party to the proceedings. This means, for example, that a cohabitee of the parent of a child can be ordered to refrain from exercising contact.

Re H (Minors)
(Prohibited Steps
Orders) [1995] 1 FLR 638

15.9 ORDERS UNDER SECTION 13 OF THE CHILDREN ACT 1989

As was explained in **15.8.1**, where a residence order is in force with respect to a child, no person may:

(a) cause a child to be known by a new surname; or
(b) remove a child from the United Kingdom without the written consent of every person who has parental responsibility for the child, or without the leave of the court.

15.9.1 Change of surname

Generally, courts have become increasingly reticent to endorse an application to change the surname of a child and tend to do so only in the most obvious of circumstances and where it is clearly in the interests of the child's welfare.

Where a father has continued to maintain contact with a child and assumed a degree of responsibility in his/her upbringing, it is unlikely that approval will be given.

The court will probably take a different view where the father has ceased to participate actively in the life of a child or has disappeared completely, and particularly where such circumstances are coupled with the mother having remarried or formed a long-term relationship with another person. Another factor will be where the child in question has a different surname from other children in the present household.

15.9.2 Removal from the United Kingdom

Courts are likely to be sympathetic towards an application for leave to remove a child from the United Kingdom for a reasonably short period of time where, for example, the purpose is to enable the child to visit relatives or for an educational purpose.

It is more difficult to anticipate the outcome of an application to remove a child from the United Kingdom permanently. Amongst the factors which may weigh heavily in the balance are:

(a) the age of a child;
(b) whether the parent with residence is going abroad to marry or for long-term employment or returning to his/her country of origin;
(c) the proposed education arrangements in the country where the child is to live and the stability of that country;
(d) the arrangements, with regard to both frequency of visits and funding of travel and accomodation which can potentially be put in place to ensure that the parent who does not have residence is able to properly maintain contact.

CHAPTER 16

WARDSHIP AND CHILD ABDUCTION

16.1   WARDSHIP

16.1.1   The process of wardship

The issuing of an originating summons for wardship vests in the High Court rights and obligations in respect of all significant aspects of the upbringing of a minor. Accordingly, once a minor is warded, no step of importance can be taken with regard to him/her, without first obtaining the leave of the court.

Re F (in Utero) [1988] Fam 122, [1988] 2 All ER 193

A child may be made a ward of court immediately upon birth but not prior to birth.

Following the introduction of the Children Act 1989, and the wide-ranging powers it confers on the court, wardship proceedings, once widely used, have become much less common. In particular, the court will almost certainly consider wardship unnecessary if the relief sought may be obtained under s 8 of the CA 1989.

C v C [1990] 1 FLR 462, CA

The most obvious examples of circumstances in which wardship may still be appropriate are:

(a)   where a parent is withholding permission for a child to receive medical treatment or a blood transfusion;

(b)   where authority is required to withdraw medical treatment or to switch off life-support equipment;

(c)   in an international abduction case where the provisions of the Child Abduction and Custody Act 1985 do not apply;

(d)   where there are surrogacy issues.

Note: For abduction matters generally see **16.2**.

16.1.2   Procedure

Wardship proceedings are commenced by issuing an originating summons in the High Court (which includes District Registries of the High Court Family Division). A court fee is payable unless the plaintiff is exempt from fees.

FPR 1991, r 5.1(1)

Unlike most other family proceedings, the parties are
referred to as plaintiff and defendant(s).

Unless otherwise directed, the originating summons must
be supported by an affidavit, which clearly sets out the
basis upon which the wardship is sought.   FPR 1991, r 5.1(1)

Wherever possible, the minor's birth certificate and, if
appropriate, a certified copy of the relevant entry in the
Adopted Children's Register must be lodged with the
court. Where the child was born or adopted in England and
Wales, a certified copy certificate can be obtained from the
Family Records Centre, 1 Myddelton Street, London
EC1R 1UW. The telephone enquiry number is
0151 471 4800.   FPR 1991, r 5.1(5)(a)

If proper proof of the date of birth cannot be immediately
obtained, the direction of the court should be sought at the
first hearing.   FPR 1991, r 5.1(5)(b)

The full name of the minor should appear in the title of the
action. If a baby has not yet been named, his/her gender
should be given, for example 'Baby Smith, a male'.

In addition to the name and, where possible, the date of
birth of the minor, the originating summons should also
provide:

(a) the full name of each party to the action together with
     the relationship to or other interest in the minor;   FPR 1991, r 5.1(6)
(b) if known, the whereabouts of the minor or otherwise a
     statement to confirm that they are not known;   FPR 1991, r 5.1(7)
(c) a notice to each defendant informing him/her of the
     requirement to keep the court informed as to the
     whereabouts of the minor, unless a defendant is
     unaware of the details.   FPR 1991, r 5.1(10)

In some limited circumstances, it may be appropriate for
the minor to be named as a defendant, for example where
he/she is of an age to understand the nature of the
proceedings. However, the Court of Appeal has   FPR 1991, r 5.3
emphasised that in the great majority of cases it is
unnecessary to join a child as a party and that it should
only be done in exceptional cicumstances.   PD of 8 December 1981

Sufficient copies of the originating summons and any
affidavit in support must be lodged for service upon each
defendant, together with the appropriate court fee unless
the plaintiff is exempt from fees.

Each defendant must be served with:

(a) a sealed copy of the originating summons;

(b)   a sealed copy of any affidavit in support;

(c)   sealed notice of the proceedings;

(d)   acknowledgement of service.

The plaintiff is responsible for service of the above documents upon each defendant. This is usually undertaken by a process server.

FPR 1991, r 10.6 and RSC Ord 11, rr 5 and 6

If the defendant is to be served outside the jurisdiction, the leave of the court will be required and the time for filing the acknowledgement extended. The application for leave must be supported by an affidavit.

Although all substantive hearings will be before a High Court judge, some interlocutory hearings may be listed before a district judge and, accordingly, practitioners should carefully check the relevant endorsement on each summons. Whilst all hearings will be in chambers, because of the nature of these proceedings, it may be thought appropriate for either counsel or a solicitor to appear as an advocate.

PD of 10 March 2000

Since all hearings will be in the High Court, it will always be necessary to prepare and lodge court bundles in accordance with the relevant President's Direction.

Where an application is being heard as a matter of urgency the Practice Direction of 10 March 2000 does not apply.

16.1.3   The effect of proceedings

Immediately upon the issue of the originating summons, the minor will become a ward of court.

FPR 1991, r 5.3(1)(a)

If an application for an appointment for the hearing of the summons is not made within a period of 21 days after issue, the minor will cease to be a ward.

No ward of court may be removed from the jurisdiction, by any person, without the leave of the court. For information as to the steps to be taken in order to obtain leave, see *Rayden*, 17th edn, paragraphs 42.23 and 42.24.

FPR 1991, r 5.1(4)

Particulars of any originating summons issued in wardship will be recorded in the Register of Wards, which is maintained by the Principal Registry of the Family Division.

SCA 1981, s 41(3)

Wardship, once confirmed by a court order, remains in force throughout the minority of a child unless previously discharged by order of the court.

16.2   CHILD ABDUCTION AND CUSTODY ACT 1985

In recent years, a much greater emphasis has been placed on the need to discourage a parent from unilaterally removing a child from one jurisdiction to another without a court order.

The Child Abduction and Custody Act 1985 (CACA 1985) ratified and implemented the provisions of:

(a)   the Hague Convention 1980, with regard to the civil aspects of international child abduction; and

(b)   the European Convention of 1980, with regard to recognition and enforcement of decisions concerning custody of children.

A comprehensive list of all countries which are signatories to the Hague Convention is set out in Sch 1 to the Child Abduction and Custody (Parties to Conventions) Order 1986 and appears in each issue of *Family Law* journal.

Broadly, the provisions of the CACA 1985 provide for a child who has been improperly brought to England and Wales to be returned to the country where he/she has previously been resident.

The court may exercise a degree of circumspection in circumstances where it is being asked to order the return of a child to a non-Hague Convention country or one which is in the throes of a civil war.

16.2.1   Procedure

Proceedings can only be issued in the Principal Registry of the High Court Family Division. They are commenced by way of an originating summons, in the form which can be found in RSC App A. The originating summons must set out comprehensive details of the child and the child's parents or guardians, together with information as to where the child is likely to be found and the facts which have given rise to the application. A court fee is payable on the issue of the originating summons unless the plaintiff is exempt from fees.

FPR 1991, r 6.2

FPR 1991, rr 6.3 and 6.4

Unlike most other family proceedings, the parties are referred to as plaintiff and defendant(s).

The plaintiff on issuing the originating summons may lodge affidavit evidence in support of the application.

FPR 1991, r 6.7(1)

If the child has been the subject of previous proceedings, copies of all relevant documents must also be lodged with the court.

A copy of the originating summons should be provided for service on each defendant. Each defendant will be served with:

(a) a sealed copy of the originating summons, with the hearing date endorsed. Such date will be not more than 21 days from the date of issue;

FPR 1991, r 6.10

(b) a sealed copy of any supporting affidavit;

(c) acknowledgement of service.

Practitioners should note that FPR 1991, r 6.5 sets out a list of persons who should be made defendants.

Once served, a defendant is required to file the acknowledgement of service within a period of seven days, unless the court has made provision for a longer period.

FPR 1991, r 6.6

The court may however dispense with service of any summons in any proceedings under the CACA 1985.

FPR 1991, r 6.9

Whilst the court may adjourn the first or any subsequent hearing, the period of such adjournment may not exceed a period of 21 days at any one time.

Where the case is one of urgency, the court may consider an ex parte application, on affidavit, for interim directions.

FPR 1991, r 6.13; CACA 1985, ss 5 and 19

All hearings of a substantive nature in relation to abduction matters are before a High Court judge and will be in chambers unless otherwise directed.

Two clear days prior to the commencement of a hearing, court bundles must be prepared and lodged in accordance with the relevant President's Direction.

PD of 10 March 2000

Where the application is being heard as a matter of urgency, the President's Direction of 10 March 2000 does not apply.

Child abduction in all its various facets is far too substantial to be dealt with in any great detail in a book of this nature. However, a comprehensive account is to be found in *Rayden*, 17th edn, Chapter 45 and para 46.17. This includes action to be taken where a child has been removed from the jurisdiction, as well as where one has been brought into the jurisdiction.

Of particular note is the fact that, in some circumstances, the Child Abduction Unit of the Lord Chancellor's Department may be prepared to instruct and pay foreign lawyers. In effect, it is a non-means tested form of Community Legal Service funding.

Note: The address of the Child Abduction Unit is 81 Chancery Lane, London WC2A 1DD, and the telephone number is 0207 911 7045/7047.

Prior to the introduction of the CA 1989, wardship proceedings were often issued in connection with the unlawful removal of a child from a foreign jurisdiction. Whilst the procedure is now infrequently used, it may still be necessary in an international abduction case where the provisions of the CACA 1985 do not apply.

Also of significance in this area of the law are the provisions of s 33 of the FLA 1986. This section enables a judge to order any person who it is believed may have relevant information concerning the whereabouts of a child to disclose that information to the court. For the relevant procedure, see Chapter 17.

FPR 1991, r 6.16

Note: See **16.1** for information on wardship proceedings.

CHAPTER 17

LOCATING THE WHEREABOUTS OF A CHILD

17.1 PROCEDURE FOR LOCATING A CHILD

The principles set out in this chapter apply to the CA 1989, wardship and child abduction.

If the whereabouts of a child is not known, an application can be made to the court in proceedings for or relating to a Part I order (for a definition of a Part I order, see below) for an order requiring any person who it has reason to believe may have relevant information to disclose it to the court.

FLA 1986, s 33(1) and
FPR 1991, r 6.17

The application is made by way of Form C4 and may be made ex parte or on notice. If it is made on notice and is related to an application for an order pursuant to Part I of the CA 1989, the period of that notice will be 14 clear days, otherwise it will be two clear days. Whether made ex parte or on notice the application attracts a court fee unless the applicant is exempt from fees.

The FLA 1986 (as amended by the CA 1989) provides the definition of a Part I order.

An application in Form C4 will only be considered ex parte in circumstances where:

(a) the whereabouts of the respondent is not known; or
(b) there is a perceived emergency.

If the district judge makes an order, the named person or body will be directed to give the information which they have, to a named official of the court and in a specified manner, usually in writing. The order in Form C30 will be endorsed with a penal notice. See Chapter 23 for the procedure to follow where the order is subsequently breached.

It is also possible, in connection with a Part I order, to apply to the court in Form C3 for an order authorising a search for, taking charge of and delivery of a child. In view of the nature of the application, it will invariably be made ex parte. The application attracts a court fee unless the applicant is exempt from fees.

Where the court makes an order requiring a person to hand over a child to another person and that order is not complied with, the court may make a further order in an attempt to force compliance. The order, in Form C31, is addressed to all police constables, the High Court tipstaff or a county court bailiff and authorises them to search for, take charge of and deliver the child to a person specified in the order. Such an order confers wide powers to ensure compliance.

FLA 1986, s 34

A Part I order can be registered in another part of the United Kingdom and, once registered, can be enforced in exactly the same way as in England and Wales.

FLA 1986, s 27

Similarly, an order made in another part of the United Kingdom can be registered in England and Wales, at the Principal Registry of the Family Division, and thereafter enforced as though made within the jurisdiction.

FLA 1986, s 27 and FPR 1991, r 7.8

All matters relating to an application for the enforcement of such orders will be heard by a High Court judge.

17.2   PORT ALERT

Where there is a possibility of a child being imminently removed from the United Kingdom, it may be appropriate to request a port alert. Police should be notified and requested to contact all ports and airports within the United Kingdom, through the police national computer. All agencies dealing with emigration will then be expected to be vigilant, although since the ending of routine embarkation controls this is somewhat dependent on the liaison between the police and security staff at individual ports and airports. The procedure to be adopted is clearly set out in *Rayden*, 17th edn, para 46.20, and a Practice Direction of 15 October 1987 (see *Rayden*, 17th edn, para 55.42).

CHAPTER 18

CHILDREN AND FINANCIAL APPLICATIONS

18.1 ANCILLARY RELIEF ORDERS

Ancillary relief orders are covered by ss 23 and 24 of the MCA 1973.

A child of the family can apply to the court for an ancillary relief order in much the same way as either a petitioner or a respondent.

The application can be made on behalf of a child by:

(a) a parent; or

FPR 1991, r 2.54(1)(a) and (b)

(b) a guardian; or

(c) any person in whose favour there is a residence order.

The rules also provide for a child to apply to the court for leave to intervene in the matrimonial proceedings of a parent or parents for the purpose of applying for ancillary

FPR 1991, r 2.54(1)(f) MCA 1973, s 23(4)

relief. Unlike the position of a party to the proceedings, the child is able to apply for more than one lump sum.

In all other respects, the procedure for an application under ss 23 and 24 is identical to that set out in Chapter 11 with regard to an application for ancillary relief by either a petitioner or a respondent. However, it should be noted that the power to make a property adjustment order, pursuant to s 24, will be exercised only very rarely in favour of a child of the family.

18.2 FINANCIAL PROVISION ORDERS UNDER SCHEDULE 1 OF THE CHILDREN ACT 1989

Subject to the provisions of the CSA 1991, s 15 of and Sch 1 to the CA 1989 empower the High Court or a county court to order a parent of a child to make financial provision to or for the benefit of that child in one or more of the following ways:

(a) periodical payments;

(b) secured periodical payments;

CA 1989, Sch 1, para 1(1)(a) and (2)(a)–(c) and (e)

(c) lump sum;

(d) transfer of property.

The court can also order a parent to make a settlement for the benefit of a child of that parent.

CA 1989, Sch 1, para 1(1)(a) and (2)(d)

A family proceedings court has the jurisdiction to make financial provision but is restricted to making periodical payments and lump sum orders.

CA 1989, Sch 1, para 1(1)(b)

Ideally, where there are existing divorce proceedings, or matrimonial proceedings in the family proceedings court, involving the parent or parents of a child, any financial matters concerning that child should be dealt with as part of those proceedings.

Practitioners should note that an application to vary an existing order is treated as a new application and the procedure to be followed is as set out at **18.8** .

18.3   MAINTENANCE

18.3.1   Maintenance orders

At any time prior to the final disposal of the application, the court may make an interim periodical payments order. The order can potentially include provision for the payment of school or college fees.

CA 1989, Sch 1, para 9(1)(a)

Unless the court thinks it appropriate in the circumstances of a case, a periodical payments order will not, in the first instance, extend beyond a seventeenth birthday of a child and in any event not beyond the eighteenth birthday.

CA 1989, Sch 1, para 3(1)(a) and (b)

18.3.2   Court or Child Support Agency?

The CSA 1991 substantially restricts the power of the court to order maintenance for a child and, before making an application, practitioners should check to ensure that it is within the residual jurisdiction of the court.

CSA 1991, s 8

The main exceptions to the Child Support Agency exercising its powers are where:

(a)   parents agree in writing to the court making a consent order;

CSA 1991, s 8(5)(a)

(b)   the application is for a variation of an existing court order;

(c)   a child is or will be receiving instruction at an educational establishment or undergoing training for a trade, profession or vocation, whether or not in gainful employment;

CSA 1991, s 8(7)(a)

(d)   a child is disabled;

CSA 1991, s 8(8)

(e)   the absent parent is habitually resident outside the United Kingdom.

CSA 1991, s 44(1)(c)

If there is an issue as to whether or not a child falls within

CSA 1991, s 55(1) and (2)

the scope of the CSA 1991, it may be necessary, in the first instance, to consider the statutory meaning of 'child'.

Where an agreement is reached for the payment of maintenance, that agreement can be made the subject of a consent order, which will be enforceable in the same way as any other maintenance order. However, there is currently some debate as to whether or not the CSA 1991 prevents an application being made to the court to vary an order made by consent. In practice most, if not all, courts are currently entertaining such applications.

18.3.3 Members of the armed forces

Where the respondent to an application for maintenance is a regular member of the armed forces it is possible to apply to his/her unit commander for a compulsory allotment of the respondent's pay. This will be simpler and quicker than proceeding through the Child Support Agency for an assessment or seeking a court order.

NF(EML)A 1947, AA 1955, s 150 and AFA 1955, s 150

18.4 LUMP SUM ORDERS

A lump sum order may include provision for payment of a sum, not exceeding £1,000, in respect of expenses relating to the birth of a child or monies otherwise incurred prior to a final order being made.

CA 1989, Sch 1, para 5(1) and (2)

Although only likely to be made in very exceptional circumstances, a lump sum order may be sought for the purpose of providing accommodation for a child.

Whereas the MCA 1973 allows one lump sum order to be made in favour of a party to the proceedings, the CA 1989 permits the court to make a second or subsequent order, provided that the child concerned has not reached the age of 18.

CA 1989, Sch 1, para 1(5)(a)

CA 1989, Sch 1, para 5(5)

An order for the payment of a lump sum, whether interim or final, can be made to be payable by instalments.

18.5 TRANSFER OF PROPERTY ORDERS

An application for a transfer of property order can be used, inter alia, as a means of asking the court to transfer a tenancy as between parents, for the benefit of a child.

CA 1989, Sch 1, para 1(5)(b)

Unlike the position with regard to lump sum provision, the court is restricted to making only one transfer of property or settlement order.

18.6 PARTIES TO AN APPLICATION AND SCOPE OF ORDERS

CA 1989, Sch 1, para 1(1)

An application can be made by a parent or guardian of a child or by any person in whose favour a residence order is in force.

If an application is granted, the resultant order can be expressed to be made either to the applicant for the benefit of a child or direct to that child.

CA 1989, Sch 1, para 1(2)

An order can be sought against one or both of a child's birth or adopted parents, or a person who, during the course of a marriage, has treated the child as a child of the family. However, as explained at the end of this section, an application, pursuant to CA 1989, Sch 1, para 2(1), by a child over the age of 18 is much more restricted in its ambit.

CA 1989, Sch 1, para 16(2)

In view of the wide definition of CA 1989, Sch 1, para 16(2) referred to above, it is clear that a putative father is included and the fact that he does not have parental responsibility is irrelevant.

CA 1989, s 3(4)

Whilst, as explained above, a person who has treated a child as a child of the family can be ordered to make financial provision, it should always be borne in mind that there is a continuing responsibility on the part of a birth parent and this is a factor which the court may properly be asked to take into account.

CA 1989, Sch 1, para 4(2)(c)

Unlike under the MCA 1973, there is no provision under the CA 1989 for a child under the age of 18 to make an application on his/her own behalf. However, once a child has reached the age of 18, he/she can then make an application in circumstances where he/she is or will be receiving instruction at an educational establishment or undergoing training for a trade, profession or vocation, whether or not while in gainful employment.

CA 1989, Sch 1, para 2(1)(a)

An application can also be made by a person over 18 years where there are special circumstances which justify the making of an order, for example where the person concerned has a mental or physical impairment and as a result is unable to work.

CA 1989, Sch 1, para 2(1)(b)

Whilst the court is granted the power to make an order in favour of a child who has reached the age of 18, that power is limited to making periodical payments and lump sum orders.

CA 1989, Sch 1, para 2(2)

The court is also prevented from making an order under the provisions of Sch 1, para 2 in circumstances where:

(a) there was already a periodical payments order in force immediately prior to a child reaching the age of 16; or
(b) the parents of that child are living together in the same household.

CA 1989, Sch 1, para 2(3) and (4)

18.7 FACTORS FOR THE COURT TO CONSIDER

In making an order pursuant to CA 1989, Sch 1, the court must have regard to all the circumstances of the case and the factors set out in Sch 1, para 4. Whilst not identical, the principles are very similar to those provided in s 25 of the MCA 1973.

CA 1989, Sch 1, para 4(1) and (2)

18.8 PROCEDURE

18.8.1 Commencement of proceedings

An application pursuant to Sch 1 to the CA 1989 is issued by way of Form C10. A court fee is payable unless the applicant is exempt from fees.

FPR 1991, r 4.4(1)(a)

If the applicant does not wish to reveal his/her address, or that of a child, Form C8 must also be completed. Once filed at court, the address should not be disclosed to any person without the leave of a judge. The Form C8 will be placed in a sealed envelope on the court file, which will be endorsed accordingly.

FPR 1991, r 10.21

The application should be supported by a statement of means in Form C10A.

FPR 1991, r 4.4(6)

A first directions appointment will be fixed taking into account the requirements regarding time for service. The prescribed time for service within the jurisdiction is 14 days, and outside the jurisdiction such additional days as provided for in FPR 1991, r 10.6.

18.8.2 Service

Once issued the respondent will be served with:

(a) copy Form C10;
(b) copy statement of means in Form C10A;
(c) Form C10A for completion as to his/her own means;
(d) Form C6 (notice of proceedings) which will be endorsed with the time, date and place of the first directions appointment;
(e) Form C7 (acknowledgement of service).

Form C9 (statement of service) will be provided by the court in order that the applicant can complete and file it before the first directions appointment.

FPR 1991, r 4.8

Practitioners may wish to note that service of any process, relating to maintenance, upon a regular member of the armed forces may be effected by registered post, on his/her commanding officer, and is deemed good service.

NDA 1957, s 101, AA 1955, s 153 and AFA 1955, s 153

Note: The requirements for service under the CA 1989 are set out in **15.2.5.**

18.8.3 Statement of means

It should be noted that it is not necessary to swear the
statement of means. However, the court will expect
complete disclosure.

FPR 1991, r 4.4(6)

18.8.4 Hearings

The first directions appointment will be listed before a
district judge who will explore the possibility of resolving
the issues between the parties. If agreement is not reached,
directions will be given leading to a final contested hearing
also before a district judge.

All hearings will be in chambers and, accordingly, counsel,
a solicitor or a legal executive will have the right of
audience.

If the final hearing has a time estimate of a half-day or
more, court bundles must be prepared and lodged in
accordance with the relevant President's Direction.

PD of 10 March 2000

18.9   INHERITANCE (PROVISION FOR FAMILY AND DEPENDANTS) ACT 1975

Section 2 of the Inheritance (Provision for Family and
Dependants) Act 1975 (I(PFD)A 1975) provides the
mechanism for an application by a child for financial
support out of the estate of a parent, in circumstances
where it is alleged that no or insufficient provision has
been made for that child in the parent's will or, where
there is no will, by operation of the laws of intestacy.

A child for the purposes of an application under s 2
includes a birth or adopted child of the deceased, or
otherwise one who has been treated as a child of the
family.

I(PFD)A 1975, s 1(1)(c)
and (d)

The application will be commenced under the provisions
of Part 8 of the CPR 1998, using Form N208.

If, at the time of the application, the child is still a minor,
it will be necessary to appoint a litigation friend. Where
there is a conflict with the surviving parent in relation to
the distribution of the estate, an alternative litigation friend
will have to be sought.

CPR 1998, r 21.2

If the child has reached the age of majority, the application
will be commenced in the usual way.

The court has unfettered power to make an order in respect
of a child in any of the forms of financial relief set out in

s 2 of the I(PFD)A 1975. However, the court will have to carefully weigh in the balance any competing claims of a surviving spouse of the deceased.

Any possible conflict between a child and a surviving spouse should be resolved as quickly as possible and, in such a situation, practitioners should apply to the court for directions at an early stage.

Note: For fuller details and the procedure to be followed, see Chapter 13.

Part IV

INJUNCTIONS AND ENFORCEMENT

CHAPTER 19

FAMILY HOMES AND DOMESTIC VIOLENCE

19.1 INTRODUCTION

The once fragmented law relating to the occupation of a family home, domestic violence and related matters has been rationalised and, with the exception of stalking, has been brought into a single codified law, by the provisions of Part IV of the Family Law Act 1996 (FLA 1996).

Note: See **19.16** below with regard to stalking.

19.2 JURISDICTION

Proceedings may be commenced in:

(a) the High Court;
(b) a divorce county court;
(c) the Principal Registry of the Family Division exercising county court jurisdiction;
(d) Lambeth, Shoreditch and Woolwich County Courts;
(e) any magistrates' court exercising family jurisdiction (family proceedings court).

FLA 1996, s 57 and FLA 1996 (Pt IV)(AP)O 1997, arts 4, 16 and 17

19.3 POWERS OF THE COURT

Subject to the limitations referred to below, a designated court has wide powers to make orders with regard to:

FLA 1996, ss 33–38

(a) rights of occupation in respect of a dwelling;

FLA 1996, ss 33 and 35–38

(b) the exclusion of a party from all or a part of a dwelling;

FLA 1996, s 42

(c) the protection of a party from domestic violence (a non-molestation order).

An order in the form of (b) above can include a restriction on a party from approaching within a set distance of the dwelling in question, or a specified locality.

FLA 1996, Pt IV also makes provision for a court to order the transfer of certain tenancies upon the pronouncement of a decree of divorce, nullity or judicial separation, or upon the separation of cohabitants.

FLA 1996, s 53 and Sch 7

The jurisdiction of the family proceedings court is more restricted than the other courts referred to in **19.2**, in that it cannot entertain any application or make any order where there is a dispute as to a party's entitlement to occupy any property by virtue of any of the matters set out in s 59.

FLA 1996, s 59(1)

A comprehensive account of the provisions of ss 33 and 36–38, with regard to rights of occupation and the scope of the orders which the court can make is to be found in *Rayden*, 17th edn, Chapter 32, section 4.

The court is also able to impose one or more of a number of additional provisions when making an occupation order under any one of ss 33, 35 or 36, for example:

(a) requiring a party to pay outgoings in respect of a dwelling-house;

(b) in some circumstances requiring a party to make periodical payments to the other party in respect of the occupation of a dwelling-house;

(c) with regard to the use and security of a dwelling-house and its contents.

FLA 1996,
s 40(1)(a)–(e)

However, the true value of one of the financial orders referred to above has been put in doubt by a decision of the Court of Appeal in which it has been made clear that the court has no related power of enforcement.

Nwogbe v Nwogbe
[2000] 2 FLR 744

19.4   FACTORS TO BE CONSIDERED

In considering an application for an occupation order under any of ss 33, 35 and 36, the court must have regard to all the circumstances of the case, taking particular account of the statutory factors set out in the FLA 1996.

FLA 1996, ss 33(6) and (7), 35(6) and (8) and 36(6)–(8)

In deciding whether to grant a non-molestation order under s 42, the court must have regard to all the circumstances of the case, including the need to secure the health, safety and well-being of the applicant and of any relevant child.

FLA 1996, s 42(5)

For the purposes of s 42, health includes physical or mental health.

FLA 1996, s 63(1)

Section 45 sets out the factors to which the court must have regard in deciding whether or not to make an ex parte order. See **19.6** and **19.6.1** with regard to an ex parte application and order.

FLA 1996, s 45(2)(a)–(c)

19.5   PARTIES TO THE PROCEEDINGS

Where the remedy sought is an injunction to protect the applicant from domestic violence, the applicant can seek an order against a person with whom he/she is associated.

For the purposes of Part IV, a person is associated with another person if:

(a) they are or have been married to each other;
(b) they are cohabitants or former cohabitants;
(c) they live or have lived in the same household, otherwise than merely by reason of one of them being the other's employee, tenant, lodger or boarder;
(d) they are relatives;
(e) they have agreed to marry one another (whether or not that agreement has been terminated);
(f) in relation to any child, both are either the parent or have or have had parental responsibility for the child in question;
(g) they are parties to the same family proceedings (other than proceedings under Part IV), for example under the CA 1989.

FLA 1996, s 62(3)(a)–(g)

An application can also be made in respect of an adopted child.

FLA 1996, s 62(5)

With regard to (e) in the list above, the court will require positive evidence of the existence of an agreement to marry in one or more of the following ways:

(a) in the form of a written document;
(b) the gift of an engagement ring by one party to the agreement to the other, in contemplation of their marriage;
(c) a ceremony entered into by the parties in the presence of one or more other persons assembled for the purpose of witnessing the ceremony.

FLA 1996, s 44(1) and (2)

Where the remedy sought is an occupation order, any of the following persons can apply:

(a) those who are or have been married to each other;
(b) those who are cohabitants or former cohabitants;
(c) an associated person, not falling within (a) and (b) above, who is already entitled to occupy the property which is the subject of the application.

Practitioners will need to carefully check under which of ss 33, 35, 36, 37 or 38 they are bringing their client's application.

An order may be made for the benefit or protection of a relevant child, such child being:

(a) any child who is living with or might reasonably be expected to live with either party to the proceedings;

(b) any child in relation to whom an order under the Adoption Act 1976 or the CA 1989 is in question in the proceedings;

(c) any other child whose interest the court considers relevant.

FLA 1996, s 62(2)

However, other than with leave of the court, a child under the age of 16 may not apply for occupation or non-molestation orders. For further details, see **19.6**.

FLA 1996, s 43(1)

Leave will be granted only where the court is satisfied that the child concerned has sufficient understanding to make the proposed application.

FLA 1996, s 43(2)

A child, whether between the ages of 16 and 18 or under 16 who has been given leave, should apply for an order with the assistance of a litigation friend.

FPR 1991, r 9.2

19.6 PROCEDURE

The application must be issued in Form FL401, and a court fee is payable unless the applicant is exempt from fees.

FPR 1991, r 3.8(1)

The proceedings can be commenced either by way of a free-standing application or within existing proceedings. If issued as a free-standing application reference should be made to the existence of the other proceedings.

If the applicant does not wish to reveal his/her address or that of a relevant child, Form C8 must be completed. Once filed at court, the address should not be revealed to any person other than by order of the court. The form will be placed, in a sealed envelope, on the court file which will be marked accordingly.

FPR 1991, r 10.21

The application should be supported by a sworn statement of the applicant.

FPR 1991, r 3.8(4)

It is good practice to provide the court with a draft of the order which is sought, particularly where the application is being made ex parte in an emergency situation.

An application for an occupation or a non-molestation order made by a child under the age of 16 must be made in Form FLA401 and is to be treated, in the first instance, as an application to the High Court for leave. This application does not attract a court fee.

FPR 1991, r 3.8(2)

An application in the first instance can be made ex parte (without notice being given to the respondent) or inter partes (on notice). Where an application is made without giving notice, the sworn statement must state the reason why notice was not given.

FPR 1991, r 3.8(5)

Where an application is made inter partes, it must be served together with a copy of the applicant's sworn statement and a notice in Form FL402 which sets out the date and time of the hearing.

FPR 1996, r 3.8(6)

The applicant is required to arrange for personal service upon the respondent, giving not less than two clear days' notice of the hearing date.

FPR 1991, r 3.8(6)

The court may abridge (shorten) the time for service specified in r 3.8(6). Where time is abridged, a judge is likely to specify, in the form of an order, the date and time by which the respondent is to be served.

FPR 1991, r 3.8(7)

The applicant must file a statement in Form FL415 to confirm that service of the application has been effected. The Form FL415 should be filed with the court prior to the hearing.

FPR 1991, r 3.8(15)

Where the applicant is acting in person, service of the application will be effected by the court if the applicant so requests.

FPR 1991, r 3.8(8)

The provisions of r 3.8(8) do not affect the court's power to order substituted service.

Note: For the procedure to follow with regard to an emergency application, see Chapter 20.

19.6.1 Action following a court order

Where an order is made on an application made ex parte, a copy of the order together with a copy of the application and of the sworn statement in support must be served by the applicant on the respondent personally.

FPR 1991, r 3.9(2)

If the court makes an ex parte order it must afford the respondent an opportunity to make representations at a full hearing, as soon as it is just and convenient.

FLA 1996, s 45(3)

A copy of an order made on an application which has been heard inter partes must also be served by the applicant on the respondent personally.

FPR 1991, r 3.9(4)

It will often be expedient to arrange for the respondent to be served before leaving the court. Not only will this be quicker and cheaper but it will also avoid the necessity of the respondent having to be pursued by a process-server.

Where the applicant is acting in person, service of a copy of any order made on the hearing of the application must be effected by the court if the applicant so requests.

FPR 1991, r 3.9(5)

19.6.2 Procedure where property mortgaged or leased

Where a dwelling to which an application for an occupation order under ss 33, 35 or 36 relates is mortgaged or rented, notice must be given to the mortgagee or landlord. A copy of the application together with a notice in Form FL416, informing the mortgagee or landlord of the right to make representations in writing or at any hearing, must be served by the applicant by first-class post.

FPR 1991, r 3.8(11)

If the application is for a transfer of tenancy, notice of the application must be served by the applicant on the spouse or cohabitant and on the landlord. Any person who has been served is entitled to be heard on the application.

FPR 1991, r 3.8(12)

In circumstances where the tenancy is either in the sole name of the respondent or is a joint tenancy, the respondent can potentially frustrate the application by either surrendering the tenancy or giving notice to quit, without consulting the applicant.

Hammersmith & Fulham London Borough Council v Monk [1992] 1 FLR 465,
Bater and Bater v Greenwich London Borough Council [1999] 2 FLR 993

Practitioners may, therefore, think it prudent in order to avoid a negligence claim, to make an interlocutory application for an injunction.

Where an occupation order is made, a copy must be served by the applicant, by first-class post, on the mortgagee or landlord of the dwelling in question.

FPR 1991, r 3.9(3)

The court may direct that a further hearing be held in order to consider any representations made by a mortgagee or a landlord.

FPR 1991, r 3.9(7)

Sections 55 and 56 set out the steps which are to be taken in circumstances where a mortgagee commences enforcement proceedings in respect of a dwelling which is the subject of a Part IV application.

19.7 DURATION OF ORDERS

As a general rule, the court can be expected to grant an exclusion or non-molestation order for a period of either three or six months, or exceptionally for a period of up to twelve months. If, at the end of the period ordered, the matter has not been satisfactorily resolved, an application can be made for an extension.

Although in practice the duration of a non-molestation order is likely to be for a specified period, the court does have jurisdiction to grant relief until further order.

FLA 1996, s 42(7)

A non-molestation order which is made in other family proceedings ceases to have effect if those proceedings are

FLA 1996, s 42(8)

withdrawn or dismissed. Although s 42 makes no reference to an exclusion order, as a matter of logic, such an order will similarly cease to have effect.

FLA 1996, s 36(10)

An occupation order under s 36, by a cohabitant or former cohabitant who has no existing rights of occupation, may be made for a maximum period of six months and may be renewed only once.

FLA 1996, s 37(5)

An occupation order under ss 37 and 38 may be made for a maximum period of six months, renewable.

FLA 1996, s 38(6)

However, where a s 37 or s 38 order is made as between cohabitants or former cohabitants, it may be renewed only once.

In any event, where the parties are married and there are separate proceedings pending for divorce, nullity or judicial separation, it will usually be more appropriate for issues relating to the matrimonial home to be determined as part of the ancillary relief application within those proceedings.

19.8 UNDERTAKINGS

FLA 1996, s 46(1)

Where the court has power to make an occupation or non-molestation order, the court may accept an undertaking, in Form N117 (county court) or Form D787 (PRFD), from any party to the proceedings.

FLA 1996, s 46(2) and (3)

No power of arrest may be attached to any undertaking given under s 46(1) and, in any event, the court is required not to accept an undertaking in circumstances where the power of arrest is required to be attached to an order in accordance with s 47(2).

FLA 1996, s 46(4)

An undertaking given to the court is enforceable in exactly the same way as a court order.

Note: See below with regard to the power of arrest.

19.9 POWER OF ARREST

FLA 1996, s 47(2)

Where the court makes an occupation or non-molestation order and it appears that the respondent has used or threatened violence against the applicant or a relevant child, it is required to attach a power of arrest to that order unless satisfied that, in all the circumstances of the case, the applicant or child will be adequately protected without such a power.

Accordingly, there is a general presumption in favour of attaching the power, although where, pursuant to s 45(1),

an order is made ex parte, the Act is less emphatic and
states that the court may attach the power.

FLA 1996, s 47(3)

The power of arrest authorises a constable to arrest,
without warrant, a person whom he/she has reasonable
cause for suspecting is in breach of any part of an order to
which the power attaches.

FLA 1996, s 47(6)

Once an order has been made with a power of arrest
attached, it is important that the respondent be served
personally, without delay.

The court office is required to complete Form FL406
setting out the parts of the order to which the power of
arrest attaches and the date it expires.

FPR 1991, r 3.9A(1)(a)

A copy of Form FL406 must be delivered to the officer
who at the time of delivery is in charge of the police
station which covers the applicant's address or such other
station as the court may specify.

FPR 1991, r 3.9A(1)(b)

The copy Form FL406 must be accompanied by a
statement showing that the respondent has been served
with the order or informed of its terms (whether by being
present when the order was made or by telephone or
otherwise).

FPR 1991, r 3.9A(1)

If the applicant is represented by solicitors, those solicitors
or a process server should effect delivery to the police. It is
also advisable for the police to be provided with details of:

(a) the applicant's name, address and telephone number
 (if any);
(b) the applicant's solicitor's name, address and
 telephone number, including emergency number (if
 any);
(c) the name and address of the person against whom the
 order is made;
(d) information as to how to contact the court in the event
 of an arrest being made outside normal business
 hours. For further information on the subject, see
 Chapter 20 and Appendix C(2).

If the person in whose favour an order has been granted is
not represented by solicitors, directions should be sought
with regard to the service of the court order and delivery to
the police of the Form FL406.

Where an order is made either varying or discharging any
relevant part of the order, the police should be notified
without delay.

19.10 PENAL NOTICE

19.10.1 Attached to a court order

All non-molestation and exclusion orders should have a penal notice endorsed on the face of the order. The notice warns the respondent that if the order is not obeyed he/she may be committed to prison for contempt.

It is unlikely that a committal order will be made in circumstances where the person against whom the order has been made is not served and, accordingly, every effort should be made to ensure that personal service does take place.

Once the order has been served, an affidavit of service should be filed with the court.

19.10.2 Attached to an undertaking

An undertaking will similarly have a penal notice endorsed on the face of the document (this is referred to as 'Important Notice' on the standard form of undertaking). This notice warns the person giving the undertaking that a failure to keep the promise that has been given to the court may result in a period of imprisonment for contempt.

The judge who accepts the undertaking should explain its nature and give a verbal warning as to the consequences of breaking the promise. If the judge does not do so, it is appropriate to provide a discreet reminder.

Although it is not strictly necessary to formally serve an undertaking, for the purpose of enforcement, it is good practice. Therefore, in order to save unnecessary expense and inconvenience, it is usually appropriate to ask the person concerned to wait in the court so that a sealed copy may be served there and then.

19.11 ACTION WHERE AN ORDER HAS BEEN BREACHED

Where there has been a breach of a non-molestation or exclusion order, the matter can be dealt with in one of the following ways:

(a) by the activation of a power of arrest;
(b) as a result of a warrant issued pursuant to FLA 1996, s 47(8);
(c) by way of an application to commit.

19.11.1 Activating a power of arrest

Where a police officer activates a power of arrest, the person who has been arrested must be brought before a court within the period of 24 hours from the time of the arrest.

FLA 1996, s 47(7)(a)

In calculating the period of 24 hours, no account is to be taken of Christmas Day, Good Friday or any Sunday.

FLA 1996, s 47(7)

Once seized of the matter, the court can immediately deal with the breach or can order a remand.

FLA 1996, s 47(7)(b)

Where the court orders a remand under FLA 1996, s 47, that remand may be:

(a) in custody; or
(b) on bail.

FLA 1996, Sch 5, para 2(1)(a) and (b)

An application for bail may be made either orally or in writing. If the application is in writing, it must contain the particulars required by r 3.10 and be signed by the person making the application or otherwise as provided by the FPR 1991. The application does not attract a court fee.

FPR 1991, r 3.10(1)

FPR 1991, r 3.10(2) and (3)

In ordering a remand on bail, the court may require a recognizance (with or without sureties) to be given.

FLA 1996, Sch 5, para 2(1)(b)(i) and (ii)

Although there are exceptions, the broad rule is that the period of remand cannot exceed eight clear days.

FLA 1996, Sch 5, para 2(5)

The main exception to the rule is where the court has reason to consider that a medical report is required. In these circumstances, an adjournment for not more than four weeks at any one time may be ordered where the person concerned is to be remanded on bail.

FLA 1996, s 48(1) and (2)

Where a person has been remanded in custody, the adjournment for the preparation of a medical report is restricted to a period of not more than three weeks at a time.

FLA 1996, s 48(3)

Where the person remanded is suffering from mental illness or severe mental impairment, the court has the same power as it would have under s 35 of the Mental Health Act 1983.

FLA 1996, s 48(4)

19.11.2 Arrest warrant

Even where a power of arrest has not been attached to an order, where the applicant considers that the respondent has failed to comply with that order, an application may be made to the court by way of Form FL407 for the issue of a

FLA 1996, s 47(8)

warrant for the arrest of the respondent. The application attracts a court fee unless the applicant is exempt from fees.

19.11.3   Application to commit

The action to be taken in the event of a breach of either an order or an undertaking is dealt with in Chapter 23.

19.12   COMMITTAL HEARING

At a committal hearing, for breach of an order or undertaking, or one which takes place following the activation of a power of arrest, the person who is alleged to have breached the order is answerable to the court. However, the person in whose favour the original order was granted or undertaking given may be required to give evidence at the hearing and indeed it will often be crucial where it is that person whose allegations give rise to the hearing.

Where the police have made an arrest, it will sometimes be the case that the alleged breach results from an act or acts witnessed by a police officer, who will then be called upon to provide evidence either orally and/or by way of a written witness statement.

In circumstances where the police have not witnessed the relevant events, the attendance of the arresting officer at the subsequent court hearing will not be necessary unless the arrest itself is in issue. A written statement from the officer concerned as to the circumstances of the arrest should normally be sufficient.

PD of 9 December 1999

If the breach is not considered serious, it may be dealt with by way of a warning or a suspended order. On the other hand, if the breach is serious, an immediate committal order is more likely to be made.

Hale v Tanner [2000] 2 FLR 879

Should the contemnor repeat the contempt, it can be anticipated that increasingly longer sentences will be passed.

The maximum sentence which can be imposed for contempt of court in respect of a breach under a Part IV order is two years' imprisonment (including the activation of a suspended sentence). Such sentence will be subject to the usual remission for good conduct provisions.

Contempt of Court Act 1981, s 14(1)

In some circumstances, it may be appropriate for a fine to be imposed rather than a period of imprisonment. However, recently the courts have been more prepared to take a firm view of domestic violence and to deal with breaches more harshly.

19.13   PURGING CONTEMPT

In circumstances where a contemnor shows genuine remorse, it may be possible for the court to allow that person to purge his/her contempt.

If a solicitor is acting for a contemnor, a formal application should be issued in the normal way; however, where a solicitor is not acting, most judges are likely to treat a letter, written by a contemnor from prison, as a notice of application. Irrespective of the form the application takes, no court fee is payable.

Whilst the application is a matter as between the contemnor and the court, practitioners can anticipate a judge requiring the other party to be notified of the application, so that if there have been continuing problems, for example with the contemnor sending threatening letters, the matter can be brought to the attention of the court and appropriate representations made.

19.14   PREPARATION FOR HEARINGS

If a hearing has a time estimate of a half-day or more or, irrespective of the time estimate, it is in the High Court or the Royal Courts of Justice at county court level, court bundles must be prepared and lodged in accordance with the relevant President's Direction.

PD of 10 March 2000

Where the application is being made as a matter of urgency, the President's Direction of 10 March 2000 does not apply.

19.15   ALLOCATION OF HEARINGS

All interlocutory and final hearings in respect of applications for a Part IV order will be heard in chambers unless the court otherwise directs. Such hearings may be before any level of judge, both full and part-time, and accordingly counsel, a solicitor or legal executive will have the right of audience.

FPR 1991, r 3.9(1)

However, all matters relating to committal, whether as a result of a power of arrest being activated or as a result of a committal application or an application for a warrant of arrest, should be heard in open court, before any level of judge other than a deputy district judge.

Family Proceedings (Allocation to Judiciary) Directions 1999 [1999] 2 FLR 799

Accordingly, counsel or a solicitor has the right of audience save that, if the matter is proceeding in the High

Court, the solicitor must have higher court rights of audience.

If, on arrival at court, the advocate finds that a committal hearing is listed before a deputy district judge, the jurisdiction should be immediately questioned.

19.16   STALKING

The Protection from Harassment Act 1997 (PHA 1997) makes provision for the protection of a person from harassment and similar conduct. The Act is a curious hybrid which provides both criminal and civil remedies. Only the civil aspects are considered here.

19.16.1   Jurisdiction

PHA 1997, s 3 and RSC
Ord 94, r 16(3)

Proceedings can be issued in either a county court or the High Court but then only in the Queen's Bench Division.

19.16.2   Procedure

An application should be commenced as a Part 8 action in Form N208 and attracts a civil procedure court fee unless the claimant is exempt from fees.

Note: For full details of the procedure to be adopted for pursuing a Part 8 claim, see **13.2**.

19.16.3   Detailed provisions of the PHA 1997

A person must not pursue a course of conduct which:

PHA 1997, s 1(1)(a) and (b)

(a)   amounts to harassment of another; and
(b)   which that person knows or ought to know amounts to harassment of that other person.

For the purposes of the PHA 1997:

PHA 1997, s 7(2)

(a)   harassment includes alarming a person or causing distress;

PHA 1997, s 7(3)
PHA 1997, s 7(4)

(b)   a course of conduct must involve offending conduct on at least two occasions;
(c)   conduct includes speech.

PHA 1997, s 1(2)

The person whose conduct is in question ought to know that it amounts to harassment of another if a reasonable person in possession of the same information would think the course of conduct amounts to harassment.

A course of conduct will not amount to harassment if:

(a)   it was pursued for the purpose of preventing or detecting crime;

(b) it was pursued under any enactment or rule of law;

(c) in the particular circumstances the course of conduct
was reasonable.

PHA 1997, s 1(3)(a)–(c)

An actual or apprehended breach of PHA 1997, s 1 may be
the subject of a civil claim by the person who is or may be
the victim of the conduct in question.

PHA 1997, s 3(1)

Where the court makes a finding that harassment has taken
place it may grant an injunction restraining the defendant
from pursuing the offending course of conduct and/or
make an award in damages.

PHA 1997, s 3(2) and
(3)(a)

However, it is likely that a claimant will be more
concerned with obtaining an injunction than seeking
financial compensation.

Practitioners are advised to check with the court of issue as
to whether the matter is to be heard in chambers or open
court and as to the level of judiciary, before deciding on
who should appear as advocate.

Where an injunction has been breached, the claimant may
apply for the issue of a warrant for the arrest of the
defendant.

PHA 1997, s 3(3)

The warrant application in Form N139 must:

(a) state that it is an application for the issue of a warrant
for the arrest of the defendant;

(b) set out the grounds for making the application, which
must be supported by an affidavit or evidence on oath;

(c) state whether the claimant has informed the police of
the defendant's conduct;

(d) state whether, to the claimant's knowledge, criminal
proceedings are being pursued.

An application for a warrant must be made to a High Court
judge where the injunction was granted by a judge of that
court. Where the injunction was granted in the county
court, an application for a warrant should be made to a
circuit judge or district judge of that or any other county
court.

PHA 1997, s 3(4)(a) and
(b)

A judge may issue a warrant only if:

(a) the application is substantiated on oath; and

(b) he/she has reasonable grounds for believing that the
defendant has done anything which he/she is
prohibited by the injunction from doing.

PHA 1997, s 3(5)(a) and
(b)

Following the arrest of the defendant, the resultant
commital proceedings will be before either a High Court
judge or circuit judge who may:

RSC Ord 94, r 5(b)(i) and (ii)

(a) adjourn the proceedings for a maximum period of 14 days from the date of arrest. Where the matter is adjourned the defendant must be released and given not less than two days' notice of the adjourned hearing;

(b) make an immediate custodial order;

(c) make a suspended custodial order;

(d) dismiss the application.

CHAPTER 20

EMERGENCY APPLICATIONS

20.1 PROCEDURE

In cases of emergency, a judge may be prepared to make an interim order and, when necessary, accept an undertaking to issue proceedings within a specified period of time, usually not more than 48 hours.

If the emergency arises outside normal court opening hours, the applicant's solicitor or counsel will need to telephone the Urgent Court Business Officer for the group of courts within whose area the application is proceeding or intended to be issued. Accordingly, all practitioners who specialise in this sphere of law should ensure that they have a record of relevant telephone numbers.

Every police station should have a pager number for the Urgent Court Business Officer who is covering that police area.

If either the police are unable to help or there is no response from the pager number, a telephone call should be made to the security office at the Royal Courts of Justice (tel: 0207 947 6000), for assistance. The Urgent Court Business Officer for the Royal Courts of Justice, having established the nature of the emergency, will then contact either the Urgent Court Business Officer for the applicant's local group of courts or the duty emergency applications judge and make such arrangements as may be necessary.

In appropriate circumstances, the judge may be prepared to deal with the application over the telephone.

A copy of an information sheet for court users, detailing how the system operates, is to be found at Appendix C(2). This information sheet should be obtainable from all county courts and the Principal Registry of the Family Division.

If the judge is not minded to grant an order ex parte but nevertheless takes the view that an early date should be fixed for an inter partes hearing, the time for service on the respondent can be abridged (shortened). He/she will determine the number of days allowed for service and usually specify the date and time by which any respondent must be served. The purpose of specifying the date and time by which the application is to be served is to allow the respondent a reasonable opportunity to obtain legal advice and/or representation.

If the duty emergency application judge is prepared to make an ex parte order, it is good practice to provide the court with a draft of the order which is being sought.

CHAPTER 21

PROCEDURES FOR THE ENFORCEMENT OF FINANCIAL AND COSTS ORDERS

21.1 INTRODUCTION

Where a party has obtained a financial order which has not been fully complied with, there are a variety of steps which can potentially be taken with a view to enforcement. However, it should be noted that before any process is issued for the enforcement of an order governed by the Family Proceedings Rules 1991, for the payment of money to any person, an affidavit must be filed which verifies the amount due under the order and showing how that amount is calculated.

FPR 1991, r 7.1(1)

21.2 MAINTENANCE ARREARS IN EXCESS OF 12 MONTHS

Leave of the court is required to enforce arrears of maintenance if those arrears became due more than 12 months prior to the issue of the enforcement proceedings.

MCA 1973, s 32(1)

The application for leave should be made on notice in accordance with FPR 1991, r 10.9.

21.3 ORAL EXAMINATION

An oral examination is a useful means of enabling a judgment creditor to have the judgment debtor orally examined, with a view to establishing:

CCR Ord 25, r 3(1)
RSC Ord 48, r 1(1)

(a) the ability or otherwise to meet the substantive order and any related order for costs; and
(b) the most appropriate method of enforcement.

FPR 1991, r 7.1(5) and
CCR Ord 25, r 3(2)

The application is made ex parte on affidavit and, in county court proceedings, is made to the divorce county court in whose jurisdiction the person to be examined resides (which for this purpose includes the Principal Registry of the Family Division).

A copy of the order which it is sought to enforce must be exhibited to the affidavit, unless the application is made to the court in which the order was made. However, there is no related requirement to transfer an existing file to the court where the oral examination is to be conducted. It may be requested simply for the hearing if the district judge or the nominated officer considers it necessary.

If the relevant order was made in the High Court, regardless of where the proceedings are at the time of the application, it must be issued in the registry in which the order was made. However, thereafter, it is possible for the judgment creditor to apply to the district judge for the examination to take place in the court in whose jurisdiction the person to be examined resides.

MFPA 1984, s 38 and RSC Ord 48, r 1

A fee is payable on the issue of the application unless the applicant (judgment creditor) is exempt from fees.

The hearing should be fixed within a reasonable time, which in practice usually means at least 14 days ahead. In the county court, service of the order for an oral examination is normally effected in the first instance by first-class post.

CCR Ord 25, r 3(3)

In the High Court, service of the order for oral examination must be served personally on the judgment debtor.

RSC Ord 48, r 1(2)

The examination is usually conducted by an authorised clerk but may very exceptionally, on written request, be conducted by a district judge. Such a request should set out the reasons why it is being made.

In the county court, if the judgment debtor fails to attend the first hearing and the oral examination is adjourned for his/her attendance, the debtor may request a sum of money sufficient to cover his/her travelling expenses in getting to and from the court for the adjourned hearing. This payment is referred to as conduct money. It must be provided by the judgment creditor not less than seven days prior to the adjourned hearing, notice of which must be served personally on the person to be examined not less than 10 days prior to the date fixed for the hearing.

CCR Ord 25, r 3(5A)

The rules for oral examination in the High Court are similar to those in the county court save that the order for the oral examination must be personally served and conduct money offered at the time of service.

RSC Ord 48, r 1

Not more than four days before the date fixed for the adjourned hearing, the judgment creditor must file a certificate stating either that the requested conduct money has been paid or that no such request has been made.

CCR Ord 25, r 3(5B)

The conduct money referred to above is not payable in circumstances where sufficient monies have been paid to the person who is to be examined at the time of service of the original order for oral examination.

Failure to attend an oral examination may ultimately result in the judgment debtor being committed to prison unless a request for conduct money has not been complied with or otherwise there has been a failure to fully comply with the rules.

CCR Ord 25, r 3(5C) and
Ord 29, r 1(1)

21.4   FAILURE TO COMPLY WITH FINANCIAL ORDERS OTHER THAN THOSE RELATING TO CURRENT PERIODICAL PAYMENTS

21.4.1   Charging order

A charging order can potentially protect the receiving party in respect of unpaid lump sum or sums, accumulated arrears of periodical payments and costs orders, by imposing a charge on an asset or assets owned by the judgment debtor.

CCR Ord 31 and RSC
Ord 50

Reference should be made to CCR Ord 31, r 1(1) for information as to the appropriate court in which to issue the application. The procedure in the county court closely follows that provided by RSC Ord 50 in the High Court.

The application for the order nisi (interim order), supported by an affidavit, is made to a district judge without giving notice to the other party. The affidavit must contain all the information required by CCR Ord 31 and RSC Ord 50.

CCR Ord 31, r 2 and RSC
Ord 50, r 1(3)

The application attracts a court fee unless the judgment creditor is exempt from fees.

Where the asset is land or buildings erected upon the land, which has or have been registered at the Land Registry, many district judges will insist on the Land Registry office copy entries being lodged with the affidavit.

An order to show cause as to why the order nisi should not be made absolute is issued for hearing and must be served on the judgment debtor at least seven days prior to the hearing, together with a sealed copy of the affidavit and any exhibit.

CCR Ord 31, r 1(8) and
RSC Ord 50, r 2(3)

All other interested parties must also be served with the order nisi, copy of the supporting affidavit and exhibits (if any) not less than seven days prior to the date fixed for the hearing.

CCR Ord 31, r 1(6) and
RSC Ord 50, r 2(2)

The district judge will need to be satisfied that the judgment debtor and other interested parties have been served.

If the judgment debtor attends court with proposals for an early payment of the monies owed, so as to ensure that such proposals are honoured, the district judge should be asked for an adjournment to a fixed date and for the charging order nisi to remain in force in the meantime.

If, on the other hand, the judgment debtor offers payment by way of instalments, the district judge should be asked to consider making the charging order absolute before considering a variation order.

If the district judge is satisfied, the order will be made absolute. If he/she is not satisfied, the charging order nisi will be discharged.

CCR Ord 31, r 2(1) and
RSC Ord 50, r 3(1)

A copy of the order should then be served in such a way so as ensure that the interest of the judgment creditor is recorded on the appropriate register, for example at HM Charges Registry, the Land Registry or with a company registry (in respect of a stock or share holding).

Failure on the part of a solicitor to ensure that a charging order is promptly registered on property which is subsequently sold would almost certainly be viewed as negligence. Accordingly, all aspects of such an application should be conducted with the absolute minimum of delay.

Although opinion on the point is divided, it may be considered expedient to register both the charging order nisi and the charging order absolute.

A charging order is not of itself a means of enforcement but the charging order absolute may be enforced by an order for sale in separate proceedings (see **21.4.2**).

Because it is not strictly an enforcement, during the currency of a charging order it is possible to issue one of the other processes described in this chapter.

21.4.2   Enforcement of charging order by sale

If, following the granting of a charging order absolute, the judgment debtor still fails to pay the amount due, either under the original substantive order or any subsequent variation, an application can be made for the property to be sold or, where property can be divided, for the sale of a part. The procedure for the enforcement of a charging order by sale of the property is governed by CCR Ord 31, r 4.

The application for an order for sale will be commenced under the provisions of the TLATA 1996, using the procedure provided by Part 8 of the CPR 1998.

The Part 8 claim form can be issued in either a county court or the High Court but, in any event, not in the Principal Registry of the Family Division. If it is intended to proceed in the High Court, the application must be made in the Chancery Division.

RSC Ord 50, r 9A

The standard Part 8 court fee will be payable, unless the claimant is exempt from fees.

If commenced in a county court, proceedings must be issued in the court which made the charging order. If, on the other hand, it is sought to enforce a High Court charging order in the county court, the application must be made in the court for the district in which the defendant resides or carries on business.

CCR Ord 31, r 4(2)(b)

The claim form must be served within four months after the date of issue, unless service is required out of the jurisdiction, in which case the period is extended to six months.

CPR 1998, r 7.5(2) and (3)

For procedure concerning service out of the jurisdiction reference should be made to RSC Ord 11. The claimant may apply for an order extending the period within which the claim form may be served.

Note: See **13.2.2** for further information concerning an application to extend time.

The application must be supported by either a witness statement or affidavit, which sets out all the information required by the rules.

CCR Ord 31, r 4(1) and CPR 1998, r 8.5

The defendant must be served not less than 21 days before the hearing and accordingly the court will usually fix a hearing date not less than 28 days ahead to take account of service by post.

CPR 1998 Part 8, PD8B, para B.10

Prior to the hearing, it is advisable to obtain a valuation of the property in question for presenting to the court. This is because the judge who hears the application will, if an order for sale is made, need to fix a minimum sale price.

A copy of the claim form should be served on the defendant together with:

CCR Ord 31, r 4(3)

(a) notice of the hearing date;
(b) a copy of the witness statement or affidavit;
(c) acknowledgement of service;

(d) a copy of a valuation if one has been obtained as suggested above.

If a valuation has taken place after service has been effected, a copy of the valuation should be sent to the defendant without delay.

The defendant must file a completed acknowledgement of service not more than 14 days after service of the claim form and must serve a copy on the claimant and any other party.

CPR 1998, r 8.3(1)(a) and (b)

The acknowledgement of service must state:

(a) whether the defendant contests the claim;
(b) if the defendant seeks some other remedy to the claim.

CPR 1998, r 8.3(2)(a) and (b)

21.4.3 Garnishee order

A garnishee order nisi (interim order) freezes assets of a judgment debtor which are in the possession of a third party (the garnishee) in order to enforce accumulated arrears of periodical payments, lump sum or sums orders, costs orders and undertakings to pay school fees. This is subject to a minimum of £50.

CCR Ord 30, r 1(1) and RSC Ord 49, r 1(1)

The application for the order nisi, supported by an affidavit, is made to a district judge without giving notice to the judgment debtor or to the garnishee.

CCR Ord 30, r 1 and RSC Ord 49, r 1

The affidavit must contain all the information set out in CCR Ord 30, r 2 and RSC Ord 49, r 2(2). The application attracts a court fee unless the judgment creditor is exempt from fees.

Obvious examples of a garnishee are high street banks and building societies but can equally be an individual.

If the garnishee order nisi is granted, the order will be endorsed with the date and time of the hearing of the application to make the order absolute.

CCR Ord 30, r 1(2) and RSC Ord 49, r 1(2)

The hearing date is normally fixed at least three weeks in advance because the garnishee must be served at least 15 days before the hearing. The judgment debtor must be served at least seven days after the order has been served on the garnishee and at least seven days before the hearing. In the High Court, the order nisi must be served personally on the garnishee.

CCR Ord 30, r 3(2)(a) and (b) and RSC Ord 49, r 3(1)(a) and (b)

For obvious reasons, it may be thought prudent in county court proceedings similarly to serve the garnishee in person.

In any event, the district judge will need to be satisfied as to service of the garnishee order nisi before making it absolute.

Where the garnishee is a deposit-taking institution, for example a bank, the garnishee order nisi should be served on the head office.

Once the garnishee order nisi is made absolute, the garnishee must pay the amount ordered to the judgment creditor, provided that at the time the garnishee was served with the order nisi sufficient funds were available and standing to the credit of the judgment debtor. If the available amount is less than that ordered then that lesser amount should be paid.

Where the garnishee is a bank or other deposit-taking institution, it is entitled to deduct a sum, currently £55, from the relevant debt as payment towards administration and clerical expenses. This is so even where the amount held by the institution is insufficient to cover the full amount of the judgment debt and the costs associated with that judgment.

CCA 1984, s 109 and
AD(E)O 1996

If the garnishee refuses to pay, the garnishee order absolute can be enforced against that garnishee in the same manner as any other judgment debt.

A garnishee order can be a particularly potent weapon where it is known that moneys are to be paid into a bank or building society account on a particular day. In these circumstances, the timing of the application is obviously vital and, where necessary, the application should be made by a practitioner in person and not by post. Having issued the application, the practitioner should ask to go before a judge and, if the garnishee order nisi is made, should request the court to kindly draw the order immediately so that service can then be effected on the garnishee without delay.

CCR Ord 30, r 3(2) and
RSC Ord 49, r 3(2)

All aspects of a garnishee application should be conducted expeditiously since any unreasonable delay on the part of a solicitor which results in a failure to secure funds, which are subsequently withdrawn from an account after instructions have been received, could well be viewed as negligence. In particular, it is important to remember that a garnishee is not bound by the terms of an order nisi until the order has been served.

21.4.4 Matrimonial judgment summons

A matrimonial judgment summons requires a judgment debtor to appear before a High Court judge or circuit judge to be examined on oath as to his means.

FPR 1991, rr 7.4 and 7.5

Orders which are enforceable by this means are orders for periodical payments (where there are accumulated arrears), lump sums and, in some circumstances, those for costs.

An order for the payment of school fees direct to a school can also be enforced by judgment summons.

L v L (Payment of School Fees) [1997] 2 FLR 252

Failure to attend court for an examination may ultimately result in the judgment debtor being committed to prison for a period not exceeding 14 days.

CCA 1984, s 110(2)

Before presenting the application to the court, practitioners should consider the Practice Direction of the President of the Family Division which has been in force since 16 March 2001, concerning the issue and conduct of committal proceedings. A copy of this direction is to be found at Appendix C. Practitioners should also refer to *Mubarak v Mubarak* [2001] 1 FLR 698, CA, and *Quinn and Cuff* [2001] EWCA Civ 36, [2001] All ER (D) 29.

The application may be issued in the case of an order of:

(a) the High Court, in the Principal Registry of the Family Division, a district registry or a divorce county court, whichever in the opinion of the judgment creditor is most convenient;

(b) a divorce county court (which includes the Principal Registry of the Family Division exercising its county court jurisdiction), in whichever divorce county court is, in the opinion of the judgment creditor, most convenient having regard in either case to the place where the judgment debtor resides or carries on business and irrespective of the court or registry in which the order was made.

FPR 1991, r 7.4(2)

The application must be made by filing a request in Form M16 together with an affidavit.

FPR 1991, r 7.4(3)

The application attracts a court fee, unless the judgment creditor is exempt from fees.

The judgment summons must be served personally and not less than 10 clear days before the hearing.

FPR 1991, r 7.4(5)

Conduct money must be paid to the judgment debtor at the time of service of the judgment summons. This money is to cover the expenses in travelling to and from the court at which he/she is summoned to appear.

FPR 1991, r 7.4(5)

At the hearing, the judge may order:

(a) the variation of an existing lump sum or costs order, either by extending the specified time for payment or by way of instalments;

FPR 1991, r 7.4(9)

(b) the payment of accumulated arrears by way of instalments;

(c) that payment be made by way of an attachment of earnings order;

AEA 1971, s 3(4)

(d) the committal of the judgment debtor, suspended on terms;

FPR 1991, r 7.4(10)

(e) an immediate committal for a specified period.

Even when a judgment debtor is committed to prison, it will not have the effect of extinguishing the judgment debt.

21.4.5 Warrant of execution

The procedure in respect of a warrant of execution is governed by CCR Ord 26. The warrant authorises a county court bailiff to seize goods belonging to a judgment debtor and to sell them in order to satisfy a sum of money, including costs, due under a court order. The application for a warrant is made by way of Form N323 supported by an affidavit, giving the information required by the rules.

CCR Ord 26, r 1 and FPR 1991, r 7.1(1)

A court fee is payable unless the judgment creditor is exempt from fees.

Unless a district judge directs otherwise, the bailiff will give the judgment debtor seven days' notice of intention to levy. If the debt remains unpaid at the end of this seven-day period, the warrant is executed by the court bailiff against goods owned by the judgment debtor.

CCR Ord 26, r 1(4)

A bailiff is empowered to seize and sell items sufficient to cover the value of the debt, although any excess monies not required to satisfy the debt are repaid to the debtor. A similar procedure exists in the High Court where the creditor can apply for a writ of fieri facias (usually referred to as a writ of fi fa).

Application is made by filing a praecipe (a High Court request form), supported by an affidavit and a prepared writ for sealing.

RSC Ord 46 and 47

21.5 FAILURE TO COMPLY WITH PERIODICAL PAYMENTS ORDERS

21.5.1 Attachment of earnings

Procedure in respect of attachment of earnings is governed by the Attachment of Earnings Act 1971 (AEA 1971). An attachment of earnings order is a means of enforcing a periodical payments order by requiring an employer to make deductions from the debtor's earnings and make regular payments direct to the court, for subsequent transmission to the applicant.

CCR Ord 27, r 17

However, it should be noted that leave of the court will be required to enforce payment of any arrears which have been outstanding for more than 12 months.

CCR Ord 27, r 17(3)

Order 27 of the CCR sets out the procedure to be followed for an attachment of earnings application. The more important aspects of the Order are set out below.

The application for an attachment is made on the prescribed Form N55, and must be issued in the court in which the maintenance order was made. The application attracts a court fee unless the applicant is exempt from fees.

CCR Ord 27, r 17(2)

The application requires the judgment creditor to certify:

(a) the amount due under the order; and
(b) whether or not there are any arrears and, if so, how such sum has been calculated.

Unlike other attachment of earnings applications, there is no requirement for any arrears to have accrued. However, where there are no arrears, the order may be refused.

CCR Ord 27, r 4(1) and AEA 1971, s 3(3) and (3A)

Once the application is issued, it is endorsed with the date and time of the hearing, which will be not less than 21 days ahead, when the application will be listed for determination.

CCR Ord 27, r 4(2)

Unlike attachment of earnings hearings in respect of county court judgments, maintenance attachments are listed for a private hearing, in chambers, before a district judge. Although CCR Ord 27 provides a discretion, in practice all county courts list in this way.

CCR Ord 27, r 17(5)

The application, endorsed with the details of the hearing, will be served on the judgment debtor together with a form of reply, in Form N56, which requires the debtor to provide to the court full financial disclosure, information which will subsequently be passed to the judgment creditor.

CCR Ord 27, r 17(3A)

The debtor is required to complete and file the Form N56 within eight days of service.

CCR Ord 27, r 5(2)

If the debtor complies and provides comprehensive information concerning both income and expenditure, the district judge will then be able to calculate fairly the appropriate deduction to be made from the debtor's earnings (referred to as the normal deduction rate) and fix a protected earnings rate. Protected earnings are, as the term implies, a level of earnings below which no deductions can properly be made by an employer. It, in effect, guarantees a minimum take-home pay.

The attachment of earnings order may be suspended in circumstances where there is a good reason to believe that the judgment debtor will make regular payments in future, and where an immediate order may have a detrimental effect on future employment.

A copy of the order which sets out the information given above should be sent by the court to the debtor's employer, without delay, together with an explanatory leaflet. If the order is not complied with and the employer fails to provide a satisfactory reason, a fine may be imposed.

AEA 1971, s 23(2) and (3)

The employer has a duty to notify the court, within 10 days, of any person bound by an attachment of earnings order ceasing to be in their employ.

AEA 1971, s 7(2)

An attachment of earnings order in respect of maintenance takes priority over other attachment of earnings orders which may have been made against the judgment debtor or any which are subsequently made. The court which makes the order has a duty to send a copy of that order to the Court Officer for the district in which the debtor resides.

AEA 1971, Sch 3, Part II, para 8(a)

CCR Ord 2, r 2(2)

If the debtor fails to disclose details of his/her financial position or details of his/her employer, he/she may be fined or committed to prison for a period not exceeding 14 days.

CCR Ord 27, r 8

As an alternative to a fine or committal, the court may simply make an attachment of earnings order on the basis of such information as is available. Both the normal deduction and protected earnings rates may be in excess of what would have otherwise been ordered had the relevant information been provided. However, in these circumstances it is always open to the judgment debtor to apply to the court for a variation order, and at the same time provide full and proper financial disclosure.

The provision set out above applies equally in circumstances where the judgment debtor fails to attend an attachment of earnings hearing and, having been given an opportunity to explain that failure, does not take that opportunity or otherwise does not provide a satisfactory reason as to why a fine or a period of imprisonment should not be imposed.

Where details of the employer have been disclosed but no financial information has been provided, the court can require the employer to disclose full details of the debtor's earnings by way of Form N338.

CCR Ord 27, r 6

It is also possible for a judgment debtor to apply on his/her own behalf for an attachment of earnings order either at the time a maintenance order is made or on any subsequent variation.

CCR Ord 27, r 17(4)

The attachment of earnings order will usually make provision for the payment of the instalments required under the order, together with a further instalment in respect of any accumulated arrears.

Where the attachment of earnings order relates to maintenance for a minor child, it may be prudent for a practitioner who is acting for the debtor to ask the court to request the creditor to provide an undertaking to notify the court when the child concerned has ceased full-time education. Without this, child maintenance orders are difficult to monitor.

Practitioners should note that any matrimonial costs order is enforced in the same way as any other judgment debt. CCR Ord 27, r 17 does not apply. Accordingly the Principal Registry of the Family Division does not have the jurisdiction to deal with the enforcement of such orders by this means.

21.5.2 Registration of a maintenance order in a magistrates' court

Procedure in respect of the registration of a maintenance order in a magistrates' court is governed by s 2(1) of the Maintenance Orders Act 1958 (MOA 1958). It applies to orders made pursuant to the MCA 1973 and CA 1989.

This procedure enables a person who is entitled to receive payments under a maintenance order to apply to register that order in a magistrates' court, where it may be more effectively and economically enforced.

The application must be made to the court which made the order, in Form M33, and should be signed by the applicant in person, unless solicitors are on the court record.

FPR 1991, r 7.23(1)

The application attracts a court fee unless the applicant is exempt from fees.

Form M33 requires the following information to be given:

(a) the full name and address of the person who is to receive payment;

(b) the full name, address, occupation and date of birth of the person who has to make the payment;

(c) the date of the order and the date when the next payment is due;

(d) the arrears, if any, and the date to which the arrears have been calculated;

(e) whether the whole or only part of the order is to be registered;

(f) confirmation that no other enforcement proceedings are pending and that the order has not been previously registered;

(g) the reasons for requesting registration;

(h) whether or not the Department of Social Security has requested registration.

MOA 1958, s 2(1) and (3)

Although the form provides for details of the arrears of maintenance to be set out, it is not a pre-condition for registration for there to be any arrears.

FPR 1991, r 7.23(3)

If the district judge gives leave to register the order, the court will send a copy of the application, together with a certified copy of the relevant order, to the appropriate magistrates' court.

The order is registered in the court that has jurisdiction over the area in which the debtor resides.

Secretariat Circular, 18 December 2000

However, where the debtor appears to be in the petty sessions area of one of the Inner London magistrates' courts (Camberwell Green, Greenwich, Highbury Corner, Horseferry Road, Marylebone, South Western, Thames and West London), the papers for registration should *not* be sent to the individual court but to the Inner London Magistrates' Courts Service, Centralised Accounts Office, PO Box 31093, London SW1P 3WT.

Magistrates' Court Rules 1981, r 52(2)

If the debtor moves from the jurisdiction of that magistrates' court, it is the duty of the Chief Executive to the Justices to transfer the order to the appropriate magistrates' court to be re-registered there.

PD of 10 March 1980

Interim orders are registered only in exceptional circumstances. This is to ensure that no confusion is created by either:

(a) the final order being for a different amount; or

(b)   a variation order being made by the magistrates' court
      before the final High Court or county court order is
      made.

Leave of the court is required to enforce arrears of
maintenance if those arrears became due more than 12
months prior to the issue of the enforcement proceedings.   MCA 1973, s 32(1)

If either party subsequently applies to vary the rate or
method of payment of a registered order, the application
must be issued in the magistrates' court unless the order is
de-registered and remitted by them back to the court of
origin.   MOA 1958, s 4(2)(a)

However, any application to extend or discharge an order
must be issued in the court of origin. There is no related
requirement to de-register.

It is important to note that any application to extend the
duration of an order must be made before the order lapses.
Once an order has expired, it cannot be revived.

It is also possible to register an order in Scotland and
Ireland and overseas under reciprocal enforcement
arrangements. This is an area of practice which is little
known to the majority of practitioners and is a complete
mystery to some. Most applications are poorly prepared,
with scant, if any, regard to the various statutory
requirements. It is for these reasons that the topic has been
made the subject of a separate chapter in this edition. See
Chapter 22.

21.6   MAINTENANCE PAYABLE BY MEMBERS OF THE ARMED FORCES

Pay and allowances made to regular members of the armed
forces are not earnings within the attachment of earnings   NF(EML)A 1947, AA
legislation; however, deductions from pay may be made   1955, s 150 and AFA
automatically from a debtor's pay.   1955, s 150

Where the respondent to an application for maintenance is
a regular member of the armed forces, it is possible to
apply to his/her unit commander for a compulsory
allotment of the respondent's pay.

A copy of any order for maintenance should be forwarded,
by the court, to the appropriate military paymaster so as to
facilitate this procedure, fuller details of which will be
found in *Rayden*, 17th edn, para 34.5.

As a result of the operation of the various provisions
referred to opposite the first paragraph of this section, none

of the methods set out in this chapter for the enforcement of maintenance will be effective in respect of any member of the armed forces.

Practitioners may wish to note that service of any process upon a regular member of the armed forces which relates to maintenance may be effected by registered post on his/her commanding officer and is deemed good service.

Note: The relevant addresses can be obtained from the various military manning and record offices whose details are provided in Appendix C(1).

NDA 1957, s 101, AA 1955, s 153 and AFA 1955, s 153

21.7 JUDICIAL AUTHORITY TO SIGN DOCUMENTS

A party may decline or otherwise be unable to sign a document, for example a contract or a deed, required in connection with the sale or transfer of property pursuant to a court order. Section 39 of the Supreme Court Act 1981 empowers a judge to sign the document on behalf of that party or alternatively direct another person to sign.

An application may be made at the time the substantive order is made, where there is little prospect of co-operation. Otherwise, a subsequent application on notice may be made, in respect of which a court fee is payable unless the applicant is exempt from paying fees.

A deed should be endorsed as follows:

Signed by District Judge   pursuant   *[signature*
to Section 39 of the Supreme Court Act 1981   *of district*
and pursuant to an order of the   *judge]*
Court dated the   day of   .
Before me,
[signature of witness]
[address of witness]
[occupation of witness]

Note: The form and wording will require some variation, for example where the document to be signed is a contract.

CHAPTER 22

RECIPROCAL ENFORCEMENT OF MAINTENANCE ORDERS

22.1 RECIPROCAL OR INTERNATIONAL ENFORCEMENT

The enforcement of maintenance orders where a party resides outside the jurisdiction of England and Wales can be defined as applications which are:

(a) outgoing, ie those made within the jurisdiction and in respect of which it is sought to enforce against a person who resides outside the jurisdiction (this includes other parts of the United Kingdom);

(b) incoming, ie those made outside the jurisdiction (this includes other parts of the United Kingdom) and in respect of which it sought to enforce against a person who resides within the jurisdiction, or against assets which are within the jurisdiction, even if the payer is not. Where the assets are within the jurisdiction but the payer is not, enforcement will proceed in the High Court.

It should be noted that for this purpose a maintenance order is defined as one which provides for periodical payments. This includes financial provision, in the nature of maintenance, under the provisions of the CA 1989. For enforcement of lump sum orders, see **22.7**.

With the exception of other countries within the United Kingdom, all applications are ultimately dealt with through the Reciprocal Enforcement of Maintenance Orders Section (REMO) at the Headquarters of the Lord Chancellor's Department. Applications concerning England, Wales, Scotland and Northern Ireland are dealt with solely by the court which made the original maintenance order, without the involvement of REMO; see paragraphs **22.10** and **22.11**.

Note: An order can be registered in one court only at any time.

22.2 CONVENTIONS AND PRIMARY AND SUBORDINATE LEGISLATION

A comprehensive list of the conventions and related primary legislation is to be found at Appendix C(5).

The related subordinate legislation is comprehensively dealt with in *Rayden*, 17th edition, chapter 34, section 5.

Note: Some countries are governed by more than one Act.

22.3   RECIPROCAL COUNTRIES

A comprehensive list of those countries with which England and Wales have reciprocal arrangements is to be found at Appendix C(5).

Within the United States of America the agreement is made with the individual state and not the federal government. It should be noted that not all the states are signatories and reference should be made to Appendix C(5), in order to establish whether or not the relevant state is a participant.

22.4   PROCEDURE

22.4.1   Incoming Applications

For the meaning of an incoming application see **22.1** (b) above. An application to enforce can be made only to the foreign court which made the original order. Under no circumstances can a court within England and Wales authorise enforcement. Once the application has been approved, all relevant documents will be sent by the originating court to the Reciprocal Enforcement of Maintenance Orders Section at the Lord Chancellor's Department, for forwarding to the magistrates' court for the area in which the payer is thought to reside. Registration is effected by the Chief Executive to the Justices entering details of the order in the register.

MO(RE) Act 1972, s 6(2) and MC(REMO)R 1974, r 8(1)

It is possible for a registered order to be re-registered in the High Court for the purpose of enforcement.

MO(RE) Act 1972, s 8(1)

In these circumstances, application is made to the Chief Executive to the Justices who will forward the documentation to the Principal Registry of the Family Division or the appropriate District Registry. Once registered the order may be enforced as though an order made within that court.

MO(RE) Act 1972, s 8(1) and MC(REMO)R 1974, r 9A

The enforcement of foreign orders, other than those made in Scotland, Northern Ireland and the Republic of Ireland, is not considered further in this book.

22.4.2   Outgoing Applications

(a) Part I MO(RE) Act 1972
For the meaning of an outgoing application see **22.1** (a) above.

An application must be made to the court which made the order by the person to whom payments should be made. This is made by way of an affidavit setting out:

MO(RE) Act 1972, s 2(3)

(a) details of the order it is sought to enforce;
(b) the applicant's reasons for believing that the payer is residing in that country;
(c) the amount of any arrears and how such figures have been calculated, the date to which they have been calculated and the date the next payment is due;
(d) confirmation that the order has been served and the manner in which such service has been effected;
(e) details of the whereabouts of the payer;
(f) a description of the payer. Where possible, a recent photograph should also be provided;
(g) as much information as possible concerning the payer's employment;
(h) whether or not the time for appealing against the order has expired and whether or not an appeal is pending.

FPR 1991, r 7.31

Once a practitioner has identified the country in which the order is to be enforced, reference should be made to the Rules as some countries require additional information to that set out above.

FPR 1991, rr 7.31, 7.38 and 7.39

In particular, it should be noted that:

(a) Canada requires a statement confirming that a child referred to in the order which it is sought to enforce is still alive and living with the applicant.
(b) Australia requires a certificate confirming that the order is enforceable in England and Wales and, where the payer has been in prison, what element of the arrears is referable to the period of imprisonment.
(c) New Zealand requires proof that a child to whom the order relates is still alive.
(d) Some foreign authorities, notably Sweden, Germany, Norway and The Netherlands, may request a 'Power of Attorney'. The applicant thereby gives the foreign authority permission to act on his/her behalf for the purpose of enforcing the order.

As a general rule, only final orders will be considered for enforcement.

MO(RE) Act 1972, s 2(2)

It should be noted that the REMO Section at the Lord Chancellor's Department require that all documents should be provided in triplicate.

FPR 1991, r 7.39(7)

If a district judge approves the application he/she will
complete and sign a certificate confirming:

(a) that the maintenance order is enforceable in the
     United Kingdom;
(b) that the arrears of maintenance are as set out in the
     affidavit;
(c) the date of birth of any child referred to in the
     maintenance order;
(d) that the affidavit contains the information in the
     possession of the court as to the whereabouts and the
     identification of the payer.

PD of 7 May 1974
MO(RE) Act 1972, s 2(4)

In addition, if registration is sought in a Hague Convention
Country, the certificate must also state:

(a) whether the payer has been served with the
     proceedings;
(b) whether he/she has appeared at any hearing and, if
     they have not –
(c) that they were served with notice of the application;
     and
(d) whether the payee has received legal aid either within
     the proceedings or in connection with the application
     to enforce.

FPR 1991, r 7.38

The court will then forward, in triplicate, the affidavit,
certificate and certified copy of the relevant order, to the
REMO Section at the Lord Chancellor's Department for
onward transmission to the appropriate authority in the
reciprocating country.

Part I of the MO(RE) Act
1972

The REMO Section will subsequently act as a form of
intermediary, forwarding mail between the originating
court and the reciprocating court.

FPR 1991, r 7.36

When the relevant authority in the reciprocating country
receives an application, the matter will normally be listed
for hearing in the receiving court. The payer is served with
notice of the application and a date is fixed for the hearing.
The applicant is not expected to attend. At the hearing the
judge (or magistrate) will either confirm or vary the order.
A variation will be by way of a provisional order only,
which is then referred back to the originating court, for
confirmation or other order.

FPR 1991, r 7.33(1)

The court which made the provisional order will
subsequently be informed of the order made in the
originating court.

FPR 1991, r 7.33(2)

The application for reciprocal enforcement attracts a fee
unless the applicant is exempt from fees.

Where the order is for enforcement in a non-English speaking country, practitioners will be delighted to learn that the Lord Chancellor's Department will arrange for the translation of all relevant documents at no additional fee.

(b) Part II MO(RE) Act 1972
Where an order is to be enforced under Part II, the procedure is somewhat different.

MO(RE) Act 1972, s 26(6)

In the first instance, an application in Form M33 should be made to the originating court to register the order in the magistrates' court for the area in which the *applicant* resides. Practitioners should refer to **21.5.2** for the procedure to be followed. It should be made clear on Form M33 that the order is to be enforced abroad.

MO(RE) Act 1972, s 26(3)

Once the order has been registered in the magistrates' court, an application should then be made to that court for the order to be enforced in the reciprocating country. The Chief Executive to the Justices will assist the applicant in completing the application in accordance with the requirements of the law of the reciprocating country.

The documentation which will normally be required by the REMO Section will include:

(a)   the birth certificate of any relevant child;
(b)   a marriage certificate if applicable;
(c)   a recent photograph of the payer;
(d)   copies of any previous orders;
(e)   a power of attorney which authorises the authorities in the reciprocating country to take all necessary steps to enforce the order;
(f)   a certificate by the Chief Executive to the Justices in accordance with s 26(3A) of the Act.

MO(RE) Act 1972, s 26

The Chief Executive to the Justices will forward the documentation to the REMO Section at the Lord Chancellor's Department for onward transmission to the authorities in the reciprocating country.

22.5   TRACING THE WHEREABOUTS OF A PAYER

Where the payer is residing outside the United Kingdom but a precise address is not known, it may be possible to trace his/her whereabouts if he/she is in Australia, Canada, New Zealand or South Africa.

Application is made by way of completing a questionnaire in Form D312 (Principal Registry of the Family Division) or Form D85 (County Court), which should be lodged with the relevant court. No fee is payable.

Solicitors may be required to give an undertaking that they will not disclose the address provided to the applicant or use it otherwise than for the purpose of the enforcement proceedings.

Practice Note of 10 February 1976

22.6   HIGH COURT OR COUNTY COURT?

Some countries will accept only a High Court order for enforcement purposes and, accordingly, practitioners may think it prudent to check with the legal department of the High Commission or Embassy of the country in question. It is possible to transfer a county court order, other than a periodical payments order, to the High Court for the purpose of enforcement.

FPR 1991, r 7.3

If the order to be enforced is for periodical payments, the suit must be transferred to the High Court.

22.7   LUMP SUM ORDERS

Although rarely used in the Family Division, practitioners should be aware that the Civil Jurisdiction and Judgments Act 1982 provides an alternative means of enforcing a lump sum order. *Rayden*, 17th edn, Chapter 34, section 82, clarifies orders which are enforceable under the 1982 Act.

Procedure is dictated by RSC Ord 71, rr 35–39.

The application is made by way of affidavit which must exhibit a certified copy of the order and confirm that the order has been served and that it is enforceable and:

(a)   give particulars of the proceedings in which the judgment was obtained;

(b)   have annexed to it a copy of the writ, originating summons or other process by which the proceedings were begun, the evidence of service thereof on the defendant, copies of the pleadings, if any, and a statement of the grounds on which the judgment was based together, where appropriate, with any document under which the applicant is entitled to public funding for the purpose of the proceedings;

(c)   state whether the defendant did or did not object to the jurisdiction, and if so, on what grounds;

(d)   show that the judgment has been served in accordance with Ord 65, r 5 and is not subject to any stay of execution;

(e)   state that the time for appealing has expired, or, as the case may be, the date on which it will expire and in either case whether notice of appeal against the judgment has been given; and

(f) state:
  (i) whether the judgment provides for the payment of a sum or sums of money; or
  (ii) whether interest is recoverable on the judgment or part thereof and if so, the rate of interest, the date from which interest is recoverable and the date on which interest ceases to accrue.

The application is made to the Central Office of the Queen's Bench Division of the Royal Courts of Justice.

RSC Ord 71, r 37

A similar procedure applies for the enforcement of an order in other parts of the United Kingdom.

22.8 PENSION ATTACHMENT (EARMARKING)

Practitioners should note that there is no provision for the reciprocal enforcement of pension attachment orders, whether made within the jurisdiction or within a foreign jurisdiction.

22.9 COSTS ORDERS

Costs orders within divorce and related matters whether in the High Court or county court are also subject to enforcement under the Civil Jurisdiction and Judgments Act 1982. Reference should be made to RSC Ord 71, r 37 and, in the county court, CCR Ord 35, which set out details of the procedure to be followed. See **22.7** above.

22.10 RECIPROCAL ENFORCEMENT IN OTHER PARTS OF THE UNITED KINGDOM

The Maintenance Orders Act 1950 provides for the enforcement of orders made in different parts of the United Kingdom.

22.10.1 Registration in London of orders made in Scotland or Northern Ireland

It is possible for the Principal Registry of the Family Division to register an order made in the Court of Session in Scotland or the Supreme Court of Northern Ireland.

FPR 1991, r 7.20(2)

The application is made to the originating court by way of affidavit or statutory declaration. Once approved, the officer of that court will forward the application to the Principal Registry together with a certified copy of the order.

It is possible for the order, once registered in London, to be re-registered in a magistrates' court pursuant to the MOA 1958. For the procedure in this respect, see **21.5.2**.

Note: It is not possible for the Principal Registry to register an order made in the Sheriff Court in Scotland or in a Court of Summary Jurisdiction in Northern Ireland. (These orders must be registered in a magistrates' court.)

MOA 1950, s 17(3)(b)

22.10.2 Registration of an English order in Scotland or Northern Ireland

It is possible to register a Maintenance Order made in the High Court in the Court of Session in Scotland or the Supreme Court of Jurisdiction in Northern Ireland.

FPR 1991, r 7.19(2) and Part II MOA 1950

Maintenance Orders made in a divorce county court must be registered in the Sheriff Court in Scotland or in the Court of Summary Jurisdiction in Northern Ireland.

FPR 1991, r 7.19(6)

The application is made by way of affidavit to the court which made the order. The affidavit must state:

(a) the address in the United Kingdom and the occupation of the payer;
(b) the date on which that order was served on the person, or if the order has not been served, the reason why this has not been done;
(c) the reason why the order should be registered in either Scotland or Northern Ireland;
(d) the amount of any arrears due under the order;
(e) that the order is not already registered.

FPR 1991, r 7.19(1)

Note: An order can be registered in one court only at any given time.

If the district judge is satisfied that the payer is resident in either Scotland or Northern Ireland, he/she will direct that a certified copy of the order, together with a copy of the affidavit, be sent to the appropriate court in that country for registration to be effected there.

FPR 1991, r 7.19(2)

22.11 RECIPROCAL ENFORCEMENT IN THE REPUBLIC OF IRELAND

Enforcement in Eire is governed by the Maintenance Orders (Reciprocal Enforcement) Act 1972 and the Reciprocal Enforcement of Maintenance Orders (Republic of Ireland) Order 1993.

The procedure is much the same as that described in **22.4.1** for incoming applications and **22.4.2** for outgoing applications, both of which must be submitted through the

REMO Section. It should be noted that the following additional information is required:

(a)   a statement by the district judge regarding whether the payee received legal aid in the original proceedings and/or in the application for registration;

(b)   a statement as to whether the payer appeared in the proceedings at which the maintenance order was made and, if not, the original or a certified copy of a document which establishes that notice of the institution of proceedings was served upon him/her;

(c)   a document which establishes that notice of the order was served on the payer.

FPR 1991, r 7.37(2)

22.12   FINAL THOUGHTS

Once an order has been registered, enforcement can potentially be effective, but practitioners should be aware, and make their clients aware at the outset, that the process of reciprocal enforcement can take many months to complete. Delay can potentially be encountered both within the Lord Chancellor's Department and in the receiving country.

The level of success may, to a large extent, depend upon the degree of co-operation provided by the country in which enforcement is sought.

Clients should also be informed that the amount which is eventually enforced may not be the same as the amount ordered by the Court in England and Wales, this is because a judge of the country in which the enforcement is sought may have the jurisdiction to order a variation, although this would be subject to confirmation by the originating court.

Should the payer move to another country, the frustrating process will then have to start all over again.

CHAPTER 23

PENAL NOTICES AND COMMITTAL APPLICATIONS

23.1 PENAL NOTICES

Some orders and undertakings referred to in this book may, or in some cases will, be endorsed with a penal notice, so as to try to ensure compliance.

23.1.1 Interlocutory orders

Where an interlocutory order has not been complied with, an application may be made to the court for a penal notice to be endorsed on that order.

The penal notice, which must be prominently endorsed on the front of the order, informs the person to whom it is directed that if the order is not complied with, he/she will be guilty of contempt of court and may be sent to prison.

Care must be taken to ensure that the penal notice is endorsed only upon an order which is capable of being complied with and it is essential that the penal notice is directed to the person who is required to comply with the order.

For the penal notice to be effective, actual service will need to be proved; accordingly, the order with the penal notice attached may need to be served personally. This will most usually be done by a process server.

If the order is not complied with and enforcement is sought, proof of service will be required. This is usually provided in the form of an affidavit of service.

Unusually, an application to commit as a result of a failure to comply with an order made under the provisions of Sch 1 to the CA 1989 may be heard in chambers and not in open court.

However, practitioners should be clear that it will be unlikely that a person will be committed to prison for breach of an interlocutory order, for example, where there is a requirement to file an affidavit of means or to provide some specific discovery. Such a breach is more likely to be

RSC Ord 45, r 7(4)

RSC Ord 45, r 7(1) and
CCR 1981 Ord 29, r 1(2)

RSC Ord 52, r 6(1)(a)

dealt with by way of an indemnity costs order and/or a trial judge simply drawing inevitable conclusions from the failure to comply.

23.1.2 Injunctions

All injunctions carry a penal notice on the front of the order, together with a clear warning as to the potential consequences of failing to comply.

RSC Ord 45, r 7(4)

Once an injunction is granted, every effort must be made to ensure that the person against whom the order has been made is personally served. This is because without proof of personal service a judge is most unlikely to commit a person to prison for an alleged breach.

Note: For information concerning specific types of order to which a penal notice may attach, see:

(a) **12.2** with regard to s 37 of the MCA 1973;
(b) **19.10.1** with regard to Part IV of the FLA 1996;
(c) **15.2.17** with regard to s 8 of the CA 1989.

23.1.3 Undertakings

Similar principles apply in circumstances where a party is in breach of an undertaking (promise) given to the court. The standard form of court undertaking is also endorsed with a clear warning to the person who is making the promise as to the potential consequences of breaking that promise.

Note: For information concerning specific types of undertaking to which a penal notice may attach, see:

(a) **12.2.3** with regard to s 37 of the MCA 1973;
(b) **19.10.2** with regard to Part IV of the FLA 1996.

23.2 COMMITTAL APPLICATIONS

If an order or undertaking which has been endorsed with a penal notice has been breached, the person in whose favour it has been granted can apply to the court for an order committing the contemnor to prison.

23.2.1 Action on breach

Practitioners are advised to ensure that an application to commit for breach of an order or undertaking should contain all the information required by, and adopt the layout of, the former county court Form N78. In particular, it is important to set out:

(a) the precise parts of the injunction or undertaking which are relevant to the committal application;

(b) a list of the ways in which it is alleged that the order has been disobeyed or the undertaking broken. It is particularly important to note that the allegations must be specific and practitioners should be clear that generalisations are most unlikely to be acceptable to the court.

As from 16 March 2001, a Practice Direction of the President of the Family Division has been in force concerning the issue and conduct of committal proceedings. A copy of that Practice Direction is to be found at Appendix C(4). Practitioners should also refer to *Mubarak v Mubarak* [2001] 1 FLR 698, CA, *Quinn and Cuff* [2001] EWCA Civ 36, [2001] All ER (D) 29.

The application attracts a court fee unless the applicant is exempt from paying fees.

Unlike a situation under Part IV of the FLA 1996, where the police activate a power of arrest and as a result bring the person who is in breach of an order to court, an application for committal must be initiated by the person in whose favour the order was granted.

Note: Further information with regard to a committal hearing is to be found at **19.12**.

23.2.2   Financial orders

It should be noted that generally an order to pay money cannot be enforced by way of committal. However, see Chapter 21 with regard to:

(a) the issue of a matrimonial judgment summons concerning the non-payment of a maintenance order;
(b) an application to commit where there has been a failure to comply with certain orders under either:
    (i)   the oral examination procedure, or
    (ii) the AEA 1971.

23.2.3   Jurisdiction

An application for committal is one of the few family matters which is heard in open court, although, where the alleged breach relates to proceedings involving a child, it may be heard in private.

RSC Ord 52, r 6(1)(a)

Other than applications under Part IV of FLA 1996, the application will be listed before either a High Court judge, a circuit judge or a district judge; this includes part-time judiciary. By reason of the application being dealt with in open court, rights of audience will be limited: in the High

Court, to counsel or a solicitor with higher court rights of audience and in the county court, counsel or a solicitor.

With regard to judicial allocation and rights of audience in FLA 1996, Part IV matters, see **19.15**.

A full-time district judge has the jurisdiction to hear a committal application even though it relates to an order made by a circuit judge.

A term of imprisonment can be suspended for a specified period of time and, as an alternative to committal, the court can impose a fine.

Part V
THE COURT RECORD

CHAPTER 24

THE COURT RECORD

24.1 DETAILS RELATING TO THE COURT RECORD

Solicitors who sign either:

(a) a document which initiates court proceedings;
(b) an acknowledgement of service; or
(c) a document which operates as a defence,

automatically put themselves on the court record as acting for the party on whose behalf the document has been signed and filed.

Signing a subsequent application will also probably have the effect of solicitors being put on the court record, but see **24.2** for the correct procedure to adopt.

Going on the court record results in the solicitors concerned receiving copies of all documents from the court which are for personal service, copies of all documents filed by other parties to the proceedings and any correspondence to the parties which is generated by the court. Whilst on the record, solicitors are obliged to accept service of all documents.

It also results in the solicitors being responsible for the payment of all court fees, whether or not their client is in receipt of legal aid or Community Legal Services funding.

Conversely, if the document initiating or defending proceedings is signed by a litigant in person, the documents referred to above will be sent direct to that litigant. It also follows that the litigant will be personally responsible for all court fees unless exempt from paying fees.

However, it is permissible in some circumstances for a litigant in person to use a solicitor's address as a care of address. Examples of such circumstances are where:

(a) a litigant has permission from the court to omit a private address because of past violence on the part of an opponent and the fear of such violence being repeated;
(b) solicitors are advising in divorce proceedings under the provisions of the Legal Help Scheme.

Unlike the situation where a litigant is in receipt of a full legal aid or Community Legal Services funding certificate, where solicitors are merely advising under the Legal Help Scheme, no court fees are payable by or on behalf of a client.

24.2 AMENDING THE COURT RECORD

Solicitors can go on the record, in place of a litigant in person, at any stage in the course of proceedings, and this is achieved simply by filing a notice of change of acting with the court and by serving a copy on all parties.

Similarly, if a litigant wishes to conclude proceedings acting in person, rather than continuing with the services of solicitors, a notice of change of acting must be filed with the court and served on all parties.

If either solicitors or a litigant in person change address, telephone number or any other details relevant to the proceedings, a notice of such change must be filed at court and served on all parties.

The reason for filing a notice of change of details is to ensure that at all times the court and other parties to the proceedings can promptly receive relevant documents or be contacted, for example, as a matter of urgency should there be a late adjournment of a court hearing.

If solicitors wish to be removed from the court record, other than with the consent of their client, they will need to apply on notice. The application must be supported by evidence (either witness statement or affidavit) and served on their client on not less than two clear days' notice unless the court directs otherwise.

CPR 1998, r 42.3(1) and (2)(b)

CPR 1998, r 42.3(2)(a)

An application to be removed from a court record may not necessarily be an automatic process and leave may be refused; particularly in circumstances where a client has already paid significant moneys on account of costs. The application attracts a court fee.

Where a litigant has the benefit of a legal aid or Community Legal Services funding certificate and subsequently has that certificate discharged or revoked, the effect of solicitors filing a copy of the discharge or revocation will be to automatically remove them from the court record. However, removal from the court record in such circumstances will not prevent the solicitors from having their legal aid or Community Legal Services funding bill of costs assessed. More specifically, the

CLA (Gen) Regs 1989, reg 84(a), and as amended by CLA (Gen)A Regs 2000

discharge or revocation will operate as an authority for the court to assess.

Note: In circumstances where solicitors have been merely advising under the Legal Help Scheme but are no longer providing advice it will be sufficient to inform the court of that fact and, where possible, to provide an alternative contact address. It is not appropriate to issue an application to be removed from the court record.

Appendices

Appendix A

PRECEDENTS AND FORMS

Petitions

(1) Divorce under Matrimonial Causes Act 1973, ss 1(2)(c) and 1(2)(a) – in tandem

IN THE   COUNTY COURT

No. of Matter

The petition of MARY DOE shows that:

1. On the 20th day of January 1977 the Petitioner, Mary Doe, was lawfully married to John Doe (hereinafter called the Respondent) at the Parish Church in the parish of St Cedric's, Hayes, Bromley, in the County of Kent.

2. The Petitioner and the Respondent last lived together as husband and wife at 1, Railways Cuttings, East Cheam, Surrey.

3. The court has jurisdiction under Article 2(1) of the Council Regulation on the following ground: The Petitioner and the Respondent are both domiciled in England and Wales. The Petitioner is by occupation a personal assistant and resides at 1, Railway Cuttings, aforesaid. The Respondent is by occupation a builder who resides at 2, Ash Grove, Littleton-on-Sea, Sussex.

4. There are two children of the family now living, namely:

   Ann Doe (born 5 December 1979) who is in full-time employment; and Michael Doe (born 31 August 1986).

5. No other child now living has been born to the Petitioner during the marriage.

6. There are or have been no other proceedings in any court in England and Wales or elsewhere with reference to the marriage (or to any child of the family) or between the Petitioner and the Respondent with reference to any property of either or both of them, save that the Petitioner issued a petition for divorce in the Littleton County Court, number of matter XY89D01111, which was dismissed by order dated 20 April 1990.

7. There are no proceedings continuing in any country outside England and Wales which are in respect of the marriage or are capable of affecting its validity or subsistence.

8. No application has been made to the Child Support Agency with reference to the maintenance of the younger child of the family.

9. The said marriage has broken down irretrievably.

10. The Respondent has deserted the Petitioner for a continuous period of at least two years immediately preceding the presentation of this Petition, and

11. The Respondent has committed adultery with Jane Roe and the Petitioner finds it intolerable to live with the Respondent.

PARTICULARS

12. On the 24th day of December 1998, the Respondent left the Petitioner and the matrimonial home, without the agreement of the Petitioner and without lawful or reasonable excuse. Since this date, on several occasions the Petitioner has invited the Respondent to return but he has declined so to do.

13. Since the 24th day of December 1998, the Respondent has committed adultery with Jane Roe at 2, Ash Grove, aforesaid, where they live together as husband and wife. The adultery is continuing.

The Petitioner therefore prays:

1. That the said marriage may be dissolved.

2. That the Respondent may be ordered to pay the costs of this suit limited to £300.

3. That she may be granted the following ancillary relief:

    maintenance pending suit
    a periodical payments order
    a secured periodical payments order
    a lump sum order
    a property adjustment order

Signed:

John Smith & Co

The name and address of the persons to be served with this petition are:

The Respondent: John Doe
                2, Ash Grove,
                Littleton-on-Sea
                Sussex

The Co-Respondent: Jane Roe
                   2, Ash Grove,
                   Littleton-on-Sea
                   Sussex

The Petitioner's address for service is: John Smith & Co
                                         9, Queensway
                                         East Cheam
                                         Surrey

Dated this 18th day of June 2001.

(2) Divorce under Matrimonial Causes Act 1973, ss 1(2)(b) and 1(2)(d) – in the alternative

IN THE   COUNTY COURT

No. of Matter

The petition of MARY DOE shows that:

1. On the 20th day of January 1977 the Petitioner, Mary Doe, then Roe spinster (and who is incorrectly described in the marriage certificate as Marie Roe) was lawfully married to John Doe (hereinafter called the Respondent) at the Parish Church in the parish of St Cedric's, Bromley, in the County of Kent.

2. The Petitioner and the Respondent last lived together as husband and wife at 1, Railways Cuttings, East Cheam, Surrey.

3. The court has jurisdiction under Article 2(1) of the Council Regulation on the following ground: The Petitioner and the Respondent are both domiciled in England and Wales. The Petitioner is by occupation a personal assistant and resides at 1, Railway Cuttings, East Cheam, Surrey. The Respondent is by occupation a builder who resides at 2, Ash Grove, Littleton-on-Sea, Sussex.

4. There are two children of the family now living, namely:

   Ann Doe (born 5 May 1979) who attends a special school for the mentally impaired; and
   Michael Doe (born 31 August 1992).

5. No other child now living has been born to the Petitioner during the marriage.

6. There are or have been no other proceedings in any court in England and Wales or elsewhere with reference to the marriage (or to any child of the family) or between the Petitioner and the Respondent with reference to any property of either or both of them.

7. There are no proceedings continuing in any country outside England and Wales which are in respect of the marriage or are capable of affecting its validity or subsistence.

8. No application has been made to the Child Support Agency with reference to the maintenance of the younger child of the family.

9. The said marriage has broken down irretrievably.

10. The Respondent has behaved in such a way that the Petitioner cannot reasonably be expected to live with the Respondent.

PARTICULARS

10.1 During the latter years of the marriage the Respondent has failed to show any or any sufficient tenderness and affection towards the Petitioner.

10.2 During the latter years of the marriage the Respondent has dedicated himself to the management of his finances at the expense of spending time with the Petitioner and the children of the family.

10.3 Throughout the marriage the Respondent has pursued his interest in motor racing at the expense of spending time with his family. The Respondent has habitually spent every other weekend from Thursday to Monday from June to September away from the matrimonial home at motor sport events, as well as at other times throughout the year.

10.4 During the period of the Petitioner's pregnancy with the second child of the family the Respondent was inconsiderate towards the Petitioner and took little or no account of the Petitioner's wishes and feelings. The nature of his comments often caused her to break down and cry.

10.5 The Respondent has habitually belittled the Petitioner.

11.   In the alternative, the parties to the marriage have lived apart for a continuous period of at least two years immediately preceding the presentation of this petition and the Respondent consents to a decree being granted.

PARTICULARS

11.1 In or about April 1999 as a result of the Respondent's behaviour the Petitioner insisted that he leave the matrimonial home, since which time the parties have lived separate and apart.

The Petitioner therefore prays:

1.   That the said marriage may be dissolved.
2.   That the Respondent may be ordered to pay the costs of this suit.
3.   That she may be granted the following ancillary relief:

     maintenance pending suit
     a periodical payments order
     a secured periodical payments order
     a lump sum order
     a property adjustment order

                                                      Signed:
                                                      Mary Doe

The name and address of the person to be served wth this petition is:

The Respondent: John Doe
                2, Ash Grove,
                Littleton-on-Sea
                Sussex

The Petitioner's address for service is: c/o Truth & Co
                                      The Strand
                                      East Cheam
                                      Surrey

Dated this 18th day of June 2001.

(3) Divorce under Matrimonial Causes Act 1973, s 1(2)(e)

IN THE   COUNTY COURT

                                    No. of Matter

The petition of MARIA DOESKI shows that:

1. On the 20th day of January 1977, the Petitioner, Maria Doeski, was lawfully married to Johan Doeski (hereinafter called the Respondent) at the City Hall in the City of Warsaw, Poland.

2. The Petitioner and the Respondent last lived together as husband and wife at 1, Krakow Street, Warsaw, Poland.

3. The court has jurisdiction under Article 2(1) of the Council Regulation on the following ground: The Petitioner is habitually resident in England and Wales and has resided there for at least one year immediately prior to the presentation of this petition in that since 1 May 1996 she has resided at 1, Railway Cuttings, East Cheam, Surrey and is by occupation a housewife. The Respondent is by occupation a mechanic and is believed to reside at an address in Poland which is unknown to the Petitioner.

4. There are no children of the family now living.

5. No other child now living has been born to the Petitioner during the marriage.

6. There are or have been no other proceedings in any court in England and Wales or elsewhere with reference to the marriage (or to any child of the family) or between the Petitioner and the Respondent with reference to any property of either or both of them.

7. There are no proceedings continuing in any country outside England and Wales which are in respect of the marriage or are capable of affecting its validity or subsistence.

8. [*This paragraph should be completed only if the petition is based on five years' separation.*] No agreement or arrangement has been made or is proposed to be made between the parties for the support of the Petitioner (and any child of the family).

9. The said marriage has broken down irretrievably.

10. The parties have lived separate and apart for a continuous period of at least five years immediately preceding the presentation of this petition.

PARTICULARS

10.1 In or about April 1992 the Petitioner left the matrimonial home, since which date the parties have not resumed cohabitation.

The Petitioner therefore prays:

1. That the said marriage be dissolved.

2. That the Petitioner may be granted the following ancillary relief:
    maintenance pending suit
    a periodical payments order
    a secured provision order
    a lump sum or sums order
    a property adjustment order.

Signed:

Maria Doeski

The name and address of the person to be served wth this petition is:

The Respondent: Johan Doeski
              Address Unknown

The Petitioner's address for service is: c/o Truth & Co
                       Hackney Chambers
                       London

Dated this 18th day of June 2001.

(4)   Judicial separation under Matrimonial Causes Act 1973, s 1(2)(b)

IN THE   COUNTY COURT

No. of Matter

The petition of MARY DOE shows that:

1.   On the 20th day of January 1977 the Petitioner, Mary Doe, was lawfully married to John Doe (hereinafter called the Respondent) at the Parish Church in the parish of St Cedric's, Hayes, Bromley, in the County of Kent.

2.   The Petitioner and the Respondent last lived together as husband and wife at 1, Railways Cuttings, East Cheam, Surrey.

3.   The court has jurisdiction under Article 2(1) of the Council Regulation on the following ground: The Petitioner and the Respondent are both domiciled in England and Wales and the Petitioner is by occupation a personal assistant who resides at an address the details of which she does not wish to disclose to the Respondent. The Respondent is by occupation a nurse who resides at 2, Ash Grove, Littleton-on-Sea, Sussex.

4.   There are two children of the family now living, namely:

Ann Doe (born 5 May 1979) who is in full-time employment; and
Michael Doe (born 31 August 1980) who is an apprentice plumber.

5.   No other child now living has been born to the Petitioner during the marriage.

6.   There are or have been no other proceedings in any court in England and Wales or elsewhere with reference to the marriage (or to any child of the family) or between the Petitioner and the Respondent with reference to any property of either or both of them.

7.   There are no proceedings continuing in any country outside England and Wales which are in respect of the marriage or are capable of affecting its validity or subsistence.

8.   No application has been made to the Child Support Agency with reference to the maintenance of the younger child of the family.

9.   The Respondent has behaved in such a way that the Petitioner cannot reasonably be expected to live with the Respondent.

PARTICULARS

9.1 The Respondent has formed an improper association with Jane Roe.

9.2 In or about May 1999 the Respondent was appointed as guardian of the said Jane Roe for the purpose of obtaining medical assistance for her whilst she was undergoing therapy in connection with a heroin addiction.

9.3 The Petitioner became suspicious about the Respondent's relationship with the said Jane Roe and accordingly had his movements observed by a private investigator. As a result, she established that during a period of four weeks from 5 October 1999 the Respondent regularly visited the property at 3, Somerset Mansions, Littleton-on-Sea, Sussex, where Jane Roe resides, and frequently did not leave the premises until the early hours of the morning.

9.4 The association continues.

9.5 On each occasion that the Petitioner confronted the Respondent with her suspicions the Respondent would fly into a rage and physically assault the Petitioner. On numerous occasions such assaults resulted in the Petitioner receiving severe bruising, cuts and lacerations to her face, arms and body.

The Petitioner therefore prays:

1. That she may be judicially separated from the Respondent.

2. That the Respondent may be ordered to pay the costs of this suit.

3. That she may be granted the following ancillary relief:
    maintenance pending suit
    a periodical payments order
    a lump sum or sums order
    a secured provision order
    a property adjustment order

Signed:
Truth & Co

The name and address of the person to be served with this petition is:

The Respondent: John Doe
      2, Ash Grove,
      Littleton-on-Sea
      Sussex

The Petitioner's address for service is: Truth & Co
              The Strand
              East Cheam
              Surrey

Dated this 18th day of June 2001.

(5) Nullity (void marriage)

IN THE   COUNTY COURT

No. of Matter

The petition of MARY DOE shows that:

1. On the 20th day of January 2001 the Petitioner, Mary Doe, was lawfully married to John Doe (hereinafter called the Respondent) at the Register Office in the District of Hackney in the London Borough of Hackney.

2. The Petitioner and the Respondent last lived together as husband and wife at 1, Railways Cuttings, East Cheam, Surrey.

3. The court has jurisdiction under Article 2(1) of the Council Regulation on the following ground: The Petitioner and the Respondent are both domiciled in England and Wales. The Petitioner is unemployed and resides at 1, Railway Cuttings, aforesaid. The Respondent is by occupation a builder and resides at 2, Ash Grove, Littleton-on-Sea, Sussex.

4. There are no children of the family now living.

5. No other child now living has been born to the Petitioner during the marriage.

6. There are or have been no other proceedings in any court in England and Wales or elsewhere with reference to the marriage (or to any child of the family) or between the Petitioner and the Respondent with reference to any property of either or both of them.

7. There are no proceedings continuing in any country outside England and Wales which are in respect of the marriage or are capable of affecting its validity or subsistence.

8. The said marriage was not a valid marriage under the provisions of the Marriage Acts 1949–1986 by reason of the matters set out in the Particulars below.

9. PARTICULARS

9.1 At the time of the marriage the Respondent was lawfully married to Jane Smith.

9.2 The Respondent fraudulently told the Petitioner that he was John Doe. After the marriage, the Petitioner discovered that the Respondent's true identity was Boris Smith and that he was already married to Jane Smith.

The Petitioner therefore prays:

1. That the marriage celebrated between the Petitioner and the Respondent be declared null and void.

2. That the Respondent may be ordered to pay the costs of this suit.

3. That the Petitioner may be granted the following ancillary relief:

   maintenance pending suit
   a periodical payments order
   a secured provision order
   a lump sum or sums order
   a property adjustment order.

                                                      Signed:
                                                           Truth & Co

The name and address of the person to be served with this petition is:

The Respondent: John Doe
                2, Ash Grove,
                Littleton-on-Sea
                Sussex

The Petitioner's address for service is: Truth & Co
                                          Hackney Chambers
                                          London

Dated this 18th day of June 2001.

(6) Nullity (voidable marriage)

IN THE   COUNTY COURT

No. of Matter

The petition of JOHN DOE shows that:

1. On the 7th day of November 2000, the Petitioner, John Doe, was lawfully married to Mary Doe, then Green, a widow (hereinafter called the Respondent) at the Register Office in the District of Hackney in the London Borough of Hackney.

2. The Petitioner and the Respondent last lived together as husband and wife at 1, Railways Cuttings, East Cheam, Surrey.

3. The court has jurisdiction under Article 2(1) of the Council Regulation on the following ground: The Petitioner and the Respondent are both domiciled in England and Wales. The Petitioner is unemployed, and resides at 1, Omega Road, Hackney, London. The Respondent is by occupation a housewife who resides at 1, Railway Cuttings, aforesaid.

4. There are no children of the family now living except Ann Doe who was born on 30 January 1989. The child is not a child of the Respondent, although for the short duration of the marriage was treated by her as a child of the family.

5. No other child now living has been born to the Respondent during the marriage as far as is known to the Petitioner.

6. There are or have been no other proceedings in any court in England and Wales or elsewhere with reference to the marriage (or to any child of the family) or between the Petitioner and the Respondent with reference to any property of either or both of them.

7. There are no proceedings continuing in any country outside England and Wales which are in respect of the marriage or are capable of affecting its validity or subsistence.

8. No application has been made to the Child Support Agency with reference to the maintenance of the child of the family.

9. The said marriage has not been consummated owing to the wilful refusal of the Respondent to consummate it.

PARTICULARS

9.1 Approximately one week prior to the marriage the Petitioner bought a double bed for use as the marital bed. The parties were married on the 7th day of November 2000 and during the first two months of the marriage, until the end of December 2000, on approximately three or four occasions each week, the Petitioner requested the Respondent to have sexual intercourse with him. The Respondent persistently refused, giving the Petitioner a variety of excuses and in particular repeatedly telling him that she would prefer to wait until after 1 January 2001 as she wished to tell her grown-up daughter that she was married before so doing.

9.2 In or about early January 2001 the Respondent told the Petitioner that she felt she had made a terrible mistake in marrying him. The Petitioner and the said child of the family moved out of the former matrimonial home on 1 February 2001, since which date the parties have not resumed cohabitation.

The Petitioner therefore prays:

That the marriage celebrated between the Petitioner and the Respondent be declared null and void.

Signed:
Truth & Co

The name and address of the person to be served with this petition is:

The Respondent: Mary Doe
                1, Railway Cuttings
                East Cheam
                Surrey

The Petitioner's address for service is: Truth & Co
                                        Hackney Chambers
                                        London

Dated this 18th day of June 2001.

(7)   Presumption of death

IN THE   COUNTY COURT
                                              No. of Matter

The petition of MARIA DOESKI shows that:

1. On the 20th day of January 1977, the Petitioner, Maria Doeski, was lawfully married to Johan Doeski (hereinafter called the Respondent) at the City Hall in the City of Warsaw, Poland.

2. The Petitioner and the Respondent last lived together as husband and wife at 1, Krakow Street, Warsaw, Poland.

3. The court has jurisdiction under Article 2(1) of the Council Regulation on the following ground: The Petitioner is habitually resident in England and Wales and has resided there for at least one year immediately prior to the presentation of this petition in that since 1 May 1996 she has resided at 1, Railway Cuttings, East Cheam, Surrey and is by occupation a housewife. The Respondent's whereabouts and occupation are not known to the Petitioner.

4. There are no children of the family now living.

5. No other child now living has been born to the Petitioner during the marriage.

6. There are or have been no other proceedings in any court in England and Wales or elsewhere with reference to the marriage (or to any child of the family) or between the Petitioner and the Respondent with reference to any property of either or both of them.

7. There are no proceedings continuing in any country outside England and Wales which are in respect of the marriage or are capable of affecting its validity or subsistence.

8. The Respondent should be presumed to have died in or about 1991.

9.   PARTICULARS

9.1   In 1990 a civil war started in Somalia. The Respondent was approached by a friend to go to that country as a mercenary. Having signed an agreement he then departed for Somalia in December 1990. In June 1991 the Petitioner received a communication which informed her that all members of the unit in which the Respondent had been serving had been either killed or captured. Since then she has received no further communications and despite having made a number of enquiries through the Polish Consulate in Somalia no trace of the Respondent has been found.

9.2 Since the Petitioner left Poland in December 1990 the Respondent has not been in contact with any of his family members.

9.3 The Petitioner believes that the Respondent was killed during the conflict.

9.4 The Petitioner knows of no other realistic enquiry which she could make in the circumstances.

10 No agreement or arrangement has been made or is proposed to be made between the parties for the support of the Petitioner.

11. In the alternative, if the Respondent should still be alive, the said marriage has broken down irretrievably.

12. The parties to the marriage have lived apart for a continuous period of at least five years immediately preceding the presentation of this petition.

13. PARTICULARS

13.1 The Respondent left the matrimonial home in December 1990 in the circumstances set out in paragraph 9.1 above since when the parties have not resumed cohabitation.

The Petitioner therefore prays:

1. That the Court will presume the death of the Respondent and dissolve the said marriage.

2. In the alternative, that the said marriage may be dissolved.

3. That the Petitioner may be granted the following ancillary relief:

   maintenance pending suit
   a periodical payments order
   a secured provision order
   a lump sum or sums order
   a property adjustment order.

Signed:
Truth & Co

It is not intended to serve this petition on any person.

The Petitioner's address for service is: Truth & Co
                                        Hackney Chambers
                                        London

Dated this 18th day of June 2001.

(8)   Declaration of parentage

IN THE HIGH COURT OF JUSTICE
FAMILY DIVISION

No. of Matter

IN THE MATTER OF SECTION 55A OF THE FAMILY LAW ACT 1986

THE PETITION OF RICHARD ROE SHOWS THAT:

1. The Petitioner's full name is Richard Roe who was born Richard Smith, his name having been changed by reason of his mother having married James Roe and having been adopted by him.

2. The Petitioner is male and was born on 5 December 1967 at Basildon Hospital in the County of Essex.

3. The Petitioner's mother was born Jane Smith, now known as Roe, at 1, Hackney Road, Basildon, Essex on 12 June 1946. She resides at 1, Railway Cottages, East Cheam, Surrey and is by occupation a secretary.

4. The Petitioner's father is John Doe who was born on 15 August 1944 at Reading General Hospital in the County of Berkshire. He resides at 2, Ash Grove, Littleton-on-Sea, Sussex, and is by occupation a merchant banker.

5. The Petitioner is domiciled in England and Wales.

6. The grounds upon which the Petitioner relies are:

   that his mother was cohabiting with the said John Doe and having a sexual relationship with him from in or about January 1966 to August 1967 and in particular in March 1967.

7. There have been no other proceedings in any court with reference to the parentage of the Petitioner by or on behalf of the Petitioner.

8. The Petitioner is a British citizen as is the Respondent by virtue of him being born in England. The declaration of parentage will have no effect on the Petitioner's status as regards his nationality.

The Petitioner therefore prays that the Court will declare:

That the said John Doe is the father of the said Petitioner.

Signed:
Truth & Co

The names and addresses of the persons to be served with this petition are:

1. John Roe, c/o Jones and Company, Merchant Bank, North Row, London, in an envelope marked 'private and confidential'.

2. Jane Roe, 1, Railway Cottages, East Cheam, Surrey.

The Petitioner's address for service is: Truth & Co
Hackney Chambers
London

Dated this 18th day of June 2001.

(9)   Answer by a respondent to a petition

In the   County Court

                                                  No. of Matter

BETWEEN:

MARY DOE	Petitioner
and	
JOHN DOE	Respondent
and	
JANE ROE	Co-Respondent
and	
JOHN SMITH	Party Cited

The Respondent in ANSWER to the petition filed herein says that:

1.   Paragraphs 1, 2, 4, 5, 6, 7, 8 and 9 are admitted.

2.   Paragraph 3 is admitted save that the Respondent resides at 10, Plaza del Matador, Tenerife, Canary Islands.

3.   He denies that he has behaved in such a way as alleged in the petition or at all.

4.   He denies that he has committed the adultery as alleged or at all.

5.   Each and every allegation set out in the Particulars under paragraph 12 of the petition is denied.

6.   The said marriage has broken down irretrievably by reason of the matters hereinafter set out.

7.   The Petitioner has committed adultery with John Smith (hereinafter called the Party Cited) and the Respondent finds it intolerable to live with the Petitioner.

8.   On divers dates between October 1999 and March 2000 at various addresses in and about London the Petitioner and the Party Cited committed adultery.

THE RESPONDENT THEREFORE PRAYS:

1. That the prayer of the petition may be rejected.

2. That the marriage may be dissolved.

3. That the Petitioner and the Party Cited may be ordered to pay the costs of this suit.

4. That the Respondent may be granted the following ancillary relief:

   maintenance pending suit
   a periodical payments order
   a lump sum or sums order
   a secured provision order
   a property adjustment order
   an order under the provisions of sections 25B and 25C of the Matrimonial Causes Act 1973, as amended by the Pensions Act 1995.

Dated the 18th day of July 2001

Signed:

Alpha Beta & Co

The Persons to be served with this Answer are Mary Doe and John Smith at the address of their solicitors Truth & Co, The Strand, East Cheam, Surrey.

The Respondent's address for service is Alpha Beta & Co, 10, The Highway, London.

(10)   Reply by a petitioner to an answer

In the   County Court

                                        No. of Matter

Between   John Doe   Petitioner
And   Mary Doe   Respondent

The Petitioner in REPLY to the Answer filed in this suit says that:

1(a) As to paragraph 4 of the Answer, he admits that he and the Respondent shared many common interests but will say that they did not necessarily share a common point of view about them.

 (b) He admits that some differences were discussed but denies that the Respondent dealt with them constructively.

 (c) He admits that, following the incident in July 1999, he felt obliged to sleep elsewhere. He further admits that they went on holiday two days later but says that the reason why they shared a bed was because there was nowhere else to sleep.

2   As to paragraph 5, he admits that rumours that he was having a relationship with another woman began to circulate but he believes that it was the Respondent herself who was responsible for spreading them. As it was not within his own knowledge, he is unable to comment on what alleged support the Respondent did or did not receive.

3(a) As to paragraph 6, he admits that he was aware that overdrafts were from time to time incurred, sometimes for quite large sums, albeit temporarily.

 (b) He admits that the Respondent settled the family bills in the latter stages of the marriage but not, as a general rule, before then.

4   As to paragraph 7, he admits that the Respondent tried to persuade him to seek marriage guidance but says that he declined because he did not believe that any useful purpose would be served by it, as by then the deterioration of the parties' relationship as a result of the Respondent's unreasonable behaviour had already gone too far. He admits that he is now committing adultery.

5   As to paragraph 12, he admits that, in an endeavour to better his career, he applied for an appointment in London. That application was unsuccessful and he remained in Carlisle. His subsequent application for his present appointment was not decided until after the Respondent had herself returned to London, from which the Petitioner concluded that the Respondent also believed that their marriage had broken down irretrievably. Since leaving Carlisle, the Respondent

has not taken any steps towards seeking a reconciliation nor has she expressed any wish to live with him again. He infers from this that the Respondent does in fact accept that the marriage has irretrievably broken down.

6   Save as aforesaid and save insofar as the same consists of admissions and opinions or beliefs said to be held by the Respondent, he denies the allegations contained in the Answer.

The Petitioner therefore prays:

That the prayer of the Answer may be rejected.

Signed:
Truth & Co

Dated the 26th day of September 2001

The person to be served with this Reply is Mary Doe at the address of her solicitors, Alpha Beta & Co, The Highway, London.

The Petitioner's address for service is Truth & Co, The Strand, East Cheam, Surrey.

(11) Request by respondent for directions for trial

No of Matter

Between	Petitioner
And	Respondent
And	Co-Respondent

Application for directions for trial (Special Procedure)

The (~~Petitioner~~) RESPONDENT applies to a district judge for directions for the trial of this undefended cause by entering it in the Special Procedure List.

The (~~Petitioner's~~) RESPONDENT'S affidavit of evidence is lodged with this application.

Signed

[Solicitor for] the (~~Petitioner~~) RESPONDENT

Dated

(12) Affidavit by respondent under Matrimonial Causes Act 1973, s 1(2)(b) in support of request for directions for trial

Affidavit by (~~Petitioner~~) RESPONDENT in support of (~~Petition~~) ANSWER under section 1(2)(b) of Matrimonial Causes Act 1973

Family Proceedings Rules 1991
Rule 2.24(3) (Form M7)

In the   County Court

                                        No. of Matter

Between   Petitioner

and   Respondent

Question	Answer
About the Suit	
(1) Have you read the Petition and Answer in this case including what is said about the behaviour of the Petitioner?	
(2) Do you wish to alter or add to any statement in paragraphs 1–8 of the Petition or the Answer? If so, state the alterations or additions.	
(3) Are all the statements in the Answer and the particulars, including any alterations or additions, true?	
(4) If you consider that the Petitioner's behaviour has affected your health, state the effect that it has had.	

Question	Answer
(5) (i) Is the Petitioner's behaviour as set out in the Answer continuing? (ii) If the Petitioner's behaviour is not continuing, what was the date of the final incident relied upon by you in the Answer?	
(6) (i) Since the date given in answer to question (5) or, if no date is given in answer to that question, since the date of the answer, have you lived at the same address as the Petitioner for a period of more than six months, or for periods which together amount to more than six months? (ii) If so, state the address and the period or periods, giving dates to the best of your knowledge or belief, and describe the arrangements for sharing the accommodation. [State: – whether you have shared a bedroom; – whether you have taken your meals together; – what arrangements you have made for cleaning the accommodation and for other domestic tasks; – what arrangements you have made for the payment of household bills and other expenses.]	
About the children of the family (7) Have you read the Statement of Arrangements filed in this case?	
(8) Do you wish to alter anything in the Statement of Arrangements or add to it? If so, state the alterations or additions.	
(9) Subject to these alterations and additions (if any), is everything stated in your Answer [and Statement of Arrangements for the child(ren)] true and correct to the best of your knowledge and belief?	

I, (full name)

of (full residential
address)

(occupation)

make oath and say as follows:

(1) I am the Respondent in this cause.

(2) The answers to Questions (1) to (9) above are true.

(3) I exhibit marked 'A' a certificate/report of Dr _____

(4) I identify the signature _____
appearing at Part IV of the Statement of Arrangements now produced to me and
marked 'B' as the signature of the petitioner.

(5) I ask the Court to grant a decree dissolving my marriage with the Petitioner on
the grounds stated in the Answer [and to order the Petitioner to pay the costs of
this suit].

Sworn at
In the County of
This   day of   20
Before me.

A Commissioner for Oaths/Solicitor
Officer of the Court appointed by the judge to take Affidavits

(13)   Affidavit by respondent under Matrimonial Causes Act 1973, s 1(2)(a) in support of request for directions for trial

Affidavit by RESPONDENT (~~Petitioner~~) in support of ANSWER (~~Petition~~) under section 1(2)(a) of Matrimonial Causes Act 1973

Family Proceedings Rules 1991
Rule 2.24(3) (Form M7)

In the   County Court

                                                No. of Matter

Between   Petitioner

and   Respondent

and   Co-Respondent

Question	Answer
About the Suit (1) Have you read the Answer and Cross-Petition filed in this case?	
(2) Do you wish to alter or add to any statement in the Answer and Cross-Petition? If so, state the alterations or additions.	
(3) Subject to these alterations and additions (if any), is everything stated in your Answer and Cross-Petition true? If any statement is not within your knowledge, indicate this and say whether it is true to the best of your information and belief.	

Question	Answer
(4) State briefly your reasons for saying that the Petitioner has committed the adultery alleged.	
(5) On what date did it first become known to you that the Petitioner had committed the adultery alleged?	
(6) Do you find it intolerable to live with the Petitioner?	
(7) Since the date given in the answer to Question (5), have you ever lived with the Petitioner in the same household? If so, state the address(es) and the period or periods, giving dates.	
About the children of the family (8) Have you read the Statement of Arrangements filed in this case?	
(9) Do you wish to alter anything in the Statement of Arrangements or add to it? If so, state the alterations or additions.	
(10) Subject to these alterations and additions (if any), is everything stated in your Answer and Cross-Petition [and Statement of Arrangements for the child(ren)] true and correct to the best of your knowledge and belief?	

I,   (full name)

of   (full residential
                                                                        address)

                                                                    (occupation)

make oath and say as follows:

(1) I am the Respondent in this cause.

(2) The answers to Questions (1) to (10) above are true.

(3) I identify the signature _____
     appearing on the copy letter now produced to me and marked 'A' as the signature
     of my husband/wife, the Petitioner in this cause.

(4) I identify the signature _____
     appearing at the foot of the document now produced to me and marked 'B' as the
     signature of the Petitioner.

(5) I identify the signature _____
     appearing at Part IV of the Statement of Arrangements now produced to me and
     marked 'C' as the signature of the Petitioner.

(6) *[Exhibit any other document on which the RESPONDENT wishes to rely]*

(7) I ask the Court to grant a decree dissolving my marriage with the Petitioner on the
     grounds stated in the Answer and Cross-Petition [and to order the Petitioner/Party
     Cited to pay the costs of this suit].

Sworn at

In the County of   _____

This   day of   20

                              Before me, _____

                                        A Commissioner for Oaths/Solicitor/
                                             Officer of a Court appointed
                                           by the Judge to take Affidavits

(14) Affidavit by wife under Matrimonial Causes Act 1973, s 1(2)(b) in support of request for directions for trial in a consolidated suit

Affidavit by (~~Petitioner~~) WIFE in support of petition under
section 1(2)(b) of Matrimonial Causes Act 1973

Family Proceedings Rules 1991
Rule 2.24(3) (Form M7)

In the   County Court

                                    No. of Matter

Between   Wife
                                           Husband

and   Husband
                                             Wife

Question	*Answer*
About the divorce petition	
(1) Have you read your petition in this case including what is said about the behaviour of (~~the Respondent~~) YOUR HUSBAND?	
(2) Do you wish to alter or add to any statement in your petition or the particulars? If so, state the alterations or additions.	
(3) Are all the statements in (~~the~~) YOUR petition and the particulars, including any alterations or additions, true?	

Question	Answer
(4) If you consider that (the Respondent's) YOUR HUSBAND's behaviour has affected your health, state the effect that it has had.	
(5) (i) Is (the Respondent's) YOUR HUSBAND's behaviour as set out in your petition and particulars continuing? (ii) If (the Respondent's) YOUR HUSBAND's behaviour is not continuing, what was the date of the final incident relied upon by you in your petition?	
(6) (i) Since the date given in answer to question (5) or, if no date is given in answer to that question, since the date of your petition, have you lived at the same address as your husband for a period of more than six months, or for periods which together amount to more than six months? (ii) If so, state the address and the period or periods, giving dates to the best of your knowledge or belief, and describe the arrangements for sharing the accommodation. [State: – whether you have shared a bedroom; – whether you have taken your meals together; – what arrangements you have made for cleaning the accommodation and for other domestic tasks; – what arrangements you have made for the payment of household bills and other expenses.]	
About the children of the family (7) Have you read the Statement of Arrangements filed in this case?	
(8) Do you wish to alter anything in the Statement of Arrangements or add to it? If so, state the alterations or additions.	

Question	Answer
(9) Subject to these alterations and additions (if any), is everything stated in your Petition [and Statement of Arrangements for the child(ren)] true and correct to the best of your knowledge and belief?	

I,   (full name)

of   (full residential
                                                                              address)

                                                                        (occupation)

make oath and say as follows:

(1) I am the wife in this cause.

(2) The answers to Questions (1) to (9) above are true.

(3) I identify the signature _____
    appearing on the copy acknowledgement of service now produced to me and
    marked 'A' as the signature of my husband, the husband in this cause.

(4) I exhibit marked 'B' a certificate/report of Dr _____

(5) I identify the signature _____
    appearing at Part IV of the Statement of Arrangements now produced to me and
    marked 'C' as the signature of my husband.

(6) I ask the Court to grant a decree dissolving my marriage with my husband on the
    grounds stated my petition [and to order my husband to pay the costs of this suit].

Sworn at
In the County of
This   day of
Before me.   20

A Commissioner for Oaths/Solicitor/
Officer of a Court appointed by the Judge to take Affidavits

(15)   Letter of consent for the purposes of Matrimonial Causes Act 1973, s 1(2)(d)

I, John Doe, of 2, Ash Grove, Littleton-on-Sea, Sussex, hereby give notice that my wife, Mary Doe, and I separated in or about April 1995 since which date we have not resumed cohabitation. I also confirm that I agree to a divorce on the ground that we have lived separate and apart for a period of at least two years with my consent to a decree being granted.

Signed

John Doe

Dated 31 May 1997

(16) Request for directions for trial of an undefended cause for a decree of divorce, judicial separation or nullity

IN THE HIGH COURT OF JUSTICE
FAMILY DIVISION
PRINCIPAL REGISTRY

Matrimonial cause proceeding in the Principal Registry treated by virtue
of Section 42 of the Matrimonial and Family Proceedings Act 1984
as pending in a divorce county court

Between   Petitioner

and   Respondent

and   Co-Respondent

The Petitioner hereby applies to the District Judge for directions for the trial of this cause.

(a) It is desired that this cause shall be heard at:

(b) The Petitioner who resides at
     intends to call   witnesses who reside at the following places:

(c) The probable length of the hearing is
(d) Other facts relevant to a decision as to the place of trial are:

The petition was served in

The time allowed in the Notice of Proceedings for giving notice of intention to defend
was   days.

        Dated the   day of   20

                                             (Solicitors for) the Petitioner

---

Directions for Trial

I am satisfied that the requirements of Rule 2.24(1) have been complied with and I
direct that this cause which is treated as pending in a divorce county court be heard at Royal
Courts of Justice, Strand, London WC2A 1LL.

        Dated the   day of   20

                                             District Judge

(17)   Request for directions for trial in a defended cause for a decree of divorce, judicial separation or nullity

IN THE HIGH COURT OF JUSTICE
FAMILY DIVISION
PRINCIPAL REGISTRY

Matrimonial cause proceeding in the Principal Registry treated by virtue
of Section 42 of the Matrimonial and Family Proceedings Act 1984
as pending in a divorce county court

Between   Petitioner

and   Respondent

and   Co-Respondent

The Petitioner hereby applies to the District Judge for directions for the trial of this cause.

(a)   It is desired that this cause shall be heard at

(b)   The Petitioner who resides at   intends to
       call witnesses who reside at the following places:

(c)   Notice has been given in accordance with Rule 2.25(3). A Statement as to Respondent
       and his witnesses has (not) been received (and is attached).

(d)   The probable length of the hearing is

(e)   Other facts relevant to a decision as to place of trial are:

The petition was served on   The time allowed in the Notice of
proceedings for giving notice of intention to defend was   days

Dated   the   day of   20

                                              Solicitors for the Petitioner

---

TAKE NOTICE that pursuant to Rule 2.24(4), proviso, you are required to
attend before District Judge   in Room
of the Principal Registry, First Avenue House, 42–49, High Holborn, London WC1V 6NP at
on the   day of   20   for consideration to be given as to the future
course of this cause and the giving of any consequential directions.

If aggrement has been reached as to the future conduct of the case, the parties need not attend
provided that they lodge at the Registry, not less than 8 days before the date of the appointment
for directions, the full terms agreed.

Unless agreement has been reached, the parties must attend, unless otherwise directed. Where
instructed, it is most desirable that counsel should attend.

DIRECTIONS FOR TRIAL

I am satisfied that the requirements of Rule 2.24(1) have been complied with and I direct that
the cause be heard at the Royal Courts of Justice, Strand, London WC2A 1LL.

Dated   the   day of   20

                                                          DISTRICT JUDGE

(18) Application by way of affidavit to omit a petitioner's address from a petition

In the   County Court

No. of Matter

Between   Mary Doe   Petitioner

and   John Doe   Respondent

Affidavit of the Petitioner

I, Mary Doe, of The Refuge, Narrow Road, West Cheam, Surrey make oath and say as follows:

1. I am the Petitioner in these proceedings.

2. I request that the court make an order authorising the omission of my address from my divorce petition.

3. The reason for my request is that I do not wish my husband to have knowledge of my present address. This is because he has previously entered my former home through an open window, in the early hours of the morning, and assaulted me whilst I was asleep in bed. I am fearful of the incident being repeated.

Sworn by the above-named

Mary Doe

At

On

Before me,

Solicitor/Commissioner of Oaths/Officer of the Court appointed by the Judge to administer oaths

(19)   Order to omit address

In the   County Court

                                                    No. of Matter

District Judge Grey   in Chambers

Between Mary Smith   Petitioner

and John Smith   Respondent

UPON the application of the Petitioner dated 4 June 1997

AND upon reading the affidavit of the Petitioner sworn on 4 June 1997

IT IS ORDERED THAT:

(1)   the Petitioner do have leave to omit her address from the petition and all other documents herein

(2)   the petition be allowed to stand in the form lodged

(3)   the affidavit sworn by the Petitioner in support of the application be placed in a sealed envelope within the Court file and not be opened without leave of a judge.

Dated 19 June 1997

(20) Notice of application for a direction pursuant to FPR 1991, r 2.7(3)

In the   County Court

No. of Matter

Between   Mary Doe   Petitioner
and   John Doe   Respondent

Take notice that the Petitioner intends to apply to a district judge sitting in chambers in the   County Court on   1997 at 10.30 am (time estimate 15 minutes) for a direction pursuant to Family Proceedings Rules 1991, rule 2.7(3) as to whether or not Jane Roe be joined in the suit as a co-respondent.

Dated the 18th day of June 1997

Signed

Truth & Co
The Strand
East Cheam
Surrey

To: John Doe
    2, Ash Grove
    Littleton-on-Sea
    Sussex

(21) Order to stay petition and proceed on answer

In the   County Court

No. of Matter

District Judge Grey   in Chambers

Between Mary Smith   Petitioner

and John Smith   Respondent

UPON hearing the solicitor for the Petitioner and Counsel for the Respondent

UPON the application dated 20 February 1998

IT IS ORDERED THAT:

(1) the prayer for dissolution contained in the petition herein be stayed

(2) the cause do proceed on the prayer of the Respondent's answer and cross-petition

(3) upon pronouncement of a decree nisi on the Respondent's cross-petition the Petitioner's prayer for dissolution be dismissed.

Dated 9 March 1998

(22)   Order to consolidate two petitions (lead suit)

In the   County Court

No. of Matter XY97D0444

District Judge Grey   in Chambers

Between Mary Smith   Petitioner

and John Smith   Respondent

UPON HEARING the solicitors for both parties

UPON the Petitioner's application dated 20 February 1998

And By Consent

IT IS ORDERED THAT:

(1) this suit be consolidated with the suit of John Smith and Mary Smith bearing
     number of matter XY97DO555 and be carried on under title:

Between   Mary Smith   Wife

And   John Smith   Husband

                              and

Between   John Smith   Husband

And   Mary Smith   Wife

(2) this suit bearing number of matter XY97D0444 be the leading suit.

Dated 9 March 1998

(23)   Order to consolidate two petitions (second suit)

In the   County Court

                                         No. of Matter XY97D0555

District Judge Grey   in Chambers

Between John Smith   Petitioner

and Mary Smith   Respondent

UPON HEARING the solicitors for both parties

UPON the Respondent's application dated 20 February 1998

And By Consent

IT IS ORDERED THAT:

(1) this suit be consolidated with the suit of Mary Smith and John Smith bearing number of matter XY97D0444

(2) the lead suit be the suit number XY97D0444

Dated 9 March 1998

(24)   Decree nisi of divorce reciting cross-decrees

In the   County Court

No. of Matter

District Judge Grey

Sitting at

Between Mary Doe   Petitioner

and John Doe   Respondent

On the 23rd day of September 1997

the District Judge held that the Respondent

has behaved in such a way that the Petitioner cannot reasonably be expected to live with the Respondent and that the Petitioner has behaved in such a way that the Respondent cannot reasonably be expected to live with the Petitioner

that the marriage solemnised

on the 20th day of January 1994

at the Parish Church in the Parish of St Cedric's, Hayes, Bromley in the County of Kent

Between Mary Doe   Petitioner

And John Doe   Respondent

has broken down irretrievably and decreed that the said marriage be dissolved unless sufficient cause be shown to the Court within six weeks from the making of this decree why such decree should not be made absolute.

THIS IS NOT THE FINAL DECREE.

(25)   Draft newspaper advertisement

A divorce petition has been filed against John Doe, late of 1, Ash Grove, Littleton-on-Sea, Sussex, who may apply to the   County Court at
referring to matter number   for a copy of the petition. If, within one month, he has not communicated with the Court, the petition may be heard in his absence.

(26)   Notice of abatement

No. of Matter

Between   Petitioner

and   Respondent

and   Co-Respondent

Take notice that owing to the death of

the Petitioner/Respondent herein on   the   day of
20   this suit has now abated.

Dated

(27)   Parental responsibility agreement

Parental Responsibility Agreement
Section 4(1)(b) Children Act 1989

Keep this form in a safe place
Date recorded at The Principal Registry of the Family Division

Read the notes on the other side before you make this agreement.

This is a Parental Responsibility Agreement regarding

the Child   *Name*

_____

Boy or Girl Date of birth   *Date of 18th birthday*

Between
the Mother   *Name*
Address

and   the Father   *Name*
Address

We declare that   we are the mother and father of the above child and we agree that the child's father shall have parental responsibility for the child (in addition to the mother having parental responsibility).

Signed **(Mother)**   Signed **(Father)**

Date   Date

Certificate of Witness

The following evidence of identity was produced by the person signing above:

The following evidence of identity was produced by the person signing above:

Signed in the presence of:
Name of Witness

Signed in the presence of:
Name of Witness

Address   *Address*

Signature of Witness   *Signature of Witness*

[A Justice of the Peace]
[Justices' Clerk]
[An Officer of the Court authorised by the judge to administer oaths]

[A Justice of the Peace]
[Justices' Clerk]
[An Officer of the Court authorised by the judge to administer oaths]

C(PRA)

Notes about the Parental Responsibility Agreement

Read these notes before you make the agreement.

About the Parental Responsibility Agreement

The making of this agreement will affect the legal position of the mother and the father. You should both seek legal advice before you make the Agreement. You can obtain the name and address of a solicitor from the Children Panel (020 7242 1222) or from

- your local family proceedings court, or county court
- a Citizens Advice Bureau
- a Law Centre
- a local library.

You may be eligible for public funding.

When you fill in the Agreement

Please use black ink (the Agreement will be copied). Put the name of one child only. If the father is to have parental responsibility for more than one child, fill in a separate form for each child. **Do not sign the Agreement**.

When you have filled in the Agreement

Take it to a local family proceedings court, or county court, or the Principal Registry of the Family Division (the address is below).

A justice of the peace, a justices' clerk, or a court official who is authorised by the judge to administer oaths, will witness your signature and he or she will sign the certificate of the witness.

To the mother: When you make the declaration you will have to prove that you are the child's mother so take to the court the child's full birth certificate.

You will also need evidence of your identity showing a photograph and signature (for example, a photocard, official pass or passport).

To the father: You will need evidence of your identity showing a photograph and signature (for example, a photocard, official pass or passport).

When the certificate has been signed and witnessed

Make 2 copies of the other side of this form. You do not need to copy these notes.

Take, or send, this form and the copies to **The Principal Registry of the Family Division, First Avenue House, 42–49 High Holborn, London WC1V 6NP**.

The Registry will record the Agreement and keep this form. The copies will be stamped and sent back to each parent at the address on the Agreement. If the Agreement is lodged by a solicitor, who needs a copy for his/her own records an additional (3rd copy) should be provided. The Agreement will not take effect until it has been received and recorded at the Principal Registry of the Family Division.

Ending the Agreement

Once a parental responsibility agreement has been made it can only end

- by an order of the court made on the application of any person who has parental responsibility for the child
- by an order of the court made on the application of the child with leave of the court
- when the child reaches the age of 18.

C(PRA) (Notes)

(28) Pension sharing annex under section 24B of the Matrimonial Causes Act 1973

Pension Sharing Annex under
Section 24B of the Matrimonial
Causes Act 1973
(Rule 2.70 (14) FPR 1991)

In the	
	[County Court] *[Principal Registry of the Family Division]*
Case No. *Always quote this*	
Applicant's Solicitor's reference	
Respondent's Solicitor's reference	

The marriage of   **and**

Take Notice that:

On _____ the court

- made a pension sharing order under Part IV of the Welfare Reform and Pensions Act 1999.
- [varied] [discharged] an order which included provision for pension sharing made under Part IV of the Welfare Reform and Pensions Act 1999 and dated _____.

This annex to the order provides the person responsible for the pension arrangement with the information required by virtue of The Family Proceedings Rules 1991 as amended.

1. Name of the Transferor:

2. Name of the Transferee:

3. The Transferor's National Insurance Number:

4. Details of the Pension Arrangement and Policy Reference Number:
    (or such other details to enable the pension arrangement to be identified).

5. The specified percentage value of the pension arrangement to be transferred:
    (The specified amount required in order to create a pension credit and debit should only be inserted where specifically ordered by the court).

    In accordance with the Divorce etc (Pensions) Regulations 2000 the court has specified that the benefits shall be valued as at the following date:

6.   Pension Sharing Charges:
(*Delete as appropriate)

It is directed that:
   *The pension sharing charges be
   apportioned between the parties as
   follows:

   _____   _____

   *The pension sharing charges be paid in
   full by the transferor.

   _____   _____

The court is satisfied that the person responsible for the pension arrangement has furnished the
information required by Regulation 4 of the Pensions on Divorce etc (Provision of Information)
Regulations 2000 and that it appears from the information that there is power to make an order
including provision under section 24B (pension sharing) of the Act of 1973.

THIS [ORDER] [PROVISION] TAKES EFFECT FROM _____

To the person responsible for the pension arrangement:
(*Delete as appropriate)

1.   *Take notice that you must discharge your liability within the period of 4 months
      beginning with the later of:

      •   the day on which this order or provision takes effect; or,

      •   the first day on which you are in receipt of –
          a. this [order] [provision] for ancillary relief, including the annex;
          b. the decree of divorce or nullity of marriage; and
          c. the information prescribed by Regulation 5 of the Pensions on Divorce etc
             (Provision of Information) Regulations 2000.

2.   *The court directs that the implementation period for discharging your liability should be
      determined by regulations made under section 34(4) or 41(2)(a) of the Welfare Reform
      and Pensions Act 1999, in that:

(29) Pension attachment annex under section 25B or 25C of the Matrimonial Causes Act 1973

Pension Attachment Annex
under Section 25B or 25C of the
Matrimonial Causes Act 1973
(Rule 2.70 (15) FPR 1991)

In the	
	*[County Court] *[Principal Registry of the Family Division]
Case No. *Always quote this*	
Applicant's Solicitor's reference	
Respondent's Solicitor's reference	

The marriage of   **and**

Take Notice that:

On _____ the court

- made an order including provision under section [25B][25C]* of the Matrimonial Causes Act 1973.
- [varied] [discharged] an order which included provision under section [25B][25C]* of the Matrimonial Causes Act 1973 and dated _____.

(*delete as appropriate)

This annex to the order provides the person responsible for the pension arrangement with the information required by virtue of the Family Proceedings Rules 1991 as amended.

1. Name of the party with the pension rights:

2. Name of the other party:

3. The National Insurance Number of the party with pension rights:

4. Details of the Pension Arrangement and Policy Reference Number:
    (or such other details to enable the pension arrangement to be identified).

5. *The specified percentage of any payment due to the party with pension rights that is to be paid for the benefit of the other party:

    *The person responsible for the pension arrangement is required to:

    (*delete as appropriate)

    In accordance with the Divorce etc (Pensions) Regulations 2000 the court has specified that the benefits shall be valued as at the following date:

To the person responsible for the pension arrangement:
(*Delete if this information has already been provided to the person responsible for the pension arrangement with Form A or pursuant to FPR 2.70(11))

1.	*You are required to serve any notice under the Divorce etc (Pensions) Regulations 2000 on the other party at the following address:

2.	*You are required to make any payments due under the pension arrangement to the other party at the following address:

3.	*If the address at 2. above is that of a bank, building society or the Department of National Savings the following details will enable you to make payment into the account of the other party (eg Account Name, Number, Bank/Building Society, etc and Sort code):

> Note: Where the order to which this annex applies was made by consent the following section should also be completed.

The court also confirms:
(*Delete as appropriate)

- *That notice under Rule 2.70(11) of the Family Proceedings Rules 1991 has been served on the person responsible for the pension arrangement and that no objection has been received under Rule 2.70(12).

- *That notice under Rule 2.70(11) of the Family Proceedings Rules 1991 has been served on the person responsible for the pension arrangement and that the court has considered any objection received under Rule 2.70(12)(b).

Appendix B

BLOOD AND DNA TESTS

(1) Scientific tests – direction form (BD1)

DIRECTION FORM

[IN THE PRINCIPAL REGISTRY OF THE FAMILY DIVISION]

[IN THE   COUNTY COURT]

CASE NO.

....

v.

....

Full name and
date of birth of   ....
person to be
tested to whom   ....
this form relates.   ....

PART 1 – Notification of direction

Insert name
and address
of court

on the   day of   [20   ] directed that scientific tests be
carried out in respect of the persons whose names are set out below for the
purpose of ascertaining the parentage of *(name of person whose parentage is in
dispute)*

and that the bodily samples be taken from the persons named below on or before
the   day of   [20   ].

*Delete as   *The name of the person appearing to the court to have the care and control of
appropriate   the person to whom this form relates who is *under 16/suffering from a mental
                    disorder within the meaning of the Mental Health Act 1959 and is incapable of
                    understanding the nature and purpose of the scientific tests, is

                                                    _____(Signed)
                                                              District Judge

          NAME   ADDRESS   AGE

PART 2 – Photograph

Below is a photograph of the person to whom this form relates, being a person who has attained the age of twelve months.

PART 3 – Declaration

If the person to whom this form relates has attained the age of sixteen years and is not suffering from a mental disability then he/she should complete paragraphs (a), (b) and (d) and delete paragraph (c) **but** if he/she is under sixteen years of age or is suffering from a mental disability then paragraphs (a), (c) and (d) should be completed by the person having the care and control of him/her and paragraph (b) should be deleted.

(a) I *(full name and address of person completing this form)*

Delete as appropriate

(b) declare that the photograph affixed in Part 2 of this form is a photograph of me and that I am a person in respect of whom the above-named court gave a direction that scientific tests be made. I hereby *consent/do not consent to the taking of a bodily sample from me for the purpose of such tests.

(c) being the person having care and control of *(name person to whom form relates)*

declare that the person whom I identify to *(identify name of sampler)*

*[and whose photograph is affixed to Part 2 of this form]
    is, to the best of my knowledge and belief

Delete if inapplicable

[who is the son/daughter of *(insert the name of mother of the person identified)*

]

I being the person having the care and control of the person to whom this form relates, *consent/do not consent to the taking of a sample.

†To be completed if the person making the declaration withholds consent and wishes to record the reasons for so doing

(d) †[I do not consent because

]

I understand that it is a serious offence punishable by imprisonment to personate another person for the purpose of providing a bodily sample or to proffer the wrong child for that purpose.

Date _____   _____ (Signed)

The above was explained to the declarant who stated that he/she understood it and signed in my presence.

Date _____   _____ (Signed)
                                                                Sampler

PART 4 – Request to sampler to take sample

To *(name and address of sampler)*

*Delete if not applicable

You are hereby requested to take a bodily sample from *(name person to whom form relates)* [*The sample is to be taken notwithstanding the refusal to consent of the person with care and control of *(name of person to whom form relates)*]

Delete if sampler is also tester

You are further requested to send the sample taken to *(name and address of accredited body)*

To be completed where all the samples from the parties named in Part 1 are not to be taken by the same sampler

[Other samples will be taken as follows:-

Name person from whom sample will be taken	*Name, address and telephone number of sampler*
_____	_____
_____	_____
_____	_____]

_____ (Signed)

For use where sampler named above nominates another sampler

[Being unable to comply with the request set out above, I have nominated *(name and address of nominee)*

to take the sample

_____ (Signed)

PART 5 – To be completed by sampler where sample is of blood

I have questioned *(insert name of person to whom form relates, or in the case of person under 16 or suffering from mental disability, person accompanying that person)*

and it appears that *he/she/the party to whom this form relates –

*Delete as appropriate

*has/has not been transfused with blood in the last three months

*has not been injected with a blood product or plasma substitute

*has been injected with a *blood product/blood plasma on or about

and that the value of any tests will thereby *be/not be affected

_____ (Signed)
Sampler

PART 6 – To be completed by sampler

I have today taken a bodily sample from

To whom this form relates, whose [apparent] age is _____ years.

Delete as appropriate

[I identified him/her from the photograph affixed to this form.]

[He/She was [also] identified to me by

]

Date _____ _____ (Signed)
Sampler

OBSERVATIONS

(Any observations by the sampler which may assist the tester shall be inserted here)

PART 7 – To be completed by sampler

The person to whom this form relates did not attend on the date originally arranged [or on a new date arranged by me].

His/Her reasons given to me for failing to attend were as follows:

Date _____ _____ (Signed)

PART 8 – Request to accredited body to carry out tests

To *(name and address of accredited body)*

You are hereby requested to carry out scientific tests on a bodily sample from *(name of person to whom form relates)*

PART 9 – To be completed by tester

I have today received at *(insert place of receipt)*

the sample referred to in Part 6 of this form.

Delete as
appropriate

[*It was received by recorded delivery]

[*It was handed to me by   ].

Date _____   _____ (Signed)
                                                                                        Tester

(2) Order for blood or DNA tests

In the   County Court

Case Number:

| *The full name(s) of the children* | *Date(s) of Birth* |
| John Smith | 1 January 1999 |

Order

Children Act 1989

Upon hearing the solicitor for the Applicant father David Green and the solicitor for the Respondent mother Ann Smith

IT IS DIRECTED THAT:

(1) Pursuant to section 20(1) of the Family Law Reform Act 1969:

  (a) scientific tests be used to ascertain whether such tests show that David Green is not excluded from being the father of the child John Smith born on 1 January 1999

  (b) for that purpose bodily samples be taken on or before 31 March 2002 from David Green, Ann Smith, the mother of the said child, and John Smith, the said child

  (c) the person appearing to the Court to have care and control of the child who is under the age of 16 years is Ann Smith

  (d) such tests be carried out by [*name of accredited body*]

(2) The matter be listed for further directions before a district judge sitting at
              Court on   at   (time estimate   ).

(3) Costs in the application.

Ordered by District Judge Grey on 4 February 2002

---

(3) List of laboratories approved by the Lord Chancellor to test bodily samples in cases of disputed parentage

ADDRESS	TEL NO	FAX NO
Department of Haematology St Bartholomew's and the Royal London School of Medicine and Dentistry Turner Street London E1 2AD	0207 377 7076	0207 377 7629
Department of Human Genetics University of Newcastle upon Tyne 19/20 Claremont Place Newcastle upon Tyne NE2 4AA	0191 222 6000 extn 7574	0191 222 7143
Cellmark Diagnostics Blacklands Way Abingdon Business Park Abingdon Oxon OX14 1DY	01235 528609	01235 528141
University Diagnostics Ltd LGC Building Queens Road Teddington Middlesex TW11 0NJ	0208 943 8420	0208 943 8401
The Forensic Science Service Wetherby Laboratory Sandbeck Way Audby Lane Wetherby West Yorkshire LS22 4DN	01937 548100	01937 548230
The Forensic Science Service Metropolitan Laboratory 109 Lambeth Road London SE1 7LP	0207 230 6700	0207 230 6253
Department of Human Sciences Loughborough University Loughborough Leics LE11 3TU	01509 223036	01509 223940

The following Forensic Science Service Laboratories may occasionally report disputed parentage cases

ADDRESS	TEL NO	FAX NO
The Forensic Science Service Chepstow Laboratory Usk Road Chepstow Gwent NP6 6YE	01291 637100	01291 629482
The Forensic Science Service Birmingham Laboratory 3rd Floor Norfolk House Smallbrook Queensway Birmingham B5 4LJ	0121 607 6939	0121 643 3476
The Forensic Science Service 6th Floor Priory House Gooch Street North Birmingham B5 6QQ	0121 607 6800	0121 622 5889

Appendix C

OTHER INFORMATION

(1)   List of armed forces contact addresses

Armed forces manning and records offices

Naval Pay and Pension Executive Office
Centurion Building
Grange Road
Gosport
Hants
PO13 9XA

Pension Division
Army Personnel Centre
Kentigern House
65 Brown Street
Glasgow
G2 8EX

RAF Pensions Office
AFPAA
RAF Innsworth
Gloucester
GL3 1EZ

Postal and Courier Services

Defence Mail and Courier Services
BFPO
Frith Lane
Mill Hill
London
NW7 1PX

(2)   Urgent court business – information for court users

Introduction

Not all the incidents which may require the attention of a judge occur within normal office hours, and some are too urgent to wait until the next day that a court is open. In order to cater for such emergencies, the Court Service provides a system known as 'urgent court business'. This system enables court users to contact an experienced member of staff at any time during the night, weekends or public holidays. If the circumstances are serious enough, the urgent court business officer will arrange a hearing with a judge. The following gives a basic guide to urgent court business, how it operates, the work it covers and how you can contact an officer in an emergency.

Nature of work covered

- Injunctions;
- Children Act applications; and
- other urgent applications where an individual's personal safety, well-being, business or assets may be at risk.

Times when the system operates

- Between 4 pm and 8.30 am each workday;
- between 4 pm on Friday until 8.30 am on Monday for each weekend; and
- from 4 pm on the last day preceding a public holiday or privilege holiday that the court is open until 8.30 am on the day the court is next open.

Publicity for the scheme

Details of the scheme must be given, locally, to:

- Police;
- Citizens Advice Bureau(x);
- the local authority social services department;
- law centres;
- the local Law Society;
- the local Bar.

Some Circuits/Group Manager's Offices also give the information to other organisations.

How it operates

Urgent court business officers all carry a radio pager. Anybody with a touch tone telephone who needs to contact one of them simply telephones the pager number provided and leaves their telephone number. **Note: the system will not accept verbal messages. When asked for your message you simply tap in your telephone number on which you wish to be contacted.** Anyone without a touch tone telephone will need to contact the Security Office at the Royal Courts of Justice on 0207 947 6000. The caller will be required to leave a contact number and the name of their local court. The Security Officer will then telephone the pager number for the area of the local court. In either case, the urgent court business officer will telephone you back and ask for details of the case. It would be of great assistance if solicitors could have any relevant orders to hand when contacting the court office. The officer will then discuss the case with a member of the judiciary who will decide whether a hearing is necessary. All urgent court business officers in a particular region, such as South Wales, will have a pager with the same number. The number therefore always remains the same.

If you have any queries about urgent court business or would like more information about how it works, please contact the Group Manager's Office for the relevant region.

(3) President's Direction of 10 March 2000

PRACTICE DIRECTION

(FAMILY PROCEEDINGS: COURT BUNDLES)

(1) The following practice applies to all hearings in family proceedings in the High Court, to all hearings of family proceedings in the Royal Courts of Justice and to hearings with a time estimate of half a day or more in all care centres, family hearing centres and divorce county courts (including the Principal Registry of the Family Division when so treated), except as specified in para (2.3) below, and subject to specific directions given in any particular case. 'Hearing' extends to all hearings before judges and district judges and includes the hearing of any application.

(2.1) A bundle for the use of the court at the hearing shall be provided by the party in the position of applicant at the hearing or by any other party who agrees to do so. It shall contain copies of all documents relevant to the hearing in chronological order, paginated and indexed and divided into separate sections, as follows:

(a) applications and orders;
(b) statements and affidavits;
(c) experts' reports and other reports including those of a guardian ad litem; and
(d) other documents, divided into further sections as may be appropriate.

(2.2) Where the nature of the hearing is such that a complete bundle of all documents is unnecessary, the bundle may comprise only those documents necessary for the hearing but the summary (para (3.1)(a) below) must commence with a statement that the bundle is limited or incomplete. The summary should be limited to those matters which the court needs to know for the purpose of the hearing and for management of the case.

(2.3) The requirement to provide a bundle shall not apply to the hearing of any urgent application where the circumstances are such that it is not reasonably practicable for a bundle to be provided.

(3.1) At the commencement of the bundle there shall be:

(a) a summary of the background to the hearing limited, if practicable, to one A4 page;
(b) a statement of the issue or issues to be determined;
(c) a summary of the order or directions sought by each party;
(d) a chronology if it is a final hearing or if the summary under (a) is insufficient;
(e) skeleton arguments as may be appropriate, with copies of all authorities relied on.

(3.2) If possible the bundle shall be agreed. In all cases, the party preparing the bundle shall paginate it and provide an index to all other parties prior to the hearing.

(3.3) The bundle should normally be contained in a ring binder or lever arch file (limited to 350pp in each file). Where there is more than one bundle, each should be clearly distinguishable. Bundles shall be lodged, if practicable, 2 clear days prior to the hearing. For hearings in the Royal Courts of Justice bundles shall be lodged with the Clerk of the Rules. All bundles shall have clearly marked on the outside, the title and number of the case, the hearing date and time and, if known, the name of the judge hearing the case.

(4) After each hearing which is not a final hearing, the party responsible for the bundle shall retrieve it from the court. The bundle with any additional documents shall be re-lodged for further hearings in accordance with the above provisions.

(5) This direction replaces paras (5) and (8) of *Practice Direction: Case Management* (31 January 1995) [1995] 1 FLR 456 and shall have effect from 2 May 2000.

(6) Issued with the approval and concurrence of the Lord Chancellor.

10 March 2000   DAME ELIZABETH BUTLER-SLOSS
                                                           President

(4)   President's Direction of 16 March 2001

THE PRINCIPAL REGISTRY OF THE FAMILY DIVISION

President's Direction
16 March 2001

(1)   Committal Applications
(2)   Proceedings in which a committal order may be made

1   As from the date of this direction, the Civil Procedure Practice Direction supplemental to RSC Ord 52 (Sch 1 to the Civil Procedure Rules) and CCR Ord 29 (Sch 2 to the CPR) ('the CPR Direction') shall apply to all applications in family proceedings for an order of committal in the same manner and to the same extent as it applies to proceedings governed by the Civil Procedure Rules ('the CPR') but subject to:

(a)   the provisions of the Family Proceedings Rules 1991 (SI 1991/1247) ('the FPR') and the rules applied by those rules namely, the Rules of the Supreme Court ('RSC') and the County Court Rules ('CCR') in force immediately before 26 April 1999, and
(b)   the appropriate modifications consequent upon the limited application of the CPR to family proceedings.

1.1   In particular, the following modifications apply.
    (a)   Where the alleged contempt is in connection with existing proceedings (other than contempt in the face of the court) or with an order made or an undertaking given in existing proceedings, the committal application shall be made in those proceedings.
    (b)   As required by FPR r 7.2, committal applications in the High Court are to be made by summons. In county court proceedings, applications are to be made in the manner prescribed by CCR Ord 29. References in the CPR Direction to 'claim form' and 'application notice' are to be read accordingly.
    (c)   In instances where the CPR Direction requires more information to be provided than is required to be provided under the RSC and the CCR, the court will expect the former to be observed.
    (d)   Having regard to the periods specified in RSC Ord 52 r 3, Ord 32 r 3(2)(a) and CCR Ord 13 r 1(2), the time specified in paragraph 4.2 of the CPR Direction shall not apply. Nevertheless, the court will ensure that adequate time is afforded to the respondent for the preparation of his defence.
    (e)   Paragraph 9 of the CPR Direction is to be read with paragraph (3) of each of the Directions issued on 17 December 1997, entitled 'Children Act 1989 – Exclusion requirement' and 'Family Law Act 1996 – Part IV'.

2   In any family proceedings (not falling within 1 above), in which a committal order may be made, including proceedings for the enforcement of an existing order

by way of judgment summons or other process, full effect will be given to the Human Rights Act 1998 and to the rights afforded under that Act. In particular, Art 6 of the Convention (as set out in the Sch 1 to the Human Rights Act 1998) is fully applicable to such proceedings. Those involved must ensure that in the conduct of the proceedings there is due observance of the Human Rights Act 1998 in the same manner as if the proceedings fell within the CPR Direction.

3   As with all family proceedings, the CPR costs provisions apply to all committal proceedings.

4   Issued with the approval and concurrence of the Lord Chancellor.

Elizabeth Butler-Sloss
President

(5)   Conventions and Legislation relating to reciprocal enforcement of maintenance orders

CONVENTION	LEGISLATION
Brussels	Civil Jurisdiction and Judgments Act 1982
Commonwealth 1920	Maintenance Orders (Facilities for Enforcement) Act 1920
Commonwealth – Part I	Part I of the Maintenance Orders (Reciprocal Enforcement) Act 1972
Hague	Part I of the Maintenance Orders (Reciprocal Enforcement) Act 1972 – as amended by the Reciprocal Enforcement of Maintenance Orders (Hague Convention Countries) Order 1993
Irish	Part I of the Maintenance Orders (Reciprocal Enforcement) Act 1972 – as amended by the Reciprocal Enforcement of Maintenance Orders (Republic of Ireland) Order 1993
Lugano	Civil Jurisdiction and Judgments Act 1982
UN	Part II of the Maintenance Orders (Reciprocal Enforcement) Act 1972
US	Part II of the Maintenance Orders (Reciprocal Enforcement) Act 1972

COUNTRIES	CONVENTIONS
Alberta†	Commonwealth – Part 1
Algeria	UN
Anguilla	Commonwealth – Part 1
Antigua	Commonwealth 1920
Australia	
Australian Capital Territory‡	Commonwealth – Part 1
Austria§	UN, Brussels, Lugano
Bahamas	Commonwealth 1920
Barbados	Commonwealth – Part 1, UN
Belgium	UN, Brussels, Lugano
Belize	Commonwealth 1920
Bermuda	Commonwealth – Part 1
Bosnia and Herzegovina	UN
Botswana	Commonwealth 1920
Brazil	UN
British Columbia	Commonwealth – Part 1
British Solomon Islands	Commonwealth 1920

COUNTRIES	CONVENTIONS
Brunei	Commonwealth 1920
Canada	
Cayman Islands	Commonwealth 1920
Central African Republic	UN
Chile	UN
Croatia	UN
Cyprus	Commonwealth 1920
Czech Republic	UN, Hague
Denmark	UN, Brussels, Hague
Dominica	Commonwealth 1920
Ecuador	UN
Falkland Islands	Commonwealth – Part 1
Fiji	Commonwealth – Part 1
Finland§	UN, Hague, Brussels
France	UN, Hague, Brussels
Gambia	Commonwealth 1920
Germany	UN, Hague, Brussels, Lugano
Ghana*	Commonwealth – Part 1
Gibraltar	Commonwealth – Part 1
Gilbert and Ellice Islands	Commonwealth 1920
Greece§	UN, Brussels
Grenada	Commonwealth 1920
Guatemala	UN
Guernsey	Commonwealth 1920
Guyana	Commonwealth 1920
Haiti	UN
Holy See	UN
Hong Kong	Commonwealth – Part 1
Hungary	UN
India*	Commonwealth – Part 1
Ireland – The Republic of	Irish, Brussels
Isle of Man	Commonwealth – Part 1
Israel	UN
Italy	UN, Hague, Brussels
Jamaica	Commonwealth 1920
Jersey	Commonwealth 1920
Kenya*	Commonwealth – Part 1
Lesotho	Commonwealth 1920
Luxembourg	UN, Hague, Brussels
Macedonia – former Yugoslav Republic of	UN
Malawi	Commonwealth 1920
Malaysia	Commonwealth 1920
Malta	Commonwealth – Part 1
Manitoba	Commonwealth – Part 1
Mauritius	Commonwealth 1920
Monaco	UN
Montserrat	Commonwealth 1920

COUNTRIES	CONVENTIONS
Morocco	UN
Naura	Commonwealth – Part 1
Netherlands	UN, Hague, Brussels
New Brunswick*	Commonwealth – Part 1
New South Wales‡	Commonwealth – Part 1
New Zealand†	Commonwealth – Part 1
Newfoundland and Prince Edward Island	Commonwealth 1920
Niger	UN
Nigeria	Commonwealth 1920
Norfolk Island‡	Commonwealth – Part 1
Northern Territory‡	Commonwealth – Part 1
Northwest Territories*	Commonwealth – Part 1
Norway	UN, Hague, Lugano
Nova Scotia‡	Commonwealth – Part 1
Ontario	Commonwealth – Part 1
Pakistan	UN
Papua New Guinea	Commonwealth – Part 1
Philippines	UN
Poland	UN
Portugal§	UN, Hague, Brussels
Queensland‡	Commonwealth – Part 1
Saskatchewan†	Commonwealth – Part 1
Serbia and Montenegro	UN
Seychelles	Commonwealth 1920
Sierra Leone	Commonwealth 1920
Singapore	Commonwealth – Part 1
Slovakia	UN, Hague
Slovenia	UN
South Africa*	Commonwealth – Part 1
South Australia‡	Commonwealth – Part 1
Spain§	UN, Brussels
Sri Lanka	UN, Commonwealth 1920
St Christopher (Kitts) and Nevis	Commonwealth 1920
St Helena	Commonwealth – Part 1
St Lucia	Commonwealth 1920
St Vincent	Commonwealth 1920
Surinam	UN
Swaziland Protectorate	Commonwealth 1920
Sweden§	UN, Hague, Brussels
Switzerland	UN, Hague, Lugano
Tanzania (except Zanzibar)*	Commonwealth – Part 1
Tasmania‡	Commonwealth – Part 1
Territory of Christmas Island	Commonwealth 1920
Territory of Cocos Islands	Commonwealth 1920
Trinidad and Tobago	Commonwealth 1920
Tunisia	UN

COUNTRIES	CONVENTIONS
Turkey	UN, Hague
Turks and Caicos Islands*	Commonwealth – Part 1
Uganda	Commonwealth 1920
United States#	US
Upper Volta	UN
Victoria‡	Commonwealth – Part 1
Virgin Islands	Commonwealth 1920
Western Australia‡	Commonwealth – Part 1
Yugoslavia (see under new names)	UN
Yukon Territory	Commonwealth 1920
Zambia	Commonwealth 1920
Zanzibar	Commonwealth 1920
Zimbabwe*	Commonwealth – Part 1

*   Not affiliation orders.
†   Not provisional affiliation orders.
‡   Not orders obtained by or in favour of a public authority.
§   Although these countries are party to the Brussels Convention through accession to the EU, there is doubt whether they will enforce maintenance orders under it.
#   See below.

The United Kingdom has reached agreement with the following states in the United States of America for the reciprocal enforcement of maintenance orders:

Alaska	Kansas	New Mexico*	Virginia
Arizona	Kentucky	New York	Washington State*
Arkansas	Louisiana	North Carolina	Wisconsin
California	Maine	North Dakota	Wyoming
Colorado*	Maryland	Ohio*	
Connecticut	Massachusetts	Oklahoma	
Delaware	Michigan*	Oregon	
Florida	Minnesota	Pennsylvania	
Georgia*	Missouri	Rhode Island*	
Hawaii*	Montana	South Dakota	
Idaho*	Nebraska	Tennessee*	
Illinois*	Nevada	Texas	
Indiana	New Hampshire*	Utah	
Iowa	New Jersey	Vermont	

The UK does **not** have reciprocal arrangements with the following states:

Alabama
Mississippi
South Carolina
The District of Columbia

*   The UK does not have agreements with these states under Part II of the Maintenance Orders (Reciprocal Enforcement) Act 1972.

(6)   CAFCASS Practice Note of March 2001

OFFICERS OF CAFCASS LEGAL SERVICES AND SPECIAL CASEWORK: APPOINTMENT IN FAMILY PROCEEDINGS

Practice notes – CAFCASS Legal Services and Special Casework – Appointment of officer as children's guardian – Terms of appointment

(1)   This Practice Note comes into effect on 1 April 2001 and supersedes the Practice Note dated 4 December 1998 issued by the Official Solicitor in relation to the representation of children in family proceedings. It is issued in conjunction with a Practice Note dealing with the appointment of the Official Solicitor in family proceedings. This Practice Note is intended to be helpful guidance, but always subject to Practice Directions, decisions of the courts and other legal guidance.

The Children and Family Court Advisory and Support Service
Appointment as children's guardian

(2)   The Children and Family Court Advisory and Support Service (CAFCASS) has responsibilities in relation to children in family proceedings as defined in s 12 of the Criminal Justice and Court Services Act 2000. CAFCASS has established CAFCASS Legal Services and Special Casework ('CAFCASS Legal') principally to take over the Official Solicitor's responsibilities of representing children who are the subject of family proceedings.

(3)   Generally it is only where it appears to the court that the child ought to have party status and be legally represented that the question of the involvement of CAFCASS Legal may arise. Normally an officer of CAFCASS in the area in which the case is proceeding will be appointed as the children's guardian, but all private law cases where it is felt necessary for the child to be joined as a party, and all High Court adoption cases, should be referred to CAFCASS Legal. CAFCASS Legal may represent children in family proceedings either in the High Court or in a county court (but not in a family proceedings court).

Private Cases

(4)   The court will normally at the first directions apppointment consider whether the child should be made a party to the proceedings. In most private law cases (non-specified proceedings), a child's interests will be sufficiently safeguarded by the commissioning of a report under s 7 of the Children Act 1989 from a children and family reporter. Children who need someone to orchestrate an investigation of the case on their behalf may need party status and legal representation: *Re A* (2001) *The Times*, February 28. Particular examples are where:

(a)   there is a significant foreign element such as a challenge to the English court's jurisdiction or a need for enquiries to be conducted abroad;
(b)   there is a need for expert medical or other evidence to be adduced on behalf of a child in circumstances where a joint instruction by the parties is impossible
(c)   where a child wants to instruct a solicitor direct but has been refused leave pursuant to Family Proceedings Rules r 9.2A to instruct a solicitor.

(d) an application is made for leave to seek contact with an adopted child
(e) there are exceptionally difficult, unusual or sensitive issues making it necessary for the child to be granted party status within the proceedings: such cases are likely to be High Court matters.

(5)   CAFCASS Legal will almost invariably accept cases where case law has pointed to the need for a child to be granted party status and to be legally represented, for instance in 'special category' medical treatment cases, notably in those cases involving an application to authorise sterilisation and cases concerning disputed life sustaining treatment. Applications in such cases should be made under the inherent jurisdiction of the High Court. The Official Solicitor will have a continuing role in such cases for adult patients and for some older children who are also patients.

(6)–(8) omitted

Non-subject children

(9)   Exceptionally, CAFCASS Legal may accept apppointment on behalf of child applicants (typically seeking contact with siblings) or children who are otherwise parties to family proceedings, such as a minor mother of a child who is the subject of the proceedings. This may be appropriate to allow continuity of representation following earlier proceedings in which the child was the subject. In all cases where the child is the applicant, CAFCASS Legal will need to be satisfied that the proposed proceedings would benefit that child before proceeding.

Advising the Court

(10)   CAFCASS Legal may be invited to act or instruct counsel as friend of the court (amicus).

Liaison with the Official Solicitor

(11)   In cases of doubt or difficulty, staff of CAFCASS Legal will liaise with staff of the Official Solicitor's office to avoid duplication and ensure the most suitable arrangements are made.

Appointment of an officer of CAFCASS Legal Services and Special Casework

(12)   Where the court considers that a child should be made a respondent to an application and represented by CAFCASS Legal it should make an order in the following terms:

(a) The Director of Legal Services, CAFCASS, is invited to nominate one of his officers to act as children's guardian for [name(s)];
(b) Upon an officer of CAFCASS Legal Services and Special Casework consenting to act as children's guardian [name(s)] will be made respondent(s) to the applications before the court.

CAFCASS Legal will normally provide a response to any invitation within 10 working days of receiving the papers referred to in paragraph 15 below.

(13)   It is often helpful to discuss the question of appointment with the duty divisional manager or a lawyer at CAFCASS Legal by telephoning 020 7904 0867. It is particularly important to do so in urgent cases.

(14)   Save in the most urgent cases a substantive hearing date should not normally be fixed before the next directions hearing following the invitation to act.

(15)   The following documents should be forwarded to CAFCASS Legal without delay:

(a)   a copy of the order and a note of the reasons for approaching CAFCASS Legal approved by the judge;
(b)   the court file;
(c)   whenever practicable, a bundle with summary, statement of issues and chronology (in the form required by the President's Direction of 10 March 2000).

The address of CAFCASS Legal Services and Special Casework is:

Newspaper House
8–16 Great New Street
London EC4A 3BN

Telephone: 020 7904 0867
Fax: 020 7904 0868/9
e-mail: legal@cafcass.gsi.gov.uk

March 2001

Charles Prest
Director of Legal Services
CAFCASS

Official Solicitor's Practice Note of 2 April 2001

PRACTICE NOTE

THE OFFICIAL SOLICITOR: APPOINTMENT IN FAMILY PROCEEDINGS

Practice directions and notes – Official Solicitor – Appointment as guardian ad litem – Appointment as next friend – Terms of appointment

(1)   This Practice Note supersedes the Practice Note dated 4 December 1998 issued by the Official Solicitor in relation to his appointment in family proceedings. It is issued in conjunction with a Practice Note dealing with the appointment of officers of CAFCASS Legal Services and Special Casework in family proceedings. This Practice Note is intended to be helpful guidance, but always subject to Practice Directions, decisions of the court and other legal guidance.

(2)   The Children and Family Court Advisory and Support Service (CAFCASS) has responsibilities in relation to children in family proceedings in which their welfare is or may be in question (Criminal Justice and Court Services Act 2000, s 12). From 1 April 2001, the Official Solicitor will no longer represent children who are the subject

of family proceedings (other than in very exceptional circumstances and after liaison with CAFCASS).

(3)   This Practice Note summarises the continuing role of the Official Solicitor in family proceedings. Since there are no provisions for parties under disability in the Family Proceedings Courts (Children Act 1989) Rules 1991, the Official Solicitor can only act in the High Court or in a county court, pursuant to Part IX of Family Proceedings Rules 1991. The Official Solicitor will shortly issue an updated Practice Note about his role for adults under disability who are the subject of declaratory proceedings in relation to their medical treatment or welfare.

(4)   *omitted*

Non-subject children

(5)   Again in the absence of any other willing and suitable person, the Official Solicitor will act as next friend or guardian ad litem of a child party whose own welfare is not the subject of family proceedings (Family Proceedings Rules 1991, r 2.57, r 9.2 and r 9.5). The most common examples will be:

(a) a child who is also the parent of a child, and who is a respondent to a Children Act or Adoption Act application. If a child respondent is already represented by a CAFCASS officer in pending proceedings of which he or she is the subject, then the Official Solicitor will liaise with CAFCASS to agree the most appropriate arrangements;
(b) a child who wishes to make an application for a Children Act order naming another child (typically a contact order naming a sibling). The Official Solicitor will need to satisfy himself that the proposed proceedings would benefit the child applicant before proceeding;
(c) a child witness to some disputed factual issue in a children case and who may require intervener status. In such circumstances the need for party status and legal representation should be weighed in the light of *Re H (Care Proceedings: Intervener)* [2000] 1 FLR 775;
(d) a child party to a petition for a declaration of status under Part III of the Family Law Act 1986;
(e) a child intervener in divorce or ancillary relief proceedings (r 2.57 or r 9.5);
(f) a child applicant for, or respondent to, an application for an order under Part IV of the Family Law Act 1996. In the case of a child applicant, the Official Solicitor will need to satisfy himself that the proposed proceedings would benefit the child before pursuing them, with leave under Family Law Act 1996, s 43 if required.

(6)   Any children who are parties to Children Act or inherent jurisdiction proceedings may rely on the provisions of Family Proceedings Rules 1991, r 9.2A, if they wish to instruct a solicitor without the intervention of a next friend or guardian ad litem. Rule 9.2A does not apply to Adoption Act, Family Law Act or Matrimonial Causes Act proceedings.

Older children who are also patients

(7)   Officers of CAFCASS will not be able to represent anyone who is over the age of 18. The Official Solicitor may therefore be the more appropriate next friend or

guardian ad litem of a child who is also a patient and whose disability will persist beyond his or her 18th birthday, especially in non-emergency cases where the substantive hearing is unlikely to take place before the child's 18th birthday. The Official Solicitor may also be the more appropriate next friend or guardian ad litem in medical treatment cases such as sterilisation or vegetative state cases, in which his staff have particular expertise deriving from their continuing role for adult patients.

Advising the court

(8)   The Official Solicitor may be invited to act or instruct counsel as a friend of the court (amicus) if it appears to the court that such an invitation is more appropriately addressed to him rather than (or in addition to) CAFCASS Legal Services and Special Casework.

Liaison with CAFCASS

(9)   In cases of doubt or difficulty, staff of the Official Solicitor's office will liaise with staff of CAFCASS Legal Services and Special Casework to avoid duplication and ensure the most suitable arrangements are made.

Invitations to act in new cases

(10)   Solicitors who have been consulted by a child or an adult under disability (or by someone acting on their behalf, or concerned about their interests) should write to the Official Solicitor setting out the background to the proposed case and explaining why there is no other willing and suitable person to act as next friend or guardian ad litem. Where the person concerned is an adult, medical evidence in the standard form of the Official Solicitor's medical certificate should be provided.

Invitations to act in pending proceedings

(11)   Where a case is already before the court, an order appointing the Official Solicitor should be expressed as being made subject to his consent. The Official Solicitor aims to provide a response to any invitation within 10 working days. He will be unable to consent to act for an adult until satisfied that the party is a 'patient'. A further directions appointment after 28 days may therefore be helpful. If he accepts appointment, the Official Solicitor will need time to prepare the case on behalf of the child or patient and may wish to make submissions about any substantive hearing date. The following documents should be forwarded to the Official Solicitor without delay:

(a)   a copy of the order inviting him to act (with a note of the reasons approved by the judge if appropriate);
(b)   the court file;
(c)   if available, a bundle with summary, statement of issues and chronology (as required by President's Direction of 10 March 2000).

Contacting the Official Solicitor

(12)   It is often helpful to discuss the question of appointment with the Official Solicitor or one of his staff by telephoning 020 7911 7127. Enquiries about family proceedings should be addressed to the Team Manager, Family Litigation.

The Official Solicitor's address is:
81 Chancery Lane,
London WC2A 1DD.

DX 0012 London Chancery Lane
Fax: 020 7911 7105
E-mail address: officialsolicitor@offsol.gsi.gov.uk

2 April 2001

Laurence Oates
Official Solicitor

(7) Guidelines for good practice on parental contact in domestic violence cases

THE ADVISORY BOARD ON FAMILY LAW:
CHILDREN ACT SUB-COMMITTEE

EXTRACTED FROM SECTION 5 OF THE REPORT OF THE CHILDREN ACT SUB-COMMITTEE TO THE
LORD CHANCELLOR ON THE QUESTION OF PARENTAL CONTACT IN CASES WHERE THERE IS
DOMESTIC VIOLENCE

Court to give early consideration to allegations of domestic violence

1.1 In every case in which domestic violence is put forward as a reason for refusing or limiting contact, the court should at the earliest opportunity consider the allegations made (and any answer to them) and decide whether the nature and effect of the violence alleged by the complainant (or admitted by the respondent) is such as to make it likely that the order of the court for contact will be affected if the allegations are proved.

Steps to be taken where the court forms the view that its order is likely to be affected if allegations of domestic violence are proved

1.2 Where the alleations are disputed and the court forms the view that the nature and effect of the violence alleged is such as to make it likely that the order of the court will be affected if the allegations are proved, the court should—

(a) consider what evidence will be required to enable the court to make findings of fact in relation to the allegations;

(b) ensure that appropriate directions under s 11(1) of the Children Act 1989 are given at an early stage in the application to enable the matters in issue to be heard as speedily as possible; including consideration of whether or not it would be appropriate for there to be an initial hearing for the purpose of enabling findings of fact to be made;

(c) consider whether an order for interim contact pending the final hearing is in the interests of the child; and in particular that the safety of the child and the residential parent can be secured before, during and after any such contact;

(d) direct a report from a children and family reporter on the question of contact unless satisfied that it is not necessary to do so in order to safeguard the child's interests;

(e) subject to the seriousness of the allegations made and the difficulty of the case consider whether or not the children in question need to be separately represented in the proceedings; and, if the case is proceeding in the Family Proceedings Court, whether or not it should be transferred to the county court; if in the county court, whether or not it should be transferred to the High Court for hearing.

Directions to the children and family reporter in cases involving domestic violence

1.3 (a) Where the court orders a welfare report under s 7 of the Children Act 1989 in a disputed application for contact in which it considers domestic violence to be a relevant issue, the order of the court should contain specific directions to the children and family reporter to address the issue of domestic violence; to make an assessment of the harm which the children have suffered or which they are at risk of suffering if contact is ordered; to assess whether the safety of the child and the residential parent can be secured before, during and after contact; and to make particular efforts to ascertain the wishes and feelings of the children concerned in the light of the allegations of violence made.

(b) Where the court has made findings of fact prior to the children and family reporter conducting his or her investigation, the court should ensure that either a note of the court's judgment or of the findings of fact made by the court is made available to the children and family reporter as soon as is practicable after the findings have been made.

(c) Where, in a case involving allegations of domestic violence, the whereabouts of the child and the residential parent are known to the court but not known to the parent seeking contact; and where the court takes the view that it is in the best interests of the child or children concerned for that position to be maintained for the time being, the court should give directions designed to ensure that any welfare report on the circumstances of the residential parent and the child does not reveal their whereabouts, whether directly or indirectly.

Interim contact pending full hearing

1.4 In deciding any question of interim contact pending a full hearing the court should:

(a) specifically take into account the matters set out in s 1(3) of the Children Act 1989 ('the welfare check-list');

(b) give particular consideration to the likely risk of harm to the child, whether physical and/or emotional, if contact is either granted or refused;

(c) consider, if it decides such contact is in the interests of the child, what directions are required about how it is to be carried into effect; and, in particular, whether it should be supervised, and if so, by whom; and generally, in so far as it can, ensure that any risk of harm to the child is minimised and the safety of the child and residential parent before, during and after any such contact is secured;

(d) consider whether it should exercise its powers under s 42(2)(b) of the Family Law Act 1996 to make a non-molestation order;

(e) consider whether the parent seeking contact should seek advice and/or treatment as a precondition to contact being ordered or as a means of assisting the court in ascertaining the likely risk of harm to the child from that person at the final hearing.

Matters to be considered at the final hearing

1.5 At the final hearing of a contact application in which there are disputed allegations of domestic violence:

(a) the court should, wherever practicable, make findings of fact as to the nature and degree of the violence which is established on the balance of probabilities and its effect on the child and the parent with whom the child is living;

(b) in deciding the issue of contact the court should, in the light of the findings of fact which it has made, apply the individual items in the welfare checklist with reference to those findings; in particular, where relevant findings of domestic violence have been made, the court should in every case consider the harm which the child has suffered as a consequence of that violence and the harm which the child is at risk of suffering if an order for contact is made and only make an order for contact if it can be satisfied that the safety of the residential parent and the child can be secured before, during and after contact.

Matters to be considered where findings of domestic violence are made

1.6 In each case where a finding of domestic violence is made, the court should consider the conduct of both parents towards each other and towards the children; in particular, the court should consider:

(a) the effect of the domestic violence which has been established on the child and on the parent with whom the child is living;

(b) whether or not the motivation of the parent seeking contact is a desire to promote the best interests of the child or as a means of continuing a process of violence against or intimidation or harassment of the other parent;

(c) the likely behaviour of the parent seeking contact during contact and its effect on the child or children concerned;

(d) the capacity of the parent seeking contact to appreciate the effect of past and future violence on the other parent and the children concerned;

(e) the attitude of the parent seeking contact to past violent conduct by that parent; and, in particular, whether that parent has the capacity to change and/or to behave appropriately.

Matters to be considered where contact is ordered in a case where findings of domestic violence have been made

1.7 Where the court has made findings of domestic violence but, having applied the welfare checklist, nonetheless considers that direct contact is in the best interests of the child or children concerned, the court should consider (in addition to the matters set out in paragraphs 5 and 6 above) what directions are required to enable the order to be carried into effect under s 11(7) of the Children Act 1989 and, in particular, should consider:

(a) whether or not contact should be supervised, and if so, by whom;

(b) what conditions (for example, by way of seeking advice or treatment) should be complied with by the party in whose favour the order for contact has been made;

(c) whether the court should exercise its powers under s42(2)(b) of the Family Law Act 1996 to make a non-molestation order;

(d) whether such contact should be for a specified period or should contain provisions which are to have effect for a specified period;

(e) setting a date for the order to be reviewed and giving directions to ensure that the court at the review has full information about the operation of the order.

Information about local facilities

1.8   The court should also take steps to inform itself (alternatively direct the children and family reporter or the parties to inform it) of the facilities available locally to the court to assist parents who have been violent to their partners and/or their children, and, where appropriate, should impose as a condition of future contact that violent parents avail themselves of those facilities.

Reasons

1.9   In its judgment or reasons the court should always explain how its findings on the issue of domestic violence have influenced its decision on the issue of contact; and, in particular where the court has found domestic violence proved but nonetheless makes an order for contact, the court should always explain, whether by way of reference to the welfare check-list or otherwise, why it takes the view that contact is in the best interests of the child.

(8) List of disability organisations

Access Audit Co UK
9 Eastbourne Grove
Swansea SA2 9DR
tel 01792 549803

Association of Disabled Professionals
170 Benton Hill
Wakefield Road
Horbury
West Yorkshire WF4 5HW
tel/text 01924 270335 (please ask for ADP)
fax 01924 276498

Centre on Accessible Environments
Nutmeg House
60 Gainsford Street
London SE1 2NY
tel/minicom 0207 357 8182
fax 0207 357 8183

Churchill and Friend Ltd
Welltech Centre
Richway
Welwyn Garden City
Herts AL7 2AA
tel 01707 324466
fax 01707 324432
(Offers consultancy and training)

Dr Stephen Duckworth
Chief Executive
Disability Matters Ltd
The Old Dairy
Tiebridge Farm
North Houghton
Stockbridge
Hants SO20 6LQ
tel 01264 811120

Mik Standing
Training and Development Officer
Disability Wales/Anabledd Cymru
Wernddu Court
Caerffili Business Park
Van Road
Caerffili
Mid Glamorgan CF83 3ED
tel 0292 088 7325
fax 0292 088 8702

Employers Forum on Disability
Nutmeg House
60 Gainsford Street
London SE1 2NY
tel 0207 403 3020
fax 0207 400 0404

Equal Ability
170 Benton Hill
Wakefield Road
Horbury
West Yorkshire WF4 5HW
minicom 01924 270335
tel 01924 270335
fax 01924 276498
(Offers consultancy and training)

Tessa Harding
Planning and Development
Help the Aged
207–211 Pentonville Road
London N19 2DZ
tel 0207 278 1114
fax 0207 278 1116

Information Department
Royal Association for Disability and Rehabilitation (RADAR)
12 City Forum
250 City Road
London EC1V 8AF
tel 0207 250 3222
minicom 0207 250 4119
fax 0207 250 0212

Deborah Cooper
Director
SKILL (National Bureau for Students with Disabilities)
Chapter House
18–20 Crucifix Lane
London SE1 3JW
tel 0207 450 0620
fax 0207 450 0650

Other contacts listed in alphabetical order of disability

AUTISM

The National Autistic Society
393 City Road
London EC1V 1NE
tel 0207 833 2299

DYSLEXIA

Adult Dyslexia Organisation
336 Brixton Road
London SW9 7AA
tel 0207 737 7646
fax 0207 207 7796

EPILEPSY

The National Society for Epilepsy
Chesham Lane
Chalfont St Peter
Bucks SL9 0RJ
tel 01494 601300

FACIAL DISFIGUREMENT

Changing Faces
The Centre for Changing Faces
1 and 2 Junction Mews
Paddington
London W2 1PN
(Offers advice in connection with people with
facial disfigurements)
tel 0207 706 4232
fax 0207 706 4234

HEARING IMPAIRMENT

Bob Peckford
Director of Operations
**Council for the Advancement of
Communication with Deaf People**
Rooms 18–19, 1st Floor
London Fruit and Wool Exchange
Rushfield Street
London E1 6EX
tel 0207 422 0500

Royal Association of Deaf People
Walsingham Road
Colchester
Essex CO2 7BP
tel 01206 509509
fax 01206 769755
minicom 01206 577090

Jim Edwards
Director of Research and Development
Royal National Institute for Deaf People
19–23 Featherstone Street
London EC1Y 8SL
tel 0207 296 8000
fax 0207 296 8199
minicom 0207 296 8001

Sally Hawkins
Director
UK Council on Deafness
59 Banner Street
London EC1Y 8PX
tel 0207 689 2080
fax 0207 689 2082

LEARNING DIFFICULTIES

Ann Watson
Head of Campaigns
Mencap
123 Golden Lane
London EC1 0RT
tel 0207 454 0454
fax 0207 608 3254

People First
3rd Floor
299 Kentish Town Road
London NW5 2TJ
tel 0207 485 6660
fax 0207 485 6664

MENTAL HEALTH PROBLEMS

MIND
Granta House
15–19 Broadway
Stratford
London E15 4BQ
tel 0208 519 2122
fax 0208 519 1725

SCOPE
6 Market Road
London N7 9PW
tel 0207 619 7100
Helpline 0808 800 3333

VISUAL IMPAIRMENT

Jill Allen-King MBE
Public Relations Officer
National Federation of the Blind
59 Silversea Drive
Westcliff-on-Sea
Essex SS0 9XD
tel 01702 477899
fax 01702 477899

Jon Sacker
Campaigns Officer
Royal National Institute for the Blind
224 Great Portland Street
London W1W 5AA
tel 0207 388 1266
fax 0207 388 2034

Appendix D

FAMILY PROCEEDINGS RULES 1991 (AS AMENDED)

Family Proceedings Rules 1991
SI 1991/1247

PART I
PRELIMINARY

1.1 Citation and commencement
These rules may be cited as the Family Proceedings Rules 1991 and shall come into force on 14 October 1991.

1.2 Interpretation
(1) In these rules, unless the context otherwise requires –

"the Act of 1973" means the Matrimonial Causes Act 1973;
"the Act of 1984" means the Matrimonial and Family Proceedings Act 1984;
"the Act of 1986" means the Family Law Act 1986;
"the Act of 1989" means the Children Act 1989;
"the Act of 1991" means the Child Support Act 1991;
"ancillary relief" means –

   (*a*) an avoidance of disposition order,
   (*b*) a financial provision order,
   (*c*) an order for maintenance pending suit,
   (*d*) a property adjustment order,
   (*e*) a variation order, or
   (*f*) a pension sharing order;

"avoidance of disposition order" means an order under section 37(2)(*b*) or (*c*) of the Act of 1973;
"business day" has the meaning assigned to it by rule 1.5(6);
"cause" means a matrimonial cause as defined by section 32 of the Act of 1984 or proceedings under section 19 of the Act of 1973 (presumption of death and dissolution of marriage);
"child" and "child of the family" have, except in Part IV, the meanings respectively assigned to them by section 52(1) of the Act of 1973;
"consent order" means an order under section 33A of the Act of 1973;
"Contracting State" means –

   (*a*) one of the original parties to the Council Regulation, that is to say Belgium, Germany, Greece, Spain, France, Ireland, Italy, Luxembourg, the Netherlands, Austria, Portugal, Finland, Sweden and the United Kingdom, and
   (*b*) a party which has subsequently adopted the Council Regulation;

"the Council Regulation" means Council Regulation (EC) No 1347/2000 of 29 May 2000 on jurisdiction and the recognition and enforcement of judgments in matrimonial matters and in matters of parental responsibility for children of both spouses;
"court" means a judge or the district judge;
"court of trial" means a divorce county court designated by the Lord Chancellor as a court of trial pursuant to section 33(1) of the Act of 1984 and, in relation to matrimonial proceedings pending in a divorce county court, the principal registry shall be treated as a court of trial having its place of sitting at the Royal Courts of Justice;
"defended cause" means a cause not being an undefended cause;

"district judge", in relation to proceedings in the principal registry, a district registry or a county court, means the district judge or one of the district judges of that registry or county court, as the case may be;

"district registry", except in rule 4.22(2A), means any district registry having a divorce county court within its district;

"divorce county court" means a county court so designated by the Lord Chancellor pursuant to section 33(1) of the Act of 1984;

"divorce town", in relation to any matrimonial proceedings, means a place at which sittings of the High Court are authorised to be held outside the Royal Courts of Justice for the hearing of such proceedings or proceedings of the class to which they belong;

"document exchange" means any document exchange for the time being approved by the Lord Chancellor;

"family proceedings" has the meaning assigned to it by section 32 of the Act of 1984;

"financial provision order" means any of the orders mentioned in section 21(1) of the Act of 1973 except an order under section 27(6) of that Act;

"financial relief" has the same meaning as in section 37 of the Act of 1973;

"judge" does not include a district judge;

"notice of intention to defend" has the meaning assigned to it by rule 10.8;

"officer of the service" has the same meaning as in the Criminal Justice and Court Services Act 2000;

"order for maintenance pending suit" means an order under section 22 of the Act of 1973;

"person named" includes a person described as "passing under the name of A.B.";

"the President" means the President of the Family Division or, in the case of his absence or incapacity through illness or otherwise or of a vacancy in the office of President, the senior puisne judge of that Division;

"principal registry" means the Principal Registry of the Family Division;

"proper officer" means –

    (*a*) in relation to the principal registry, the family proceedings department manager, and

    (*b*) in relation to any other court or registry, the court manager,

    or other officer of the court or registry acting on his behalf in accordance with directions given by the Lord Chancellor;

"property adjustment order" means any of the orders mentioned in section 21(2) of the Act of 1973;

"registry for the divorce town" shall be construed in accordance with rule 2.32(6);

"Royal Courts of Justice", in relation to matrimonial proceedings pending in a divorce county court, means such place, being the Royal Courts of Justice or elsewhere, as may be specified in directions given by the Lord Chancellor pursuant to section 42(2)(*a*) of the Act of 1984;

"senior district judge" means the senior district judge of the Family Division or, in his absence from the principal registry, the senior of the district judges in attendance at the registry;

"special procedure list" has the meaning assigned to it by rule 2.24(3);

"undefended cause" means –

    (i) a cause in which no answer has been filed or any answer filed has been struck out, or

    (ii) a cause which is proceeding only on the respondent's answer and in which no reply or answer to the respondent's answer has been filed or any such reply or answer has been struck out, or

    (iii) a cause to which rule 2.12(4) applies and in which no notice has been given under that rule or any notice so given has been withdrawn, or

    (iv) a cause in which an answer has been filed claiming relief but in which no pleading has been filed opposing the grant of a decree on the petition or answer or any pleading or part of a pleading opposing the grant of such relief has been struck out, or

(v) any cause not within (i) to (iv) above in which a decree has been pronounced;

"variation order" means an order under section 31 of the Act of 1973.

(2) Unless the context otherwise requires, a cause begun by petition shall be treated as pending for the purposes of these rules notwithstanding that a final decree or order has been made on the petition.

(3) Unless the context otherwise requires, a rule or Part referred to by number means the rule or Part so numbered in these rules.

(4) In these rules a form referred to by number means the form so numbered in Appendix 1 or 1A to these rules with such variation as the circumstances of the particular case may require.

(5) In these rules any reference to an Order and rule is –

(a) if prefixed by the letters "CCR", a reference to that Order and rule in the County Court Rules 1981, and

(b) if prefixed by the letters "RSC", a reference to that Order and rule in the Rules of the Supreme Court 1965.

(5A) In these rules a reference to a Part or rule, if prefixed by the letters "CPR", is a reference to that Part or rule in the Civil Procedure Rules 1998.

(6) References in these rules to a county court shall, in relation to matrimonial proceedings, be construed as references to a divorce county court.

(7) In this rule and in rule 1.4, "matrimonial proceedings" means proceedings of a kind with respect to which divorce county courts have jurisdiction by or under section 33, 34 or 35 of the Act of 1984.

1.3 Application of other rules

(1) Subject to the provisions of these rules and of any enactment the County Court Rules 1981 and the Rules of the Supreme Court 1965 shall continue to apply, with the necessary modifications, to family proceedings in a county court and the High Court respectively.

(2) For the purposes of paragraph (1) any provision of these rules authorising or requiring anything to be done in family proceedings shall be treated as if it were, in the case of proceedings pending in a county court, a provision of the County Court Rules 1981 and, in the case of proceedings pending in the High Court, a provision of the Rules of the Supreme Court 1965.

1.4 County court proceedings in principal registry

(1) Subject to the provisions of these rules, matrimonial proceedings pending at any time in the principal registry which, if they had been begun in a divorce county court, would be pending at that time in such a court, shall be treated, for the purposes of these rules and of any provision of the County Court Rules 1981 and the County Courts Act 1984, as pending in a divorce county court and not in the High Court.

(2) Unless the context otherwise requires, any reference to a divorce county court in any provision of these rules which relates to the commencement or prosecution of proceedings in a divorce county court, or the transfer of proceedings to or from such a court, includes a reference to the principal registry.

1.5 Computation of time

(1) Any period of time fixed by these rules, or by any rules applied by these rules, or by any decree, judgment, order or direction for doing any act shall be reckoned in accordance with the following provisions of this rule.

(2) Where the act is required to be done not less than a specified period before a specified date, the period starts immediately after the date on which the act is done and ends immediately before the specified date.

(3) Where the act is required to be done within a specified period after or from a specified date, the period starts immediately after that date.

(4) Where, apart from this paragraph, the period in question, being a period of seven days or less, would include a day which is not a business day, that day shall be excluded.

(5) Where the time so fixed for doing an act in the court office expires on a day on which the office is closed, and for that reason the act cannot be done on that day, the act shall be in time if done on the next day on which the office is open.

(6) In these rules "business day" means any day other than –

> (*a*) a Saturday, Sunday, Christmas Day or Good Friday; or
> (*b*) a bank holiday under the Banking and Financial Dealings Act 1971, in England and Wales.

PART II
MATRIMONIAL CAUSES

2.1 Application of Part II

This Part applies –

> (*a*) to causes;
> (*b*) to applications under Part II of the Act of 1973, except sections 27, 32, 33, 35, 36 and 38; and
> (*c*) for specifying the procedure for complying with the requirements of section 41 of the Act of 1973.

Commencement etc of proceedings

2.2 Cause to be begun by petition

(1) Every cause shall be begun by petition.

(2) Where a petition for divorce, nullity or judicial separation discloses that there is a minor child of the family who is under 16 or who is over that age and is receiving instruction at an educational establishment or undergoing training for a trade or profession, the petition shall be accompanied by a statement, signed by the petitioner personally and if practicable agreed with the respondent, containing the information required by Form M4, to which shall be attached a copy of any medical report mentioned therein.

2.3 Contents of petition

Unless otherwise directed, every petition shall contain the information required by Appendix 2 to these rules.

2.4 Petitioner relying on section 11 or 12 of the Civil Evidence Act 1968

(1) A petitioner who, in reliance on section 11 or 12 of the Civil Evidence Act 1968, intends to adduce evidence that a person –

    (*a*) was convicted of an offence by or before a court in the United Kingdom or by a court-martial there or elsewhere, or

    (*b*) was found guilty of adultery in matrimonial proceedings or to be the father of a child in relevant proceedings before any court in England and Wales, or was adjudged to be the father of a child in affiliation proceedings before a court in the United Kingdom,

must include in his petition a statement of his intention with particulars of –

        (i) the conviction, finding or adjudication and the date thereof,

        (ii) the court or court-martial which made the conviction, finding or adjudication and, in the case of a finding or adjudication, the proceedings in which it was made, and

        (iii) the issue in the proceedings to which the conviction, finding or adjudication is relevant.

(2) In this rule "matrimonial proceedings", "relevant proceedings" and "affiliation proceedings" have the same meaning as in the said section 12.

2.5 Signing of petition

Every petition shall be signed by counsel if settled by him or, if not, by the petitioner's solicitor in his own name or the name of his firm, or by the petitioner if he sues in person.

2.6 Presentation of petition

(1) A petition may be presented to any divorce county court.

(2) Unless otherwise directed on an application made ex parte, a certificate of the marriage to which the cause relates shall be filed with the petition.

(3) Where a solicitor is acting for a petitioner for divorce or judicial separation, a certificate in Form M3 shall be filed with the petition, unless otherwise directed on an application made ex parte.

(4) Where there is before a divorce county court or the High Court a petition which has not been dismissed or otherwise disposed of by a final order, another petition by the same petitioner in respect of the same marriage shall not be presented without leave granted on an application made in the pending proceedings:

Provided that no such leave shall be required where it is proposed, after the expiration of the period of one year from the date of the marriage, to present a petition for divorce alleging such of the facts mentioned in section 1(2) of the Act of 1973 as were alleged in a petition for judicial separation presented before the expiration of that period.

(5) The petition shall be presented by filing it, together with any statement and report required by rule 2.2(2) in the court office, with as many copies of the petition as there are persons to be served and a copy of the statement and report required by rule 2.2(2) for service on the respondent.

(6) CCR Order 3, rule 4(2) (which, as applied by rule 5 of that Order, deals with the filing and service of petitions) shall not apply, but on the filing of the petition the proper officer shall annex to every copy of the petition for service a notice in Form M5 with Form M6 attached and shall also annex to the copy petition for service on a respondent the copy of any statement and report filed pursuant to paragraph (5) of this rule.

2.7 Parties

(1) Subject to paragraph (2), where a petition alleges that the respondent has committed adultery, the person with whom the adultery is alleged to have been committed shall be made a co-respondent in the cause unless –

    (*a*) that person is not named in the petition, or
    (*b*) the court otherwise directs.

(2) Where a petition alleges that the respondent has been guilty of rape upon a person named, then, notwithstanding anything in paragraph (1) that person shall not be made a co-respondent in the cause unless the court so directs.

(3) Where a petition alleges that the respondent has been guilty of an improper association (other than adultery) with a person named, the court may direct that the person named be made co-respondent in the cause, and for that purpose the district judge may require the proper officer to give notice to the petitioner and to any other party who has given notice of intention to defend of a date, time and place at which the court will consider giving such a direction.

(4) An application for directions under paragraph (1) may be made ex parte if no notice of intention to defend has been given.

(5) Paragraphs (1) and (3) of this rule do not apply where the person named has died before the filing of the petition.

2.8 Discontinuance of cause before service of petition

Before a petition is served on any person, the petitioner may file a notice of discontinuance and the cause shall thereupon stand dismissed.

Service of petition etc

2.9 Service of petition

(1) Subject to the provisions of this rule and rules 9.3 and 10.6, a copy of every petition shall be served personally or by post on every respondent or co-respondent.

(2) Service may be effected –

    (*a*) where the party to be served is a person under disability within the meaning of rule 9.1, through the petitioner, and
    (*b*) in any other case, through the court or, if the petitioner so requests, through the petitioner.

(3) Personal service shall in no case be effected by the petitioner himself.

(4) A copy of any petition which is to be served through the court shall be served by post by an officer of the court or, if on a request by the petitioner the district judge so directs, by a bailiff delivering a copy of the petition to the party personally.

(5) For the purposes of the foregoing paragraphs, a copy of a petition shall be deemed to be duly served if –

    (*a*) an acknowledgement of service in Form M6 is signed by the party to be served or by a solicitor on his behalf and is returned to the court office, and
    (*b*) where the form purports to be signed by the respondent, his signature is proved at the hearing or, where the cause is undefended, in the affidavit filed by the petitioner under rule 2.24(3).

(6) Where a copy of a petition has been sent to a party and no acknowledgment of service has been returned to the court office, the district judge, if satisfied by affidavit or otherwise that the party has nevertheless received the document, may direct that the document shall be deemed to have been duly served on him.

(6A) Paragraph (6) shall not apply in cases where –

(*a*) the petition alleges two years' separation coupled with the respondent's consent to a decree being granted; and

(*b*) none of the other facts mentioned in section 1(2) of the Act of 1973 is alleged,

unless the petititioner produces to the court a written statement containing the respondent's consent to the grant of a decree.

(7) Where a copy of a petition has been served on a party personally and no acknowledgement of service has been returned to the court office, service shall be proved by filing an affidavit of service (or, in the case of service by bailiff, an indorsement of service under CCR Order 7, rule 6) showing, in the case of a respondent, the server's means of knowledge of the identity of the party served.

(8) Where an acknowledgement of service is returned to the court office, the proper officer shall send a photographic copy thereof to the petitioner.

(9) An application for leave to substitute some other mode of service for the modes of service prescribed by paragraph (1) or to substitute notice of the proceedings by advertisement or otherwise, shall be made ex parte by lodging an affidavit setting out the grounds on which the application is made; and the form of any advertisement shall be settled by the district judge:

Provided that no order giving leave to substitute notice of the proceedings by advertisement shall be made unless it appears to the district judge that there is a reasonable probability that the advertisement will come to the knowledge of the person concerned.

(10) CCR Order 7, rule 8 shall apply in relation to service by bailiff under this rule as it applies to service of a summons by bailiff in accordance with rule 10 of that Order.

(11) Where in the opinion of the district judge it is impracticable to serve a party in accordance with any of the foregoing paragraphs or it is otherwise necessary or expedient to dispense with service of a copy of a petition on the respondent or on any other person, the district judge may make an order dispensing with such service.

An application for an order under this paragraph shall be made in the first instance ex parte by lodging an affidavit setting out the grounds of the application, but the district judge may, if he thinks fit, require the attendance of the petitioner on the application.

2.10 Consent to grant of decree

(1) Where, before the hearing of a petition alleging two years' separation coupled with the respondent's consent to a decree being granted, the respondent wishes to indicate to the court that he consents to the grant of a decree, he shall do so by filing a notice to that effect signed by the respondent personally.

For the purposes of this paragraph an acknowledgement of service containing a statement that the respondent consents to the grant of a decree shall be treated as such a notice if the acknowledgement is signed –

(*a*) in the case of a respondent acting in person, by the respondent, or

(*b*) in the case of a respondent represented by a solicitor, by the respondent as well as by the solicitor.

(2) A respondent to a petition which alleges any such fact as is mentioned in paragraph (1) may give notice to the court either that he does not consent to a decree being granted or that he withdraws any consent which he has already given.

Where any such notice is given and none of the other facts mentioned in section 1(2) of the Act of 1973 is alleged, the proceedings on the petition shall be stayed and the proper officer shall thereupon give notice of the stay to all parties.

Pleadings and amendment

2.11 Supplemental petition and amendment of petition

(1) Subject to rule 2.14 –

    (*a*) a supplemental petition may be filed without leave at any time before an answer is filed but thereafter only with leave; and

    (*b*) a petition may be amended without leave at any time before an answer is filed but thereafter only with leave.

(2) Subject to paragraph (3) an application for leave under this rule –

    (*a*) may if every opposite party consents in writing to the supplemental petition being filed or the petition being amended, be made by lodging in the court office the supplemental petition or a copy of the petition as proposed to be amended; and

    (*b*) shall, in any other case, be made on notice (or in the High Court by summons) to be served, unless otherwise directed, on every opposite party.

(3) The district judge may, if he thinks fit, require an application for leave to be supported by an affidavit.

(4) An order granting leave shall –

    (*a*) where any party has given notice of intention to defend, fix the time within which his answer must be filed or amended;

    (*b*) where the order is made after directions for trial have been given, provide for a stay of the hearing until after the directions have been renewed.

(5) An amendment authorised to be made under this rule shall be made by filing a copy of the amended petition.

(6) Rules 2.5 and 2.7 shall apply to a supplemental or amended petition as they apply to the original petition.

(7) Unless otherwise directed, a copy of a supplemental or amended petition, together with a copy of the order (if any) made under this rule shall be served on every respondent and co-respondent named in the original petition or in the supplemental or amended petition.

(8) The petitioner shall file the documents required by paragraph (7) to be served on any person and thereupon, unless otherwise directed, rules 2.6(6) and 2.9 shall apply in relation to that person as they apply in relation to a person required to be served with an original petition.

2.12 Filing of answer to petition

(1) Subject to paragraph (2) and to rules 2.10, 2.14 and 2.37, a respondent or co-respondent who –

    (*a*) wishes to defend the petition or to dispute any of the facts alleged in it,

    (*b*) being the respondent wishes to make in the proceedings any charge against the petitioner in respect of which the respondent prays for relief, or

(*c*) being the respondent to a petition to which section 5(1) of the Act of 1973 applies,
wishes to oppose the grant of a decree on the ground mentioned in that subsection,
shall, within 21 days after the expiration of the time limited for giving notice of intention
to defend, file an answer to the petition.

(2) An answer may be filed notwithstanding that the person filing the answer has not
given notice of intention to defend.

(3) Any reference in these rules to a person who has given notice of intention to defend
shall be construed as including a reference to a person who has filed an answer without
giving notice of intention to defend.

(4) Where in a cause in which relief is sought under section 12(*d*) of the Act of 1973 the
respondent files an answer containing no more than a simple denial of the facts stated in
the petition, he shall, if he intends to rebut the charges in the petition, give the court notice
to that effect when filing his answer.

2.13 Filing of reply and subsequent pleadings

(1) A petitioner may file a reply to an answer within 14 days after he has received a copy
of the answer pursuant to rule 2.17.

(2) If the petitioner does not file a reply to an answer, he shall, unless the answer prays for
a degree, be deemed, on making a request for directions for trial, to have denied every
material allegation of fact made in the answer.

(3) No pleading subsequent to a reply shall be filed without leave.

2.14 Filing and amendment of pleadings after directions for trial

No pleading shall be filed or amended without leave after directions for trial have been
given.

2.15 Contents of answer and subsequent pleadings

(1) Where an answer, reply or subsequent pleading contains more than a simple denial of
the facts stated in the petition, answer or reply, as the case may be, the pleading shall set
out with sufficient particularity the facts relied on but not the evidence by which they are
to be proved and, if the pleading is filed by the husband or wife, it shall, in relation to
those facts, contain the information required in the case of a petition by paragraph 1(*k*) of
Appendix 2.

(2) Unless otherwise directed, an answer by a husband or wife who disputes any statement
required by paragraphs 1(*f*), (*g*) and (*h*) of Appendix 2 to be included in the petition shall
contain full particulars of the facts relied on.

(3) Paragraph 4(*a*) of Appendix 2 shall, where appropriate, apply with the necessary
modifications, to a respondent's answer as it applies to a petition:

 Provided that it shall not be necessary to include in the answer any claim for costs against
the petitioner.

(4) Where an answer to any petition contains a prayer for relief, it shall contain the
information required by paragraph 1(*j*) of Appendix 2 in the case of the petition in so far
as it has not been given by the petitioner.

(5) Where a party's pleading includes such a statement as is mentioned in rule 2.4, then if
the opposite party –

(*a*) denies the conviction, finding or adjudication to which the statement relates, or

(*b*) alleges that the conviction, finding or adjudication was erroneous, or

(*c*) denies that the conviction, finding or adjudication is relevant to any issue in the proceedings,

he must make the denial or allegation in his pleading.

(6) Rules 2.4 and 2.5 shall apply, with the necessary modifications, to a pleading other than a petition as they apply to a petition.

2.16 Allegation against third person in pleading

(1) Rules 2.7 and 2.9 shall apply, with the necessary modifications, to a pleading other than a petition as they apply to a petition, so however that for the references in those rules to a co-respondent there shall be substituted references to a party cited.

(2) Rule 2.12 shall apply, with the necessary modifications, to a party cited as it applies to a co-respondent.

2.17 Service of pleadings

A party who files an answer, reply or subsequent pleading shall at the same time file a copy for service on every opposite party, and thereupon the proper officer shall annex to every copy for service on a party cited in the pleading a notice in Form M5 with Form M6 attached and shall send a copy to every other opposite party.

2.18 Supplemental answer and amendment of pleadings

Rule 2.11 shall apply, with the necessary modifications, to the filing of a supplemental answer, and the amendment of a pleading or other document not being a petition, as it applies to the filing of a supplemental petition and the amendment of a petition.

2.19 Particulars

(1) A party on whom a pleading has been served may in writing request the party whose pleading it is to give particulars of any allegation or other matter pleaded and, if that party fails to give the particulars within a reasonable time, the party requiring them may apply for an order that the particulars be given.

(2) The request or order in pursuance of which particulars are given shall be incorporated with the particulars, each item of the particulars following immediately after the corresponding item of the request or order.

(3) A party giving particulars, whether in pursuance of an order or otherwise, shall at the same time file a copy of them.

Preparations for trial

2.20 Discovery of documents in defended cause

(1) RSC Order 24 (discovery and inspection of documents) shall apply to a defended cause begun by petition whether pending in the High Court or county court as it applies to an action begun by writ, with the following modifications –

(*a*) the second paragraph of rule 2(1) and rules 2(2) to (4), rules 4(2), 6 and 7A shall be omitted,

(*b*) in rule 16(1) the words from "including" to the end shall be omitted,

(*c*) in rule 2(7) for the words "the summons for directions in the action is taken out" there shall be substituted the words "directions for trial are given".

(2) For the purposes of RSC Order 24, rule 2(1) as applied by paragraph (1) of this rule, pleadings shall be deemed to be closed at the expiration of 14 days after service of the answer, and are deemed to be closed then notwithstanding that any request or order for particulars previously made has not been complied with.

(3) The petitioner and any party who has filed an answer shall be entitled to have a copy of any list of documents served on any other party under RSC Order 24 as applied by paragraph (1) of this rule, and such copy shall, on request, be supplied to him free of charge by the party who served the list.

In this paragraph "list of documents" includes an affidavit verifying the list.

2.21 Discovery by interrogatories in defended cause

(1) RSC Order 26 (which deals with discovery by interrogatories) shall apply to a defended cause begun by petition and pending in the High Court as it applies to a cause within the meaning of that Order, but with the omission of –

(*a*) rule 2(1)(*b*),

(*b*) in rule 4(1) the words "or the notice under Order 25, rule 7," and

(*c*) in rule 6(1) the words from "including" to the end.

(2) A copy of the proposed interrogatories shall be filed when they are served under RSC Order 26, rule 3(1) or when a summons for an order under RSC Order 26, rule 1(2) is issued.

(3) Where a defended cause is pending in a divorce county court RSC Order 26 as applied by CCR Order 14, rule 11, shall apply, and references in this rule to provisions of the said Order 26 shall be construed as references to those provisions as so applied.

2.22 Medical examination in proceedings for nullity

(1) In proceedings for nullity on the ground of incapacity to consummate the marriage the petitioner shall, subject to paragraph (2), apply to the district judge to determine whether medical inspectors should be appointed to examine the parties.

(2) An application under paragraph (1) shall not be made in an undefended cause –

(*a*) if the husband is the petitioner, or

(*b*) if the wife is the petitioner and –

    (i) it appears from the petition that she was either a widow or divorced at the time of the marriage in question, or

    (ii) it appears from the petition or otherwise that she has borne a child, or

    (iii) a statement by the wife that she is not a virgin is filed;

unless, in any such case, the petitioner is alleging his or her own incapacity.

(3) References in paragraphs (1) and (2) to the petitioner shall, where the cause is proceeding only on the respondent's answer or where the allegation of incapacity is made only in the respondent's answer, be construed as references to the respondent.

(4) An application under paragraph (1) by the petitioner shall be made –

(*a*) where the respondent has not given notice of intention to defend, after the time limited for giving the notice has expired;

(*b*) where the respondent has given notice of intention to defend, after the expiration of the time allowed for filing his answer or, if he has filed an answer, after it has been filed;

and an application under paragraph (1) by the respondent shall be made after he has filed an answer.

(5) Where the party required to make an application under paragraph (1) fails to do so within a reasonable time, the other party may, if he is prosecuting or defending the cause, make an application under that paragraph.

(6) In proceedings for nullity on the ground that the marriage has not been consummated owing to the wilful refusal of the respondent, either party may apply to the district judge for the appointment of medical inspectors to examine the parties.

(7) If the respondent has not given notice of intention to defend, an application by the petitioner under paragraph (1) or (6) may be made ex parte.

(8) If the district judge hearing an application under paragraph (1) or (6) considers it expedient to do so, he shall appoint a medical inspector or, if he thinks it necessary, two medical inspectors to examine the parties and report to the court the result of the examination.

(9) At the hearing of any such proceedings as are referred to in paragraph (1) the court may, if it thinks fit, appoint a medical inspector or two medical inspectors to examine any party who has not been examined or to examine further any party who has been examined.

(10) The party on whose application an order under paragraph (8) is made or who has the conduct of proceedings in which an order under paragraph (9) has been made for the examination of the other party, shall serve on the other party notice of the date, time and place appointed for his or her examination.

2.23 Conduct of medical examination

(1) Every medical examination under rule 2.22 shall be held at the consulting room of the medical inspector or, as the case may be, of one of the medical inspectors appointed to conduct the examination:

 Provided that the district judge may, on the application of a party, direct that the examination of that party shall be held at the court office or at such other place as the district judge thinks convenient.

(2) Every party presenting himself for examination shall sign, in the presence of the inspector or inspectors, a statement that he is the person referred to as the petitioner or respondent, as the case may be, in the order for the examination, and at the conclusion of the examination the inspector or inspectors shall certify on the statement that it was signed in his or their presence by the person who has been examined.

(3) Every report made in pursuance of rule 2.22 shall be filed and either party shall be entitled to be supplied with a copy on payment of the prescribed fee.

(4) In an undefended cause it shall not be necessary for the inspector or inspectors to attend and give evidence at the trial unless so directed.

(5) In a defended cause, if the report made in pursuance of rule 2.22 is accepted by both parties, notice to that effect shall be given by the parties to the district judge and to the inspector or inspectors not less than seven clear days before the date fixed for the trial; and where such notice is given, it shall not be necessary for the inspector or inspectors to attend and give evidence at the trial.

(6) Where pursuant to paragraphs (4) or (5) the evidence of the inspector or inspectors is not given at the trial, his or their report shall be treated as information furnished to the court by a court expert and be given such weight as the court thinks fit.

2.24 Directions for trial

(1) On the written request of the petitioner or of any party who is defending a cause begun by petition the district judge shall give directions for the trial of the cause if he is satisfied –

> (*a*) that a copy of the petition (including any supplemental or amended petition) and any subsequent pleading has been duly served on every party required to be served and, where that party is a person under disability, that an affidavit required by rule 9.3(2) has been filed;
>
> (*b*) if no notice of intention to defend has been given by any party entitled to give it, that the time limited for giving such notice has expired;
>
> (*c*) if notice of intention to defend has been given by any party, that the time allowed him for filing an answer has expired;
>
> (*d*) if an answer has been filed, that the time allowed for filing any subsequent pleadings has expired;
>
> (*e*) in proceedings for nullity –
>> (i) that any application required by rule 2.22(1) has been made, and
>> (ii) where an order for the examination of the parties has been made on an application under rule 2.22, that the notice required by paragraph (10) of that rule has been served and that the report of the inspector or inspectors has been filed.

(2) Subject to paragraph (3), where the cause is pending in a divorce county court other than the principal registry and is to be tried at that court, the district judge shall, if he considers it practicable to do so, give directions for trial.

(3) Where the cause is an undefended cause for divorce or judicial separation and, in a case to which section 1(2)(*d*) of the Act of 1973 applies, the respondent has filed a notice under rule 2.10(1) that he consents to the grant of a decree, then, unless otherwise directed, there shall be filed with the request for directions for trial an affidavit by the petitioner –

> (*a*) containing the information required by Form M7(*a*), (*b*), (*c*), (*d*), or (*e*) (whichever is appropriate) as near as may be in the order there set out, together with any corroborative evidence on which the petitioner intends to rely, and
>
> (*b*) verifying, with such amendments as the circumstances may require, the contents of any statement of arrangements filed by the petitioner under rule 2.2(2),

and the district judge shall give directions for trial by entering the cause in a list to be known as the special procedure list.

(4) In the case of a defended cause the district judge may treat the request for directions for trial as a summons or application for directions so as to enable him to give such directions with regard to –

> (*a*) the future course of the cause,
>
> (*b*) any application made therein for ancillary relief or for an order relating to a child, and
>
> (*c*) the provision of evidence relating to the arrangements or proposed arrangements for the children of the family,

as appear to be necessary or desirable for securing the just, expeditious and economical disposal of the cause or application; and the proper officer shall give the parties notice of a date, time and place at which the request will be considered.

(5) In any other case the district judge shall give directions for trial by requiring the proper officer to set the cause down for trial and give notice that he has done so to every party to the cause.

(6) Except where evidence has been provided under paragraph (3)(*b*), directions for trial under this rule shall, unless the court orders otherwise, include a direction to the petitioner to file an affidavit verifying, with such amendments as the circumstances may require, the contents of any statement of arrangements filed by the petitioner under rule 2.2(2).

(7) In the case of an undefended cause proceeding on the respondent's answer, paragraphs (3) and (6) shall have effect as if for the references to the petitioner and respondent there were substituted references to the respondent and the petitioner respectively.

2.25 Determination of place of trial

(1) Directions for trial, except where given under rule 2.24(3), shall determine the place of trial.

(2) In the case of an undefended cause to which rule 2.24(3) does not apply, the request for directions shall state –

- (*a*) the place of trial desired,
- (*b*) the place where the witnesses whom it is proposed to call at the trial reside,
- (*c*) an estimate of the probable length of trial, and
- (*d*) any other fact which may be relevant for determining the place of trial.

(3) In the case of a defended cause, the party intending to make a request for directions shall, not less than eight days before making his request, give notice of the place of trial desired to every other party who has given notice of intention to defend and, if the party intending to make the request is the respondent, to the petitioner.

The notice shall state the number of witnesses to be called on behalf of the party giving the notice and the places where he and his witnesses reside.

(4) If any party to whom notice is given under paragraph (3) does not consent to the place of trial specified in the notice, he may, within eight days after receiving it, apply to the district judge to direct trial at some other place; and if he does consent to the place so specified, he shall within that period send to the party by whom the notice was given a statement signed by his solicitor (or by him, if he is acting in person) indicating that the notice has been received and specifying the number of witnesses to be called on his behalf and the places where he and his witnesses reside.

(5) Where no application for trial at some other place is made under paragraph (4) within the period specified in that paragraph, the party making the request for directions shall state in his request –

- (*a*) the place of trial desired;
- (*b*) the number of witnesses to be called on his behalf and the places where he and his witnesses reside;
- (*c*) if it be the case, that no statement has been received from any party (naming him) to whom notice was given under paragraph (3); and
- (*d*) an estimate of the probable length of trial;

and shall file with the request any statement sent to him by any other party in accordance with paragraph (4).

(6) If circumstances arise tending to show that the estimate of the probable length of the trial given under paragraph (2)(*c*) or (5)(*d*) or made on an application under paragraph (4) is inaccurate, a further estimate shall be filed.

(7) In determining the place of trial the district judge shall have regard to all the circumstances of the case so far as it is possible for him to do so on the basis of the information available to him, including the convenience of the parties and their witnesses, the costs likely to be incurred, the date on which the trial can take place and the estimated length of the trial.

(8) Directions determining the place of trial of any cause may be varied by the district judge of the court or registry in which the cause is proceeding on the application of any party to the cause.

2.26 Directions as to allegations under section 1(2)(b) of Act of 1973

(1) Where in a defended cause the petitioner alleges that the respondent has behaved in such a way that the petitioner cannot reasonably be expected to live with the respondent, the district judge may, of his own motion on giving directions for trial or on the application of any party made at any time before the trial, order or authorise the party who has made the request for or obtained such directions to file a schedule of the allegations and counter-allegations made in the pleadings or particulars.

(2) Where such an order is made or authority given, the allegations and counter-allegations shall, unless otherwise directed, be listed concisely in chronological order, each counter-allegation being set out against the allegation to which it relates, and the party filing the schedule shall serve a copy of it on any other party to the cause who has filed a pleading.

2.27 Stay under Domicile and Matrimonial Proceedings Act 1973

(1) An application to the court by the petitioner or respondent in proceedings for divorce for an order under paragraph 8 of Schedule 1 to the Domicile and Matrimonial Proceedings Act 1973 (in this rule referred to as "Schedule 1") shall be made to the district judge, who may determine the application or refer the application, or any question arising thereon, to a judge for his decision as if the application were an application for ancillary relief.

(2) An application for an order under paragraph 9 of Schedule 1 shall be made to a judge.

(3) Where, on giving directions for trial, it appears to the district judge from any information given in pursuant to paragraph 1(*j*) of Appendix 2 or rule 2.15(4) or paragraph (4) of this rule that any proceedings which are in respect of the marriage in question or which are capable of affecting its validity or subsistence are continuing in any country outside England and Wales and he considers that the question whether the proceedings on the petition should be stayed under paragraph 9 of Schedule 1 ought to be determined by the court, he shall fix a date, time and place for the consideration of that question by a judge and give notice thereof to all parties.

In this paragraph "proceedings continuing in any country outside England and Wales" has the same meaning as in paragraph 1(*j*) of Appendix 2.

(4) Any party who makes a request for directions for trial in matrimonial proceedings within the meaning of paragraph 2 of Schedule 1 shall, if there has been a change in the information given pursuant to paragraph 1(*j*) of Appendix 2 and rule 2.15(4) file a statement giving particulars of the change.

(5) An application by a party to the proceedings for an order under paragraph 10 of Schedule 1 may be made to the district judge, and he may determine the application or may refer the application, or any question arising thereon, to a judge as if the application were an application for ancillary relief.

2.27A Stay under the Council Regulation

(1) An application for an order under Article 11 of the Council Regulation shall be made to a district judge, who may determine the application or refer the application, or any question arising thereon, to a judge for his decision as if the application were an application for ancillary relief.

(2) Where at any time after the presentation of a petition, it appears to the court that, under Articles 9, 10 or 11 of the Council Regulation, the court does not have jurisdiction to hear the petition and is required or may be required to stay the proceedings, the Court shall stay the proceedings and fix a date for a hearing to determine the questions of jurisdiction and whether there should be a stay or other order and shall serve notice of the hearing on the parties to the proceedings.

(3) The court must give reasons for its decision under Articles 9, 10 or 11 of the Council Regulation and, where it makes a finding of fact, state such finding of fact.

(4) An order under Article 9 of the Council Regulation that the court has no jurisdiction over the proceedings shall be recorded by the court or the proper officer in writing.

(5) The court may, if all parties agree, deal with any question about the jurisdiction of the court without a hearing.

Evidence

2.28 Evidence at trial of cause

(1) Subject to the provisions of this rule and rules 2.29, 2.36 and 10.14 and of the Civil Evidence Act 1995 and any other enactment, any fact required to be proved by the evidence of witnesses at the trial of a cause begun by petition shall be proved by the examination of the witnesses orally and in open court.

(2) Nothing in this rule and rules 2.29 and 10.14 shall affect the power of the judge at the trial to refuse to admit any evidence if in the interest of justice he thinks fit to do so.

(3) The court may order –

    (*a*) that the affidavit of any witnesses may be read at the trial on such conditions as the court thinks reasonable;

    (*b*) that the evidence of any particular fact shall be given at the trial in such manner as may be specified in the order and in particular –

        (i) by statement on oath of information or belief, or

        (ii) by the production of documents or entries in books, or

        (iii) by copies of documents or entries in books, or

        (iv) in the case of a fact which is or was a matter of common knowledge either generally or in a particular district, by the production of a specified newspaper containing a statement of that fact; and

    (*c*) that not more than a specified number of expert witnesses may be called.

(4) An application to the district judge for an order under paragraph (3) shall –

    (*a*) if no notice of intention to defend has been given, or

    (*b*) if the petitioner and every party who has given notice of intention to defend consents to the order sought, or

    (*c*) if the cause is undefended and directions for trial have been given, be made ex parte by filing an affidavit stating the grounds on which the application is made.

(5) Where an application is made before the trial for an order that the affidavit of a witness may be read at the trial or that evidence of a particular fact may be given at the trial by affidavit, the proposed affidavit or a draft thereof shall be submitted with the

application; and where the affidavit is sworn before the hearing of the application and sufficiently states the ground on which the application is made, no other affidavit shall be required under paragraph (4).

2.29 Evidence by deposition

The court may, on the application of any party to a cause begun by petition, make an order under CCR Order 20, rule 13, or (if the cause is pending in the High Court) under RSC Order 39, rule 1, for the examination on oath of any person; and CCR Order 20, rule 13 or (if the cause is pending in the High Court) RSC Order 38, rule 9, and Order 39, rules 1 to 14 (which regulate the procedure where evidence is to be taken by deposition) shall have effect accordingly with the appropriate modifications.

2.30 Issue of witness summons or subpoena

(1) A witness summons in a cause pending in a divorce county court may be issued in that court or in the court of trial at which the cause is to be tried.

(2) A writ of subpoena in a cause pending in the High Court may issue out of –

  (*a*) the registry in which the cause is proceeding; or
  (*b*) if the cause is to be tried at the Royal Courts of Justice, the principal registry; or
  (*c*) if the cause is to be tried at a divorce town, the registry for that town.

2.31

(*revoked*)

Trial etc

2.32 Mode and place of trial

(1) Unless otherwise directed and subject to rule 2.36 every cause and any issue arising therein shall be tried by a judge without a jury.

(2) Any cause begun by petition (except one entered in the special procedure list) which is pending in a divorce county court may be tried at any court of trial.

(3) Any cause begun by petition which is pending in the High Court may be tried at the Royal Courts of Justice or at any divorce town.

(4) A judge or the district judge of the registry for the divorce town at which any cause has been set down for trial may, where it appears to him that the cause cannot conveniently be tried at that town, order that it be tried at some other divorce town; and rule 10.10(4) and (5) shall apply to such an order as it applies to an order under paragraph (1) of that rule.

(5) As soon as practicable after a cause pending in a divorce county court has been set down for trial, the proper officer of the court of trial shall fix the date, place and, as nearly as may be, the time of the trial and give notice thereof to every party to the cause.

(6) In these rules any reference to the registry for the divorce town at which a cause is to be tried shall, in relation to a divorce town in which there is no district registry, be construed as a reference to such district registry as the Lord Chancellor may designate for the purpose or, if the divorce town is not situated within the district of any district registry, as a reference to the principal registry.

2.33 Trial of issue

Where directions are given for the separate trial of any issue and those directions have been complied with, the district judge shall –

    (*a*) if the issue arises on an application for ancillary relief or an application with respect to any child or alleged child of the family, proceed as if the issue were a question referred to a judge on an application for ancillary relief and rule 2.65 shall apply accordingly;

    (*b*) in any other case, set the issue down for trial and thereupon rule 2.32(5) and (6) shall apply as if the issue were a cause.

2.34 Exercise of district judge's jurisdiction in causes set down for trial

(1) The district judge of the registry for the divorce town at which a cause has been set down for trial, or, in the case of a cause set down for a trial at the Royal Courts of Justice, a district judge of the principal registry may, if it appears to him to be desirable having regard to the proximity of the date of trial or otherwise, exercise in the cause any jurisdiction of the district judge of the registry in which the cause is proceeding.

(2) RSC Order 34, rule 5(3) shall apply, with the necessary modifications, to a defended cause pending in the High Court as it applies to an action begun by writ.

2.35 Further provisions as to date of trial

Except with the consent of the parties or by leave of a judge, no cause, whether defended or undefended, shall be tried until after the expiration of 10 days from the date on which directions for trial were given:

Provided that nothing in this rule shall apply to a cause entered in the special procedure list.

2.36 Disposal of causes in special procedure list

(1) As soon as practicable after a cause has been entered in the special procedure list, the district judge shall consider the evidence filed by the petitioner and –

    (*a*) if he is satisfied that the petitioner has sufficiently proved the contents of the petition and is entitled to a decree the district judge shall so certify;

    (*b*) if he is not so satisfied he may either give the petitioner an opportunity of filing further evidence or remove the cause from the special procedure list whereupon rule 2.24(3) shall cease to apply.

(2) On the making of a certificate under paragraph (1) a date shall be fixed for the pronouncement of a decree by a judge or district judge in open court and the proper officer shall send to each party notice of the date and place so fixed and a copy of the certificate, but subject to paragraph (3) it shall not be necessary for any party to appear on that occasion.

(3) Where the district judge makes a certificate under paragraph (1) and the petition contains a prayer for costs, the district judge may –

    (*a*) if satisfied that the petitioner is entitled to such costs, include in his certificate a statement to that effect;

    (*b*) if not so satisfied, give to any party who objects to paying such costs notice that, if he wishes to proceed with his objection, he must attend before the court on the date fixed pursuant to paragraph (2).

(4) Within 14 days after the pronouncement of a decree in accordance with a certificate under paragraph (1) any person may inspect the certificate and the evidence filed under rule 2.24(3) (except the statement of arrangements) and may bespeak copies on payment of the prescribed fee.

2.37 Right to be heard on question of costs

(1) A respondent, co-respondent or party cited may, without filing an answer, be heard on any question as to costs, but the court may at any time order any party objecting to a claim for costs to file and serve on the party making the claim a written statement setting out the reasons for his objection.

(2) A party shall be entitled to be heard on any question pursuant to paragraph (1) whether or not he has returned to the court office an acknowledgment of service stating his wish to be heard on that question.

(3) In proceedings after a decree nisi of divorce or a decree of judicial separation no order the effect of which would be to make a co-respondent or party cited liable for costs which are not directly referable to the decree shall be made unless the co-respondent or party cited is a party to such proceedings or has been given notice of the intention to apply for such an order.

2.38 Respondent's statement as to arrangements for children

(1) A respondent on whom there is served a statement in accordance with rule 2.2(2) may, whether or not he agreed that statement, file in the court office a written statement of his views on the present and proposed arrangements for the children, and on receipt of such a statement from the respondent the proper officer shall send a copy to the petitioner.

(2) Any such statement of the respondent's views shall, if practicable, be filed within the time limited for giving notice of intention to defend and in any event before the district judge considers the arrangements or proposed arrangements for the upbringing and welfare of the children of the family under section 41(1) of the Act of 1973.

2.39 Procedure for complying with section 41 of Act of 1973

(1) Where no such application as is referred to in rule 2.40(1) is pending the district judge shall, after making his certificate under rule 2.36(1)(*a*) or after the provision of evidence pursuant to a direction under rule 2.24(4), as the case may be, proceed to consider the matters specified in section 41(1) of the Act of 1973 in accordance with the following provisions of this rule.

(2) Where, on consideration of the relevant evidence, including any further evidence or report provided pursuant to this rule and any statement filed by the respondent under rule 2.38, the district judge is satisfied that –

(*a*) there are no children of the family to whom section 41 of the Act of 1973 applies, or
(*b*) there are such children but the court need not exercise its powers under the Act of 1989 with respect to any of them or give any direction under section 41(2) of the Act of 1973,

the district judge shall certify accordingly and, in a case to which sub-paragraph (*b*) applies, the petitioner and the respondent shall each be sent a copy of the certificate by the proper officer.

(3) Where the district judge is not satisfied as mentioned in paragraph (2) above he may, without prejudice to his powers under the Act of 1989 or section 41(2) of the Act of 1973, give one or more of the following directions –

    (*a*) that the parties, or any of them, shall file further evidence relating to the arrangements for the children (and the direction shall specify the matters to be dealt with in further evidence);

    (*b*) that a welfare report on the children, or any of them, be prepared;

    (*c*) that the parties, or any of them, shall attend before him at the date, time and place specified in the direction;

and the parties shall be notified accordingly.

(4) Where the court gives a direction under section 41(2) of the Act of 1973, notice of the direction shall be given to the parties.

(5) In this rule "parties" means the petitioner, the respondent and any person who appears to the court to have the care of the child.

2.40 Applications relating to children of the family

(1) Where a cause is pending, an application by a party to the cause or by any other person for an order under any provision of Part I or Part II of the Act of 1989 in relation to a child of the family shall be made in the cause; and where the applicant is not a party and has obtained such leave as is required under the Act of 1989 to make the application, no leave to intervene in the cause shall be necessary.

(2) If, while a cause is pending, proceedings relating to any child of the family are begun in any other court, a concise statement of the nature of the proceedings shall forthwith be filed by the person beginning the proceedings or, if he is not a party to the cause, by the petitioner.

(3) A cause shall be treated as pending for the purposes of this rule for a period of one year after the last hearing or judicial intervention in the cause and rule 1.2(2) shall not apply.

2.41 Restoration of matters adjourned at the hearing

Where at the trial of a cause any application is adjourned by the court for hearing in chambers, it may be restored –

    (*a*) in the High Court, by notice without a summons;

    (*b*) in a divorce county court, on notice under CCR Order 13, rule 1 (which deals with applications in the course of proceedings); or

    (*c*) in the High Court or a divorce county court, by notice given by the district judge when in his opinion the matter ought to be further considered;

and the notice shall state the date, time and place for the hearing of the restored application and be served on every party concerned.

2.42 Application for re-hearing

(1) An application for re-hearing of a cause tried by a judge alone (whether in the High Court or a divorce county court) where no error of the court at the hearing is alleged, shall be made to a judge.

(2) Unless otherwise directed, the application shall be made to the judge by whom the cause was tried and shall be heard in open court.

(3) The application shall be made –

> (*a*) in the High Court, by a notice to attend before the judge on a day specified in the notice, and
> (*b*) in the county court, on notice in accordance with CCR Order 13, rule 1 (which deals with applications in the course of proceedings),

and the notice shall state the grounds of the application.

(4) Unless otherwise directed, the notice must be issued within six weeks after the judgment and served on every other party to the cause not less than 14 days before the day fixed for the hearing of the application.

(5) The applicant shall file a certificate that the notice has been duly served on each person required to be served therewith.

(6) The application shall be supported by an affidavit setting out the allegations on which the applicant relies or exhibiting a copy of any pleading which he proposes to file if the application is granted, and a copy of the affidavit shall be served on every other party to the cause.

(7) Not less than seven days before the application is heard the applicant shall file a copy of a transcript of so much as is relevant of any official shorthand note of the proceedings at the trial.

(8) Where a party wishes to appeal against a decree absolute of divorce or nullity of marriage, the question whether he has had the time and opportunity to appeal from the decree nisi on which the decree absolute was founded shall be determined on an application for a re-hearing under this rule.

(9) Any other application for re-hearing shall be made by way of appeal to the Court of Appeal.

(10) This rule shall apply, with the necessary modifications, to a cause disposed of under rule 2.36 as it applies to a cause tried by a judge alone, save that where in such a case the decree was pronounced by a district judge the application shall be made to a district judge.

Decrees and orders

2.43 Decrees and orders

(1) Except in a case to which rule 2.61 (consent orders) applies, every decree, every order made in open court and every other order which is required to be drawn up shall be drawn up –

> (*a*) in the case of a decree or order made at a divorce county court, by the proper officer of that court;
> (*b*) in the case of a decree or order made at the Royal Courts of Justice, by the proper officer of the principal registry;
> (*c*) in the case of a decree or order made at a divorce town, by the proper officer of the registry for that town.

(2) CCR Order 22, rule 7 (which deals among other things with the settlement of judgments) shall not apply to a decree made in a cause pending in a divorce county court.

2.44 Application for rescission of decree

(1) An application by a respondent under section 10(1) of the Act of 1973 for the rescission of a decree of divorce shall be made to a judge and shall be heard in open court,

save that where the decree was pronounced by a district judge the application shall be made to a district judge.

(2) Paragraphs (3) and (5) of rule 2.42 shall apply to an application under this rule as they apply to an application under that rule.

(3) Unless otherwise directed, the notice of the application shall be served on the petitioner not less than 14 days before the day fixed for the hearing of the application.

(4) The application shall be supported by an affidavit setting out the allegations on which the applicant relies and a copy of the affidavit shall be served on the petitioner.

2.45 Application under section 10(2) of Act of 1973

(1) An application by a respondent to a petition for divorce for the court to consider the financial position of the respondent after the divorce shall be made by notice in Form B.

(2), (3) (*revoked*)

(4) The powers of the court on hearing the application may be exercised by the district judge.

(5) Where the petitioner has relied on the fact of two or five years' separation and the court has granted a decree nisi without making any finding as to any other fact mentioned in section 1(2) of the Act of 1973, rules 2.51B to 2.70 and 10.10 shall apply as if the application were an application for ancillary relief and, unless the context otherwise requires, those rules shall be read as if all references to Form A were references to Form B.

(6) A statement of any of the matters mentioned in section 10(3) of the Act of 1973 with respect to which the court is satisfied, or, where the court has proceeded under section 10(4), a statement that the conditions for which that subsection provides have been fulfilled, shall be entered in the records of the court.

2.46 Intervention to show cause by Queen's Proctor

(1) If the Queen's Proctor wishes to show cause against a decree nisi being made absolute, he shall give notice to that effect to the court and to the party in whose favour it was pronounced.

(2) Within 21 days after giving notice under paragraph (1) the Queen's Proctor shall file his plea setting out the grounds on which he desires to show cause, together with a copy for service on the party in whose favour the decree was pronounced and every other party affected by the decree.

(3) The proper officer shall serve a copy of the plea on each of the persons mentioned in paragraph (2).

(4) Subject to the following provisions of this rule, these rules shall apply to all subsequent pleadings and proceedings in respect of the plea as if it were a petition by which a cause is begun.

(5) If no answer to the plea is filed within the time limited or, if an answer is filed and struck out or not proceeded with, the Queen's Proctor may apply forthwith by motion for an order rescinding the decree and dismissing the petition.

(6) Rule 2.24 shall apply to proceedings in respect of a plea by the Queen's Proctor as it applies to the trial of a cause, so however that if all the charges in the plea are denied in the answer the application for directions shall be made by the Queen's Proctor and in any other case it shall be made by the party in whose favour the decree nisi has been pronounced.

2.47 Intervention to show cause by person other than Queen's Proctor

(1) If any person other than the Queen's Proctor wishes to show cause under section 9 of the Act of 1973 against a decree nisi being made absolute, he shall file an affidavit stating the facts on which he relies and a copy shall be served on the party in whose favour the decree was pronounced.

(2) A party on whom a copy of the affidavit has been served under paragraph (1) may, within 14 days after service, file an affidavit in answer and, if he does so, a copy thereof shall be served on the person showing cause.

(3) The person showing cause may file an affidavit in reply within 14 days after service of the affidavit in answer and, if he does so, a copy shall be served on each party who was served with a copy of his original affidavit.

(4) No affidavit after an affidavit in reply shall be served without leave.

(5) Any person who files an affidavit under paragraphs (1), (2) or (3) shall at the same time file a copy for service on each person required to be served therewith and the proper officer shall thereupon serve the copy on that person.

(6) A person showing cause shall apply to the judge (or, where a district judge has pronounced the decree nisi, a district judge) for directions within 14 days after expiry of the time allowed for filing an affidavit in reply or, where an affidavit in answer has been filed, within 14 days after the expiry of the time allowed for filing such an affidavit.

(7) If the person showing cause does not apply under paragraph (6) within the time allowed, the person in whose favour the decree was pronounced may do so.

2.48 Rescission of decree nisi by consent

(1) Where a reconciliation has been effected between the petitioner and the respondent –

    (*a*) after a decree nisi has been pronounced but before it has been made absolute, or
    (*b*) after a decree of judicial separation has been pronounced,
either party may apply for an order rescinding the decree by consent.

(2) Where the cause is pending in a divorce county court, the application shall be made on notice to the other spouse and to any other party against whom costs have been awarded or who is otherwise affected by the decree, and where the cause is pending in the High Court a copy of the summons by which the application is made shall be served on every such person.

(3) The application shall be made to a district judge and may be heard in chambers.

2.49 Decree absolute on lodging notice

(1) Subject to rule 2.50(1) an application by a spouse to make absolute a decree nisi pronounced in his favour may be made by lodging with the court a notice in Form M8.

(2) On the lodging of such a notice, the district judge shall cause the records of the court to be searched, and if he is satisfied –

    (*a*) that no application for rescission of the decree or for re-hearing of the cause and no appeal against the decree or the dismissal of an application for re-hearing of the cause is pending;

(*b*) that no order has been made by the court extending the time for making an application for re-hearing of the cause or by the Court of Appeal extending the time for appealing against the decree or the dismissal of an application for re-hearing of the cause or, if any such order has been made, that the time so extended has expired;

(*c*) that no application for such an order as is mentioned in sub-paragraph (*b*) is pending;

(*d*) that no intervention under rule 2.46 or 2.47 is pending;

(*e*) that the court has complied with section 41(1) of the Act of 1973 and has not given any direction under section 41(2);

(*f*) where a certificate has been granted under section 12 of the Administration of Justice Act 1969 in respect of the decree –

    (i) that no application for leave to appeal directly to the House of Lords is pending;

    (ii) that no extension of the time to apply for leave to appeal directly to the House of Lords has been granted or, if any such extension has been granted, that the time so extended has expired; and

    (iii) that the time for any appeal to the Court of Appeal has expired; and

(*g*) that the provisions of section 10(2) to (4) of the Act of 1973 do not apply or have been complied with,

the district judge shall make the decree absolute:

Provided that if the notice is lodged more than 12 months after the decree nisi there shall be lodged with the notice an explanation in writing:

(*a*) giving reasons for the delay;

(*b*) stating whether the parties have lived with each other since the decree nisi and, if so, between what dates; and

(*c*) stating whether the applicant being the wife has, or being the husband has reason to believe that his wife has, given birth to any child since the decree nisi and, if so, stating the relevant facts and whether or not it is alleged that the child is or may be a child of the family;

and the district judge may require the applicant to file an affidavit verifying the said explanation and may make such order on the application as he thinks fit.

2.50 Decree absolute on application

(1) In the following cases an application for a decree nisi to be made absolute shall be made to a judge, that is to say –

(*a*) where the Queen's Proctor gives to the court and to the party in whose favour the decree was pronounced a notice that he requires more time to decide whether to show cause against the decree being made absolute and the notice has not been withdrawn, or

(*b*) where there are other circumstances which ought to be brought to the attention of the court before the decree nisi is made absolute.

Unless otherwise directed, the summons by which the application is made (or, where the cause is pending in a divorce county court, notice of the application) shall be served on every party to the cause (other than the applicant) and, in a case to which sub-paragraph (*a*) applies, on the Queen's Proctor.

(2) An application by a spouse for a decree nisi pronounced against him to be made absolute may be made to a judge or the district judge, and the summons by which the application is made (or, where the cause is pending in a divorce county court, notice of the application) shall be served on the other spouse not less than four clear days before the day on which the application is heard.

(3) An order granting an application under this rule shall not take effect until the district judge has caused the records of the court to be searched and is satisfied as to the matters mentioned in rule 2.49(2).

2.51 Indorsement and certificate of decree absolute

(1) Where a decree nisi is made absolute, the proper officer shall make an indorsement to that effect on the decree, stating the precise time at which it was made absolute.

(2) On a decree nisi being made absolute, the proper officer shall send to the petitioner and the respondent a certificate in Form M9 or M10 whichever is appropriate, authenticated by the seal of the divorce county court or registry from which it is issued.

(3) A central index of decrees absolute shall be kept under the control of the principal registry and any person shall be entitled to require a search to be made therein, and to be furnished with a certificate of the result of the search, on payment of the prescribed fee.

(4) A certificate in Form M9 or M10 that a decree nisi has been made absolute shall be issued to any person requiring it on payment of the prescribed fee.

Ancillary relief

2.51A Application of ancillary relief rules

(1) The procedures set out in rules 2.51B to 2.70 ("the ancillary relief rules") apply to any ancillary relief application and to any application under section 10(2) of the Act of 1973.

(2) In the ancillary relief rules, unless the context otherwise requires:

"applicant" means the party applying for ancillary relief;
"respondent" means the respondent to the application for ancillary relief;
"FDR appointment" means a Financial Dispute Resolution appointment in accordance with rule 2.61E.

2.51B The overriding objective

(1) The ancillary relief rules are a procedural code with the overriding objective of enabling the court to deal with cases justly.

(2) Dealing with a case justly includes, so far as is practicable –

(*a*) ensuring that the parties are on an equal footing;
(*b*) saving expense;
(*c*) dealing with the case in ways which are proportionate –
   (i) to the amount of money involved;
   (ii) to the importance of the case;
   (iii) to the complexity of the issues; and
   (iv) to the financial position of each party;
(*d*) ensuring that it is dealt with expeditiously and fairly; and
(*e*) allotting to it an appropriate share of the court's resources, while taking into account the need to allot resources to other cases.

(3) The court must seek to give effect to the overriding objective when it –

(*a*) exercises any power given to it by the ancillary relief rules; or
(*b*) interprets any rule.

(4) The parties are required to help the court to further the overriding objective.

(5) The court must further the overriding objective by actively managing cases.

(6) Active case management includes –

    (*a*) encouraging the parties to co-operate with each other in the conduct of the proceedings;

    (*b*) encouraging the parties to settle their disputes through mediation, where appropriate;

    (*c*) identifying the issues at an early date;

    (*d*) regulating the extent of disclosure of documents and expert evidence so that they are proportionate to the issues in question;

    (*e*) helping the parties to settle the whole or part of the case;

    (*f*) fixing timetables or otherwise controlling the progress of the case;

    (*g*) making use of technology; and

    (*h*) giving directions to ensure that the trial of a case proceeds quickly and efficiently.

2.52 Right to be heard on ancillary questions

A respondent may be heard on any question of ancillary relief without filing an answer and whether or not he has returned to the court office an acknowledgement of service stating his wish to be heard on that question.

2.53 Application by petitioner or respondent for ancillary relief

(1) Any application by a petitioner, or by a respondent who files an answer claiming relief, for –

    (*a*) an order for maintenance pending suit,

    (*b*) a financial provision order,

    (*c*) a property adjustment order,

    (*d*) a pension sharing order

shall be made in the petition or answer, as the case may be.

(2) Notwithstanding anything in paragraph (1), an application for ancillary relief which should have been made in the petition or answer may be made subsequently –

    (*a*) by leave of the court, either by notice in Form A or at the trial, or

    (*b*) where the parties are agreed upon the terms of the proposed order, without leave by notice in Form A.

(3) An application by a petitioner or respondent for ancillary relief, not being an application which is required to be made in the petition or answer, shall be made by notice in Form A.

2.54 Application by parent, guardian etc for ancillary relief in respect of children

(1) Any of the following persons, namely –

    (*a*) a parent or guardian of any child of the family,

    (*b*) any person in whose favour a residence order has been made with respect to a child of the family, and any applicant for such an order,

    (*c*) any other person who is entitled to apply for a residence order with respect to a child,

    (*d*) a local authority, where an order has been made under section 30(1)(*a*) of the Act of 1989 placing a child in its care,

    (*e*) the Official Solicitor, if appointed the guardian ad litem of a child of the family under rule 9.5, and (*f*) a child of the family who has been given leave to intervene in the cause for the purpose of applying for ancillary relief,

may apply for an order for ancillary relief as respects that child by notice in Form A.

(2) In this rule "residence order" has the meaning assigned to it by section 8(1) of the Act of 1989.

2.55, 2.56

(*revoked*)

2.57 Children to be separately represented on certain applications

(1) Where an application is made to the High Court or a divorce county court for an order for a variation of settlement, the court shall, unless it is satisfied that the proposed variation does not adversely affect the rights or interests of any children concerned, direct that the children be separately represented on the application, either by a solicitor or by a solicitor and counsel, and may appoint the Official Solicitor or other fit person to be guardian ad litem of the children for the purpose of the application.

(2) On any other application for ancillary relief the court may give such a direction or make such appointment as it is empowered to give or make by paragraph (1).

(3) Before a person other than the Official Solicitor is appointed guardian ad litem under this rule there shall be filed a certificate by the solicitor acting for the children that the person proposed as guardian has no interest in the matter adverse to that of the children and that he is a proper person to be such guardian.

2.58

(*revoked*)

2.59 Evidence on application for property adjustment or avoidance of disposition order

(1) (*revoked*)

(2) Where an application for a property adjustment order or an avoidance of disposition order relates to land, the notice in Form A shall identify the land and –

> (*a*) state whether the title to the land is registered or unregistered and, if registered, the Land Registry title number; and
> (*b*) give particulars, so far as known to the applicant, of any mortgage of the land or any interest therein.

(3) Copies of Form A and of Form E completed by the applicant, shall be served on the following persons as well as on the respondent to the application, that is to say –

> (*a*) in the case of an application for an order for a variation of settlement, the trustees of the settlement and the settlor if living;
> (*b*) in the case of an application for an avoidance of disposition order, the person in whose favour the disposition is alleged to have been made;

and such other persons, if any, as the district judge may direct.

(4) In the case of an application to which paragraph (2) refers, a copy of Form A shall be served on any mortgagee of whom particulars are given pursuant to that paragraph; any

person so served may apply to the court in writing, within 14 days after service, for a copy of the applicant's Form E.

(5) Any person who –

    (*a*) is served with copies of Forms A and E pursuant to paragraph (3), or

    (*b*) receives a copy of Form E following an application made in accordance with paragraph (4),

may, within 14 days after service or receipt, as the case may be, file a statement in answer.

(6) A statement filed under paragraph (5) shall be sworn to be true.

2.60 Service of statement in answer

(1) Where a form or other document filed with the court contains an allegation of adultery or of an improper association with a named person ("the named person"), the court may direct that the party who filed the relevant form or document serve a copy of all or part of that form or document on the named person, together with Form F.

(2) If the court makes a direction under paragraph (1), the named person may file a statement in answer to the allegations.

(3) A statement under paragraph (2) shall be sworn to be true.

(4) Rule 2.37(3) shall apply to a person served under paragraph (1) as it applies to a co-respondent.

2.61 Information on application for consent order for financial relief

(1) Subject to paragraphs (2) and (3), there shall be lodged with every application for a consent order under any of sections 23, 24 or 24A of the Act of 1973 two copies of a draft of the order in the terms sought, one of which shall be indorsed with a statement signed by the respondent to the application signifying his agreement, and a statement of information (which may be made in more than one document) which shall include –

    (*a*) the duration of the marriage, the age of each party and of any minor or dependent child of the family;

    (*b*) an estimate in summary form of the approximate amount of value or the capital resources and net income of each party and of any minor child of the family;

    (*c*) what arrangements are intended for the accommodation of each of the parties and any minor child of the family;

    (*d*) whether either party has remarried or has any present intention to marry or to cohabit with another person;

    (*dd*) where the order includes provision to be made under section 24B, 25B or 25C of the Act of 1973, a statement confirming that the person responsible for the pension arrangement in question has been served with the documents required by rule 2.70(11) and that no objection to such an order has been made by that person within 14 days from such service;

    (*e*) where the terms of the order provide for a transfer of property, a statement confirming that any mortgagee of that property has been served with notice of the application and that no objection to such a transfer has been made by the mortgagee within 14 days from such service; and

    (*f*) any other especially significant matters.

(2) Where an application is made for a consent order varying an order for periodical payments paragraph (1) shall be sufficiently complied with if the statement of information required to be lodged with the application includes only the information in respect of net income mentioned in paragraph (1)(*b*) (and, where appropriate, a statement under

paragraph (1)(*dd*)), and an application for a consent order for interim periodical payments pending the determination of an application for ancillary relief may be made in like manner.

(3) Where all or any of the parties attend the hearing of an application for financial relief the court may dispense with the lodging of a statement of information in accordance with paragraph (1) and give directions for the information which would otherwise be required to be given in such a statement to be given in such a manner as it sees fit.

2.61A Application for ancillary relief

(1) A notice of intention to proceed with an application for ancillary relief made in the petition or answer or an application for ancillary relief must be made by notice in Form A.

(2) The notice must be filed:

    (*a*) if the case is pending in a divorce county court, in that court; or
    (*b*) if the case is pending in the High Court, in the registry in which it is proceeding.

(3) Where the applicant requests an order for ancillary relief that includes provision to be made by virtue of section 24B, 25B or 25C of the Act of 1973 the terms of the order requested must be specified in the notice in Form A.

(4) Upon the filing of Form A the court must:

    (*a*) fix a first appointment not less than 12 weeks and not more than 16 weeks after the date of the filing of the notice and give notice of that date;
    (*b*) serve a copy on the respondent within 4 days of the date of the filing of the notice.

(5) The date fixed under paragraph (4) for the first appointment, or for any subsequent appointment, must not be cancelled except with the court's permission and, if cancelled, the court must immediately fix a new date.

2.61B Procedure before the first appointment

(1) Both parties must, at the same time, exchange with each other, and each file with the court, a statement in Form E, which –

    (*a*) is signed by the party who made the statement;
    (*b*) is sworn to be true, and
    (*c*) contains the information and has attached to it the documents required by that Form.

(2) Form E must be exchanged and filed not less than 35 days before the date of the first appointment.

(3) Form E must have attached to it:

    (*a*) any documents required by Form E;
    (*b*) any other documents necessary to explain or clarify any of the information contained in Form E; and
    (*c*) any documents furnished to the party producing the form by a person responsible for a pension arrangement, either following a request under rule 2.70(2) or as part of a "relevant valuation" as defined in rule 2.70(4).

(4) Form E must have no documents attached to it other than the documents referred to in paragraph (3).

(5) Where a party was unavoidably prevented from sending any document required by Form E, that party must at the earliest opportunity:

    (*a*) serve copies of that document on the other party, and (*b*) file a copy of that document with the court, together with a statement explaining the failure to send it with Form E.

(6) No disclosure or inspection of documents may be requested or given between the filing of the application for ancillary relief and the first appointment, except –

(*a*) copies sent with Form E, or in accordance with paragraph (5); or
(*b*) in accordance with paragraph (7).

(7) At least 14 days before the hearing of the first appointment, each party must file with the court and serve on the other party –

(*a*) a concise statement of the issues between the parties;
(*b*) a chronology;
(*c*) a questionnaire setting out by reference to the concise statement of issues any further information and documents requested from the other party or a statement that no information and documents are required;
(*d*) a notice in Form G stating whether that party will be in a position at the first appointment to proceed on that occasion to a FDR appointment.

(8) (*revoked*)

(9) At least 14 days before the hearing of the first appointment, the applicant must file with the court and serve on the respondent, confirmation of the names of all persons served in accordance with rule 2.59(3) and (4), and that there are no other persons who must be served in accordance with those paragraphs.

2.61C Expert evidence

CPR rules 35.1 to 35.14 relating to expert evidence (with appropriate modifications), except CPR rules 35.5(2) and 35.8(4)(*b*), apply to all ancillary relief proceedings.

2.61D The first appointment

(1) The first appointment must be conducted with the objective of defining the issues and saving costs.

(2) At the first appointment the district judge –

(*a*) must determine –
(i) the extent to which any questions seeking information under rule 2.61B must be answered, and
(ii) what documents requested under rule 2.61B must be produced,
and give directions for the production of such further documents as may be necessary;
(*b*) must give directions about –
(i) the valuation of assets (including, where appropriate, the joint instruction of joint experts);
(ii) obtaining and exchanging expert evidence, if required; and
(iii) evidence to be adduced by each party and, where appropriate, about further chronologies or schedules to be filed by each party;
(*c*) must, unless he decides that a referral is not appropriate in the circumstances, direct that the case be referred to a FDR appointment;
(*d*) must, where he decides that a referral to a FDR appointment is not appropriate, direct one of the following:
(i) that a further directions appointment be fixed;
(ii) that an appointment be fixed for the making of an interim order;

      (iii) that the case be fixed for final hearing and, where that direction is given, the district judge must determine the judicial level at which the case should be heard; or

      (iv) that the case be adjourned for out-of-court mediation or private negotiation or, in exceptional circumstances, generally;

(*e*) must consider whether, having regard to all the circumstances (including the extent to which each party has complied with this Part, and in particular the requirement to send documents with Form E), to make an order about the costs of the hearing; and

(*f*) may –

      (i) make an interim order where an application for it has been made in accordance with rule 2.69F returnable at the first appointment;

      (ii) having regard to the contents of Form G filed by the parties, treat the appointment (or part of it) as a FDR appointment to which rule 2.61E applies;

      (iii) in a case where an order for ancillary relief is requested that includes provision to be made under section 25B or 25C of the Act of 1973, require any party to request a valuation under regulation 4 of the Divorce etc (Pensions) Regulations 1996 from the trustees or managers of any pension scheme under which the party has, or is likely to have, any benefits.

(3) After the first appointment, a party is not entitled to production of any further documents except in accordance with directions given under paragraph (2)(*a*) above or with the permission of the court.

(4) At any stage:

(*a*) a party may apply for further directions or a FDR appointment;

(*b*) the court may give further directions or direct that the parties attend a FDR appointment.

(5) Both parties must personally attend the first appointment unless the court orders otherwise.

2.61E The FDR appointment

(1) The FDR appointment must be treated as a meeting held for the purposes of discussion and negotiation and paragraphs (2) to (9) apply.

(2) The district judge or judge hearing the FDR appointment must have no further involvement with the application, other than to conduct any further FDR appointment or to make a consent order or a further directions order.

(3) Not later than 7 days before the FDR appointment, the applicant must file with the court details of all offers and proposals, and responses to them.

(4) Paragraph (3) includes any offers, proposals or responses made wholly or partly without prejudice, but paragraph (3) does not make any material admissible as evidence if, but for that paragraph, it would not be admissible.

(5) At the conclusion of the FDR appointment, any documents filed under paragraph (3), and any filed documents referring to them, must, at the request of the party who filed them, be returned to him and not retained on the court file.

(6) Parties attending the FDR appointment must use their best endeavours to reach agreement on the matters in issue between them.

(7) The FDR appointment may be adjourned from time to time.

(8) At the conclusion of the FDR appointment, the court may make an appropriate consent order, but otherwise must give directions for the future course of the proceedings, including, where appropriate, the filing of evidence and fixing a final hearing date.

(9) Both parties must personally attend the FDR appointment unless the court orders otherwise.

2.61F Costs

(1) At every court hearing or appointment each party must produce to the court an estimate in Form H of the costs incurred by him up to the date of that hearing or appointment.

(2) The parties' obligation under paragraph (1) is without prejudice to their obligations under paragraph 4.1 to 4.11 of the Practice Direction relating to CPR Part 44.

2.62 Investigation by district judge of application for ancillary relief

(1) (*revoked*)

(2) An application for an avoidance of disposition order shall, if practicable, be heard at the same time as any related application for financial relief.

(3) (*revoked*)

(4) At the hearing of an application for ancillary relief the district judge shall, subject to rules 2.64, 2.65 and 10.10 investigate the allegations made in support of and in answer to the application, and may take evidence orally and may at any stage of the proceedings, whether before or during the hearing, order the attendance of any person for the purpose of being examined or cross-examined and order the disclosure and inspection of any document or require further statements.

(4A) A statement filed under paragraph (4) shall be sworn to be true.

(5), (6) (*revoked*)

(7) Any party may apply to the court for an order that any person do attend an appointment (an "inspection appointment") before the court and produce any documents to be specified or described in the order, the inspection of which appears to the court to be necessary for disposing fairly of the application for ancillary relief or for saving costs.

(8) No person shall be compelled by an order under paragraph (7) to produce any document at an inspection appointment which he could not be compelled to produce at the hearing of the application for ancillary relief.

(9) The court shall permit any person attending an inspection appointment pursuant to an order under paragraph (7) above to be represented at the appointment.

2.63

(*revoked*)

2.64 Order on application for ancillary relief

(1) Subject to rule 2.65 the district judge shall, after completing his investigation under rule 2.62, make such order as he thinks just.

(2) Pending the final determination of the application, and subject to rule 2.69F, the district judge may make an interim order upon such terms as he thinks just.

(3) RSC Order 31, rule 1 (power to order sale of land) shall apply to applications for ancillary relief as it applies to causes and matters in the Chancery Division.

2.65 Reference of application to judge

The district judge may at any time refer an application for ancillary relief, or any question arising thereon, to a judge for his decision.

2.66 Arrangements for hearing of application etc by judge

(1) Where an application for ancillary relief or any question arising thereon has been referred or adjourned to a judge, the proper officer shall fix a date, time and place for the hearing of the application or the consideration of the question and give notice thereof to all parties.

(2) The hearing or consideration shall, unless the court otherwise directs, take place in chambers.

(3) Where the application is proceeding in a divorce county court which is not a court of trial or is pending in the High Court and proceedings in a district registry which is not in a divorce town, the hearing or consideration shall take place at such court of trial or divorce town as in the opinion of the district judge is the nearest or most convenient.

 For the purposes of this paragraph the Royal Courts of Justice shall be treated as a divorce town.

(4) In respect of any application referred to him under this rule, a judge shall have the same powers to make directions as a district judge has under these rules.

2.67 Request for periodical payments order at same rate as order for maintenance pending suit

(1) Where at or after the date of a decree nisi of divorce or nullity of marriage an order for maintenance pending suit is in force, the party in whose favour the order was made may, if he has made an application for an order for periodical payments for himself in his petition or answer, as the case may be, request the district judge in writing to make such an order (in this rule referred to as a "corresponding order") providing for payments at the same rate as those provided for by the order for maintenance pending suit.

(2) Where such a request is made, the proper officer shall serve on the other spouse a notice in Form I requiring him, if he objects to the making of a corresponding order, to give notice to that effect to the court and to the applicant within 14 days after service of the notice on Form I.

(3) If the other spouse does not give notice of objection within the time aforesaid, the district judge may make a corresponding order without further notice to that spouse and without requiring the attendance of the applicant or his solicitor, and shall in that case serve a copy of the order on the applicant as well as on the other spouse.

2.68 Application for order under section 37(2)(a) of Act of 1973

(1) An application under section 37(2)(*a*) of the Act of 1973 for an order restraining any person from attempting to defeat a claim for financial provision or otherwise for protecting the claim may be made to the district judge.

(2) Rules 2.65 and 2.66 shall apply, with the necessary modifications, to the application as if it were an application for ancillary relief.

2.69 Offers to settle

(1) Either party to the application may at any time make a written offer to the other party which is expressed to be "without prejudice except as to costs" and which relates to any issue in the proceedings relating to the application.

(2) Where an offer is made under paragraph (1), the fact that such an offer has been made shall not be communicated to the court, except in accordance with rule 2.61E(3), until the question of costs falls to be decided.

2.69A Interpretation of rules 2.69B to 2.69D

In rules 2.69B to 2.69D, "base rate" has the same meaning as in the Civil Procedure Rules 1998.

2.69B Judgment or order more advantageous than an offer made by the other party

(1) This rule applies where the judgment or order in favour of the applicant or respondent is more advantageous to him than an offer made under rule 2.69(1) by the other party.

(2) The court must, unless it considers it unjust to do so, order that other party to pay any costs incurred after the date beginning 28 days after the offer was made.

2.69C Judgment or order more advantageous than offers made by both parties

(1) This rule applies where –

    (*a*) both the applicant and the respondent have made offers under rule 2.69(1); and

    (*b*) the judgment or order in favour of the applicant or the respondent, as the case may be, is more advantageous to him than both of the offers referred to in paragraph (*a*).

(2) The court may, where it considers it just, order interest in accordance with paragraph (3) on the whole or part of any sum of money (excluding interest and periodical payments) to be awarded to the applicant or respondent, as the case may be.

(3) Interest under paragraph (2) may be at a rate not exceeding 10% above base rate for some or all of the period beginning 28 days after the offer was made.

(4) The court may also order that the applicant or respondent, as the case may be, is entitled to:

    (*a*) his costs on the indemnity basis beginning 28 days after the offer was made; and

    (*b*) interest on those costs at a rate not exceeding 10% above base rate.

(5) The court's powers under this rule are in addition to its powers under rule 2.69B.

2.69D Factors for court's consideration under rules 2.69B and 2.69C

(1) In considering whether it would be unjust, or whether it would be just, to make the orders referred to in rules 2.69B and 2.69C, the court must take into account all the circumstances of the case, including –

(*a*) the terms of any offers made under rule 2.69(1);

(*b*) the stage in the proceedings when any offer was made;

(*c*) the information available to the parties at the time when the offer was made;

(*d*) the conduct of the parties with regard to the giving or refusing to give information for the purposes of enabling the offer to be made or evaluated: and

(*e*) the respective means of the parties.

(2) The power of the court to award interest under rule 2.69C(2) and (4)(*b*) is in addition to any other power it may have to award interest.

2.69E Open proposals

(1) Not less than 14 days before the date fixed for the final hearing of an application for ancillary relief, the applicant must (unless the court directs otherwise) file with the court and serve on the respondent an open statement which sets out concise details, including the amounts involved, of the orders which he proposes to ask the court to make.

(2) Not more than 7 days after service of a statement under paragraph (1), the respondent must file with the court and serve on the applicant an open statement which sets out concise details, including the amounts involved, of the orders which he proposes to ask the court to make.

2.69F Application for interim orders

(1) A party may apply at any stage of the proceedings for an order for maintenance pending suit, interim periodical payments or an interim variation order.

(2) An application for such an order must be made by notice of application and the date fixed for the hearing of the application must be not less than 14 days after the date the notice of application is issued.

(3) The applicant shall forthwith serve the respondent with a copy of the notice of application.

(4) Where an application is made before a party has filed Form E, that party must file with the application and serve on the other party, a draft of the order requested and a short sworn statement explaining why the order is necessary and giving the necessary information about his means.

(5) Not less than 7 days before the date fixed for the hearing, the respondent must file with the court and serve on the other party, a short sworn statement about his means, unless he has already filed Form E.

(6) A party may apply for any other form of interim order at any stage of the proceedings with or without notice.

(7) Where an application referred to in paragraph (6) is made with notice, the provisions of paragraphs (1) to (5) apply to it.

(8) Where an application referred to in paragraph (6) is made without notice, the provisions of paragraph (1) apply to it.

2.70 Pensions

(1) This rule applies where an application for ancillary relief has been made, or notice of intention to proceed with the application has been given, in Form A, or an application has been made in Form B, and the applicant or respondent has or is likely to have any benefits under a pension arrangement.

(2) When the court fixes a first appointment as required by rule 2.61A(4)(*a*), the party with pension rights shall, within seven days after receiving notification of the date of that appointment, request the person responsible for each pension arrangement under which he has or is likely to have benefits to furnish the information referred to in regulation 2(2) and (3)(*b*) to (*f*) of the Pensions on Divorce etc (Provision of Information) Regulations 2000.

(3) Within seven days of receiving information under paragraph (2) the party with pension rights shall send a copy of it to the other party, together with the name and address of the person responsible for each pension arrangement.

(4) A request under paragraph (2) above need not be made where the party with pension rights is in possession of, or has requested, a relevant valuation of the pension rights or benefits accrued under the pension arrangement in question.

(5) In this rule, a relevant valuation means a valuation of pension rights or benefits as at a date not more than twelve months earlier than the date fixed for the first appointment which has been furnished or requested for the purposes of any of the following provisions –

    (*a*) the Pensions on Divorce etc (Provision of Information) Regulations 2000;

    (*b*) regulation 5 of and Schedule 2 to the Occupational Pension Schemes (Disclosure of Information) Regulations 1996 and regulation 11 of and Schedule 1 to the Occupational Pension Schemes (Transfer Value) Regulations 1996;

    (*c*) section 93A or 94(1)(*a*) or (*aa*) of the Pension Schemes Act 1993;

    (*d*) section 94(1)(*b*) of the Pension Schemes Act 1993 or paragraph 2(*a*) (or, where applicable, 2(*b*)) of Schedule 2 to the Personal Pension Schemes (Disclosure of Information) Regulations 1987.

(6) Upon making or giving notice of intention to proceed with an application for ancillary relief including provision to be made under section 24B (pension sharing) of the Act of 1973, or upon adding a request for such provision to an existing application for ancillary relief, the applicant shall send to the person responsible for the pension arrangement concerned a copy of Form A.

(7) Upon making or giving notice of intention to proceed with an application for ancillary relief including provision to be made under section 25B or 25C (pension attachment) of the Act of 1973, or upon adding a request for such provision to an existing application for ancillary relief, the applicant shall send to the person responsible for the pension arrangement concerned –

    (*a*) a copy of Form A;

    (*b*) an address to which any notice which the person responsible is required to serve on the applicant under the Divorce etc (Pensions) Regulations 2000 is to be sent;

    (*c*) an address to which any payment which the person responsible is required to make to the applicant is to be sent; and

    (*d*) where the address in sub-paragraph (*c*) is that of a bank, a building society or the Department of National Savings, sufficient details to enable payment to be made into the account of the applicant.

(8) A person responsible for a pension arrangement on whom a copy of a notice under paragraph (7) is served may, within 21 days after service, require the applicant to provide him with a copy of section 2.16 of the statement in Form E supporting his application; and the applicant must then provide that person with the copy of that section of the statement

within the time limited for filing it by rule 2.61B(2), or 21 days after being required to do so, whichever is the later.

(9) A person responsible for a pension arrangement who receives a copy of section 2.16 of Form E as required pursuant to paragraph (8) may within 21 days after receipt send to the court, the applicant and the respondent a statement in answer.

(10) A person responsible for a pension arrangement who files a statement in answer pursuant to paragraph (9) shall be entitled to be represented at the first appointment, and the court must within 4 days of the date of filing of the statement in answer give the person notice of the date of the first appointment.

(11) Where the parties have agreed on the terms of an order including provision under section 25B or 25C (pension attachment) of the Act of 1973, then unless service has already been effected under paragraph (7), they shall serve on the person responsible for the pension arrangement concerned –

(a) the notice of application for a consent order under rule 2.61(1);
(b) a draft of the proposed order under rule 2.61(1), complying with paragraph (13) below; and
(c) the particulars set out in sub-paragraphs (b), (c) and (d) of paragraph (7) above.

(12) No consent order under paragraph (11) shall be made unless either –

(a) the person responsible has not made any objection within 21 days after the service on him of such notice; or
(b) the court has considered any such objection

and for the purpose of considering any objection the court may make such direction as it sees fit for the person responsible to attend before it or to furnish written details of his objection.

(13) An order for ancillary relief, whether by consent or not, including provision under section 24B (pension sharing), 25B or 25C (pension attachment) of the Act of 1973, shall –

(a) in the body of the order, state that there is to be provision by way of pension sharing or pension attachment in accordance with the annex or annexes to the order; and
(b) be accompanied by an annex containing the information set out in paragraph (14) or paragraph (15) as the case may require; and if provision is made in relation to more than one pension arrangement there shall be one annex for each pension arrangement.

(14) Where provision is made under section 24B (pension sharing) of the Act of 1973, the annex shall state –

(a) the name of the court making the order, together with the case number and the title of the proceedings;
(b) that it is a pension sharing order made under Part IV of the Welfare Reform and Pensions Act 1999;
(c) the names of the transferor and the transferee;
(d) the national insurance number of the transferor;
(e) sufficient details to identify the pension arrangement concerned and the transferor's rights or benefits from it (for example a policy reference number);
(f) the specified percentage, or where appropriate the specified amount, required in order to calculate the appropriate amount for the purposes of section 29(1) of the Welfare Reform and Pensions Act 1999 (creation of pension debits and credits);
(g) how the pension sharing charges are to be apportioned between the parties or alternatively that they are to be paid in full by the transferor;

(*h*) that the person responsible for the pension arrangement has furnished the information required by regulation 4 of the Pensions on Divorce etc (Provision of Information) Regulations 2000 and that it appears from that information that there is power to make an order including provision under section 24B (pension sharing) of the Act of 1973;

(*i*) the day on which the order or provision takes effect; and

(*j*) that the person responsible for the pension arrangement concerned must discharge his liability in respect of the pension credit within a period of 4 months beginning with the day on which the order or provision takes effect or, if later, with the first day on which the person responsible for the pension arrangement concerned is in receipt of –

    (i) the order for ancillary relief, including the annex;

    (ii) the decree of divorce or nullity of marriage; and

    (iii) the information prescribed by regulation 5 of the Pensions on Divorce etc (Provision of Information) Regulations 2000;

provided that if the court knows that the implementation period is different from that stated in sub-paragraph (*j*) by reason of regulations under section 34(4) or 41(2)(*a*) of the Welfare Reform and Pensions Act 1999, the annex shall contain details of the implementation period as determined by those regulations instead of the statement in sub-paragraph (*j*).

(15) Where provision is made under section 25B or 25C (pension attachment) of the Act of 1973, the annex shall state –

(*a*) the name of the court making the order, together with the case number and the title of the proceedings;

(*b*) that it is an order making provision under section 25B or 25C, as the case may be, of the Act of 1973;

(*c*) the names of the party with pension rights and the other party;

(*d*) the national insurance number of the party with pension rights;

(*e*) sufficient details to identify the pension arrangement concerned and the rights or benefits from it to which the party with pension rights is or may become entitled (for example a policy reference number);

(*f*) in the case of an order including provision under section 25B(4) of the Act of 1973, what percentage of any payment due to the party with pension rights is to be paid for the benefit of the other party;

(*g*) in the case of an order including any other provision under section 25B or 25C of the Act of 1973, what the person responsible for the pension arrangement is required to do;

(*h*) the address to which any notice which the person responsible for the pension arrangement is required to serve on the other party under the Divorce etc (Pensions) Regulations 2000 is to be sent, if not notified under paragraph (7)(*b*);

(*i*) an address to which any payment which the person responsible for the pension arrangement is required to make to the other party is to be sent, if not notified under paragraph (7)(*c*);

(*j*) where the address in sub-paragraph (*i*) is that of a bank, a building society or the Department of National Savings, sufficient details to enable payment to be made into the account of the other party, if not notified under paragraph (7)(*d*); and

(*k*) where the order is made by consent, that no objection has been made by the person responsible for the pension arrangement, or that an objection has been received and considered by the court, as the case may be.

(16) A court which makes, varies or discharges an order including provision under section 24B (pension sharing), 25B or 25C (pension attachment) of the Act of 1973, shall send to the person responsible for the pension arrangement concerned –

(*a*) a copy of the decree of divorce, nullity of marriage or judicial separation;

(b) in the case of divorce or nullity of marriage, a copy of the certificate under rule 2.51 that the decree has been made absolute; and

(c) a copy of that order, or as the case may be of the order varying or discharging that order, including any annex to that order relating to that pension arrangement but no other annex to that order.

(17) The documents referred to in paragraph (16) shall be sent within 7 days after the making of the relevant order, or within 7 days after the decree absolute of divorce or nullity or decree of judicial separation, whichever is the later.

(18) In this rule –

(a) all words and phrases defined in sections 25D(3) and (4) of the Act of 1973 have the meanings assigned by those subsections;

(b) all words and phrases defined in section 46 of the Welfare Reform and Pensions Act 1999 have the meanings assigned by that section.

2.71–2.77

(*revoked*)

PART III
OTHER MATRIMONIAL ETC PROCEEDINGS

3.1 Application in case of failure to provide reasonable maintenance

(1) Every application under section 27 of the Act of 1973 shall be made by originating application in Form M19.

(2) The application may be made to any divorce county court and there shall be filed with the application an affidavit by the applicant and also a copy of the application and of the affidavit for service on the respondent.

(3) The affidavit shall state –

(a) the same particulars regarding the marriage, the court's jurisdiction, the children and the previous proceedings as are required in the case of a petition by sub-paragraphs (a), (c), (d), (f) and (i) of paragraph 1 of Appendix 2;

(b) particulars of the respondent's failure to provide reasonable maintenance for the applicant, or, as the case may be, of the respondent's failure to provide, or to make a proper contribution towards, reasonable maintenance for the children of the family; and

(c) full particulars of the applicant's property and income and of the respondent's property and income, so far as may be known to the applicant.

(4) A copy of the application and of the affidavit referred to in paragraph (2) shall be served on the respondent, together with a notice in Form M20 with Form M6.

(5) Subject to paragraph (6), the respondent shall, within 14 days after the time allowed for sending the acknowledgement of service, file an affidavit stating –

(a) whether the alleged failure to provide, or to make proper contribution towards, reasonable maintenance is admitted or denied, and, if denied, the grounds on which he relies;

(b) any allegation which he wishes to make against the applicant; and

(c) full particulars of his property and income, unless otherwise directed.

(6) Where the respondent challenges the jurisdiction of the court to hear the application he shall, within 14 days after the time allowed for sending the acknowledgement of service,

file an affidavit setting out the grounds of the challenge; and the obligation to file an affidavit under paragraph (5) shall not arise until 14 days after the question of jurisdiction has been determined and the court has decided that the necessary jurisdiction exists.

(7) Where the respondent's affidavit contains an allegation of adultery or of an improper association with a person named, the provisions of rule 2.60 (which deal with service on, and filing of a statement in answer by, a named person) shall apply.

(8) If the respondent does not file an affidavit in accordance with paragraph (5), the court may order him to file an affidavit containing full particulars of his property and income, and in that case the respondent shall serve a copy of any such affidavit on the applicant.

(9) Within 14 days after being served with a copy of any affidavit filed by the respondent, the applicant may file a further affidavit as to means and as to any fact in the respondent's affidavit which is disputed, and in that case the applicant shall serve a copy on the respondent.

No further affidavit shall be filed without leave.

(10) Rules 2.61 to 2.66 and rule 10.10 shall apply, with such modifications as may be appropriate, to an application for an order under section 27 of the Act of 1973 as if the application were an application for ancillary relief.

3.2 Application for alteration of maintenance agreement during lifetime of parties

(1) An application under section 35 of the Act of 1973 for the alteration of a maintenance agreement shall be made by originating application containing, unless otherwise directed, the information required by Form M21.

(2) The application may be made to any divorce county court and may be heard and determined by the district judge.

(3) There shall be filed with the application an affidavit by the applicant exhibiting a copy of the agreement and verifying the statements in the application and also a copy of the application and of the affidavit for service on the respondent.

(4) A copy of the application and of the affidavit referred to in paragraph (3) shall be served on the respondent, together with a notice in Form M20 with Form M6 attached.

(5) The respondent shall, within 14 days after the time limited for giving notice of intention to defend, file an affidavit in answer to the application containing full particulars of his property and income and, if he does not do so, the court may order him to file an affidavit containing such particulars.

(6) A respondent who files an affidavit under paragraph (5) shall at the same time file a copy which the proper officer shall serve on the applicant.

3.3 Application of alteration of maintenance agreement after death of one party

(1) An application under section 36 of the Act of 1973 for the alteration of a maintenance agreement after the death of one of the parties shall be made –

    (*a*) in the High Court, by originating summons out of the principal registry or any district registry, or

    (*b*) in a county court, by originating application,

in Form M22.

(2) There shall be filed in support of the application an affidavit by the applicant exhibiting a copy of the agreement and an official copy of the grant of representation to the deceased's estate and of every testamentary document admitted to proof and stating –

(a) whether the deceased died domiciled in England and Wales;

(b) the place and date of the marriage between the parties to the agreement and the name and status of the wife before the marriage;

(c) the name of every child of the family and of any other child for whom the agreement makes financial arrangements, and –

    (i) the date of birth of each such child who is still living (or, if it be the case, that he has attained 18) and the place where and the person with whom any such minor child is residing,

    (ii) the date of death of any such child who has died since the agreement was made;

(d) whether there have been in any court any, and if so what, previous proceedings with reference to the agreement or to the marriage or to the children of the family or any other children for whom the agreement makes financial arrangements, and the date and effect of any order or decree made in such proceedings;

(e) whether there have been in any court any proceedings by the applicant against the deceased's estate under the Inheritance (Provision for Family and Dependants) Act 1975 or any Act repealed by that Act and the date and effect of any order made in such proceedings;

(f) in the case of an application by the surviving party, the applicant's means;

(g) in the case of an application by the personal representatives of the deceased, the surviving party's means, so far as they are known to the applicants, and the information mentioned in sub-paragraphs (a), (b) and (c) of rule 3.4(4);

(h) the facts alleged by the applicant as justifying an alteration in the agreement and the nature of the alteration sought;

(i) if the application is made after the end of the period of six months from the date on which representation in regard to the deceased's estate was first taken out, the grounds on which the court's permission to entertain the application is sought.

(3) CCR Order 48, rules 3(1), 7 and 9 shall apply to an originating application under the said section 36 as they apply to an application under section 1 of the Inheritance (Provision for Family and Dependants) Act 1975.

(4) In this rule and the next following rule "the deceased" means the deceased party to the agreement to which the application relates.

3.4 Further proceedings on application under rule 3.3

(1) Without prejudice to his powers under RSC Order 15 (which deals with parties and other matters), the district judge may at any stage of the proceedings direct that any person be added as a respondent to an application under rule 3.3.

(2) RSC Order 15, rule 13 (which enables the court to make representation orders in certain cases), shall apply to the proceedings as if they were mentioned in paragraph (1) of the said rule 13.

(3) Where the application is in a county court, the references in paragraphs (1) and (2) to RSC Order 15 and Order 15, rule 13 shall be construed as references to CCR Order 5 and Order 5, rule 6 respectively.

(4) A respondent who is a personal representative of the deceased shall, within 14 days after the time limited for giving notice of intention to defend, file an affidavit in answer to the application stating –

(a) full particulars of the value of the deceased's estate for probate, after providing for the discharge of the funeral, testamentary and administration expenses, debts and liabilities payable thereout, including the amount of the inheritance tax or any other tax replaced by that tax and interest thereon;

(b) the persons or classes of persons beneficially interested in the estate (giving the names and addresses of all living beneficiaries) and the value of their interests so far as ascertained, and

(c) if such be the case, that any living beneficiary (naming him) is a minor or a patient within the meaning of rule 9.1.

(5) If a respondent who is a personal representative of the deceased does not file an affidavit stating the matters mentioned in paragraph (4) the district judge may order him to do so.

(6) A respondent who is not a personal representative of the deceased may, within 14 days after the time limited for giving notice of intention to defend, file an affidavit in answer to the application.

(7) Every respondent who files an affidavit in answer to the application shall at the same time lodge a copy, which the proper officer shall serve on the applicant.

3.5 Application of other rules to proceedings under section 35 or 36 of Act of 1973

(1) The following rules shall apply, with the necessary modifications, to an application under section 35 or 36 of the Act of 1973, as if it were an application for ancillary relief –

(a) in the case of an application under either section, rules 2.60, 2.62(4) to (6), 2.63, 2.64, 2.65 and 10.10;

(b) in the case of an application under section 35, rule 2.66; and

(c) in the case of an application under section 36, rule 2.66(1) and (2).

(2) Subject to paragraph (1) and to the provisions of rules 3.2 to 3.4, these rules shall, so far as applicable, apply with the necessary modifications to an application under section 35 or section 36 (as the case may be) of the Act of 1973, as if the application were a cause, the originating application or summons a petition, and the applicant the petitioner.

3.6 Married Women's Property Act 1882

(1) Subject to paragraph (2) below, an application under section 17 of the Married Women's Property Act 1882 (in this and the next following rule referred to as "section 17") shall be made –

(a) in the High Court, by originating summons, which may be issued out of the principal registry or any district registry, or

(b) in a county court, by originating application,

in Form M23 and shall be supported by affidavit.

(2) An order under section 17 may be made in any ancillary relief proceedings upon the application of any party thereto in Form M11 by notice of application or summons.

(3) An application under section 17 to a county court shall be filed –

(a) subject to sub-paragraph (b), in the court for the district in which the applicant or respondent resides, or

(b) in the divorce county court in which any pending matrimonial cause has been commenced by or on behalf of either the applicant or the respondent, or in which any matrimonial cause is intended to be commenced by the applicant.

(4) Where the application concerns the title to or possession of land, the originating summons or application shall –

    (*a*) state whether the title to the land is registered or unregistered and, if registered, the Land Registry title number; and

    (*b*) give particulars, so far as known to the applicant, of any mortgage of the land or any interest therein.

(5) The application shall be served on the respondent, together with a copy of the affidavit in support and an acknowledgement of service in Form M6.

(6) Where particulars of a mortgage are given pursuant to paragraph (4), the applicant shall file a copy of the originating summons or application, which shall be served on the mortgagee; and any person so served may apply to the court in writing, within 14 days after service, for a copy of the affidavit in support; and within 14 days of receiving such affidavit may file an affidavit in answer and shall be entitled to be heard on the application.

(7) If the respondent intends to contest the application, he shall, within 14 days after the time allowed for sending the acknowledgement of service, file an affidavit in answer to the application setting out the grounds on which he relies, and lodge in the court office a copy of the affidavit for service on the applicant.

(8) If the respondent fails to comply with paragraph (7), the applicant may apply for directions; and the district judge may give such directions as he thinks fit, including a direction that the respondent shall be debarred from defending the application unless an affidavit is filed within such time as the district judge may specify.

(9) A district judge may grant an injunction in proceedings under section 17 if, but only so far as, the injunction is ancillary or incidental to any relief sought in those proceedings.

(10) Rules 2.62(4) to (6) and 2.63 to 2.66 shall apply, with the necessary modifications, to an application under section 17 as they apply to an application for ancillary relief.

(11) Subject to the provisions of this rule, these rules shall apply, with the necessary modifications, to an application under section 17 as if the application were a cause, the originating summons or application a petition, and the applicant a petitioner.

3.7 Exercise in principal registry of county court jurisdiction under section 17 of Married Women's Property Act 1882

(1) Where any proceedings for divorce, nullity or judicial separation which are either pending in the principal registry, or are intended to be commenced there by the applicant are or will be treated as pending in a divorce county court, an application under section 17 by one of the parties to the marriage may be made to the principal registry as if it were a county court.

(2) In relation to proceedings commenced or intended to be commenced in the principal registry under paragraph (1) of this rule or transferred from the High Court to the principal registry by an order made under section 38 of the Act of 1984 –

    (*a*) section 42 of the Act of 1984 and the rules made thereunder shall have effect, with the necessary modifications, as they have effect in relation to proceedings commenced in or transferred to the principal registry under that section; and

    (*b*) CCR Order 4, rule 8 and rule 3.6(3) (which relate to venue) shall not apply.

(3) Rule 1.4(1) shall apply, with the necessary modifications, to proceedings in, or intended to be commenced in, the principal registry under paragraph (1) of this rule as it applies to matrimonial proceedings.

3.8 Applications under Part IV of the Family Law Act 1996 (Family Homes and Domestic Violence)

(1) An application for an occupation order or a non-molestation order under Part IV of the Family Law Act 1996 shall be made in Form FL401.

(2) An application for an occupation order or a non-molestation order made by a child under the age of sixteen shall be made in Form FLA401 but shall be treated, in the first instance, as an application to the High Court for leave.

(3) An application for an occupation order or a non-molestation order which is made in other proceedings which are pending shall be made in Form FL401.

(4) An application in Form FL401 shall be supported by a statement which is signed by the applicant and is sworn to be true.

(5) Where an application is made without giving notice, the sworn statement shall state the reasons why notice was not given.

(6) An application made on notice (together with the sworn statement and a notice in Form FL402) shall be served by the applicant on the respondent personally not less than 2 days before the date on which the application will be heard.

(7) The court may abridge the period specified in paragraph (6).

(8) Where the applicant is acting in person, service of the application shall be effected by the court if the applicant so requests.

This does not affect the court's power to order substituted service.

(9) Where an application for an occupation order or a non-molestation order is pending, the court shall consider (on the application of either party or of its own motion) whether to exercise its powers to transfer the hearing of that application to another court and shall make an order for transfer in Form FL417 if it seems necessary or expedient to do so.

(10) Rule 9.2A shall not apply to an application for an occupation order or a non-molestation order under Part IV of the Family Law Act 1996.

(11) A copy of an application for an occupation order under section 33, 35 or 36 of the Family Law Act 1996 shall be served by the applicant by first-class post on the mortgagee or, as the case may be, the landlord of the dwelling-house in question, with a notice in Form FL416 informing him of his right to make representations in writing or at any hearing.

(12) Where the application is for the transfer of a tenancy, notice of the application shall be served by the applicant on the other cohabitant or spouse and on the landlord (as those terms are defined by paragraph 1 of Schedule 7 to the Family Law Act 1996) and any person so served shall be entitled to be heard on the application.

(13) Rules 2.62(4) to (6) and 2.63 (investigation, requests for further information) shall apply, with the necessary modifications, to –

    (*a*) an application for an occupation order under section 33, 35 or 36 of the Family Law Act 1996, and
    (*b*) an application for the transfer of a tenancy,
as they apply to an application for ancillary relief.

(14) Rule 3.6(7) to (9) (Married Women's Property Act 1882) shall apply, with the necessary modifications, to an application for the transfer of a tenancy, as they apply to an application under rule 3.6.

(15) The applicant shall file a statement in Form FL415 after he has served the application.

3.9 Hearing of applications under Part IV of the Family Law Act 1996

(1) An application for an occupation order or a non-molestation order under Part IV of the Family Law Act 1996 shall be dealt with in chambers unless the court otherwise directs.

(2) Where an order is made on an application made ex parte, a copy of the order together with a copy of the application and of the sworn statement in support shall be served by the applicant on the respondent personally.

(3) Where the application is for an occupation order under section 33, 35 or 36 of the Family Law Act 1996, a copy of any order made on the application shall be served by the applicant by first-class post on the mortgagee or, as the case may be, the landlord of the dwelling-house in question.

(4) A copy of an order made on an application heard inter partes shall be served by the applicant on the respondent personally.

(5) Where the applicant is acting in person, service of a copy of any order made on the hearing of the application shall be effected by the court if the applicant so requests.

(6) The following forms shall be used in connection with hearings of applications under Part IV of the Family Law Act 1996 –

   (*a*) a record of the hearing shall be made on Form FL405, and
   (*b*) any order made on the hearing shall be issued in Form FL404.

(7) The court may direct that a further hearing be held in order to consider any representations made by a mortgagee or a landlord.

(8) An application to vary, extend or discharge an order made under Part IV of the Family Law Act 1996 shall be made in Form FL403 and this rule shall apply to the hearing of such an application.

3.9A Enforcement of orders made on applications under Part IV of the Family Law Act 1996

(1) Where a power of arrest is attached to one or more of the provisions ("the relevant provisions") of an order made under Part IV of the Family Law Act 1996 –

   (*a*) the relevant provisions shall be set out in Form FL406 and the form shall not include any provisions of the order to which the power of arrest was not attached; and
   (*b*) a copy of the form shall be delivered to the officer for the time being in charge of any police station for the applicant's address or of such other police station as the court may specify.

The copy of the form delivered under sub-paragraph (*b*) shall be accompanied by a statement showing that the respondent has been served with the order or informed of its terms (whether by being present when the order was made or by telephone or otherwise).

(2) Where an order is made varying or discharging the relevant provisions, the proper officer shall –

   (*a*) immediately inform the officer who received a copy of the form under paragraph (1) and, if the applicant's address has changed, the officer for the time being in charge of the police station for the new address; and
   (*b*) deliver a copy of the order to any officer so informed.

(3) An application for the issue of a warrant for the arrest of the respondent shall be made in Form FL407 and the warrant shall be issued in Form FL408.

(4) The court before whom a person is brought following his arrest may –

(*a*) determine whether the facts, and the circumstances which led to the arrest, amounted to disobedience of the order, or

(*b*) adjourn the proceedings and, where such an order is made, the arrested person may be released and –

(i) be dealt with within 14 days of the day on which he was arrested; and

(ii) be given not less than 2 days' notice of the adjourned hearing.

Nothing in this paragraph shall prevent the issue of a a notice under CCR Order 29, rule 1(4) if the arrested person is not dealt with within the period mentioned in sub-paragraph (*b*)(i) above.

(5) The following provisions shall apply, with the necessary modifications, to the enforcement of orders made on applications under Part IV of the Family Law Act 1996 –

(*a*) RSC Order 52, rule 7 (power to suspend execution of committal order);

(*b*) (in a case where an application for an order of committal is made to the High Court) RSC Order 52, rule 2 (application for leave);

(*c*) CCR Order 29, rule 1 (committal for breach of order);

(*d*) CCR Order 29, rule 1A (undertakings);

(*e*) CCR Order 29, rule 3 (discharge of person in custody);

and CCR Order 29, rule 1 shall have effect, as if for paragraph (3), there were substituted the following –

"(3) At the time when the order is drawn up, the proper officer shall –

(*a*) where the order made is (or includes) a non-molestation order and

(*b*) where the order made is an occupation order and the court so directs,

issue a copy of the order, indorsed with or incorporating a notice as to the consequences of disobedience, for service in accordance with paragraph (2)."

(6) The court may adjourn consideration of the penalty to be imposed for contempts found provided and such consideration may be restored if the respondent does not comply with any conditions specified by the court.

(7) Where the court makes a hospital order in Form FL413 or a guardianship order in Form FL414 under the Mental Health Act 1983, the proper officer shall –

(*a*) send to the hospital any information which will be of assistance in dealing with the patient;

(*b*) inform the applicant when the respondent is being transferred to hospital.

(8) Where a transfer direction given by the Secretary of State under section 48 of the Mental Health Act 1983 is in force in respect of a person remanded in custody by the court under Schedule 5 to the Family Law Act 1996, the proper officer shall notify –

(*a*) the governor of the prison to which that person was remanded; and

(*b*) the hospital where he is detained,

of any committal hearing which that person is required to attend and the proper officer shall give notice in writing to the hospital where that person is detained of any further remand under paragraph 3 of Schedule 5 to the Family Law Act 1996.

(9) An order for the remand of the respondent shall be in Form FL409.

(10) In paragraph (4) "arrest" means arrest under a power of arrest attached to an order or under a warrant of arrest.

3.10 Applications under Part IV of the Family Law Act 1996: bail

(1) An application for bail made by a person arrested under a power of arrest or a warrant of arrest may be made either orally or in writing.

(2) Where an application is made in writing, it shall contain the following particulars –

(*a*) the full name of the person making the application;

(*b*) the address of the place where the person making the application is detained at the time when the application is made;

(*c*) the address where the person making the application would reside if he were to be granted bail;

(*d*) the amount of the recognizance in which he would agree to be bound; and

(*e*) the grounds on which the application is made and, where a previous application has been refused, full particulars of any change in circumstances which has occurred since that refusal.

(3) An application made in writing shall be signed by the person making the application or by a person duly authorised by him in that behalf or, where the person making the application is a minor or is for any reason incapable of acting, by a guardian ad litem acting on his behalf and a copy shall be served by the person making the application on the applicant for the Part IV order.

(4) The persons prescribed for the purposes of paragraph 4 of Schedule 5 to the Family Law Act 1996 (postponement of taking of recognizance) are –

(*a*) a district judge

(*b*) a justice of the peace

(*c*) a justices' clerk

(*d*) a police officer of the rank of inspector or above or in charge of a police station, and

(*e*) (where the person making the application is in his custody) the governor or keeper of a prison.

(5) The person having custody of the person making the application shall –

(*a*) on receipt of a certificate signed by or on behalf of the district judge stating that the recognizance of any sureties required have been taken, or on being otherwise satisfied that all such recognizances have been taken; and

(*b*) on being satisfied that the person making the application has entered into his recognizance,

release the person making the application.

(6) The following forms shall be used –

(*a*) the recognizance of the person making the application shall be in Form FL410 and that of a surety in Form FL411;

(*b*) a bail notice in Form FL412 shall be given to the respondent where he is remanded on bail.

3.11 Proceedings in respect of polygamous marriage

(1) The provisions of this rule shall have effect where a petition, originating application or originating summons asks for matrimonial relief within the meaning of section 47(2) of the Act of 1973 in respect of a marriage where either party to the marriage is, or has during the subsistence of the marriage been, married to more than one person (in this rule referred to as a polygamous marriage).

(2) The petition, originating application or originating summons –

(*a*) shall state that the marriage in question is polygamous;

(*b*) shall state whether or not there is, to the knowledge of the petitioner or applicant, any living spouse of his or hers additional to the respondent or, as the case may be, any living spouse of the respondent additional to the petitioner or applicant (in this rule referred to as an additional spouse); and (*c*) if there is any additional spouse, shall give his or her full name and address and the date and place of his or her marriage to the petitioner or applicant or, as the case may be, to the respondent, or state, so far as may be applicable, that such information is unknown to the petitioner or applicant.

(3) Without prejudice to its powers under RSC Order 15 (which deals with parties) or CCR Order 15 (which deals with amendment) the court may order that any additional spouse –

  (*a*) be added as a party to the proceedings; or
  (*b*) be given notice of –
    (i) the proceedings; or
    (ii) of any application in the proceedings for any such order as is mentioned in section 47(2)(*d*) of the Act of 1973.

(4) Any order under paragraph (3) may be made at any stage of the proceedings and either on the application of any party or by the court of its own motion and, where an additional spouse is mentioned in a petition or an acknowledgement of service of a petition, the petitioner shall, on making any application in the proceedings or, if no previous application has been made in the proceedings, on making a request for directions for trial, ask for directions as to whether an order should be made under paragraph (3).

(5) Any person to whom notice is given pursuant to an order under paragraph (3) shall be entitled, without filing an answer or affidavit, to be heard in the proceedings or on the application to which the notice relates.

3.12 Application under section 55 of Act of 1986 for declaration as to marital status

(1) Unless otherwise directed, a petition by which proceedings are begun under section 55 of the Act of 1986 for a declaration as to marital status shall state –

  (*a*) the names of the parties to the marriage to which the application relates and the residential address of each of them at the date of the presentation of the petition;
  (*b*) the place and date of any ceremony of marriage to which the application relates;
  (*c*) the grounds on which the application is made and all other material facts alleged by the petitioner to justify the making of the declaration;
  (*d*) whether there have been or are continuing any proceedings in any court, tribunal or authority in England and Wales or elsewhere between the parties which relate to, or are capable of affecting, the validity or subsistence of the marriage, divorce, annulment or legal separation to which the application relates, or which relate to the matrimonial status of either of the parties, and, if so –
    (i) the nature, and either the outcome or present state of those proceedings,
    (ii) the court, tribunal or authority before which they were begun,
    (iii) the date when they were begun,
    (iv) the names of the parties to them,
    (v) the date or expected date of the trial,
    (vi) any other facts relevant to the question whether the petition should be stayed under Schedule 1 to the Domicile and Matrimonial Proceedings Act of 1973;
  and any such proceedings shall include any which are instituted otherwise than in a court of law in any country outside England and Wales, if they are instituted before a tribunal or other authority having power under the law having effect there to determine questions of status, and shall be treated as continuing if they have begun and have not been finally disposed of;

(e) where it is alleged that the court has jurisdiction based on domicile, which of the parties to the marriage to which the application relates is domiciled in England and Wales on the date of the presentation of the petition, or died before that date and was at death domiciled in England and Wales.

(f) where it is alleged that the court has jurisdiction based on habitual residence, which of the parties to the marriage to which the application relates has been habitually resident in England and Wales, or died before that date and had been habitually resident in England and Wales throughout the period of one year ending with the date of death;

(g) where the petitioner was not a party to the marriage to which the application relates, particulars of his interest in the determination of the application.

(2) Where the proceedings are for a declaration that the validity of a divorce, annulment or legal separation obtained in any country outside England or Wales in respect of the marriage either is or is not entitled to recognition in England and Wales, the petition shall in addition state the date and place of the divorce, annulment or legal separation.

(3) There shall be annexed to the petition a copy of the certificate of any marriage to which the application relates, or, as the case may be, a certified copy of any decree of divorce, annulment or order for legal separation to which the application relates.

(4) Where a document produced by virtue of paragraph (3) is not in English it shall, unless otherwise directed, be accompanied by a translation certified by a notary public or authenticated by affidavit.

(5) The parties to the marriage in respect of which a declaration is sought shall be petitioner and respondent respectively to the application, unless a third party is applying for a declaration, in which case he shall be the petitioner and the parties to the marriage shall be respondents to the application.

3.13 Application under section 55A of Act of 1986 for declaration of parentage

(1) Unless otherwise directed, a petition by which proceedings are begun under section 55A of the Act of 1986 for a declaration of parentage shall state –

(a) the full name and the sex, date and place of birth and residential address of the petitioner (except where the petitioner is the Secretary of State);

(b) where the case is not an excepted case within section 55(A)(4) of the Act of 1986; either the petitioner's interest in the determination of the application, or that section 27(2) of the Act of 1991 applies;

(c) if they are known, the full name and the sex, date and place of birth and residential address of each of the following persons (unless that person is the petitioner) –
(i) the person whose parentage is in issue;
(ii) the person whose parenthood is in issue; and
(iii) any person who is acknowledged to be the father or mother of the person whose parentage is in issue;

(d) if the petitioner, the person whose parentage is in issue or the person whose parenthood is in issue, is known by a name other than that which appears in the certificate of his birth, that other name shall also be stated in the petition and in any decree made thereon;

(e) if it is known, the full name of the mother, or alleged mother of the person whose parentage is in issue, at the date of –
(i) her birth;
(ii) her first marriage;
(iii) the birth of the person whose parentage is in issue; and

       (iv) her most recent marriage;
      if it was at any of those times different from her full name at the date of the
      presentation of the petition;

  (*f*) the grounds on which the petitioner relies and all other material facts alleged by
      him to justify the making of the declaration;

  (*g*) whether there are or have been any other proceedings in any court, tribunal or
      authority in England and Wales or elsewhere relating to the parentage of the
      person whose parentage is in issue or to the parenthood of the person whose
      parenthood is in issue, and, if so –

       (i) particulars of the proceedings, including the court, tribunal or authority
           before which they were begun, and their nature, outcome or present state,
       (ii) the date they were begun,
     (iii) the names of the parties, and
     (iv) the date or expected date of any trial in the proceedings;

  (*h*) that either the person whose parentage is in issue or the person whose parenthood
      is in issue –

       (i) is domiciled in England and Wales on the date of the presentation of the
           petition;
       (ii) has been habitually resident in England and Wales throughout the period of
           one year ending with that date; or
     (iii) died before that date and either was at death domiciled in England and
           Wales or had been habitually resident in England and Wales throughout the
           period of one year ending with the date of death; and

  (*i*) the nationality, citizenship or immigration status of the person whose parentage is
      in issue and of the person whose parenthood is in issue, and the effect which the
      granting of a declaration of parentage would have upon the status of each of them
      as regards his nationality, citizenship or right to be in the United Kingdom.

(2) Unless otherwise directed, there shall be annexed to the petition a copy of the birth
certificate of the person whose parentage is in issue.

(3) The respondents to the application shall be –

    (i) the person whose parentage is in issue; and
   (ii) any person who is, or who is alleged to be, the mother or father of the person
       whose parentage is in issue;
excluding the petitioner.

(4) The prescribed officer for the purposes of section 55A(7) of the Act of 1986 shall be
the family proceedings department manager of the principal registry.

(5) Within 21 days after a declaration of parentage has been made, the prescribed officer
shall send to the Registrar General a copy of the declaration in Form M30 and the petition.

3.14 Application under section 56(1)(b) and (2) of Act of 1986 for declaration of legitimacy or legitimation

(1) Unless otherwise directed, a petition by which proceedings are begun under section
56(1)(*b*) and (2) of the Act of 1986 for a declaration of legitimacy or legitimation shall
state –

  (*a*) the name of the petitioner, and if the petitioner is known by a name other than that
      which appears in the certificate of his birth, that other name shall be stated in the
      petition and in any decree made thereon;
  (*b*) the date and place of birth of the petitioner;
  (*c*) if it is known, the name of the petitioner's father and the maiden name of the
      petitioner's mother and, if it is different, her current name, and the residential
      address of each of them at the time of the presentation of the petition;

(*d*) the grounds on which the petitioner relies and all other material facts alleged by him to justify the making of the declaration; and

(*e*) either that the petitioner is domiciled in England and Wales on the date of the presentation of the petition or that he has been habitually resident in England and Wales throughout the period of one year ending with that date.

(2) Unless otherwise directed, there shall be annexed to the petition a copy of the petitioner's birth certificate.

(3) The petitioner's father and mother, or the survivor of them, shall be respondents to the application.

3.15 Application under section 57 of Act of 1986 for declaration as to adoption effected overseas

(1) Unless otherwise directed, a petition by which proceedings are begun under section 57 of the Act of 1986 for a declaration as to an adoption effected overseas shall state –

(*a*) the names of those persons who are to be respondents pursuant to paragraph (4) and the residential address of each of them at the date of the presentation of the petition;

(*b*) the date and place of the petitioner's birth;

(*c*) the date and place of the adoption order and the court or other tribunal or authority which made it;

(*d*) all other material facts alleged by the petitioner to justify the making of the declaration and the grounds on which the application is made;

(*e*) either that the petitioner is domiciled in England and Wales on the date of the presentation of the petition or that he has been habitually resident in England and Wales throughout the period of one year ending with that date.

(2) There shall be annexed to the petition a copy of the petitioner's birth certificate (if it is available this certificate should be the one made after the adoption referred to in the petition) and, unless otherwise directed, a certified copy of the adoption order effected under the law of any country outside the British Islands.

(3) Where a document produced by virtue of paragraph (2) is not in English, it shall, unless otherwise directed, be accompanied by a translation certified by a notary public or authenticated by affidavit.

(4) The following shall, if alive, be respondents to the application, either –

(*a*) those whom the petitioner claims are his adoptive parents for the purposes of section 39 of the Adoption Act 1976; or

(*b*) those whom the petitioner claims are not his adoptive parents for the purposes of that section.

3.16 General provisions as to proceedings under rules 3.12, 3.13, 3.14 and 3.15

(1) A petition under rule 3.12, 3.13, 3.14 or 3.15 shall be supported by an affidavit by the petitioner verifying the petition and giving particulars of every person whose interest may be affected by the proceedings and his relationship to the petitioner.

 Provided that if the petitioner is under the age of 18, the affidavit shall, unless otherwise directed, be made by his next friend.

(2) Where the jurisdiction of the court to entertain a petition is based on habitual residence the petition shall include a statement of the addresses of the places of residence of the person so resident and the length of residence at each place either during the period of one

year ending with the date of the presentation of the petition or, if that person is dead, throughout the period of one year ending with the date of death.

(3) An affidavit for the purposes of paragraph (1) may contain statements of information or belief with the sources and grounds thereof.

(4) Except in the case of a petition under rule 3.13, a copy of the petition and every document accompanying it shall be sent by the petitioner to the Attorney General at least one month before the petition is filed and it shall not be necessary thereafter to serve these documents upon him.

(5) If the Attorney General has notified the court that he wishes to intervene in the proceedings, the proper officer shall send to him a copy of any answer and, in the case of a petition under rule 3.13, of the petition and every document accompanying it.

(6) When all answers to the petition have been filed the petitioner shall issue and serve on all respondents to the application a request for directions as to any other persons who should be made respondents to the petition or given notice of the proceedings.

(7) When giving directions in accordance with paragraph (6) the court shall consider whether it is desirable that the Attorney General should argue before it any question relating to the proceedings, and if it does so consider and the Attorney General agrees to argue that question, the Attorney General need not file an answer and the court shall give directions requiring him to serve on all parties to the proceedings a summary of his argument.

(8) Persons given notice of proceedings pursuant to directions given in accordance with paragraph (6) shall within 21 days after service of the notice upon them be entitled to apply to the court to be joined as parties.

(9) The Attorney General may file an answer to the petition within 21 days after directions have been given under paragraph (7) and no directions for trial shall be given until that period and the period referred to in paragraph (8) have expired.

(10) The Attorney General, in deciding whether it is necessary or expedient to intervene in the proceedings, may have a search made for, and may inspect and bespeak a copy of, any document filed or lodged in the court offices which relates to any other family proceedings referred to in proceedings.

(11) Declarations made in accordance with section 55, section 56(1)(*a*), section 56(1)(*b*) and (2) and section 57 of the Act of 1986 shall be in the forms prescribed respectively in Forms M29, M30, M31 and M32.

(12) Subject to rules 3.12, 3.13, 3.14 and 3.15 and this rule, these rules shall, so far as applicable and with the exception of rule 2.6(1), apply with the necessary modifications to the proceedings as if they were a cause.

3.17 Application for leave under section 13 of Act of 1984

(1) An application for leave to apply for an order for financial relief under Part III of the Act of 1984 shall be made ex parte by originating summons issued in Form M25 out of the principal registry and shall be supported by an affidavit by the applicant stating the facts relied on in support of the application with particular reference to the matters set out in section 16(2) of that Act.

(2) The affidavit in support shall give particulars of the judicial or other proceedings by means of which the marriage to which the application relates were dissolved or annulled or by which the parties to the marriage were legally separated and shall state, so far as is known to the applicant –

(*a*) the names of the parties to the marriage and the date and place of the marriage;

(*b*) the occupation and residence of each of the parties to the marriage;

(*c*) whether there are any living children of the family and, if so, the number of such children and the full names (including surname) of each and his date of birth or, if it be the case, that he is over 18;

(*d*) whether either party to the marriage has remarried;

(*e*) an estimate in summary form of the appropriate amount or value of the capital resources and net income of each party and of any minor child of the family;

(*f*) the grounds on which it is alleged that the court has jurisdiction to entertain an application for an order for financial relief under Part III of the Act of 1984.

(3) The proper officer shall fix a date, time and place for the hearing of the application by a judge in chambers and give notice thereof to the applicant.

3.18 Application for order for financial relief or avoidance of transaction order under Part III of the Act of 1984

(1) An application for an order for financial relief under Part III of the Act of 1984 shall be made by originating summons issued in Form M26 out of the principal registry and at the same time the applicant, unless otherwise directed, shall file an affidavit in support of the summons giving full particulars of his property and income.

(2) The applicant shall serve a sealed copy of the originating summons on the respondent and shall annex thereto a copy of the affidavit in support, if one has been filed, and a notice of proceedings and acknowledgement of service in Form M28, and rule 10.8 shall apply to such an acknowledgement of service as if the references in paragraph (1) of that rule to Form M6 and in paragraph (2) of that rule to seven days were, respectively, references to Form M28 and 31 days.

(3) Rules 2.57, 2.59, 2.61, 2.62(5) and (6), 2.63 and 2.66(1) and (2) shall apply, with the necessary modifications, to an application for an order for financial relief under this rule as they apply to an application for ancillary relief made by notice in Form M11 and the court may order the attendance of any person for the purpose of being examined or cross-examined and the discovery and production of any document.

(4) An application for an interim order for maintenance under section 14 or an avoidance of transaction order under section 23 of the Act of 1984 may be made, unless the court otherwise directs, in the originating summons under paragraph (1) or by summons in accordance with rule 10.9(1) and an application for an order under section 23 shall be supported by an affidavit, which may be the affidavit filed under paragraph (1), stating the facts relied on.

(5) If the respondent intends to contest the application he shall, within 28 days after the time limited for giving notice to defend, file an affidavit in answer to the application setting out the grounds on which he relies and shall serve a copy on the applicant.

(6) In respect of any application for an avoidance of transaction order the court may give such a direction or make such appointment as it is empowered to give or make by paragraph (3) and rule 2.59 shall apply, with the necessary modifications, to an application for an avoidance of transaction order as it applies to an application for an avoidance of disposition order.

(7) Where the originating summons contains an application for an order under section 22 of the Act of 1984 the applicant shall serve a copy on the landlord of the dwelling house and he shall be entitled to be heard on the application.

(8) An application for an order for financial relief under Part III of the Act of 1984 or for an avoidance of transaction order shall be determined by a judge.

3.19 Application for order under section 24 of Act of 1984 preventing transaction

(1) An application under section 24 of the Act of 1984 for an order preventing a transaction shall be made by originating summons issued in Form M27 out of the principal registry and shall be supported by an affidavit by the applicant stating the facts relied on in support of the application.

(2) The applicant shall serve a sealed copy of the originating summons on the respondent and shall annex thereto a copy of the affidavit in support and a notice of proceedings and acknowledgement of service in Form M28 and rule 10.8 shall apply to such an acknowledgement of service as if the references in paragraph (1) of that rule to Form M6 and in paragraph (2) of that rule to seven days were, respectively, references to Form M28 and 31 days.

(3) If the respondent intends to contest the application he shall, within 28 days after the time limited for giving notice of intention to defend, file an affidavit in answer to the application setting out the grounds on which he relies and shall serve a copy on the applicant.

(4) The application shall be determined by a judge.

(5) Rule 2.66 (except paragraph (3)) shall apply, with the necessary modifications, to the application as if it were an application for ancillary relief.

3.20 Consent to marriage of minor

(1) An application under section 3 of the Marriage Act 1949 (in this rule referred to as "section 3") for the consent of the court to the marriage of a minor shall be dealt with in chambers unless the court otherwise directs.

(2) The application may be heard and determined by a district judge.

(3) An application under section 3 may be brought without the intervention of the applicant's next friend, unless the court otherwise directs.

(4) Where an application under section 3 follows a refusal to give consent to the marriage every person who has refused consent shall be made a defendant to the summons or a respondent to the application, as appropriate.

(5) The application shall, unless the court orders otherwise, be served not less than seven days before the date upon which the application is to be heard.

3.21 Application under section 27 of the Act of 1991 for declaration of parentage

(1) Rule 4.6 shall apply to an application under section 55A of the Act of 1986 (declarations of parentage) as it applies to an application under the Act of 1989.

(2) Where an application under section 55A of the Act of 1986 has been transferred to the High Court or a county court the court shall, as soon as practicable after a transfer has occurred, consider what directions to give for the conduct of the proceedings.

(3) Without prejudice to the generality of paragraph (2), the court may, in particular, direct that –

    (*a*) the proceedings shall proceed as if they had been commenced by originating summons or originating application;

(*b*) any document served or other thing done while the proceedings were pending in another court, including a magistrates' court, shall be treated for such purposes as may be specified in the direction as if it had been such document or other thing, being a document or other thing provided for by the rules of court applicable in the court to which the proceedings have been transferred, as may be specified in the direction and had been served or done pursuant to any such rule;

(*c*) a pre-trial hearing shall be held to determine what further directions, if any, should be given.

(4) The application may be heard and determined by a district judge.

3.22 Appeal under section 20 of Act of 1991

(1) Rule 4.6 shall apply to an appeal under section 20 of the Act of 1991 (appeals to appeal tribunals) as it applies to an application under the Act of 1989.

(2) Where an appeal under section 20 of the Act of 1991 is transferred to the High Court or a county court, Rule 3.21(2) and (3) shall apply to the appeal as it applies to an application under section 55A of the Act of 1986.

3.23 Appeal from Child Support Commissioner

(1) This rule shall apply to any appeal to the Court of Appeal under section 25 of the Act of 1991 (appeal from Child Support Commissioner on question of law).

(2) Where leave to appeal is granted by the Commissioner, the notice of appeal must be served within 6 weeks from the date on which notice of the grant was given in writing to the appellant.

(3) Where leave to appeal is granted by the Court of Appeal upon an application made within 6 weeks of the date on which notice of the Commissioner's refusal of leave to appeal was given in writing to the appellant, the notice of appeal must be served –

(*a*) before the end of the said period of 6 weeks; or
(*b*) within 7 days after the date on which leave is granted,
whichever is the later, or within such other period as the Court of Appeal may direct.

PART IV
PROCEEDINGS UNDER THE CHILDREN ACT 1989

4.1 Interpretation and application

(1) In this Part of these rules, unless a contrary intention appears –

a section or schedule referred to means the section or schedule so numbered in the Act of 1989;
"a section 8 order" has the meaning assigned to it by section 8(2);
"application" means an application made under or by virtue of the Act of 1989 or under these rules, and "applicant" shall be construed accordingly;
"child", in relation to proceedings to which this Part applies –
(*a*) means, subject to sub-paragraph (*b*), a person under the age of 18 with respect to whom the proceedings are brought, and
(*b*) where the proceedings are under Schedule 1, also includes a person who has reached the age of 18;

"children and family reporter" means an officer of the service who has been asked to prepare a welfare report under section 7(1)(*a*);

"children's guardian" –

(*a*) means an officer of the service appointed under section 41 for the child with respect to whom the proceedings are brought; but

(*b*) does not include such an officer appointed in relation to proceedings specified by Part IVA;

"directions appointment" means a hearing for directions under rule 4.14(2);

"emergency protection order" means an order under section 44;

"leave" includes permission and approval;

"note" includes a record made by mechanical means;

"parental responsibility" has the meaning assigned to it by section 3;

"recovery order" means an order under section 50;

"specified proceedings" has the meaning assigned to it by section 41(6) and rule 4.2(2); and

"welfare officer" means a person who has been asked to prepare a welfare report under section 7(1)(*b*).

(2) Except where the contrary intention appears, the provisions of this Part apply to proceedings in the High Court and the county courts –

(*a*) on an application for a section 8 order;

(*b*) on an application for a care order or a supervision order;

(*c*) on an application under section 4(1)(*a*), 4(3), 5(1), 6(7), 13(1), 16(6), 33(7), 34(2), 34(3), 34(4), 34(9), 36(1), 38(8)(*b*), 39(1), 39(2), 39(3), 39(4), 43(1), 43(12), 44, 45, 46(7), 48(9), 50(1) or 102(1);

(*d*) under Schedule 1, except where financial relief is also sought by or on behalf of an adult;

(*e*) on an application under paragraph 19(1) of Schedule 2;

(*f*) on an application under paragraph 6(3), 15(2) or 17(1) of Schedule 3;

(*g*) on an application under paragraph 11(3) or 16(5) of Schedule 14; or

(*h*) under section 25.

4.2 Matters prescribed for the purposes of the Act of 1989

(1) The parties to proceedings in which directions are given under section 38(6), and any person named in such a direction, form the prescribed class for the purposes of section 38(8) (application to vary directions made with interim care or interim supervision order).

(2) The following proceedings are specified for the purposes of section 41 in accordance with subsection (6)(i) thereof –

(*a*) proceedings under section 25;

(*b*) applications under section 33(7);

(*c*) proceedings under paragraph 19(1) of Schedule 2;

(*d*) applications under paragraph 6(3) of Schedule 3;

(*e*) appeals against the determination of proceedings of a kind set out in sub-paragraphs (*a*) to (*d*).

(3) The applicant for an order that has been made under section 43(1) and the persons referred to in section 43(11) may, in any circumstances, apply under section 43(12) for a child assessment order to be varied or discharged.

(4) The following persons form the prescribed class for the purposes of section 44(9) (application to vary directions) –

(*a*) the parties to the application for the order in respect of which it is sought to vary the directions;

(*b*) the children's guardian;

(*c*) the local authority in whose area the child concerned is ordinarily resident;

(*d*) any person who is named in the directions.

4.3 Application for leave to commence proceedings

(1) Where the leave of the court is required to bring any proceedings to which this Part applies, the person seeking leave shall file –

(*a*) a written request for leave in Form C2 setting out the reasons for the application; and

(*b*) a draft of the application (being the documents referred to in rule 4.4(1A)) for the making of which leave is sought together with sufficient copies for one to be served on each respondent.

(2) On considering a request for leave filed under paragraph (1), the court shall –

(*a*) grant the request, whereupon the proper officer shall inform the person making the request of the decision, or

(*b*) direct that a date be fixed for the hearing of the request, whereupon the proper officer shall fix such a date and give such notice as the court directs to the person making the request and such other persons as the court requires to be notified, of the date so fixed.

(3) Where leave is granted to bring proceedings to which this Part applies the application shall proceed in accordance with rule 4.4; but paragraph (1)(*a*) of that rule shall not apply.

(4) In the case of a request for leave to bring proceedings under Schedule 1, the draft application under paragraph (1) shall be accompanied by a statement setting out the financial details which the person seeking leave believes to be relevant to the request and containing a declaration that it is true to the maker's best knowledge and belief, together with sufficient copies for one to be served on each respondent.

4.4 Application

(1) Subject to paragraph (4), an applicant shall –

(*a*) file the documents referred to in paragraph (1A) below (which documents shall together be called the "application") together with sufficient copies for one to be served on each respondent, and

(*b*) serve a copy of the application together with Form C6 and such (if any) of Forms C7 and C10A as are given to him by the proper officer under paragraph (2)(*b*) on each respondent such number of days prior to the date fixed under paragraph (2)(*a*) as is specified for that application in column (ii) of Appendix 3 to these rules.

(1A) The documents to be filed under paragraph (1)(*a*) above are –

(*a*) (i) whichever is appropriate of Forms C1 to C4 or C51, and

(ii) such of the supplemental Forms C10 or C11 to C20 as may be appropriate, or

(*b*) where there is no appropriate form a statement in writing of the order sought,

and where the application is made in respect of more than one child, all the children shall be included in one application.

(2) On receipt of the documents filed under paragraph (1)(*a*) the proper officer shall –

(*a*) fix the date for a hearing or a directions appointment, allowing sufficient time for the applicant to comply with paragraph (1)(*b*),

(*b*) endorse the date so fixed upon Form C6 and, where appropriate, Form C6A, and (*c*) return forthwith to the applicant the copies of the application and Form C10A if filed with it, together with Form C6 and such of Forms C6A and C7 as are appropriate.

(3) The applicant shall, at the same time as complying with paragraph (1)(*b*), serve Form C6A on the persons set out for the relevant class of proceedings in column (iv) of Appendix 3 to these rules.

(4) An application for –

    (*a*) a section 8 order,
    (*b*) an emergency protection order,
    (*c*) a warrant under section 48(9),
    (*d*) a recovery order, or
    (*e*) a warrant under section 102(1)

may be made ex parte in which case the applicant shall –

    (i) file the application in the appropriate form in Appendix 1 to these rules –
        (*a*) where the application is made by telephone, within 24 hours after the making of the application, or
        (*b*) in any other case, at the time when the application is made, and
    (ii) in the case of an application for a section 8 order or an emergency protection order, serve a copy of the application on each respondent within 48 hours after the making of the order.

(5) Where the court refuses to make an order on an ex parte application it may direct that the application be made inter partes.

(6) In the case of proceedings under Schedule 1, the application under paragraph (1) shall be accompanied by a statement in Form C10A setting out the financial details which the applicant believes to be relevant to the application, together with sufficient copies for one to be served on each respondent.

4.5 Withdrawal of application

(1) An application may be withdrawn only with leave of the court.

(2) Subject to paragraph (3), a person seeking leave to withdraw an application shall file and serve on the parties a written request for leave setting out the reasons for the request.

(3) The request under paragraph (2) may be made orally to the court if the parties and either the children's guardian or the welfare officer or children and family reporter are present.

(4) Upon receipt of a written request under paragraph (2) the court shall –

    (*a*) if –
        (i) the parties consent in writing,
        (ii) the children's guardian has had an opportunity to make representations, and
        (iii) the court thinks fit,
    grant the request, in which case the proper officer shall notify the parties, the children's guardian and the welfare officer or children and family reporter of the granting of the request, or
    (*b*) direct that a date be fixed for the hearing of the request in which case the proper officer shall give at least 7 days' notice to the parties, the children's guardian and the welfare officer or children and family reporter, of the date fixed.

4.6 Transfer

(1) Where an application is made, in accordance with the provisions of the Allocation Order, to a county court for an order transferring proceedings from a magistrates' court following the refusal of the magistrates' court to order such a transfer, the applicant shall –

    (*a*) file the application in Form C2, together with a copy of the certificate issued by the magistrates' court, and

    (*b*) serve a copy of the documents mentioned in sub-paragraph (*a*) personally on all parties to the proceedings which it is sought to have transferred,

within 2 days after receipt by the applicant of the certificate.

(2) Within 2 days after receipt of the documents served under paragraph (1)(*b*), any party other than the applicant may file written representations.

(3) The court shall, not before the fourth day after the filing of the application under paragraph (1), unless the parties consent to earlier consideration, consider the application and either –

    (*a*) grant the application, whereupon the proper officer shall inform the parties of that decision, or

    (*b*) direct that a date be fixed for the hearing of the application, whereupon the proper officer shall fix such a date and give not less than 1 day's notice to the parties of the date so fixed.

(4) Where proceedings are transferred from a magistrates' court to a county court in accordance with the provisions of the Allocation Order, the county court shall consider whether to transfer those proceedings to the High Court in accordance with that Order and either –

    (*a*) determine that such an order need not be made,

    (*b*) make such an order,

    (*c*) order that a date be fixed for the hearing of the question whether such an order should be made, whereupon the proper officer shall give such notice to the parties as the court directs of the date so fixed, or

    (*d*) invite the parties to make written representations, within a specified period, as to whether such an order should be made; and upon receipt of the representations the court shall act in accordance with sub-paragraph (*a*), (*b*) or (*c*).

(5) The proper officer shall notify the parties of an order transferring the proceedings from a county court or from the High Court made in accordance with the provisions of the Allocation Order.

(6) Before ordering the transfer of proceedings from a county court to a magistrates' court in accordance with the Allocation Order, the county court shall notify the magistrates' court of its intention to make such an order and invite the views of the clerk to the justices on whether such an order should be made.

(7) An order transferring proceedings from a county court to a magistrates' court in accordance with the Allocation Order shall –

    (*a*) be in Form C49, and

    (*b*) be served by the court on the parties.

(8) In this rule "the Allocation Order" means the Children (Allocation of Proceedings) Order 1991 or any Order replacing that Order.

4.7 Parties

(1) The respondents to proceedings to which this Part applies shall be those persons set out in the relevant entry in column (iii) of Appendix 3 to these rules.

(2) In proceedings to which this Part applies, a person may file a request in Form C2 that he or another person –

   (*a*) be joined as a party, or
   (*b*) cease to be a party.

(3) On considering a request under paragraph (2) the court shall, subject to paragraph (4) –

   (*a*) grant it without a hearing or representations, save that this shall be done only in the case of a request under paragraph (2)(*a*), whereupon the proper officer shall inform the parties and the person making the request of that decision, or
   (*b*) order that a date be fixed for the consideration of the request, whereupon the proper officer shall give notice of the date so fixed, together with a copy of the request –
      (i) in the case of a request under paragraph (2)(*a*), to the applicant, and
      (ii) in the case of a request under paragraph (2)(*b*), to the parties, or
   (*c*) invite the parties or any of them to make written representations, within a specified period, as to whether the request should be granted; and upon the expiry of the period the court shall act in accordance with sub-paragraph (*a*) or (*b*).

(4) Where a person with parental responsibility requests that he be joined under paragraph (2)(*a*), the court shall grant his request.

(5) In proceedings to which this Part applies the court may direct –

   (*a*) that a person who would not otherwise be a respondent under these rules be joined as a party to the proceedings, or
   (*b*) that a party to the proceedings cease to be a party.

4.8 Service

(1) Subject to the requirement in rule 4.6(1)(*b*) of personal service, where service of a document is required under this Part (and not by a provision to which section 105(8) (Service of notice or other document under the Act) applies) it may be effected –

   (*a*) if the person to be served is not known by the person serving to be acting by solicitor –
      (i) by delivering it to him personally, or
      (ii) by delivering it at, or by sending it by first-class post to, his residence or his last known residence, or
   (*b*) if the person to be served is known by the person serving to be acting by solicitor –
      (i) by delivering the document at, or sending it by first-class post to, the solicitor's address for service,
      (ii) where the solicitor's address for service includes a numbered box at a document exchange, by leaving the document at that document exchange or at a document exchange which transmits documents on every business day to that document exchange, or
      (iii) by sending a legible copy of the document by facsimile transmission to the solicitor's office.

(2) In this rule "first-class post" means first-class post which has been pre-paid or in respect of which pre-payment is not required.

(3) Where a child who is a party to proceedings to which this Part applies is not prosecuting or defending them without a next friend or guardian ad litem under rule 9.2A and is required by these rules or other rules of court to serve a document, service shall be effected by –

   (*a*) the solicitor acting for the child, or

(*b*) where there is no such solicitor, the children's guardian or the guardian ad litem, or

(*c*) where there is neither such a solicitor nor a children's guardian nor a guardian ad litem, the court.

(4) Service of any document on a child who is not prosecuting or defending the proceedings concerned without a next friend or guardian ad litem under rule 9.2A shall, subject to any direction of the court, be effected by service on –

(*a*) the solicitor acting for the child, or

(*b*) where there is no such solicitor, the children's guardian or the guardian ad litem, or

(*c*) where there is neither such a solicitor nor a children's guardian nor a guardian ad litem, with leave of the court, the child.

(5) Where the court refuses leave under paragraph (4)(*c*) it shall give a direction under paragraph (8).

(6) A document shall, unless the contrary is proved, be deemed to have been served –

(*a*) in the case of service by first-class post, on the second business day after posting, and

(*b*) in the case of service in accordance with paragraph (1)(*b*)(ii), on the second business day after the day on which it is left at the document exchange.

(7) At or before the first directions appointment in, or hearing of, proceedings to which this Part applies the applicant shall file a statement in Form C9 that service of –

(*a*) a copy of the application and other documents referred to in rule 4.4(1)(*b*) has been effected on each respondent, and

(*b*) notice of the proceedings has been effected under rule 4.4(3);

and the statement shall indicate –

(i) the manner, date, time and place of service, or

(ii) where service was effected by post, the date, time and place of posting.

(8) In proceedings to which this Part applies, where these rules or other rules of court require a document to be served, the court may, without prejudice to any power under rule 4.14, direct that –

(*a*) the requirement shall not apply;

(*b*) the time specified by the rules for complying with the requirement shall be abridged to such extent as may be specified in the direction;

(*c*) service shall be effected in such manner as may be specified in the direction.

4.9 Answer to application

(1) Within 14 days of service of an application for a section 8 order or an application under Schedule 1, each respondent shall file, and serve on the parties, an acknowledgement of the application in Form C7.

(2) (*deleted*)

(3) Following service of an application to which this Part applies, other than an application under rule 4.3 or for a section 8 order, a respondent may, subject to paragraph (4), file a written answer, which shall be served on the other parties.

(4) An answer under paragraph (3) shall, except in the case of an application under section 25, 31, 34, 38, 43, 44, 45, 46, 48 or 50, be filed, and served, not less than 2 days before the date fixed for the hearing of the application.

4.10 Appointment of children's guardian

(1) As soon as practicable after the commencement of specified proceedings, or the transfer of such proceedings to the court, the court shall appoint a children's guardian, unless –

   (*a*) such an appointment has already been made by the court which made the transfer and is subsisting, or
   (*b*) the court considers that such an appointment is not necessary to safeguard the interests of the child.

(2) At any stage in specified proceedings a party may apply, without notice to the other parties unless the court directs otherwise, for the appointment of a children's guardian.

(3) The court shall grant an application under paragraph (2) unless it considers such an appointment not to be necessary to safeguard the interests of the child, in which case it shall give its reasons; and a note of such reasons shall be taken by the proper officer.

(4) At any stage in specified proceedings the court may, of its own motion, appoint a children's guardian.

(4A) The court may, in specified proceedings, appoint more than one children's guardian in respect of the same child.

(5) The proper officer shall, as soon as practicable, notify the parties and any welfare officer or children and family reporter of an appointment under this rule or, as the case may be, of a decision not to make such an appointment.

(6) Upon the appointment of a children's guardian the proper officer shall, as soon as practicable, notify him of the appointment and serve on him copies of the application and of documents filed under rule 4.17(1).

(7) A children's guardian appointed by the court under this rule shall not –

   (*a*) be a member, officer or servant of a local authority which, or an authorised person (within the meaning of section 31(9)) who, is a party to the proceedings;
   (*b*) be, or have been, a member, officer or servant of a local authority or voluntary organisation (within the meaning of section 105(1)) who has been directly concerned in that capacity in arrangements relating to the care, accommodation or welfare of the child during the five years prior to the commencement of the proceedings; or
   (*c*) be a serving probation officer who has, in that capacity, been previously concerned with the child or his family.

(8) When appointing a children's guardian the court shall consider the appointment of anyone who has previously acted as children's guardian of the same child.

(9) The appointment of a children's guardian under this rule shall continue for such time as is specified in the appointment or until terminated by the court.

(10) When terminating an appointment in accordance with paragraph (9), the court shall give its reasons in writing for so doing.

(11) Where the court appoints a children's guardian in accordance with this rule or refuses to make such an appointment, the court or the proper officer shall record the appointment or refusal in Form C47.

4.11 Powers and duties of officers of the service

(1) In carrying out his duty under section 7(1)(*a*) or section 41(2), the officer of the service shall have regard to the principle set out in section 1(2) and the matters set out in

section 1(3)(*a*) to (*f*) as if for the word "court" in that section there were substituted the words "officer of the service".

(2) The officer of the service shall make such investigations as may be necessary for him to carry out his duties and shall, in particular –

(*a*) contact or seek to interview such persons as he thinks appropriate or as the court directs;
(*b*) obtain such professional assistance as is available to him which he thinks appropriate or which the court directs him to obtain.

(3) In addition to his duties, under other paragraphs of this rule, or rules 4.11A and 4.11B, the officer of the service shall provide to the court such other assistance as it may require.

(4) A party may question the officer of the service about oral or written advice tendered by him to the court.

4.11A   Additional powers and duties of children's guardian

(1) The children's guardian shall –

(*a*) appoint a solicitor to represent the child unless such a solicitor has already been appointed; and
(*b*) give such advice to the child as is appropriate having regard to his understanding and, subject to rule 4.12(1)(*a*), instruct the solicitor representing the child on all matters relevant to the interests of the child including possibilities for appeal, arising in the course of the proceedings.

(2) Where the children's guardian is an officer of the service authorised by the Service in the terms mentioned by and in accordance with section 15(1) of the Criminal Justice and Courts Services Act 2000, paragraph 1(*a*) shall not require him to appoint a solicitor for the child if he intends to have conduct of the proceedings on behalf of the child unless –

(*a*) the child wishes to instruct a solicitor direct; and
(*b*) the children's guardian or the court considers that he is of sufficient understanding to do so.

(3) Where it appears to the children's guardian that the child –

(*a*) is instructing his solicitor direct, or
(*b*) intends to conduct and is capable of conducting the proceedings on his own behalf,

he shall inform the court and from then he –

(i) shall perform all of his duties set out in rule 4.11 and this rule, other than duties under paragraph (1)(*a*) of this rule, and such other duties as the court may direct;
(ii) shall take such part in the proceedings as the court may direct; and
(iii) may, with leave of the court, have legal representation in the conduct of those duties.

(4) Unless excused by the court, the children's guardian shall attend all directions appointments in and hearings of the proceedings and shall advise the court on the following matters –

(*a*) whether the child is of sufficient understanding for any purpose including the child's refusal to submit to a medical or psychiatric examination or other assessment that the court has power to require, direct or order;
(*b*) the wishes of the child in respect of any matter relevant to the proceedings, including his attendance at court;
(*c*) the appropriate forum for the proceedings;
(*d*) the appropriate timing of the proceedings or any part of them;

    (*e*) the options available to it in respect of the child and the suitability of each such option including what order should be made in determining the application; and

    (*f*) any other matter concerning which the court seeks his advice or concerning which he considers that the court should be informed.

(5) The advice given under paragraph (4) may, subject to any order of the court, be given orally or in writing; and if the advice be given orally, a note of it shall be taken by the court or the proper officer.

(6) The children's guardian shall, where practicable, notify any person whose joinder as a party to those proceedings would be likely, in the opinion of the children's guardian, to safeguard the interests of the child of that person's right to apply to be joined under rule 4.7(2) and shall inform the court –

    (*a*) of any such notification given;

    (*b*) of anyone whom he attempted to notify under this paragraph but was unable to contact; and

    (*c*) of anyone whom he believes may wish to be joined to the proceedings.

(7) The children's guardian shall, unless the court otherwise directs, not less than 14 days before the date fixed for the final hearing of the proceedings –

    (*a*) file a written report advising on the interests of the child; and

    (*b*) serve a copy of the filed report on the other parties.

(8) The children's guardian shall serve and accept service of documents on behalf of the child in accordance with rule 4.8(3)(*b*) and (4)(*b*) and, where the child has not himself been served, and has sufficient understanding, advise the child of the contents of any document so served.

(9) If the children's guardian inspects records of the kinds referred to in section 42, he shall bring to the attention of –

    (*a*) the court; and

    (*b*) unless the court otherwise directs, the other parties to the proceedings,

all records and documents which may, in his opinion, assist in the proper determination of the proceedings.

(10) The children's guardian shall ensure that, in relation to a decision made by the court in the proceedings –

    (*a*) if he considers it appropriate to the age and understanding of the child, the child is notified of that decision; and

    (*b*) if the child is notified of the decision, it is explained to the child in a manner appropriate to his age and understanding.

4.11B Additional powers and duties of a children and family reporter

(1) The children and family reporter shall –

    (*a*) notify the child of such contents of his report (if any) as he considers appropriate to the age and understanding of the child, including any reference to the child's own views on the application and the recommendation of the children and family reporter; and

    (*b*) if he does notify the child of any contents of his report, explain them to the child in a manner appropriate to his age and understanding.

(2) Where the court has –

    (*a*) directed that a written report be made by a children and family reporter; and

    (*b*) notified the children and family reporter that his report is to be considered at a hearing,

the children and family reporter shall –

    (i) file the report; and
    (ii) serve a copy on the other parties and on the children's guardian (if any),
    by such time as the court may direct and if no direction is given, not less than 14
    days before that hearing.

(3) The court may direct that the children and family reporter attend any hearing at which his report is to be considered.

(4) The children and family reporter shall advise the court if he considers that the joinder of a person as a party to the proceedings would be likely to safeguard the interests of the child.

(5) The children and family reporter shall consider whether it is in the best interests of the child for the child to be made a party to the proceedings.

(6) If the children and family reporter considers the child should be made a party to the proceedings he shall notify the court of his opinion together with the reasons for that opinion.

4.12 Solicitor for child

(1) A solicitor appointed under section 41(3) or in accordance with rule 4.11A(1)(*a*) shall represent the child –

    (*a*) in accordance with instructions received from the children's guardian (unless the solicitor considers, having taken into account the views of the children's guardian and any direction of the court under rule 4.11A(3), that the child wishes to give instructions which conflict with those of the children's guardian and that he is able, having regard to his understanding, to give such instructions on his own behalf in which case he shall conduct the proceedings in accordance with instructions received from the child), or

    (*b*) where no children's guardian has been appointed for the child and the condition in section 41(4)(*b*) is satisfied, in accordance with instructions received from the child, or

    (*c*) in default of instructions under (*a*) or (*b*), in furtherance of the best interests of the child.

(2) A solicitor appointed under section 41(3) or in accordance with rule 4.11A(1)(*a*) shall serve and accept service of documents on behalf of the child in accordance with rule 4.8(3)(*a*) and (4)(*a*) and, where the child has not himself been served and has sufficient understanding, advise the child of the contents of any document so served.

(3) Where the child wishes an appointment of a solicitor under section 41(3) or in accordance with rule 4.11A(1)(*a*) to be terminated, he may apply to the court for an order terminating the appointment; and the solicitor and the children's guardian shall be given an opportunity to make representations.

(4) Where the children's guardian wishes an appointment of a solicitor under section 41(3) to be terminated, he may apply to the court for an order terminating the appointment; and the solicitor and, if he is of sufficient understanding, the child, shall be given an opportunity to make representations.

(5) When terminating an appointment in accordance with paragraph (3) or (4), the court shall give its reasons for so doing, a note of which shall be taken by the court or the proper officer.

(6) Where the court appoints a solicitor under section 41(3) or refuses to make such an appointment, the court or the proper officer shall record the appointment or refusal in Form C48.

4.13 Welfare officer

(1) Where the court has directed that a written report be made by a welfare officer in accordance with section 7(1)(*b*), the report shall be filed at or by such time as the court directs or, in the absence of such a direction, at least 14 days before a relevant hearing; and the proper officer shall, as soon as practicable, serve a copy of the report on the parties and any children's guardian.

(2) In paragraph (1), a hearing is relevant if the proper officer has given the welfare officer notice that his report is to be considered at it.

(3) After the filing of a report by a welfare officer, the court may direct that the welfare officer attend any hearing at which the report is to be considered; and

>   (*a*) except where such a direction is given at a hearing attended by the welfare officer the proper officer shall inform the welfare officer of the direction; and
>   (*b*) at the hearing at which the report is considered any party may question the welfare officer about his report.

(3A) The welfare officer shall consider whether it is in the best interests of the child for the child to be made a party to the proceedings.

(3B) If the welfare officer considers the child should be made a party to the proceedings he shall notify the court of his opinion together with the reasons for that opinion.

(4) This rule is without prejudice to any power to give directions under rule 4.14.

4.14 Directions

(1) In this rule, "party" includes the children's guardian and, where a request or a direction concerns a report under section 7, the welfare officer or children and family reporter.

(2) In proceedings to which this Part applies the court may, subject to paragraph (3), give, vary or revoke directions for the conduct of the proceedings, including –

>   (*a*) the timetable for the proceedings;
>   (*b*) varying the time within which or by which an act is required, by these rules or by other rules of court, to be done;
>   (*c*) the attendance of the child;
>   (*d*) the appointment of a children's guardian, a guardian ad litem, or of a solicitor under section 41(3);
>   (*e*) the service of documents;
>   (*f*) the submission of evidence including experts' reports;
>   (*g*) the preparation of welfare reports under section 7;
>   (*h*) the transfer of the proceedings to another court;
>   (*i*) consolidation with other proceedings.

(3) Directions under paragraph (2) may be given, varied or revoked either –

>   (*a*) of the court's own motion having given the parties notice of its intention to do so, and an opportunity to attend and be heard or to make written representations,
>   (*b*) on the written request in Form C2 of a party specifying the direction which is sought, filed and served on the other parties, or
>   (*c*) on the written request in Form C2 of a party specifying the direction which is sought, to which the other parties consent and which they or their representatives have signed.

(4) In an urgent case the request under paragraph (3)(*b*) may, with the leave of the court, be made –

>   (*a*) orally, or

(*b*) without notice to the parties, or

(*c*) both as in sub-paragraph (*a*) and as in sub-paragraph (*b*).

(5) On receipt of a written request under paragraph (3)(*b*) the proper officer shall fix a date for the hearing of the request and give not less than 2 days' notice in Form C6 to the parties of the date so fixed.

(6) On considering a request under paragraph (3)(*c*) the court shall either –

(*a*) grant the request, whereupon the proper officer shall inform the parties of the decision, or

(*b*) direct that a date be fixed for the hearing of the request, whereupon the proper officer shall fix such a date and give not less than 2 days' notice to the parties of the date so fixed.

(7) A party may apply for an order to be made under section 11(3) or, if he is entitled to apply for such an order, under section 38(1) in accordance with paragraph (3)(*b*) or (*c*).

(8) Where a court is considering making, of its own motion, a section 8 order, or an order under section 31, 34 or 38, the power to give directions under paragraph (2) shall apply.

(9) Directions of a court which are still in force immediately prior to the transfer of proceedings to which this Part applies to another court shall continue to apply following the transfer, subject to any changes of terminology which are required to apply those directions to the court to which the proceedings are transferred, unless varied or discharged by directions under paragraph (2).

(10) The court or the proper officer shall take a note of the giving, variation or revocation of a direction under this rule and serve, as soon as practicable, a copy of the note on any party who was not present at the giving, variation or revocation.

4.15 Timing of proceedings

(1) Where these rules or other rules of court provide a period of time within which or by which a certain act is to be performed in the course of proceedings to which this Part applies, that period may not be extended otherwise than by direction of the court under rule 4.14.

(2) At the –

(*a*) transfer to a court of proceedings to which this Part applies,

(*b*) postponement or adjournment of any hearing or directions appointment in the course of proceedings to which this Part applies, or

(*c*) conclusion of any such hearing or directions appointment other than one at which the proceedings are determined, or so soon thereafter as is practicable, the court or the proper officer shall –

(i) fix a date upon which the proceedings shall come before the court again for such purposes as the court directs, which date shall, where paragraph (*a*) applies, be as soon as possible after the transfer, and

(ii) give notice to the parties, the children's guardian or the welfare officer or children and family reporter of the date so fixed.

4.16 Attendance at directions appointment and hearing

(1) Subject to paragraph (2), a party shall attend a directions appointment of which he has been given notice in accordance with rule 4.14(5) unless the court otherwise directs.

(2) Proceedings or any part of them shall take place in the absence of any party, including the child, if –

(*a*) the court considers it in the interests of the child, having regard to the matters to be discussed or the evidence likely to be given, and

(*b*) the party is represented by a children's guardian or solicitor;

and when considering the interests of the child under sub-paragraph (*a*) the court shall give the children's guardian, the solicitor for the child and, if he is of sufficient understanding, the child an opportunity to make representations.

(3) Subject to paragraph (4), where at the time and place appointed for a hearing or directions appointment the applicant appears but one or more of the respondents do not, the court may proceed with the hearing or appointment.

(4) The court shall not begin to hear an application in the absence of a respondent unless –

(*a*) it is proved to the satisfaction of the court that he received reasonable notice of the date of the hearing; or

(*b*) the court is satisfied that the circumstances of the case justify proceeding with the hearing.

(5) Where, at the time and place appointed for a hearing or directions appointment one or more of the respondents appear but the applicant does not, the court may refuse the application or, if sufficient evidence has previously been received, proceed in the absence of the applicant.

(6) Where at the time and place appointed for a hearing or directions appointment neither the applicant nor any respondent appears, the court may refuse the application.

(7) Unless the court otherwise directs, a hearing of, or directions appointment in, proceedings to which this Part applies shall be in chambers.

4.17 Documentary evidence

(1) Subject to paragraphs (4) and (5), in proceedings to which this Part applies a party shall file and serve on the parties, any welfare officer or children and family reporter and any children's guardian of whose appointment he has been given notice under rule 4.10(5) –

(*a*) written statements of the substance of the oral evidence which the party intends to adduce at a hearing of, or a directions appointment in, those proceedings, which shall –
　　(i) be dated,
　　(ii) be signed by the person making the statement,
　　(iii) contain a declaration that the maker of the statement believes it to be true and understands that it may be placed before the court; and
　　(iv) show in the top right hand corner of the first page –
　　　　(*a*) the initials and surname of the person making the statement,
　　　　(*b*) the number of the statement in relation to the maker,
　　　　(*c*) the date on which the statement was made, and
　　　　(*d*) the party on whose behalf it is filed; and

(*b*) copies of any documents, including experts' reports, upon which the party intends to rely at a hearing of, or a directions appointment in, those proceedings,

at or by such time as the court directs or, in the absence of a direction, before the hearing or appointment.

(2) A party may, subject to any direction of the court about the timing of statements under this rule, file and serve on the parties a statement which is supplementary to a statement served under paragraph (1).

(3) At a hearing or a directions appointment a party may not, without the leave of the court –

(*a*) adduce evidence, or

(*b*) seek to rely on a document,

in respect of which he has failed to comply with the requirements of paragraph (1).

(4) In proceedings for a section 8 order a party shall –

(*a*) neither file nor serve any document other than as required or authorised by these rules, and

(*b*) in completing a form prescribed by these rules, neither give information, nor make a statement, which is not required or authorised by that form,

without the leave of the court.

(5) In proceedings for a section 8 order no statement or copy may be filed under paragraph (1) until such time as the court directs.

4.18 Expert evidence – examination of child

(1) No person may, without the leave of the court, cause the child to be medically or psychiatrically examined, or otherwise assessed, for the purpose of the preparation of expert evidence for use in the proceedings.

(2) An application for leave under paragraph (1) shall, unless the court otherwise directs, be served on all parties to the proceedings and on the children's guardian.

(3) Where the leave of the court has not been given under paragraph (1), no evidence arising out of an examination or assessment to which that paragraph applies may be adduced without the leave of the court.

4.19 Amendment

(1) Subject to rule 4.17(2), a document which has been filed or served in proceedings to which this Part applies, may not be amended without the leave of the court which shall, unless the court otherwise directs, be requested in writing.

(2) On considering a request for leave to amend a document the court shall either –

(*a*) grant the request, whereupon the proper officer shall inform the person making the request of that decision, or

(*b*) invite the parties or any of them to make representations, within a specified period, as to whether such an order should be made.

(3) A person amending a document shall file it and serve it on those persons on whom it was served prior to amendment; and the amendments shall be identified.

4.20 Oral evidence

The court or the proper officer shall keep a note of the substance of the oral evidence given at a hearing of, or directions appointment in, proceedings to which this Part applies.

4.21 Hearing

(1) The court may give directions as to the order of speeches and evidence at a hearing or directions appointment, in the course of proceedings to which this Part applies.

(2) Subject to directions under paragraph (1), at a hearing of, or directions appointment in, proceedings to which this Part applies, the parties and the children's guardian shall adduce their evidence in the following order –

(*a*) the applicant,

(*b*) any party with parental responsibility for the child,

(*c*) other respondents,

(*d*) the children's guardian,

(*e*) the child, if he is a party to the proceedings and there is no children's guardian.

(3) After the final hearing of proceedings to which this Part applies, the court shall deliver its judgment as soon as is practicable.

(4) When making an order or when refusing an application, the court shall –

(*a*) where it makes a finding of fact state such finding and complete Form C22; and

(*b*) state the reasons for the court's decision.

(5) An order made in proceedings to which this Part applies shall be recorded, by the court or the proper officer, either in the appropriate form in Appendix 1 to these rules or, where there is no such form, in writing.

(6) Subject to paragraph (7), a copy of an order made in accordance with paragraph (5) shall, as soon as practicable after it has been made, be served by the proper officer on the parties to the proceedings in which it was made and on any person with whom the child is living.

(7) Within 48 hours after the making ex parte of –

(*a*) a section 8 order, or

(*b*) an order under section 44, 48(4), 48(9) or 50,

the applicant shall serve a copy of the order in the appropriate form in Appendix 1 to these Rules on –

(i) each party,

(ii) any person who has actual care of the child or who had such care immediately prior to the making of the order, and

(iii) in the case of an order referred to in sub-paragraph (*b*), the local authority in whose area the child lives or is found.

(8) At a hearing of, or directions appointment in, an application which takes place outside the hours during which the court office is normally open, the court or the proper officer shall take a note of the substance of the proceedings.

4.21A Attachment of penal notice to section 8 order

CCR Order 29, rule 1 (committal for breach of order or undertaking) shall apply to section 8 orders as if for paragraph (3) of that rule there were substituted the following –

"(3) In the case of a section 8 order (within the meaning of section 8(2) of the Children Act 1989) enforceable by committal order under paragraph (1), the judge or the district judge may, on the application of the person entitled to enforce the order, direct that the proper officer issue a copy of the order, indorsed with or incorporating a notice as to the consequences of disobedience, for service in accordance with paragraph (2), and no copy of the order shall be issued with any such notice indorsed or incorporated save in accordance with such a direction".

4.22 Appeals

(1) Where an appeal lies –

(*a*) to the High Court under section 94, or

(*b*) from any decision of a district judge to the judge of the court in which the decision was made, it shall be made in accordance with the following provisions; and references to "the court below" are references to the court from which, or person from whom, the appeal lies.

(2) The appellant shall file and serve on the parties to the proceedings in the court below, and on any children's guardian –

> (*a*) notice of the appeal in writing, setting out the grounds upon which he relies;
> (*b*) a certified copy of the summons or application and of the order appealed against, and of any order staying its execution;
> (*c*) a copy of any notes of the evidence;
> (*d*) a copy of any reasons given for the decision.

(2A) In relation to an appeal to the High Court under section 94, the documents required to be filed by paragraph (2) shall, –

> (*a*) where the care centre listed in column (ii) of Schedule 2 to the Children (Allocation of Proceedings) Order 1991 against the entry in column (i) relating to the petty sessions area or London commission area in which the court below is situated –
>> (i) is the principal registry, or
>> (ii) has a district registry in the same place,
>> be filed in that registry, and
> (*b*) in any other case, be filed in the district registry, being in the same place as a care centre within the meaning of article 2(*c*) of the said Order, which is nearest to the court below.

(3) The notice of appeal shall be filed and served in accordance with paragraph (2)(*a*) –

> (*a*) within 14 days after the determination against which the appeal is brought, or
> (*b*) in the case of an appeal against an order under section 38(1), within 7 days after the making of the order, or
> (*c*) with the leave of the court to which, or judge to whom, the appeal is to be brought, within such other time as that court or judge may direct.

(4) The documents mentioned in paragraph (2)(*b*) to (*d*) shall, subject to any direction of the court to which, or judge to whom, the appeal is to be brought, be filed and served as soon as practicable after the filing and service of the notice of appeal under paragraph (2)(*a*).

(5) Subject to paragraph (6), a respondent who wishes –

> (*a*) to contend on the appeal that the decision of the court below should be varied, either in any event or in the event of the appeal being allowed in whole or in part, or
> (*b*) to contend that the decision of the court below should be affirmed on grounds other than those relied upon by that court, or
> (*c*) to contend by way of cross-appeal that the decision of the court below was wrong in whole or in part,

shall, within 14 days of receipt of notice of the appeal, file and serve on all other parties to the appeal a notice in writing, setting out the grounds upon which he relies.

(6) No notice under paragraph (5) may be filed or served in an appeal against an order under section 38.

(7) In the case of an appeal mentioned in paragraph (1)(*a*) an application to –

> (*a*) withdraw the appeal,
> (*b*) have the appeal dismissed with the consent of all the parties, or
> (*c*) amend the grounds of appeal,

may be heard by a district judge.

(8) An appeal of the kind mentioned in paragraph (1)(*a*) shall, unless the President otherwise directs, be heard and determined by a single judge.

4.23 Confidentiality of documents

(1) Notwithstanding any rule of court to the contrary, no document, other than a record of an order, held by the court and relating to proceedings to which this Part applies shall be disclosed, other than to –

    (*a*) a party,
    (*b*) the legal representative of a party,
    (*c*) the children's guardian,
    (*d*) the Legal Aid Board, or
    (*e*) a welfare officer or children and family reporter,
    (*f*) an expert whose instruction by a party has been authorised by the court,
without leave of the judge or district judge.

(2) Nothing in this rule shall prevent the notification by the court or the proper officer of a direction under section 37(1) to the authority concerned.

(3) Nothing in this rule shall prevent the disclosure of a document prepared by an officer of the service for the purpose of –

    (*a*) enabling a person to perform functions required by regulations under section 62(3A) of the Justices of the Peace Act 1997;
    (*b*) assisting an officer of the service who is appointed by the court under any enactment to perform his functions.

(4) Nothing in this rule shall prevent the disclosure of any document relating to proceedings by an officer of the service to any other officer of the service unless that other officer is involved in the same proceedings but on behalf of a different party.

4.24 Notification of consent

(1) Consent for the purposes of –

    (*a*) section 16(3), or
    (*b*) section 38A(2)(*b*)(ii) or 44A(2)(*b*)(ii), or
    (*c*) paragraph 19(3)(*c*) or (*d*) of Schedule 2,
shall be given either –

        (i) orally in court, or
        (ii) in writing to the court signed by the person giving his consent.

(2) Any written consent given for the purposes of subsection (2) of section 38A or section 44A, shall include a statement that the person giving consent –

    (*a*) is able and willing to give to the child the care which it would be reasonable to expect a parent to give him; and
    (*b*) understands that the giving of consent could lead to the exclusion of the relevant person from the dwelling-house in which the child lives.

4.24A Exclusion requirements: interim care orders and emergency protection orders

(1) This rule applies where the court includes an exclusion requirement in an interim care order or an emergency protection order.

(2) The applicant for an interim care order or emergency protection order shall –

    (*a*) prepare a separate statement of the evidence in support of the application for an exclusion requirement;

(*b*) serve the statement personally on the relevant person with a copy of the order containing the exclusion requirement (and of any power of arrest which is attached to it);

(*c*) inform the relevant person of his right to apply to vary or discharge the exclusion requirement.

(3) Where a power of arrest is attached to an exclusion requirement in an interim care order or an emergency protection order, a copy of the order shall be delivered to the officer for the time being in charge of the police station for the area in which the dwelling-house in which the child lives is situated (or of such other station as the court may specify) together with a statement showing that the relevant person has been served with the order or informed of its terms (whether by being present when the order was made or by telephone or otherwise).

(4) Rules 3.9(5), 3.9A (except paragraphs (1) and (3)) and 3.10 shall apply, with the necessary modifications, for the service, variation, discharge and enforcement of any exclusion requirement to which a power of arrest is attached as they apply to an order made on an application under Part IV of the Family Law Act 1996.

(5) The relevant person shall serve the parties to the proceedings with any application which he makes for the variation or discharge of the exclusion requirement.

(6) Where an exclusion requirement ceases to have effect whether –

(*a*) as a result of the removal of a child under section 38A(10) or 44A(10),

(*b*) because of the discharge of the interim care order or emergency protection order, or

(*c*) otherwise,

the applicant shall inform –

(i) the relevant person,

(ii) the parties to the proceedings

(iii) any officer to whom a copy of the order was delivered under paragraph (3), and

(iv) (where necessary) the court.

(7) Where the court includes an exclusion requirement in an interim care order or an emergency protection order of its own motion, paragraph (2) shall apply with the omission of any reference to the statement of the evidence.

4.25 Secure accommodation – evidence

In proceedings under section 25, the court shall, if practicable, arrange for copies of all written reports before it to be made available before the hearing to –

(*a*) the applicant;

(*b*) the parent or guardian of the child;

(*c*) any legal representative of the child;

(*d*) the children's guardian; and

(*e*) the child, unless the court otherwise directs;

and copies of such reports may, if the court considers it desirable, be shown to any person who is entitled to notice of the proceedings in accordance with these rules.

4.26 Investigation under section 37

(1) This rule applies where a direction is given to an appropriate authority by the High Court or a county court under section 37(1).

(2) On giving a direction the court shall adjourn the proceedings and the court or the proper officer shall record the direction in Form C40.

(3) A copy of the direction recorded under paragraph (2) shall, as soon as practicable after the direction is given, be served by the proper officer on the parties to the proceedings in which the direction is given and, where the appropriate authority is not a party, on that authority.

(4) When serving the copy of the direction on the appropriate authority the proper officer shall also serve copies of such of the documentary evidence which has been, or is to be, adduced in the proceedings as the court may direct.

(5) Where a local authority informs the court of any of the matters set out in section 37(3)(*a*) to (*c*) it shall do so in writing.

4.27 Direction to local education authority to apply for education supervision order

(1) For the purposes of section 40(3) and (4) of the Education Act 1944 a direction by the High Court or a county court to a local education authority to apply for an education supervision order shall be given in writing.

(2) Where, following such a direction, a local education authority informs the court that they have decided not to apply for an education supervision order, they shall do so in writing.

4.28 Transitional provision

Nothing in any provision of this Part of these rules shall affect any proceedings which are pending (within the meaning of paragraph 1 of Schedule 14 to the Act of 1989) immediately before these rules come into force.

PART IVA
PROCEEDINGS UNDER SECTION 30 OF THE HUMAN FERTILISATION AND EMBRYOLOGY ACT 1990

4A.1 Interpretation

(1) In this Part of these Rules –

"the 1990 Act" means the Human Fertilisation and Embryology Act 1990;
"the birth father" means the father of the child, including a person who is treated as being the father of the child by section 28 of the 1990 Act where he is not the husband within the meaning of section 30 of the 1990 Act;
"the birth mother" means the woman who carried the child;
"the birth parents" means the birth mother and the birth father;
"the husband and wife" means the persons who may apply for a parental order where the conditions set out in section 30(1) of the 1990 Act are met;
"parental order" means an order under section 30 of the 1990 Act (parental orders in favour of gamete donors) providing for a child to be treated in law as a child of the parties to a marriage.
"parental order reporter" means an officer of the service appointed under section 41 of the Children Act 1989 in relation to proceedings specified by paragraph (2).

(2) Applications under section 30 of the 1990 Act are specified proceedings for the purposes of section 41 of the Children Act 1989 in accordance with section 41(6)(i) of that Act.

4A.2 Application of Part IV

Subject to the provisions of this Part, the provisions of Part IV of these Rules shall apply as appropriate with any necessary modifications to proceedings under this Part except that rules 4.7(1), 4.9, 4.10(1)(*b*), 4.10(11), 4.11A(1), 4.11A(3) and 4.12 shall not apply.

4A.3 Parties

The applicants shall be the husband and wife and the respondents shall be the persons set out in the relevant entry in column (iii) of Appendix 3.

4A.4 Acknowledgement

Within 14 days of the service of an application for a parental order, each respondent shall file and serve on all the other parties an acknowledgement in Form C52.

4A.5 Appointment and duties of the parental order reporter

(1) As soon as practicable after the application has been filed the court shall consider the appointment of a parental order reporter in accordance with section 41(1) of the Children Act 1989.

(2), (3) (*revoked*)

(4) In addition to such of the matters set out in rules 4.11 and 4.11A as are appropriate to the proceedings, the parental order reporter shall –

   (i) investigate the matters set out in section 30(1) to (7) of the 1990 Act;
  (ii) so far as he considers necessary, investigate any matter contained in the application form or other matter which appears relevant to the making of a parental order;
 (iii) advise the court on whether there is any reason under section 6 of the Adoption Act 1976, as applied with modifications by the Parental Orders (Human Fertilisation and Embryology) Regulations 1994, to refuse the parental order.

4A.6 Personal attendance of applicants

The court shall not make a parental order except upon the personal attendance before it of the applicants.

4A.7 Copies of orders

(1) Where a parental order is made by a court sitting in Wales in respect of a child who was born in Wales and the applicants so request before the order is drawn up, the proper officer shall obtain a translation into Welsh of the particulars set out in the order.

(2) Within 7 days after the making of a parental order, the proper officer shall send a copy of the order to the Registrar General.

(3) A copy of any parental order may be supplied to the Registrar General at his request.

4A.8 Amendment and revocation of orders

(1) An application under paragraph 4 of Schedule 1 to the Adoption Act 1976 as modified by the Parental Orders (Human Fertilisation and Embryology) Regulations 1994 for the amendment of a parental order or the revocation of a direction to the Registrar General may be made ex parte in the first instance but the court may require notice of the application to be served on such persons as it thinks fit.

(2) Where the application is granted, the proper officer shall send to the Registrar General a notice specifying the amendments or informing him of the revocation and shall give sufficient particulars of the order to enable the Registrar General to identify the case.

4A.9 Custody, inspection and disclosure of documents and information

(1) All documents relating to proceedings for a parental order shall, while they are in the custody of the court, be kept in a place of special security.

(2) Any person who obtains any information in the course of, or relating to proceedings for a parental order shall treat that information as confidential and shall only disclose it if –

> (*a*) the disclosure is necessary for the proper exercise of his duties, or
> (*b*) the information is requested –
>> (i) by a court or public authority (whether in Great Britain or not) having power to determine proceedings for a parental order and related matters, for the purpose of discharge of its duties in that behalf, or
>> (ii) by a person who is authorised in writing by the Secretary of State to obtain the information for the purposes of research.

4A.10 Application for removal, return etc of child

(1) An application under sections 27(1), 29(1) or 29(2) of the Adoption Act 1976 as applied with modifications by the Parental Orders (Human Fertilisation and Embryology) Regulations 1994 shall be made on notice in proceedings under section 30 of the 1990 Act.

(2) The proper officer shall serve a copy of the application and a notice of the date of the hearing on all the parties to the proceedings under section 30, on the guardian ad litem and on any other person or body, not being the child, as the court thinks fit.

(3) The court may at any time give directions as to the conduct of the application under this rule.

PART V
WARDSHIP

5.1 Application to make a minor a ward of court

(1) An application to make a minor a ward of court shall be made by originating summons and, unless the court otherwise directs, the plaintiff shall file an affidavit in support of the application when the originating summons is issued.

(2) Rule 4.3 shall, so far as applicable, apply to an application by a local authority for the leave of the court under section 100(3) of the Act of 1989.

(3) Where there is no person other than the minor who is a suitable defendant, an application may be made ex parte to a district judge for leave to issue either an ex parte originating summons or an originating summons with the minor as defendant thereto; and,

except where such leave is granted, the minor shall not be made a defendant to an originating summons under this rule in the first instance.

(4) Particulars of any summons issued under this rule in a district registry shall be sent by the proper officer to the principal registry for recording in the register of wards.

(5) The date of the minor's birth shall, unless otherwise directed, be stated in the summons, and the plaintiff shall –

    (*a*) on issuing the summons or before or at the first hearing thereof lodge in the registry out of which the summons issued a certified copy of the entry in the Register of Births or, as the case may be, in the Adopted Children Register relating to the minor, or

    (*b*) at the first hearing of the summons apply for directions as to proof of birth of the minor in some other manner.

(6) The name of each party to the proceedings shall be qualified by a brief description, in the body of the summons, of his interest in, or relation to, the minor.

(7) Unless the court otherwise directs, the summons shall state the whereabouts of the minor or, as the case may be, that the plaintiff is unaware of his whereabouts.

(8) Upon being served with the summons, every defendant other than the minor shall forthwith lodge in the registry out of which the summons issued a notice stating the address of the defendant and the whereabouts of the minor or, as the case may be, that the defendant is unaware of his whereabouts and, unless the court otherwise directs, serve a copy of the same upon the plaintiff.

(9) Where any party other than the minor changes his address or becomes aware of any change in the whereabouts of the minor after the issue, or, as the case may be, service of the summons, he shall, unless the court otherwise directs, forthwith lodge notice of the change in the registry out of which the summons issued and serve a copy of the notice on every other party.

(10) The summons shall contain a notice to the defendant informing him of the requirements of paragraphs (8) and (9).

(11) In this rule any reference to the whereabouts of a minor is a reference to the address at which and the person with whom he is living and any other information relevant to the question where he may be found.

5.2 Enforcement of order by tipstaff

The power of the High Court to secure, through an officer attending upon the court, compliance with any direction relating to a ward of court may be exercised by an order addressed to the tipstaff.

5.3 Where minor ceases to be a ward of court

(1) A minor who, by virtue of section 41(2) of the Supreme Court Act 1981, becomes a ward of court on the issue of a summons under rule 5.1 shall cease to be a ward of court –

    (*a*) if an application for an appointment for the hearing of the summons is not made within the period of 21 days after the issue of the summons, at the expiration of that period;

    (*b*) if an application for such an appointment is made within that period, on the determination of the application made by the summons unless the court hearing it orders that the minor be made a ward of court.

(2) Nothing in paragraph (1) shall be taken as affecting the power of the court under section 41(3) of the said Act to order that any minor who is for the time being a ward of court shall cease to be a ward of court.

(3) If no application for an appointment for the hearing of a summons under rule 5.1 is made within the period of 21 days after the issue of the summons, a notice stating whether the applicant intends to proceed with the application made by the summons must be left at the registry in which the matter is proceeding immediately after the expiration of that period.

5.4 Adoption of minor who is a ward of court

(1) An application for leave –

    (*a*) to commence proceedings to adopt a minor who is a ward, or
    (*b*) to commence proceedings to free such a minor for adoption,
may be ex parte to a district judge.

(2) Where a local authority has been granted leave to place a minor who is a ward with foster parents with a view to adoption it shall not be necessary for an application to be made for leave under paragraph (1)(*a*) or (*b*) unless the court otherwise directs.

(3) If the applicant for leave under paragraph (1)(*a*) or (*b*), or a local authority which has applied for leave as referred to in paragraph (2), or a foster parent so requests, the district judge may direct that any subsequent proceedings shall be conducted with a view to securing that the proposed adopter is not seen by or made known to any respondent or prospective respondent who is not already aware of his identity except with his consent.

(4) In paragraphs (1) and (3) "proceedings" means proceedings in the High Court or in a county court.

5.5 Orders for use of secure accommodation

No order shall be made with the effect of placing or keeping a minor in secure accommodation, within the meaning of section 25(1) of the Act of 1989 unless the minor has been made a party to the summons.

5.6 Notice to provider of refuge

Where a child is staying in a refuge which is certified under section 51(1) or 51(2) of the Act of 1989, the person who is providing that refuge shall be given notice of any application under this Part of these rules in respect of that child.

PART VI
CHILD ABDUCTION AND CUSTODY

6.1 Interpretation

In this Part, unless the context otherwise requires –

    (*a*) "the Act" means the Child Abduction and Custody Act 1985 and words or expressions bear the same meaning as in that Act;

(*b*) "the Hague Convention" means the convention defined in section 1(1) of the Act and "the European Convention" means the convention defined in section 12(1) of the Act.

6.2 Mode of application

(1) Except as otherwise provided by this Part, every application under the Hague Convention and the European Convention shall be made by originating summons, which shall be in Form No 10 in Appendix A to the Rules of the Supreme Court 1965 and issued out of the principal registry.

(2) An application in custody proceedings for a declaration under section 23(2) of the Act shall be made by summons in those proceedings.

6.3 Contents of originating summons: general provisions

(1) The originating summons by which any application is made under the Hague Convention or the European Convention shall state –

    (*a*) the name and date of birth of the child in respect of whom the application is made;
    (*b*) the names of the child's parents or guardians;
    (*c*) the whereabouts or suspected whereabouts of the child;
    (*d*) the interest of the plaintiff in the matter and the grounds of the application; and
    (*e*) particulars of any proceedings (including proceedings out of the jurisdiction and concluded proceedings) relating to the child,

and shall be accompanied by all relevant documents including but not limited to the documents specified in Article 8 of the Hague Convention or, as the case may be, Article 13 of the European Convention.

6.4 Contents of originating summons: particular provisions

(1) In applications under the Hague Convention, in addition to the matters specified in rule 6.3 –

    (*a*) the originating summons under which an application is made for the purposes of Article 8 for the return of a child shall state the identity of the person alleged to have removed or retained the child and, if different, the identity of the person with whom the child is presumed to be;
    (*b*) the originating summons under which an application is made for the purposes of Article 15 for a declaration shall identify the proceedings in which the request that such a declaration be obtained was made.

(2) In applications under the European Convention, in addition to the matters specified in rule 6.3, the originating summons shall identify the decision relating to custody or rights of access which is sought to be registered or enforced or in relation to which a declaration that it is not to be recognised is sought.

6.5 Defendants

The defendants to an application under the Act shall be –

    (*a*) the person alleged to have brought into the United Kingdom the child in respect of whom an application under the Hague Convention is made;
    (*b*) the person with whom the child is alleged to be;
    (*c*) any parent or guardian of the child who is within the United Kingdom and is not otherwise a party;

(*d*) the person in whose favour a decision relating to custody has been made if he is not otherwise a party; and

(*e*) any other person who appears to the court to have a sufficient interest in the welfare of the child.

6.6 Acknowledgement of service

The time limit for acknowledging service of an originating summons by which an application is made under the Hague Convention or the European Convention shall be seven days after service of the originating summons (including the day of service) or, in the case of a defendant referred to in rule 6.5(*d*) or (*e*), such further time as the Court may direct.

6.7 Evidence

(1) The plaintiff, on issuing an originating summons under the Hague Convention or the European Convention, may lodge affidavit evidence in the principal registry in support of his application and serve a copy of the same on the defendant with the originating summons.

(2) A defendant to an application under the Hague Convention or the European Convention may lodge affidavit evidence in the principal registry and serve a copy of the same on the plaintiff within seven days after service of the originating summons on him.

(3) The plaintiff in an application under the Hague Convention or the European Convention may within seven days thereafter lodge in the principal registry a statement in reply and serve a copy thereof on the defendant.

6.8 Hearing

Any application under the Act (other than an application (*a*) to join a defendant, (*b*) to dispense with service or extend the time for acknowledging service, or (*c*) for the transfer of proceedings) shall be heard and determined by a judge and shall be dealt with in chambers unless the court otherwise directs.

6.9 Dispensing with service

The court may dispense with service of any summons (whether originating or ordinary) in any proceedings under the Act.

6.10 Adjournment of summons

The hearing of the originating summons under which an application under the Hague Convention or the European Convention is made may be adjourned for a period not exceeding 21 days at any one time.

6.11 Stay of proceedings

(1) A party to proceedings under the Hague Convention shall, where he knows that an application relating to the merits of rights of custody is pending in or before a relevant authority, file in the principal registry a concise statement of the nature of the application which is pending, including the authority before which it is pending.

(2) A party –

(*a*) to pending proceedings under section 16 of the Act, or

(*b*) to proceedings as a result of which a decision relating to custody has been registered under section 16 of the Act,

shall, where he knows that such an application as is specified in section 20(2) of the Act or section 42(2) of the Child Custody Act 1987 (an Act of Tynwald) is pending in or before a relevant authority, file a concise statement of the nature of the application which is pending.

(3) The proper officer shall on receipt of such a statement as is mentioned in paragraph (1) or (2) notify the relevant authority in which or before whom the application is pending and shall subsequently notify it or him of the result of the proceedings.

(4) On the court receiving notification under paragraph (3) above or equivalent notification from the Court of Session, the High Court in Northern Ireland or the High Court of Justice of the Isle of Man –

(*a*) where the application relates to the merits of rights of custody, all further proceedings in the action shall be stayed unless and until the proceedings under the Hague Convention in the High Court, Court of Session, the High Court in Northern Ireland or the High Court of Justice of the Isle of Man, as the case may be, are dismissed, and the parties to the action shall be notified by the proper officer of the stay and of any such dismissal accordingly, and

(*b*) where the application is such a one as is specified in section 20(2) of the Act, the proper officer shall notify the parties to the action.

(5) In this rule "relevant authority" includes the High Court, a county court, a magistrates' court, the Court of Session, a sheriff court, a children's hearing within the meaning of Part III of the Social Work (Scotland) Act 1968, the High Court in Northern Ireland, a county court in Northern Ireland, a court of summary jurisdiction in Northern Ireland, the High Court of Justice of the Isle of Man, a court of summary jurisdiction in the Isle of Man or the Secretary of State.

6.12 Transfer of proceedings

(1) At any stage in the proceedings under the Act the court may, of its own motion or on the application by summons of any party to the proceedings issued on two days' notice, order that the proceedings be transferred to the Court of Session, the High Court in Northern Ireland or the High Court of Justice of the Isle of Man.

(2) Where an order is made under paragraph (1) the proper officer shall send a copy of the order, which shall state the grounds therefor, together with the originating summons, the documents accompanying it and any evidence, to the Court of Session, the High Court in Northern Ireland or the High Court of Justice of the Isle of Man, as the case may be.

(3) Where proceedings are transferred to the Court of Session, the High Court in Northern Ireland or the High Court of Justice of the Isle of Man the costs of the whole proceedings both before and after the transfer shall be at the discretion of the Court to which the proceedings are transferred.

(4) Where proceedings are transferred to the High Court from the Court of Session, the High Court in Northern Ireland or the High Court of Justice of the Isle of Man the proper officer shall notify the parties of the transfer and the proceedings shall continue as if they had begun by originating summons under rule 6.2.

6.13 Interim directions

An application for interim directions under section 5 or section 19 of the Act may where the case is one of urgency be made ex parte on affidavit but shall otherwise be made by summons.

6.14

(*revoked*)

6.15 Revocation and variation of registered decisions

(1) This rule applies to decisions which have been registered under section 16 of the Act and are subsequently varied or revoked by an authority in the Contracting State in which they were made.

(2) The court shall, on cancelling the registration of a decision which has been revoked, notify –

  (*a*) the person appearing to the court to have care of the child,
  (*b*) the person on whose behalf the application for registration of the decision was made, and
  (*c*) any other party to that application,
of the cancellation.

(3) The court shall, on being notified of the variation of a decision, notify –

  (*a*) the person appearing to the court to have care of the child, and
  (*b*) any party to the application for registration of the decision
of the variation and any such person may apply by summons in the proceedings for the registration of the decision, for the purpose of making representations to the court before the registration is varied.

(4) Any person appearing to the court to have an interest in the matter may apply by summons in the proceedings for the registration of a decision for the cancellation or variation of the registration.

6.16 Orders for disclosure of information

At any stage in proceedings under the European Convention the court may, if it has reason to believe that any person may have relevant information about the child who is the subject of those proceedings, order that person to disclose such information and may for that purpose order that the person attend before it or file affidavit evidence.

6.17 Applications and orders under sections 33 and 34 of the Family Law Act 1986

(1) In this rule "the 1986 Act" means the Family Law Act 1986.

(2) An application under section 33 of the 1986 Act shall be in Form C4 and an order made under that section shall be in Form C30.

(3) An application under section 34 of the 1986 Act shall be in Form C3 and an order made under that section shall be in Form C31.

(4) An application under section 33 or section 34 of the 1986 Act may be made ex parte in which case the applicant shall file the application –

(*a*)   where the application is made by telephone, within 24 hours after the making of the application, or

(*b*)   in any other case at the time when the application is made,

and shall serve a copy of the application on each respondent 48 hours after the making of the order.

(5) Where the court refuses to make an order on an ex parte application it may direct that the application be made inter partes.

PART VII
ENFORCEMENT OF ORDERS

Chapter 1. General

7.1 Enforcement of order for payment of money etc

(1) Before any process is issued for the enforcement of an order made in family proceedings for the payment of money to any person, an affidavit shall be filed verifying the amount due under the order and showing how that amount is arrived at.

In a case to which CCR Order 25 rule 11 (which deals with the enforcement of a High Court judgment in the county court) applies, the information required to be given in an affidavit under this paragraph may be given in the affidavit filed pursuant to that rule.

(2) Except with the leave of the district judge, no writ of fieri facias or warrant of execution shall be issued to enforce payment of any sum due under an order for ancillary relief or an order made under the provisions of section 27 of the Act of 1973 where an application for a variation order is pending.

(3) Where a warrant of execution has been issued to enforce an order made in family proceedings pending in the principal registry which are treated as pending in a divorce county court, the goods and chattels against which the warrant has been issued shall wherever they are situate, be treated for the purposes of section 103 of the County Courts Act 1984 as being out of the jurisdiction of the principal registry.

(4) The Attachment of Earnings Act 1971 and CCR Order 27 (which deals with attachment of earnings) shall apply to the enforcement of an order made in family proceedings in the principal registry which are treated as pending in a divorce county court as if the order were an order made by such a court.

(5) Where an application under CCR Order 25, rule 3 (which deals with the oral examination of a judgment debtor) relates to an order made by a divorce county court –

(*a*)   the application shall be made to such divorce county court as in the opinion of the applicant is nearest to the place where the debtor resides or carries on business, and

(*b*)   there shall be filed with the application the affidavit required by paragraph (1) of this rule and, except where the application is made to the court in which the order sought to be enforced was made, a copy of the order shall be exhibited to the affidavit;

and accordingly paragraph (2) of the said rule 3 shall not apply.

7.2 Committal and injunction

(1) Subject to RSC Order 52, rule 6 (which, except in certain cases, requires an application for an order of committal to be heard in open court) an application for an order of committal in family proceedings pending in the High Court shall be made by summons.

(2) Where no judge is conveniently available to hear the application, then, without prejudice to CCR Order 29, rule 3(2) (which in certain circumstances gives jurisdiction to a district judge) an application for –

    (*a*) the discharge of any person committed, or
    (*b*) the discharge by consent of an injunction granted by a judge,

may be made to the district judge who may, if satisfied of the urgency of the matter and that it is expedient to do so, make any order on the application which a judge could have made.

(3) Where an order or warrant for the committal of any person to prison has been made or issued in family proceedings pending in the principal registry which are treated as pending in a divorce county court or a county court, that person shall, wherever he may be, be treated for the purposes of section 122 of the County Courts Act 1984 as being out of the jurisdiction of the principal registry; but if the committal is for failure to comply with the terms of an injunction, the order or warrant may, if the court so directs, be executed by the tipstaff within any county court district.

(3A) Where an order or warrant for the arrest or committal of any person has been made or issued in proceedings under Part IV of the Family Law Act 1996 pending in the principal registry which are treated as pending in a county court, the order or warrant may, if the court so directs, be executed by the tipstaff within any county court district.

(4) For the purposes of section 118 of the County Courts Act 1984 in its application to the hearing of family proceedings at the Royal Courts of Justice or the principal registry, the tipstaff shall be deemed to be an officer of the court.

7.3 Transfer of county court order to High Court

(1) Any person who desires the transfer to the High Court of any order made by a divorce county court in family proceedings except an order for periodical payments or for the recovery of arrears of periodical payments shall apply to the court ex parte by affidavit stating the amount which remains due under the order, and on the filing of the application the transfer shall have effect.

(2) Where an order is so transferred, it shall have the same force and effect and the same proceedings may be taken on it as if it were an order of the High Court.

Chapter 2. Judgment summonses

7.4 General provisions

(1) In this chapter, unless the context otherwise requires –

    "order" means an order made in family proceedings for the payment of money;
    "judgment creditor" means a person entitled to enforce an order under section 5 of the Debtors Act 1869;
    "debtor" means a person liable under an order;
    "judgment summons" means a summons under the said section 5 requiring a debtor to appear and be examined on oath as to his means.

(2) An application for the issue of a judgment summons may be made –

(*a*) in the case of an order of the High Court, to the principal registry, a district registry or a divorce county court, whichever in the opinion of the judgment creditor is most convenient,

(*b*) in the case of an order of a divorce county court, to whichever divorce county court is in the opinion of the judgment creditor most convenient,

having regard (in either case) to the place where the debtor resides or carries on business and irrespective of the court or registry in which the order was made.

(3) The application shall be made by filing a request in Form M16 together with the affidavit required by rule 7.1(1) and, except where the application is made to the registry or divorce county court in which the order was made, a copy of the order shall be exhibited to the affidavit.

(4) A judgment summons shall not be issued without the leave of a judge if the debtor is in default under an order of commitment made on a previous judgment summons in respect of the same order.

(5) Every judgment summons shall be in Form M17 and shall be served on the debtor personally not less than 10 days before the hearing and at the time of service there shall be paid or tendered to the debtor a sum reasonably sufficient to cover his expenses in travelling to and from the court at which he is summoned to appear.

(6) CCR Order 28, rule 3 (which deals among other things with the issue of successive judgment summonses) shall apply to a judgment summons, whether issued in the High Court or a divorce county court, but as if the said rule 3 did not apply CCR Order 7, rule 19(2).

(7) Successive judgment summonses may be issued notwithstanding that the judgment debtor has ceased to reside or carry on business at the address stated in Form M16 since the issue of the original judgment summons.

(8) Where an applicant has obtained one or more orders in the same application but for the benefit of different persons –

(*a*) he shall be entitled to issue a judgment summons in respect of those orders on behalf of any judgment creditor without (where the judgment creditor is a child) seeking leave to act as his next friend; and

(*b*) only one judgment summons need be issued in respect of those orders.

(9) On the hearing of the judgment summons the judge may –

(*a*) where the order is for lump sum provision or costs, or

(*b*) where the order is for maintenance pending suit or other periodical payments and it appears to him that the order would have been varied or suspended if the debtor had made an application for that purpose,

make a new order for payment of the amount due under the original order, together with the costs of the judgment summons, either at a specified time or by instalments.

(10) If the judge makes an order of committal, he may direct its execution to be suspended on terms that the debtor pays to the judgment creditor the amount due, together with the costs of the judgment summons, either at a specified time or by instalments, in addition to any sums accruing due under the original order.

(11) All payments under a new order or an order of committal shall be made to the judgment creditor unless the judge otherwise directs.

(12) Where an order of committal is suspended on such terms as are mentioned in paragraph (10) –

(a) all payments thereafter made under the said order shall be deemed to be made, first, in or towards the discharge of any sums from time to time accruing due under the original order and, secondly, in or towards the discharge of a debt in respect of which the judgment summons was issued and the costs of the summons;

(b) CCR Order 28, rule 7(4) and (5) (which deal with an application for a further suspension) shall apply to the said order, whether it was made in the High Court or a divorce county court; and

(c) the said order shall not be issued until the judgment creditor has filed an affidavit of default on the part of the debtor.

7.5 Special provisions as to judgment summonses in the High Court

(1) RSC Order 38, rule 2(3) (which enables evidence to be given by affidavit in certain cases) shall apply to a judgment summons issued in the High Court as if it were an originating summons.

(2) Witnesses may be summoned to prove the means of the debtor in the same manner as witnesses are summoned to give evidence on the hearing of a cause, and writs of subpoena may for that purpose be issued out of the registry in which the judgment summons is issued.

(3) Where the debtor appears at the hearing, the travelling expenses paid to him may, if the judge so directs, be allowed as expenses of a witness, but if the debtor appears at the hearing and no order of committal is made, the judge may allow to the debtor, by way of set-off or otherwise, his proper costs, including compensation for loss of time, as upon an attendance by a defendant at a trial in court.

(4) Where a new order or an order of committal is made, the proper officer of the registry in which the judgment summons was issued shall send notice of the order to the debtor and, if the original order was made in another registry, to the proper officer of that registry.

(5) An order of committal shall be directed to the tipstaff, for execution by him, or to the proper officer of the county court within the district of which the debtor is to be found, for execution by a deputy tipstaff.

(6) Unless the judge otherwise directs, the judgment creditor's costs of and incidental to the judgment summons shall be fixed and allowed without taxation in accordance with RSC Order 62, rule 7(4).

(7) Where the judge directs that the judgment creditor's costs of and incidental to a judgment summons are to be taxed, RSC Order 62 shall have effect in relation to those costs with such modifications as may be necessary.

7.6 Special provisions as to judgment summonses in divorce county courts

(1) CCR Order 25, rules 3, 4 and 11 (which deal with the oral examination of debtors and the execution of High Court orders in county courts) and Order 28, rules 1, 2, 3(2), 7(3) and 9(2) (which deal with the issue of a judgment summons in a county court and the subsequent procedure) shall not apply to a judgment summons issued in a divorce county court.

(2) CCR Order 28, rule 9(1) (which relates to a judgment summons heard in a county court on a judgment or order of the High Court) shall apply to such a summons as if for the words "the High Court" there were substituted the words "any other court" where they first appear and "that other court" where they next appear.

(3) CCR Order 28, rule 7(1) and (2) (which relates to the suspension of a committal order) shall apply to such a summons subject to rule 7.4(10) and (11) of these Rules.

Chapter 3. Registration and enforcement of custody orders

7.7 Registration under Family Law Act 1986

(1) In this Chapter, unless the context otherwise requires –

"the appropriate court" means, in relation to Scotland, the Court of Session and, in relation to Northern Ireland, the High Court and, in relation to a specified dependent territory, the corresponding court in that territory;

"the appropriate officer" means, in relation to the Court of Session, the Deputy Principal Clerk of Session, in relation to the High Court in Northern Ireland, the Master (Care and Protection) of that court and, in relation to the appropriate court in a specified dependent territory, the corresponding officer of that court;

"Part I order" means an order under Part I of the Act of 1986;

"registration" means registration under Part I of the Act of 1986, and "register" and "registered" shall be construed accordingly;

"specified dependent territory" means a dependent territory specified in column 1 of Schedule 1 to the Family Law Act 1986 (Specified Dependent Territories) Order 1991.

(2) The prescribed officer for the purposes of sections 27(4) and 28(1) of the Act shall be the family proceedings department manager of the principal registry and the functions of the court under sections 27(3) and 28(1) of the Act of 1986 shall be performed by the proper officer.

7.8 Application to register English Part I order

(1) An application under section 27 of the Act of 1986 for the registration of a Part I order made by the High Court shall be made by lodging in the principal registry or the district registry, as the case may be, a certified copy of the order, together with a copy of any order which has varied any of the terms of the original order and an affidavit by the applicant in support of his application, with a copy thereof.

(2) An application under section 27 of the Act of 1986 for the registration of a Part I order made by a county court shall be made by filing in that court a certified copy of the order, together with a certified copy of any order which has varied any of the terms of the original order and an affidavit in support of the application, with a copy thereof.

(3) The affidavit in support under paragraphs (1) and (2) above shall state –

(a) the name and address of the applicant and his interest under the order;

(b) the name and date of birth of the child in respect of whom the order was made, his whereabouts or suspected whereabouts and the name of any person with whom he is alleged to be;

(c) the name and address of any other person who has an interest under the order and whether it has been served on him;

(d) in which of the jurisdictions of Scotland, Northern Ireland or a specified dependent territory the order is to be registered;

(e) that, to the best of the applicant's information and belief, the order is in force;

(f) whether, and if so where, the order is already registered; and

(g) details of any order known to the applicant which affects the child and is in force in the jurisdiction in which the Part I order is to be registered;

and there shall be exhibited to the affidavit any document relevant to the application.

(4) Where the documents referred to in paragraphs (1) and (3), or (2) and (3), as the case may be are to be sent to the appropriate court, the proper officer shall –

    (*a*) retain the original affidavit and send the other documents to the appropriate officer;

    (*b*) record the fact of transmission in the records of the court; and

    (*c*) file a copy of the documents.

(5) On receipt of notice of the registration of a Part I order in the appropriate court the proper officer shall record the fact of registration in the records of the court.

(6) If it appears to the proper officer that the Part I order is no longer in force or that the child has attained the age of 16, he shall refuse to send the documents to the appropriate court and shall within 14 days of such refusal give notice of it, and the reason for it, to the applicant.

(7) If the proper officer refuses to send the documents to the appropriate court, the applicant may apply to the judge in chambers for an order that the documents (or any of them) be sent to the appropriate court.

7.9 Registration of orders made in Scotland, Northern Ireland or a specified dependent territory

On receipt of a certified copy of an order made in Scotland, Northern Ireland or a specified dependent territory for registration, the prescribed officer shall –

    (*a*) record the order in the register by entering particulars of –

        (i) the name and address of the applicant and his interest under the order;

        (ii) the name and whereabouts or suspected whereabouts of the child, his date of birth, and the date on which he will attain the age of 16; and

        (iii) the terms of the order, its date and the court which made it;

    (*b*) file the certified copy and accompanying documents; and

    (*c*) give notice to the court which sent the certified copy and to the applicant for registration that the order has been registered.

7.10 Revocation and variation of English order

(1) Where a Part I order which is registered in the appropriate court is revoked or varied, the proper officer of the court making the subsequent order shall –

    (*a*) send a certified copy of that order to the appropriate officer, and to the court which made the Part I order, if that court is different from the court making the subsequent order, for filing by that court;

    (*b*) record the fact of transmission in the records of the court; and

    (*c*) file a copy of the order.

(2) On receipt of notice from the appropriate court of the amendment of its register, the proper officer in the court which made the Part I order and in the court which made the subsequent order shall each record the fact of amendment.

7.11 Registration of revoked, recalled or varied orders made in Scotland, Northern Ireland or a specified dependent territory

(1) On receipt of a certified copy of an order made in Scotland, Northern Ireland or a specified dependent territory which revokes, recalls or varies a registered Part I order, the proper officer shall enter particulars of the revocation, recall or variation, as the case may be, in the register, and give notice of the entry to –

    (*a*) the court which sent the certified copy,

(*b*) if different, the court which made the Part I order,

(*c*) the applicant for registration, and

(*d*) if different, the applicant for the revocation, recall or variation of the order.

(2) An application under section 28(2) of the Act of 1986 shall be made by summons and may be heard and determined by a district judge.

(3) If the applicant for the Part I order is not the applicant under section 28(2) of the Act of 1986 he shall be made a defendant to the application.

(4) Where the court cancels a registration of its own motion or on an application under paragraph (2), the proper officer shall amend the register accordingly and shall give notice of the amendment to the court which made the Part I order.

7.12 Interim directions

(1) An application for interim directions under section 29 of the Act of 1986 may be heard and determined by a district judge.

(2) The parties to the proceedings for enforcement and, if he is not a party thereto, the applicant for the Part I order, shall be made parties to the application.

7.13 Staying and dismissal of enforcement proceedings

(1) An application under section 30(1) or 31(1) of the Act of 1986 may be heard and determined by a district judge.

(2) The parties to the proceedings for enforcement which are sought to be stayed and, if he is not a party thereto, the applicant for the Part I order shall be made parties to an application under either of the said sections.

(3) Where the court makes an order under section 30(2) or (3) or section 31(3) of the Act of 1986, the proper officer shall amend the register accordingly, and shall give notice of the amendment to the court which made the Part I order and to the applicants for registration, for enforcement and for the stay or dismissal of the proceedings for enforcement.

7.14 Particulars of other proceedings

A party to proceedings for or relating to a Part I order who knows of other proceedings (including proceedings out of the jurisdiction and concluded proceedings) which relate to the child concerned shall file an affidavit stating –

(*a*) in which jurisdiction and court the other proceedings were instituted;

(*b*) the nature and current state of such proceedings and the relief claimed or granted;

(*c*) the names of the parties to such proceedings and their relationship to the child; and

(*d*) if applicable, and if known, the reasons why the relief claimed in the proceedings for or relating to the Part I order was not claimed in the other proceedings.

7.15 Inspection of register

The following persons, namely –

(*a*) the applicant for registration of a registered Part I order,

(*b*) any person who satisfies a district judge that he has an interest under the Part I order, and

(*c*) any person who obtains the leave of a district judge, may inspect any entry in the register relating to the order and may bespeak copies of the order and of any document relating thereto.

Chapter 4. Enforcement of maintenance orders

7.16 Interpretation

In this chapter –

> "the Act of 1920" means the Maintenance Orders (Facilities for Enforcement) Act 1920;
> "the Act of 1950" means the Maintenance Orders Act 1950;
> "the Act of 1958" means the Maintenance Orders Act 1958;
> "the Act of 1965" means the Matrimonial Causes Act 1965;
> "the Act of 1971" means the Attachment of Earnings Act 1971;
> "the Act of 1972" means the Maintenance Orders (Reciprocal Enforcement) Act 1972;
> "English maintenance order" means a maintenance order made in the High Court.

7.17 Registration etc of orders under Act of 1920

(1) The prescribed officer for the purposes of section 1(1) of the Act of 1920 shall be the senior district judge, and on receiving from the Secretary of State a copy of a maintenance order made by a court in any part of Her Majesty's dominions outside the United Kingdom to which the Act of 1920 extends he shall cause the order to be registered in the register kept for the purpose of that Act (in this rule referred to as "the register").

 The copy of the order received from the Secretary of State shall be filed in the principal registry.

(2) An application for the transmission of an English maintenance order under section 2 of the Act of 1920 shall be made to the district judge by lodging in the principal registry a certified copy of the order and an affidavit stating the applicant's reasons for believing that the person liable to make payments under the order is resident in some part of Her Majesty's dominions outside the United Kingdom to which the Act of 1920 extends, together with full particulars, so far as known to the applicant, of that person's address and occupation and any other information which may be required by the law of that part of Her Majesty's dominions for the purpose of the enforcement of the order.

(3) If it appears to the district judge mentioned in paragraph (2) that the person liable to make payments under the English maintenance order is resident in some part of Her Majesty's dominions outside the United Kingdom to which the Act of 1920 extends, he shall send the certified copy of the order to the Secretary of State for transmission to the Governor of that part of Her Majesty's dominions.

 Particulars of any English maintenance order sent to the Secretary of State under the said section 2 shall be entered in the register and the fact that this has been done shall be noted in the records of the court.

(4) Where an English maintenance order has been made in a cause or matter proceeding in a district registry, an application for the transmission of the order under the said section 2 may be made to the district judge of that registry and paragraphs (2) and (3) of this rule shall have effect as if for reference to the principal registry there were substituted references to the district registry.

 The proper officer shall send to the principal registry for entry in the register particulars of any order sent by him to the Secretary of State.

(5) Any person who satisfies a district judge that he is entitled to or liable to make payments under an English maintenance order or a maintenance order made by a court in any part of Her Majesty's dominions outside the United Kingdom to which the Act of 1920 extends or a solicitor acting on behalf of any such person or, with the leave of a district judge, any other person may inspect the register and bespeak copies of any order which has been registered and of any document filed therewith.

Proceedings under Part II of Act of 1950

7.18 Interpretation of rules 7.18 to 7.21

In this rule and rules 7.19 to 7.21 –

"the clerk of the Court of Session" means the deputy principal clerk in charge of the petition department of the Court of Session;

"maintenance order" means a maintenance order to which section 16 of the Act of 1950 applies;

"Northern Irish order" means a maintenance order made by the Supreme Court of Northern Ireland;

"register" means the register kept for the purposes of the Act of 1950;

"the registrar in Northern Ireland" means the chief registrar of the Queen's Bench Division (Matrimonial) of the High Court of Justice in Northern Ireland;

"registration" means registration under Part II of the Act of 1950 and "registered" shall be construed accordingly;

"Scottish order" means a maintenance order made by the Court of Session.

7.19 Registration etc of English order

(1) An application for the registration of an English maintenance order may be made by lodging with the proper officer a certified copy of the order, together with an affidavit by the applicant (and a copy thereof) stating –

(*a*) the address in the United Kingdom, and the occupation, of the person liable to make payments under the order;

(*b*) the date of service of the order on the person liable to make payments thereunder or, if the order has not been served, the reason why service has not been effected;

(*c*) the reason why it is convenient that the order should be enforceable in Scotland or Northern Ireland, as the case may be;

(*d*) the amount of any arrears due to the applicant under the order; and

(*e*) that the order is not already registered.

(2) If it appears to the district judge that the person liable to make payments under the order resides in Scotland or Northern Ireland and that it is convenient that the order should be enforceable there, the proper officer shall (subject to paragraph (6) below) send a certified copy of the order and the applicant's affidavit to the clerk of the Court of Session or to the registrar in Northern Ireland, as the case may be.

(3) On receipt of notice of the registration of an English maintenance order in the Court of Session or the Supreme Court of Northern Ireland, the proper officer shall –

(*a*) cause particulars of the notice to be entered in the register;

(*b*) note the fact of registration in the records of the court; and

(*c*) send particulars of the notice to the principal registry.

(4) Where an English order registered in the Court of Session or the Supreme Court of Northern Ireland is discharged or varied the proper officer of the court ordering the discharge or variation shall give notice thereof to the clerk of the Court of Session or to the

registrar in Northern Ireland, as the case may be, by sending him a certified copy of the order discharging or varying the maintenance order.

(5) Where the registration of an English maintenance order registered in the Court of Session or the Supreme Court of Northern Ireland is cancelled under section 24(1) of the Act of 1950, notice of the cancellation shall be sent (as required by section 24(3)(*a*) of that Act) to the proper officer, and on receipt of such notice he shall cause particulars of it to be entered in Part I of the register.

(6) Where the order sought to be registered was made in a county court, this rule shall apply as though references to the Court of Session, the clerk of the Court of Session, the Supreme Court of Northern Ireland and the registrar of Northern Ireland were references to the sheriff court, the sheriff-clerk of the sheriff court, the court of summary jurisdiction and the clerk of the court of summary jurisdiction respectively.

7.20 Registration etc of Scottish and Northern Irish orders

(1) In relation to a Scottish or Northern Irish order the prescribed officer for the purposes of section 17(2) of the Act of 1950 shall be the proper officer of the principal registry.

(2) On receipt of a certified copy of a Scottish or Northern Irish order for registration, the proper officer shall –

    (*a*) cause the order to be registered in Part II of the register and notify the clerk of the Court of Session or the registrar in Northern Ireland, as the case may be, that this has been done; and

    (*b*) file the certified copy and any statutory declaration or affidavit as to the amount of any arrears due under the order.

(3) An application under section 21(2) of the Act of 1950 by a person liable to make payments under a Scottish order registered in the High Court to adduce before that court such evidence as is mentioned in that section shall be made by lodging a request for an appointment before a district judge of the principal registry; and notice of the date, time and place fixed for the hearing shall be sent by post to the applicant and to the person entitled to payments under the order.

(4) The prescribed officer to whom notice of the discharge or variation of a Scottish or Northern Irish order registered in the High Court is to be given under section 23(1)(*a*) of the Act of 1950 shall be the proper officer, and on receipt of the notice he shall cause particulars of it to be registered in Part II of the register.

(5) An application under section 24(1) of the Act of 1950 for the cancellation of the registration of a Scottish or Northern Irish order shall be made ex parte by affidavit to a district judge of the principal registry who, if he cancels the registration, shall note the cancellation in Part II of the register, whereupon the proper officer shall send notice of the cancellation to the clerk of the Court of Session or the registrar in Northern Ireland, as the case may be, and also to the clerk of any magistrates' court in which the order has been registered in accordance with section 2(5) of the Act of 1958.

(6) A person entitled to payments under a Scottish or Northern Irish order registered in the High Court who wishes to take proceedings for or with respect to the enforcement of the order in a district registry may apply by letter to the senior district judge of the principal registry who may, if satisfied that the order ought to be enforceable in the district registry, make an order accordingly on such terms, if any, as may be just.

7.21 Inspection of register

Any person who satisfies a district judge of the principal registry that he is entitled to or liable to make payments under a maintenance order of a superior court or a solicitor acting on behalf of any such person or, with the leave of the district judge, any other person may inspect the register and bespeak copies of any such order which is registered in the High Court under Part II of the Act of 1950 and of any statutory declaration or affidavit filed therewith.

Registration etc of certain orders under the Act of 1958

7.22 Application and interpretation of rules 7.22 to 7.29

Section 21 of the Act of 1958 shall apply to the interpretation of this rule and rules 7.23 to 7.29 as it applies to the interpretation of that Act; and in those rules –

"cause book" includes cause card; and
"the register" means any register kept for the purposes of the Act of 1958.

7.23 Application for registration

(1) An application under section 2(1) of the Act of 1958 for the registration in a magistrates' court of a maintenance order shall be made by lodging with the proper officer –

        (i) a certified copy of the maintenance order, and
        (ii) two copies of the application in Form M33.

(2) The period required to be prescribed by rules of court for the purpose of section 2(2) of the Act of 1958 shall be 14 days.

(3) The proper officer shall cause the certified copy of an order required by the said section 2(2) to be sent to the justices' chief executive for a magistrates' court to be endorsed with a note that the application for registration of the order has been granted and to be accompanied by a copy of the application lodged under paragraph (1).

(4) On receipt of notice that a maintenance order has been registered in a magistrates' court in accordance with section 2(5) of the Act of 1958, the proper officer shall enter particulars of the registration in the records of the court.

7.24 Registration in a magistrates' court of an order registered in the High Court

On receipt of notice that a maintenance order registered in the High Court in accordance with section 17(4) of the Act of 1950 has been registered in a magistrates' court in accordance with section 2(5) of the Act of 1958, the proper officer shall cause particulars of the registration to be entered in Part II of the register.

7.25 Registration of magistrates' court order

On receipt of a certified copy of a magistrates' court order sent to him pursuant to section 2(4)(c) of the Act of 1958, the proper officer shall cause the order to be registered in the High Court by filing the copy and making an entry in the register or, where the copy order is received in a district registry, in the cause book and shall send notice to the justices' chief executive for the magistrates' court that the order has been duly registered.

7.26 Registration in the High Court of an order registered in a magistrates' court

(1) This rule applies where a sheriff court in Scotland or a magistrates' court in Northern Ireland has made an order for the registration in the High Court of an order previously registered in a magistrates' court in England and Wales in accordance with section 17(4) of the Act of 1950, and has sent a certified copy of the maintenance order to the proper officer of the High Court, pursuant to section 2(4)(c) of the Act of 1958.

(2) On receipt of the certified copy, the proper officer shall cause the order to be registered in the High Court by filing the copy and making an entry in the register, and shall send notice of the registration to the justices' chief executive for the original court and also to the justices' chief executive for the magistrates' court in which the order was registered in accordance with section 17(4) of the Act of 1950.

7.27 Variation or discharge of registered order

(1) Where the court makes an order varying or discharging an order registered in a magistrates' court under Part I of the Act of 1958, the proper officer shall send a certified copy of the first-mentioned order to the justices' chief executive for the magistrates' court.

(2) Where a certified copy of an order varying an order registered in a magistrates' court under Part I of the Act of 1958 is received from the justices' chief executive for the magistrates' court, the proper officer shall file the copy and enter particulars of the variation on the same documents or in the same records as particulars of registration are required by rule 7.23(4) to be entered.

(3) Where a certified copy of an order varying or discharging an order made by a magistrates' court and registered in the High Court under Part I of the Act of 1958 is received from the justices' chief executive for the magistrates' court, the proper officer shall –

　(a)　file the copy,
　(b)　enter particulars of the variation or discharge in the register or, where the copy order is received in a district registry, in the cause book, and
　(c)　send notice of the variation or discharge to any proper officer of a county court –
　　　(i)　who has given notice to the proper officer of proceedings taken in that court for the enforcement of the registered order, or
　　　(ii)　to whom any payment is to be made under an attachment of earnings order made by the High Court for the enforcement of the registered order.

7.28 Appeal from variation etc of order by magistrates' court

An appeal to the High Court under section 4(7) of the Act of 1958 shall be heard and determined by a Divisional Court of the Family Division, and rule 8.2 shall apply as it applies in relation to an appeal from a magistrates' court under the Domestic Proceedings and Magistrates' Courts Act 1978.

7.29 Cancellation of registration

(1) A notice under section 5 of the Act of 1958 by a person entitled to receive payments under an order registered in the High Court must be given to the proper officer.

(2) Where the High Court gives notice under the said section 5, the proper officer shall endorse the notice on the certified copy mentioned in rule 7.27(1).

(3) Where notice under the said section 5 is given in respect of an order registered in the High Court, the proper officer on being satisfied by an affidavit by the person entitled to receive payments under the order that no process for the enforcement of the order issued before the giving of the notice remains in force, shall –

    (*a*) cancel the registration by entering particulars of the notice in the register or cause book, as the case may be, and

    (*b*) send notice of the cancellation to the justices' chief executive for the court by which the order was made and, where applicable, to the justices' chief executive for the magistrates' court in which the order was registered in accordance with section 17(4) of the Act of 1950 stating, if such be the case, that the cancellation is in consequence of a notice given under subsection (1) of the said section 5.

(4) On receipt of notice from the justices' chief executive for a magistrates' court that the registration in that court under the Act of 1958 of an order made by the High Court or a county court has been cancelled, the proper officer shall enter particulars of the cancellation on the same documents or in the same records as particulars of registration are required by rule 7.23(4) to be entered.

(5) On receipt of notice from the justices' chief executive for a magistrates' court that the registration in that court under the Act of 1958 of an order registered in the High Court in accordance with section 17(4) of the Act of 1950 has been cancelled, the proper officer shall note the cancellation in Part II of the register.

Proceedings under Act of 1972

7.30 Interpretation of rules 7.31 to 7.39

(1) Expressions used in rules 7.31 to 7.39 which are used in the Act of 1972 have the same meanings as in that Act.

(2) The references in the Act of 1972 to the prescribed officer shall be construed as references to the proper officer within the meaning of rule 1.2(1).

(3) The reference in section 21 of the Act of 1972 to the proper officer shall be the proper officer within the meaning of rule 1.2(1).

7.31 Application for transmission of maintenance order to reciprocating country

An application for a maintenance order to be sent to a reciprocating country under section 2 of the Act of 1972 shall be made by lodging with the court –

    (*a*) an affidavit by the applicant stating –
        (i) the applicant's reason for believing that the payer under the maintenance order is residing in that country, and
        (ii) the amount of any arrears due to the applicant under the order, the date to which those arrears have been calculated and the date on which the next payment under the order falls due;

    (*b*) a certified copy of the maintenance order,

    (*c*) a statement giving such information as the applicant possesses as to the whereabouts of the payer,

    (*d*) a statement giving such information as the applicant possesses for facilitating the identification of the payer (including, if known to the applicant, the name and address of any employer of the payer, his occupation and the date and place of issue of any passport of the payer) and

    (*e*) if available to the applicant, a photograph of the payer.

7.32 Certification of evidence given on provisional order

Where the court makes a provisional order under section 5 of the Act of 1972 the document required by subsection (4) of that section to set out or summarise the evidence given in the proceedings shall be authenticated by a certificate signed by the district judge.

7.33 Confirmation of provisional order

(1) On receipt of a certified copy of a provisional order made in a reciprocating country, together with the document mentioned in section 5(5) of the Act of 1972, the proper officer shall fix a date, time and place for the court to consider whether or not the provisional order should be confirmed, and shall send to the payee under the maintenance order notice of the date, time and place so fixed together with a copy of the provisional order and that document.

(2) The proper officer shall send to the court which made the provisional order a certified copy of any order confirming or refusing to confirm that order.

7.34 Taking of evidence for court in reciprocating country

(1) The High Court shall be the prescribed court for the purposes of taking evidence pursuant to a request by a court in a reciprocating country under section 14 of the Act of 1972 where –

   (*a*) the request for evidence relates to a maintenance order made by a superior court in the United Kingdom, and
   (*b*) the witness resides in England and Wales.

(2) The evidence may be taken before a judge or officer of the High Court as the court thinks fit, and the provisions of RSC Order 39 shall apply with the necessary modifications as if the evidence were required to be taken pursuant to an order made under rule 1 of that Order.

(3) The county court shall be the prescribed court for the purposes of taking evidence pursuant to a request by a court in a reciprocating country pursuant to section 14 of the Act of 1972 where the request for evidence relates to a maintenance order made by a county court which has not been registered in a magistrates' court under the Act of 1958.

(4) Paragraph (2) shall apply to the taking of such evidence as though references therein to the High Court and RSC Order 39 were to the county court and CCR Order 20, rule 13 respectively.

7.35 Notification of variation or revocation

Where the court makes an order (other than a provisional order) varying or revoking a maintenance order a copy of which has been sent to a reciprocating country in pursuance of section 2 of the Act of 1972, the proper officer shall send a certified copy of the order to the court in the reciprocating country.

7.36 Transmission of documents

Any document required to be sent to a court in a reciprocating country under section 5(4) or section 14(1) of the Act of 1972 or by rule 7.33(2) or 7.36 shall be sent to the Lord Chancellor for transmission to that court unless the district judge is satisfied that, in accordance with the law of that country, the document may properly be sent by him direct to that court.

7.37 Application of rules 7.30 to 7.36 to Republic of Ireland

(1) In relation to the Republic of Ireland rules 7.30 to 7.36 shall have effect subject to the provisions of this rule.

(1A) A reference to the Act of 1972 in this rule, and in any rule which has effect in relation to the Republic of Ireland by virtue of this rule, shall be a reference to the said Act as modified by Schedule 2 to the Reciprocal Enforcement of Maintenance Orders (Republic of Ireland) Order 1993.

(2) The following paragraphs shall be added to rule 7.31 –

"(*f*) a statement as to whether or not the payer appeared in the proceedings in which the maintenance order was made and, if he did not, the original or a copy certified by the applicant or his solicitor to be a true copy of a document which establishes that notice of the institution of the proceedings was served on the payer;

(*g*) a document which establishes that notice of the order was sent to the payer, and

(*h*) if the payer received legal aid in the proceedings in which the order was made, a copy certified by the applicant or his solicitor to be a true copy of the legal aid certificate.".

(3) For rule 7.32 there shall be substituted the following rule –

"7.32 Certification of evidence given on application for variation or revocation

(1) Where an application is made to the court for the variation or revocation of an order to which section 5 of the Act of 1972 applies, the certified copy of the application and the documents required by subsection (3) of that section to set out or summarise the evidence in support of the application shall be authenticated by a certificate signed by the district judge.".

(4) Rule 7.33 shall not apply.

(5) For rule 7.35 there shall be substituted the following rule –

"7.35 Notification of variation or revocation

Where the High Court makes an order varying or revoking a maintenance order to which section 5 of the Act of 1972 applies, the proper officer shall send a certified copy of the order and a statement as to the service on the payer of the documents mentioned in subsection (3) of that section to the court in the Republic of Ireland by which the maintenance order is being enforced.".

(6) Rule 7.36 shall not apply.

7.38 Application of rules 7.30 to 7.36 to the Hague Convention countries

(1) In relation to the Hague Convention countries, rules 7.30, 7.31, 7.34, 7.35 and 7.36 shall have effect subject to the provisions of this rule, but rules 7.32 and 7.33 shall not apply.

(1A) A reference to the Act of 1972 in this rule, and in any rule which has effect in relation to the Hague Convention countries by virtue of this rule, shall be a reference to the said Act as modified by Schedule 3 to the Reciprocal Enforcement of Maintenance Orders (Hague Convention Countries) Order 1993.

(2) A reference in rules 7.31 and 7.34 to a reciprocating country shall be construed as a reference to a Hague Convention country.

(3) The following words shall be inserted after paragraph (*a*)(ii) of rule 7.31 –

"and
    (iii) whether the time for appealing against the order has expired and whether an appeal is pending;".

(4) The following paragraphs shall be inserted after paragraph (*e*) of rule 7.31 –

"(*f*) a statement as to whether or not the payer appeared in the proceedings in which the maintenance order was made, and, if he did not, the original or a copy certified by the applicant or his solicitor to be a true copy of a document which establishes that notice of the institution of proceedings, including notice of the substance of the claim, was served on the payer;

(*g*) a document which establishes that notice of the order was sent to the payer;

(*h*) a written statement as to whether or not the payee received legal aid in the proceedings in which the order was made, or in connection with the application under section 2 of the Act of 1972 and, if he did, a copy certified by the applicant or his solicitor to be a true copy of the legal aid certificate.".

(5) In relation to the Hague Convention countries the following rules shall apply in place of rules 7.35 and 7.36 –

"7.35 Notification of variation or revocation

(1) Where the court makes an order varying or revoking a maintenance order to which section 5 of the Act of 1972, as modified, applies, and the time for appealing has expired without an appeal having been entered, the proper officer shall send to the Lord Chancellor such documents as are required by subsection (8) of that section, as it applies to Hague Convention countries, including a certificate signed by the district judge that the order of variation or revocation is enforceable and that it is no longer subject to the ordinary forms of review.

(2) Where either party enters an appeal against the order of variation or revocation he shall, at the same time, inform the proper officer thereof by a notice in writing.

7.36 Transmission of documents

Any document required to be sent to a court in a Hague Convention country shall be sent to the Lord Chancellor for transmission to the court.".

7.39 Application of rules 7.30 to 7.36 to a specified State of the United States of America

(1) In this rule unless the context otherwise requires –

"specified State" means a State of the United States of America specified in Schedule 1 to the Reciprocal Enforcement of Maintenance Orders (United States of America) Order 1995.

(2) In relation to a specified State, rules 7.30, 7.31, 7.34, 7.35 and 7.36 shall have effect subject to the provisions of this rule, but rules 7.32 and 7.33 shall not apply.

(3) A reference to the Act of 1972 in this rule, and in any rule which has effect in relation to a specified State by virtue of this rule, shall be a reference to the said Act as modified by Schedule 3 to the Reciprocal Enforcement of Maintenance Orders (United States of America) Order 1995.

(4) A reference in rules 7.31 and 7.34 to a reciprocating country shall be construed as a reference to a specified State.

(5) Paragraph (*c*) of rule 7.31 shall not apply to a specified State.

(6) The following paragraphs shall be inserted after paragraph (*a*)(ii) of rule 7.31 –

> "(iii) the address of the payee;
> (iv) such information as is known as to the whereabouts of the payer; and
> (v) a description, so far as is known, of the nature and location of any assets of the payer available for execution.".

(7) A reference in paragraph (*b*) of rule 7.31 to a certified copy shall be construed as a reference to 3 certified copies.

(8) In relation to a specified State the following rules shall apply in place of rules 7.35 and 7.36 –

"7.35 Notification of variation of revocation

Where the court makes an order varying or revoking a maintenance order to which section 5 of the Act of 1972, as modified, applies, the proper officer shall send to the Secretary of State such documents as are required by subsection (7) of that section, as it applies to specified States.

7.36 Transmission of documents

Any document required to be sent to a court in a specified State shall be sent to the Secretary of State for transmission to the court."

Chapter 5. Registration and enforcement under the Council Regulation

7.40 Interpretation

In this chapter "judgment" is to be construed in accordance with the definition in Article 13 of the Council Regulation.

7.41 Filing of applications

Every application to the High Court under the Council Regulation, other than an application under rule 7.49 for a certified copy of a judgment, shall be filled with the principal registry.

7.42 Application for registration

An application for registration of a judgment under Article 21(2) of the Council Regulation shall be made without notice being served on any other party.

7.43 Evidence in support of application

(1) An application for registration under Article 21(2) of the Council Regulation must be supported by a statement that is sworn to be true or an affidavit –

> (*a*) exhibiting –
> > (i) the judgment or a verified or certified or otherwise duly authenticated copy thereof together with such other document or documents as may be requisite to show that, according to the law of the Contracting State in which it has been given, the judgment is enforceable and has been served;
> > (ii) in the case of a judgment given in default, the original or a certified true copy of the document which establishes that the party in default was served

with the document instituting the proceedings or with an equivalent document;

(iii) where it is the case, a document showing that the party making the application is in receipt of legal aid in the Contracting State in which the judgment was given;

(iv) where the judgment or document is not in the English language, a translation thereof into English certified by a notary public or a person qualified for the purpose in one of the Contracting States or authenticated by witness statement or affidavit;

(v) the certificate, in the form set out in Annex IV or Annex V of the Council Regulation, issued by the Contracting State in which judgment was given;

(b) stating –

(i) whether the judgment provides for the payment of a sum or sums of money;

(ii) whether interest is recoverable on the judgment or part thereof in accordance with the law of the State in which the judgment was given, and if such be the case, the rate of interest, the date from which interest is recoverable, and the date on which interest ceases to accrue;

(c) giving an address within the jurisdiction of the court for service of process on the party making the application and stating, so far as is known to the witness, the name and the usual or last known address or place of business of the person against whom judgment was given; and

(d) stating to the best of the information or belief of the witness –

(i) the grounds on which the right to enforce the judgment is vested in the party making the application;

(ii) as the case may require, either that at that date of the application the judgment has not been satisfied, or the part or amount in respect of which it remains unsatisfied.

(2) Where the party making the application does not produce the documents referred to in paragraphs (1)(a)(ii) and (iii) of this rule, the court may –

(a) fix a time within which the documents are to be produced;

(b) accept equivalent documents; or

(c) dispense with production of the documents.

7.44 Order for registration

(1) An order giving permission to register a judgment under Article 21(2) of the Council Regulation must be drawn up by the court.

(2) Every such order shall state the period within which an appeal may be made against the order for registration and shall contain a notification that the court will not enforce the judgment until after the expiration of that period.

(3) The notification referred to in paragraph (2) shall not prevent any application for protective measures under Article 12 of the Council Regulation pending final determination of any issue relating to enforcement of the judgment.

7.45 Register of judgments

There shall be kept in the principal registry by the proper officer a register of the judgments ordered to be registered under Article 21(2) of the Council Regulation.

7.46 Notice of registration

(1) Notice of the registration of a judgment under Article 21(2) of the Council Regulation must be served on the person against whom judgment was given by delivering it to him personally or by sending it to him at his usual or last known address or place of business or in such other manner as the court may direct.

(2) Permission is not required to serve such a notice out of the jurisdiction and rule 10.6 shall apply in relation to such a notice.

(3) The notice of the registration must state –

    (*a*) full particulars of the judgment registered and the order for registration;
    (*b*) the name of the party making the application and his address for service within the jurisdiction;
    (*c*) the right of the person against whom judgment was given to appeal against the order for registration; and
    (*d*) the period within which an appeal against the order for registration may be made.

7.47 Enforcement of judgment

(1) A judgment registered under Article 21(2) of the Council Regulation shall not be enforced until after the expiration of the period specified in accordance with rule 7.44(2) or, if that period has been extended by the Court, until after the expiration of the period so extended.

(2) Any party wishing to apply for the enforcement of a judgment registered under Article 21(2) of the Council Regulation must produce to the proper officer a witness statement or affidavit of service of the notice of registration of the judgment and of any order made by the court in relation to the judgment.

(3) Nothing in this rule shall prevent the court from granting protective measures under Article 12 of the Council Regulation pending final determination of any issue relating to enforcement of the judgment.

7.48 Application for recognition

(1) Registration of the judgment under these rules shall serve for the purposes of Article 14(3) of the Council Regulation as a decision that the judgment is recognised.

(2) Where it is sought to apply for recognition of a judgment, the rules of this chapter shall apply to such application as they apply to an application for registration under Article 21(2) of the Council Regulation, with the exception that the applicant shall not be required to produce –

    (*a*) a document or documents which establish that according to the law of the Contracting State in which it has been given the judgment is enforceable and has been served, or
    (*b*) the document referred to in rule 7.43(1)(*a*)(iii).

7.49 Enforcement of judgments in other Contracting States

(1) Subject to rules 10.16(2) and 10.20, an application for a certified copy of a judgment referred to in Article 32(1) of the Council Regulation must be made to the court which made the order on a witness statement or affidavit without notice being served on any other party.

(2) A witness statement or affidavit by which such an application is made must –

  (a) give particulars of the proceedings in which the judgment was obtained;
  (b) have annexed to it a copy of the petition or application by which the proceedings
       were begun, the evidence of service thereof on the respondent, copies of the
       pleadings and particulars, if any, and a statement of the grounds on which the
       judgment was based together, where appropriate, with any document showing that
       the applicant is entitled to legal aid or assistance by way of representation for the
       purposes of the proceedings;
  (c) state whether the respondent did or did not object to the jurisdiction, and, if so, on
       what grounds;
  (d) show that the judgment has been served in accordance with rules 4.8, 10.2, 10.3,
       10.4, 10.5, 10.6, 10.16 or 10.17 and is not subject to any order for the stay of
       proceedings;
  (e) state that the time for appealing has expired, or, as the case may be, the date on
       which it will expire and in either case whether notice of appeal against the
       judgment has been given; and
  (f) state –
       (i)   whether the judgment provides for the payment of a sum of money;
       (ii) whether interest is recoverable on the judgment or part thereof and if so, the
             rate of interest, the date from which interest is recoverable, and the date on
             which interest ceases to accrue.
(3) The certified copy of the judgment shall be an office copy sealed with the seal of the
court and signed by the district judge and there shall be issued with the copy of the
judgment a certified copy of any order which has varied any of the terms of the original
order.

7.50 Authentic instruments and court settlements

Rules 7.40 to 7.49 (except rule 7.43(1)(a)(ii)) shall apply to an authentic instrument and a
settlement to which Article 13(3) of the Council Regulation applies, as they apply to a
judgment subject to any necessary modifications.

PART VIII
APPEALS

8.1 Appeals from district judges

(1) Except where paragraph (2) applies, any party may appeal from an order or decision
made or given by the district judge in family proceedings in a county court to a judge on
notice; and in such a case –

  (a) CCR Order 13 rule 1(10) (which enables the judge to vary or rescind an order
       made by the district judge in the course of proceedings), and
  (b) CCR Order 37 rule 6 (which gives a right of appeal to the judge from a judgment
       or final decision of the district judge),
shall not apply to the order or decision.

(2) Any order or decision granting or varying an order (or refusing to do so) –

  (a) on an application for ancillary relief, or
  (b) in proceedings to which rules 3.1, 3.2, 3.3 or 3.6 apply,
shall be treated as a final order for the purposes of CCR Order 37, rule 6.

(3) On hearing an appeal to which paragraph (2) above applies, the judge may exercise his
own discretion in substitution for that of the district judge.

(4) Unless the court otherwise orders, any notice under this rule must be issued within 14 days of the order or decision appealed against and served not less than 14 days before the day fixed for the hearing of the appeal.

(5) Appeals under this rule shall be heard in chambers unless the judge otherwise directs.

(6) Unless the court otherwise orders, an appeal under this rule shall not operate as a stay of proceedings on the order or decision appealed against.

8.1A Appeals from orders made under Part IV of the Family Law Act 1996

(1) This rule applies to all appeals from orders made under Part IV of the Family Law Act 1996 and on such an appeal –

    (*a*) paragraphs (2), (3), (4), (5), (7) and (8) of rule 4.22,
    (*b*) paragraphs (5) and (6) of rule 8.1, and
    (*c*) paragraphs (4)(*e*) and (6) of rule 8.2,

shall apply subject to the following provisions of this rule and with the necessary modifications.

(2) The justices' chief executive for the magistrates' court from which an appeal is brought shall be served with the documents mentioned in rule 4.22(2).

(3) Where an appeal lies to the High Court, the documents required to be filed by rule 4.22(2) shall be filed in the registry of the High Court which is nearest to the magistrates' court from which the appeal is brought.

(4) Where the appeal is brought against the making of a hospital order or a guardianship order under the Mental Health Act 1983, a copy of any written evidence considered by the magistrates' court under section 37(1)(*a*) of the 1983 Act shall be sent by the justices' chief executive to the registry of the High Court in which the documents relating to the appeal are filed in accordance with paragraph (3).

(5) A district judge may dismiss an appeal to which this rule applies for want of prosecution and may deal with any question of costs arising out of the dismissal or withdrawal of an appeal.

(6) Any order or decision granting or varying an order (or refusing to do so) in proceedings in which an application is made in accordance with rule 3.8 for –

    (*a*) an occupation order as described in section 33(4) of the Family Law Act 1996,
    (*b*) an occupation order containing any of the provisions specified in section 33(3) where the applicant or the respondent has matrimonial home rights, or
    (*c*) a transfer of tenancy,

shall be treated as a final order for the purposes of CCR Order 37, rule 6 and, on an appeal from such an order, the judge may exercise his own discretion in substitution for that of the district judge and the provisions of CCR Order 37, rule 6 shall apply.

8.2 Appeals under Domestic Proceedings and Magistrates' Courts Act 1978

(1) Subject to paragraph (9) below, every appeal to the High Court under the Domestic Proceedings and Magistrates' Courts Act 1978 shall be heard by a Divisional Court of the Family Division and shall be entered by lodging three copies of the notice of motion in the principal registry.

(2) The notice must be served, and the appeal entered, within 6 weeks after the date of the order appealed against.

(3) Notice of the motion may be served in accordance with RSC Order 65, rule 5.

(4) On entering the appeal, or as soon as practicable thereafter, the appellant shall, unless otherwise directed, lodge in the principal registry –

(*a*) three certified copies of the summons and of the order appealed against, and of any order staying its execution,

(*b*) three copies of the clerk's notes of the evidence,

(*c*) three copies of the justices' reasons for their decision,

(*d*) a certificate that notice of the motion has been duly served on the clerk and on every party affected by the appeal, and

(*e*) where the notice of the motion includes an application to extend the time for bringing the appeal, a certificate (and a copy thereof) by the appellant's solicitor, or the appellant if he is acting in person, setting out the reasons for the delay and the relevant dates.

(5) If the clerk's notes of the evidence are not produced, the court may hear and determine the appeal on any other evidence or statement of what occurred in the proceedings before the magistrates' court as appears to the court to be sufficient.

(6) The court shall not be bound to allow the appeal on the ground merely of misdirection or improper reception or rejection of evidence unless, in the opinion of the court, substantial wrong or miscarriage of justice has been thereby occasioned.

(7) A district judge may dismiss an appeal to which this rule applies for want of prosecution or, with the consent of the parties, may dismiss the appeal or give leave for it to be withdrawn, and may deal with any question of costs arising out of the dismissal or withdrawal.

(8) Any interlocutory application in connection with or for the purpose of any appeal to which this rule applies may be heard and disposed of before a single judge.

(9) Where an appeal to which this rule applies relates only to the amount of any periodical or lump sum payment ordered to be made, it shall, unless the President otherwise directs, be heard and determined by a single judge, and in that case –

(*a*) for the references in paragraphs (1) and (4)(*a*), (*b*) and (*c*) to three copies of the documents therein mentioned there shall be substituted references to one copy;

(*b*) the parties may agree in writing or the President may direct that the appeal be heard and determined at a divorce town.

8.3 Appeals under section 13 of the Administration of Justice Act 1960

Proceedings within paragraph 3(*d*) of Schedule 1 to the Supreme Court Act 1981 shall be heard and determined by a Divisional Court of the Family Division and rule 8.2(4) shall apply, with the necessary modifications, to such proceedings.

PART IX
DISABILITY

9.1 Interpretation and application of Part IX

(1) In this Part –

"patient" means a person who, by reason of mental disorder within the meaning of the Mental Health Act 1983, is incapable of managing and administering his property and affairs;

"person under disability" means a person who is a minor or a patient;

"Part VII" means Part VII of the Mental Health Act 1983.

(2) So far as they relate to minors who are the subject of applications, the provisions of this Part of these rules shall not apply to proceedings which are specified proceedings within the meaning of section 41(6) of the Children Act 1989 and, with respect to proceedings which are dealt with together with specified proceedings, this Part shall have effect subject to the said section 41 and Part IV of these rules.

(3) Rule 9.2A shall apply only to proceedings under the Act of 1989 or the inherent jurisdiction of the High Court with respect to minors.

9.2 Person under disability must sue by next friend etc

(1) Except where rule 9.2A or any other rule otherwise provides, a person under disability may begin and prosecute any family proceedings only by his next friend and may defend any such proceedings only by his guardian ad litem and, except as otherwise provided by this rule, it shall not be necessary for a guardian ad litem to be appointed by the court.

(2) No person's name shall be used in any proceedings as next friend of a person under disability unless he is the Official Solicitor or the documents mentioned in paragraph (7) have been filed.

(3) Where a person is authorised under Part VII to conduct legal proceedings in the name of a patient or on his behalf, that person shall, subject to paragraph (2) be entitled to be next friend or guardian ad litem of the patient in any family proceedings to which his authority extends.

(4) Where a person entitled to defend any family proceedings is a patient and there is no person authorised under Part VII to defend the proceedings in his name or on his behalf, then –

    (*a*) the Official Solicitor shall, if he consents, be the patient's guardian ad litem, but at any stage of the proceedings an application may be made on not less than four days' notice to the Official Solicitor, for the appointment of some other person as guardian;

    (*b*) in any other case, an application may be made on behalf of the patient for the appointment of a guardian ad litem;

and there shall be filed in support of any application under this paragraph the documents mentioned in paragraph (7).

(5) Where a petition, answer, originating application or originating summons has been served on a person whom there is reasonable ground for believing to be a person under disability and no notice of intention to defend has been given, or answer or affidavit in answer filed, on his behalf, the party at whose instance the document was served shall, before taking any further steps in the proceedings, apply to a district judge for directions as to whether a guardian ad litem should be appointed to act for that person in the cause, and on any such application the district judge may, if he considers it necessary in order to protect the interests of the person served, order that some proper person be appointed his guardian ad litem.

(6) Except where a minor is prosecuting or defending proceedings under rule 9.2A, no notice of intention to defend shall be given, or answer or affidavit in answer filed, by or on behalf of a person under disability unless the person giving the notice or filing the answer or affidavit –

    (*a*) is the Official Solicitor or, in a case to which paragraph (4) applies, is the Official Solicitor or has been appointed by the court to be guardian ad litem; or

    (*b*) in any other case, has filed the documents mentioned in paragraph (7).

(7) The documents referred to in paragraphs (2), (4) and (6) are –

    (*a*) a written consent to act by the proposed next friend or guardian ad litem;

(b) where the person under disability is a patient and the proposed next friend or guardian ad litem is authorised under Part VII to conduct the proceedings in his name or on his behalf, an office copy, sealed with the seal of the Court of Protection, of the order or other authorisation made or given under Part VII; and

(c) except where the proposed next friend or guardian ad litem is authorised as mentioned in sub-paragraph (b), a certificate by the solicitor acting for the person under disability –

    (i) that he knows or believes that the person to whom the certificate relates is a minor or patient, stating (in the case of a patient) the grounds of his knowledge or belief and, where the person under disability is a patient, that there is no person authorised as aforesaid, and

    (ii) that the person named in the certificate as next friend or guardian ad litem has no interest in the cause or matter in question adverse to that of the person under disability and that he is a proper person to be next friend or guardian.

9.2A Certain minors may sue without next friend etc

(1) Where a person entitled to begin, prosecute or defend any proceedings to which this rule applies, is a minor to whom this Part applies, he may subject to paragraph (4), begin, prosecute or defend, as the case may be, such proceedings without a next friend or guardian ad litem –

(a) where he has obtained the leave of the court for that purpose; or

(b) where a solicitor –

    (i) considers that the minor is able, having regard to his understanding, to give instructions in relation to the proceedings; and

    (ii) has accepted instructions from the minor to act for him in the proceedings and, where the proceedings have begun, is so acting.

(2) A minor shall be entitled to apply for the leave of the court under paragraph (1)(a) without a next friend or guardian ad litem either –

(a) by filing a written request for leave setting out the reasons for the application, or

(b) by making an oral request for leave at any hearing in the proceedings.

(3) On considering a request for leave filed under paragraph (2)(a), the court shall either –

(a) grant the request, whereupon the proper officer shall communicate the decision to the minor and, where the leave relates to the prosecution or defence of existing proceedings, to the other parties to those proceedings, or

(b) direct that the request be heard ex parte, whereupon the proper officer shall fix a date for such a hearing and give to the minor making the request such notice of the date so fixed as the court may direct.

(4) Where a minor has a next friend or guardian ad litem in proceedings and the minor wishes to prosecute or defend the remaining stages of the proceedings without a next friend or guardian ad litem, the minor may apply to the court for leave for that purpose and for the removal of the next friend or guardian ad litem; and paragraph (2) shall apply to the application as if it were an application under paragraph (1)(a).

(5) On considering a request filed under paragraph (2) by virtue of paragraph (4), the court shall either –

(a) grant the request, whereupon the proper officer shall communicate the decision to the minor and next friend or guardian ad litem concerned and to all other parties to the proceedings, or

(b) direct that the request be heard, whereupon the proper officer shall fix a date for such a hearing and give to the minor and next friend or guardian ad litem concerned such notice of the date so fixed as the court may direct;

provided that the court may act under sub-paragraph (*a*) only if it is satisfied that the next friend or guardian ad litem does not oppose the request.

(6) Where the court is considering whether to –

    (*a*) grant leave under paragraph (1)(*a*), or
    (*b*) grant leave under paragraph (4) and remove a next friend or guardian ad litem,

it shall grant the leave sought and, as the case may be, remove the next friend or guardian ad litem if it considers that the minor concerned has sufficient understanding to participate as a party in the proceedings concerned or proposed without a next friend or guardian ad litem.

(6A) In exercising its powers under paragraph (6) the court may order the next friend or guardian ad litem to take such part in the proceedings as the court may direct.

(7) Where a request for leave is granted at a hearing fixed under paragraph (3)(*b*) (in relation to the prosecution or defence of proceedings already begun) or (5)(*b*), the proper officer shall forthwith communicate the decision to the other parties to the proceedings.

(8) The court may revoke any leave granted under paragraph (1)(*a*) where it considers that the child does not have sufficient understanding to participate as a party in the proceedings concerned without a next friend or guardian ad litem.

(9) Without prejudice to any requirement of CCR Order 50, rule 5 or RSC Order 67, where a solicitor is acting for a minor in proceedings which the minor is prosecuting or defending without a next friend or guardian ad litem by virtue of paragraph (1)(*b*) and either of the conditions specified in the paragraph (1)(*b*)(i) and (ii) cease to be fulfilled, he shall forthwith so inform the court.

(10) Where –

    (*a*) the court revokes any leave under paragraph (8), or
    (*b*) either of the conditions specified in paragraph (1)(*b*)(i) and (ii) is no longer fulfilled,

the court may, if it considers it necessary in order to protect the interests of the minor concerned, order that some proper person be appointed his next friend or guardian ad litem.

(11) Where a minor is of sufficient understanding to begin, prosecute or defend proceedings without a next friend or guardian ad litem –

    (*a*) he may nevertheless begin, prosecute or defend them by his next friend or guardian ad litem; and
    (*b*) where he is prosecuting or defending proceedings by his next friend or guardian ad litem, the respective powers and duties of the minor and next friend or guardian ad litem, except those conferred or imposed by this rule shall not be affected by the minor's ability to dispense with a next friend or guardian ad litem under the provisions of this rule.

9.3 Service on person under disability

(1) Where a document to which rule 2.9 applies is required to be served on a person under disability, it shall be served –

    (*a*) in the case of a minor who is not also a patient, on his father or guardian or, if he has no father or guardian, on the person with whom he resides or in whose care he is;
    (*b*) in the case of a patient –

(i) on the person (if any) who is authorised under Part VII to conduct in the name of the patient or on his behalf the proceedings in connection with which the document is to be served, or

(ii) if there is no person so authorised, on the Official Solicitor if he has consented under rule 9.2(4) to be the guardian ad litem of the patient, or

(iii) in any other case, on the person with whom the patient resides or in whose care he is:

Provided that the court may order that a document which has been, or is to be served on the person under disability or on a person other than one mentioned in sub-paragraph (*a*) or (*b*) shall be deemed to be duly served on the person under disability.

(2) Where a document is served in accordance with paragraph (1) it shall be indorsed with a notice in Form M24; and after service has been effected the person at whose instance the document was served shall, unless the Official Solicitor is the guardian ad litem of the person under disability or the court otherwise directs, file an affidavit by the person on whom the document was served stating whether the contents of the document were, or its purport was, communicated to the person under disability and, if not, the reasons for not doing so.

9.4 Petition for nullity on ground of mental disorder

(1) Where a petition for nullity has been presented on the ground that at the time of the marriage the respondent was suffering from mental disorder within the meaning of the Mental Health Act 1983 of such a kind or to such an extent as to be unfitted for marriage, then, whether or not the respondent gives notice of intention to defend, the petitioner shall not proceed with the cause without the leave of the district judge.

(2) The district judge by whom an application for leave is heard may make it a condition of granting leave that some proper person be appointed to act as guardian ad litem of the respondent.

9.5 Separate representation of children

(1) Without prejudice to rules 2.57 and 9.2A, if in any family proceedings it appears to the court that it is in the best interests of any child to be made a party to the proceedings, the court may appoint –

(*a*) an officer of the service;

(*b*) (if he consents) the Official Solicitor; or

(*c*) (if he consents) some other proper person,

to be the guardian ad litem of the child with authority to take part in the proceedings on the child's behalf.

(2) An order under paragraph (1) may be made by the court of its own motion or on the application of a party to the proceedings or of the proposed guardian ad litem.

(3) The court may at any time direct that an application be made by a party for an order under paragraph (1) and may stay the proceedings until the application has been made.

(4) (*revoked*)

(5) Unless otherwise directed, a person appointed under this rule or rule 2.57 to be the guardian ad litem of a child in any family proceedings shall be treated as a party for the purpose of any provision of these rules requiring a document to be served on or notice to be given to a party to the proceedings.

(6) Where the guardian ad litem appointed under this rule is an officer of the service, rules 4.11 and 4.11A shall apply to him as they apply to a children's guardian appointed under section 41 of the Children Act 1989.

PART X
PROCEDURE (GENERAL)

10.1 Application

The provisions of this Part apply to all family proceedings, but have effect subject to the provisions of any other Part of these rules.

10.2 Service on solicitors

(1) Where a document is required by these rules to be sent to any person who is acting by a solicitor, service shall, subject to any other direction or order, be effected –

    (*a*) by sending the document by first class post to the solicitor's address for service; or

    (*b*) where that address includes a numbered box at a document exchange, at that document exchange or at a document exchange which transmits documents every business day to that document exchange; or

    (*c*) by fax (as defined by RSC Order 1, rule 4(1)) in accordance with the provisions of RSC Order 65, rule 5(2B).

(2) Any document which is left at a document exchange in accordance with paragraph (1)(*b*) shall, unless the contrary is proved, be deemed to have been served on the second day after the day on which it is left.

(3) Where no other mode of service is prescribed, directed or ordered, service may additionally be effected by leaving the document at the solicitor's address.

10.3 Service on person acting in person

(1) Subject to paragraph (3) and to any other direction or order, where a document is required by these rules to be sent to any person who is acting in person, service shall be effected by sending the document by first class post to the address given by him or, if he has not given an address for service, to his last known address.

(2) Subject to paragraph (3), where no other mode of service is prescribed, directed or ordered, service may additionally be effected by delivering the document to him or by leaving it at the address specified in paragraph (1).

(3) Where it appears to the district judge that it is impracticable to deliver the document to the person to be served and that, if the document were left at or sent by post to, the address specified in paragraph (1) it would be unlikely to reach him, the district judge may dispense with service of the document.

10.4 Service by bailiff in proceedings in principal registry

Where, in any proceedings pending in the principal registry which are treated as pending in a divorce county court, a document is to be served by bailiff, it shall be sent for service to the proper officer of the county court within the district of which the document is to be served.

10.5 Proof of service by officer of court etc

(1) Where a petition is sent to any person by an officer of the court, he shall note the date of posting in the records of the court.

(2) Without prejudice to section 133 of the County Court Act 1984 (proof of service of summonses etc) a record made pursuant to paragraph (1) shall be evidence of the facts stated therein.

(3) Where the court has authorised notice by advertisement to be substituted for service and the advertisement has been inserted by some person other than the proper officer, that person shall file copies of the newspapers containing the advertisement.

10.6 Service out of England and Wales

(1) Any document in family proceedings may be served out of England and Wales without leave either in the manner prescribed by these rules or –

- (*a*) where the proceedings are pending in the High Court, in accordance with RSC Order 11, rules 5 and 6 (which relates to the service of a writ abroad); or
- (*b*) where the proceedings are pending in a divorce county court, in accordance with CCR Order 8, rules 8 to 10 (which relate to the service of process abroad).

(2) Where the document is served in accordance with RSC Order 11, rules 5 and 6, those rules and rule 8 of the said Order 11 (which deals with expenses incurred by the Secretary of State) shall have effect in relation to service of the document as they have effect in relation to service of notice of a writ, except that the official certificate of service referred to in paragraph (5) of the said rule 5 shall, if the document was served personally, show the server's means of knowledge of the identity of the person served.

(3) Where the document is served in accordance with CCR Order 8, rules 8 to 10, those rules shall have effect subject to the following modifications –

- (*a*) the document need not be served personally on the person required to be served so long as it is served in accordance with the law of the country in which service is effected;
- (*b*) the official certificate or declaration with regard to service referred to in paragraph (6) of the said rule 10 shall, if the document was served personally, show the server's means of knowledge of the identity of the person served; and
- (*c*) in paragraph (7) of the said rule 10 the words "or in the manner in which default summonses are required to be served" shall be omitted.

(4) Where a petition is to be served on a person out of England and Wales, then –

- (*a*) the time within which that person must give notice of intention to defend shall be determined having regard to the practice adopted under RSC Order 11, rule 4(4) (which requires an order for leave to serve a writ out of the jurisdiction to limit the time for appearance) and the notice in Form M5 shall be amended accordingly;
- (*b*) if the petition is to be served otherwise than in accordance with RSC Order 11, rules 5 and 6, or CCR Order 8, rules 8 to 10, and there is reasonable ground for believing that the person to be served does not understand English, the petition shall be accompanied by a translation, approved by the district judge, of the notice in Form M5, in the official language of the country in which service is to be effected or, if there is more than one official language of that country, in any one of those languages which is appropriate to the place where service is to be effected; but this sub-paragraph shall not apply in relation to a document which is to be served in a country in which the official language, or one of the official languages, is English.

(5) Where a document specifying the date of hearing of any proceedings is to be served out of England and Wales, the date shall be fixed having regard to the time which would

be limited under paragraph (4)(*a*) for giving notice of intention to defend if the document were a petition.

10.7 Mode of giving notice

Unless otherwise directed, any notice which is required by these rules to be given to any person shall be in writing and, may be given in any manner in which service may be effected under RSC Order 65, rule 5.

10.8 Notice of intention to defend

(1) In these rules any reference to a notice of intention to defend is a reference to an acknowledgement of service in Form M6 containing a statement to the effect that the person by whom or on whose behalf it is signed intends to defend the proceedings to which the acknowledgement relates, and any reference to giving notice of intention to defend is a reference to returning such a notice to the court office.

(2) In relation to any person on whom there is served a document requiring or authorising an acknowledgement of service to be returned to the court office, references in these rules to the time limited for giving notice of intention to defend are references –

(*a*) to seven days after service of the document, in the case of notice of intention to defend a petition under Part II of these rules, and

(*b*) in any other case, to 14 days or such other time as may be fixed.

(3) Subject to paragraph (2) a person may give notice of intention to defend notwithstanding that he has already returned to the court office an acknowledgement of service not constituting such a notice.

10.9 Mode of making applications

Except where these rules, or any rules applied by these rules, otherwise provide, every application in family proceedings –

(*a*) shall be made to a district judge;

(*b*) shall, if the proceedings are pending in the High Court, be made by summons or, if the proceedings are pending in a divorce county court, be made in accordance with CCR Order 13, rule 1 (which deals with applications in the course of proceedings).

10.10 Orders for transfer of family proceedings

(1) Where a cause is pending in the High Court, the district judge of the registry in which the cause is pending or a judge may order that the cause be transferred to another registry.

(2) Where a cause is pending in a divorce county court, the court may order that the cause be transferred to another divorce county court.

(3) Paragraphs (1) and (2) shall apply to applications in causes as they apply to causes; but before making an order for transfer of an application the court shall consider whether it would be more convenient to transfer the cause under paragraph (1) or (2), as the case may be.

(4) The court shall not, either of its own motion or on the application of any party, make an order under paragraph (1), (2) or (3) unless the parties have either –

(*a*) had an opportunity of being heard on the question, or

(*b*) consented to such an order.

(5) Where the parties, or any of them, desire to be heard on the question of a transfer, the court shall give the parties notice of a date, time and place at which the question will be considered.

(6) Paragraphs (4) and (5) shall apply with the necessary modifications to an order for the transfer of family proceedings under section 38 or 39 of the Act of 1984 as they apply to an order under paragraph (1) or (2) of this rule.

(7) Paragraphs (4) and (5) shall not apply where the court makes an order for transfer under paragraphs (1), (2) or (3) in compliance with the provisions of any Order made under Part I of Schedule 11 to the Children Act 1989.

10.11 Procedure on transfer of cause or application

(1) Where any cause or application is ordered to be transferred from one court or registry to another, the proper officer of the first-mentioned court or registry shall, unless otherwise directed, give notice of the transfer to the parties.

(2) Any provision in these rules, or in any order made or notice given pursuant to these rules, for the transfer of proceedings between a divorce county court and the High Court shall, in relation to proceedings which, after the transfer, are to continue in the principal registry, be construed –

 (*a*) in the case of a transfer from the High Court to a divorce county court, as a provision for the proceedings to be treated as pending in a divorce county court, and

 (*b*) in the case of a transfer from a divorce county court to the High Court, as a provision for the proceedings no longer to be treated as pending in a divorce county court.

(3) Proceedings transferred from a divorce county court to the High Court pursuant to any provision in these rules shall, unless the order of transfer otherwise directs, proceed in the registry nearest to the divorce county court from which they are transferred, but nothing in this paragraph shall prejudice any power under these rules to order the transfer of the proceedings to a different registry.

10.12 Evidence by affidavit

On any application made –

 (*a*) in a county court, by originating application or in accordance with CCR Order 13, rule 1 (which deals with applications in the course of proceedings), or

 (*b*) in the High Court, by originating summons, notice or motion,

evidence may be given by affidavit unless these rules otherwise provide or the court otherwise directs, but the court may, on the application of any party, order the attendance for cross-examination of the person making any such affidavit; and where, after such an order has been made, that person does not attend, his affidavit shall not be used as evidence without the leave of the court.

10.13 Taking of affidavit in county court proceedings

In relation to family proceedings pending or treated as pending in a divorce county court, section 58(1) of the County Courts Act 1984 shall have effect as if after paragraph (*c*) there were inserted the following words –

  "or

 (*d*) a district judge of the principal registry; or

(*e*) any officer of the principal registry authorised by the President under section 2 of the Commissioners for Oaths Act 1889; or

(*f*) any clerk in the Central Office of the Royal Courts of Justice authorised to take affidavits for the purposes of proceedings in the Supreme Court.".

10.14 Evidence of marriage outside England and Wales

(1) The celebration of a marriage outside England and Wales and its validity under the law of the country where it was celebrated may, in any family proceedings in which the existence and validity of the marriage is not disputed, be proved by the evidence of one of the parties to the marriage and the production of a document purporting to be –

(*a*) a marriage certificate or similar document issued under the law in force in that country; or

(*b*) a certified copy of an entry in a register of marriages kept under the law in force in that country.

(2) Where a document produced by virtue of paragraph (1) is not in English it shall, unless otherwise directed, be accompanied by a translation certified by a notary public or authenticated by affidavit.

(3) This rule shall not be construed as precluding the proof of marriage in accordance with the Evidence (Foreign, Dominion and Colonial Documents) Act 1933 or in any other manner authorised apart from this rule.

10.14A Power of court to limit cross-examination

The court may limit the issues on which an officer of the service may be cross-examined.

10.15 Official shorthand note etc of proceedings

(1) Unless the judge otherwise directs, an official shorthand note shall be taken of the proceedings at the trial in open court of every cause pending in the High Court.

(2) An official shorthand note may be taken of any other proceedings before a judge or district judge if directions for the taking of such a note are given by the Lord Chancellor.

(3) The shorthand writer shall sign the note and certify it to be a correct shorthand note of the proceedings and shall retain the note unless he is directed by the district judge to forward it to the court.

(4) On being so directed the shorthand writer shall furnish the court with a transcript of the whole or such part as may be directed of the shorthand note.

(5) Any party, any person who has intervened in a cause, the Queen's Proctor or, where a declaration of parentage has been made under section 55A of the Act of 1986, the Registrar General shall be entitled to require from the shorthand writer a transcript of the shorthand note, and the shorthand writer shall, at the request of any person so entitled, supply that person with a transcript of the whole or any part of the note on payment of the shorthand writer's charges authorised by any scheme in force providing for the taking of official shorthand notes of legal proceedings.

(6) Except as aforesaid, the shorthand writer shall not, without the permission of the court, furnish the shorthand note or a transcript of the whole or any part thereof to anyone.

(7) In these Rules references to a shorthand note include references to a record of the proceedings made by mechanical means and in relation to such a record references to the shorthand writer shall have effect as if they were references to the person responsible for transcribing the record.

10.16 Copies of decrees and orders

(1) A copy of every decree shall be sent by the proper officer to every party to the cause.

(2) A sealed or other copy of a decree or order made in open court shall be issued to any person requiring it on payment of the prescribed fee.

10.17 Service of order

(1) Where an order made in family proceedings has been drawn up, the proper officer of the court where the order is made shall, unless otherwise directed, send a copy of the order to every party affected by it.

(2) Where a party against whom the order is made is acting by a solicitor, a copy may, if the district judge thinks fit, be sent to that party as if he were acting in person, as well as to his solicitor.

(3) It shall not be necessary for the person in whose favour the order was made to prove that a copy of the order has reached any other party to whom it is required to be sent.

(4) This rule is without prejudice to RSC Order 45, rule 7 (which deals with the service of an order to do or abstain from doing an act), CCR Order 29, rule 1 (which deals with orders enforceable by committal) and any other rule or enactment for the purposes of which an order is required to be served in a particular way.

10.18 No notice of intention to proceed after year's delay

RSC Order 3, rule 6 (which requires a party to give notice of intention to proceed after a year's delay) shall not apply to any proceedings pending in the High Court.

10.19 Filing of documents at place of hearing etc

Where the file of any family proceedings has been sent from one divorce county court or registry to another for the purpose of a hearing or for some other purpose, any document needed for that purpose and required to be filed shall be filed in the other court or registry.

10.20 Inspection etc of documents retained in court

(1) Subject to rule 10.21, a party to any family proceedings or his solicitor or the Queen's Proctor or a person appointed under rule 2.57 or 9.5 to be the guardian ad litem of a child in any family proceedings may have a search made for, and may inspect and bespeak a copy of, any document filed or lodged in the court office in those proceedings.

(2) Any person not entitled to a copy of a document under paragraph (1) above who intends to make an application under the Hague Convention (as defined in section 1(1) of the Child Abduction and Custody Act 1985) in a Contracting State (as defined in section 2 of that Act) other than the United Kingdom shall, if he satisfies the court that he intends to make such an application, be entitled to obtain a copy bearing the seal of the court of any order relating to the custody of the child in respect of whom the application is to be made.

(3) Except as provided by rules 2.36(4) and 3.16(10) and paragraphs (1) and (2) of this rule, no document filed or lodged in the court office other than a decree or order made in open court shall be open to inspection by any person without the leave of the district judge, and no copy of any such document, or of an extract from any such document, shall be taken by, or issued to, any person without such leave.

10.21 Disclosure of addresses

(1) Subject to rule 2.3 nothing in these rules shall be construed as requiring any party to reveal the address of their private residence (or that of any child) save by order of the court.

(2) Where a party declines to reveal an address in reliance upon paragraph (1) above, he shall give notice of that address to the court in Form C8 and that address shall not be revealed to any person save by order of the court.

10.21A Disclosure of information under the Act of 1991

Where the Secretary of State requires a person mentioned in regulation 2(2) or (3)(*a*) of the Child Support (Information, Evidence and Disclosure) Regulations 1992 to furnish information or evidence for a purpose mentioned in regulation 3(1) of those Regulations, nothing in rules 4.23 (confidentiality of documents), 10.20 (inspection etc of documents in court) or 10.21 (disclosure of addresses) shall prevent that person from furnishing the information or evidence sought or require him to seek leave of the court before doing so.

10.22 Practice to be observed in district registries and divorce county courts

(1) The President and the senior district judge may, with the concurrence of the Lord Chancellor, issue directions for the purpose of securing in the district registries and the divorce county courts due observance of statutory requirements and uniformity of practice in family proceedings.

(2) RSC Order 63, rule 11 (which requires the practice of the Central Office to be followed in the district registries) shall not apply to family proceedings.

10.23 Transitional provisions

(1) Subject to paragraph (2) below, these rules shall apply, so far as practicable, to any proceedings pending on the day on which they come into force.

(2) Rule 8.1 shall not apply to an appeal from an order or decision made or given by a district judge in matrimonial proceedings in a divorce county court where notice of appeal has been filed before the day on which these rules come into force.

(3) Where, by reason of paragraph (1) above, these rules do not apply to particular proceedings pending on the day on which they come into force, the rules in force immediately before that day shall continue to apply to those proceedings.

(4) Nothing in this rule shall be taken as prejudicing the operation of the provisions of the Interpretation Act 1978 as regards the effect of repeals.

(5) Without prejudice to the generality of paragraph (1) above (and for the avoidance of doubt) rule 2.39 shall not apply to any proceedings which are pending within the meaning of paragraph 1(1) of Schedule 14 to the Children Act 1989.

10.24 Applications for relief which is precluded by the Act of 1991

(1) Where an application is made for an order which, in the opinion of the district judge, the court would be prevented from making by section 8 or 9 of the Act of 1991, the proper officer may send a notice in Form M34 to the applicant.

(2) In the first instance, the district judge shall consider the matter under paragraph (1) himself, without holding a hearing.

(3) Where a notice is sent under paragraph (1), no requirement of these rules, except for those of this rule, as to the service of the application by the proper officer or as to any other procedural step to follow the making of an application of the type in question, shall apply unless and until the court directs that they shall apply or that they shall apply to such extent and subject to such modifications as may be specified in the direction.

(4) Where an applicant who has been sent a notice under paragraph (1) informs the proper officer in writing, within 14 days of the date of the notice, that he wishes to persist with his application, the proper officer shall refer the matter to the district judge for action in accordance with paragraph (5).

(5) Where the district judge acts in accordance with this paragraph, he shall give such directions as he considers appropriate for the matter to be heard and determined by the court and, without prejudice to the generality of the foregoing, such directions may provide for the hearing to be ex parte.

(6) Where directions are given under paragraph (5), the proper officer, shall inform the applicant of the directions and, in relation to the other parties, –

    (*a*) send them a copy of the application;
    (*b*) where the hearing is to be ex parte, inform them briefly –
        (i) of the nature and effect of the notice under this rule,
        (ii) that the matter is being resolved ex parte, and
        (iii) that they will be informed of the result in due course; and
    (*c*) where the hearing is to be inter partes, inform them of –
        (i) the circumstances which led to the directions being given, and
        (ii) the directions.

(7) Where a notice has been sent under paragraph (1) and the proper officer is not informed under paragraph (4), the application shall be treated as having been withdrawn.

(8) Where the matter is heard pursuant to directions under paragraph (5) and the court determines that it would be prevented by section 8 or 9 of the Act of 1991 from making the order sought by the application, it shall dismiss the application.

(9) Where the court dismisses an application under this rule it shall give its reasons in writing, copies of which shall be sent to the parties by the proper officer.

(10) In this rule, "the matter" means the question whether the making of an order in the terms sought by the application would be prevented by section 8 or 9 of the Act of 1991.

10.25 Modification of rule 10.24 in relation to non-free-standing applications

Where a notice is sent under rule 10.24(1) in respect of an application which is contained in a petition or other document ("the document") which contains material extrinsic to the application –

    (*a*) the document shall, until the contrary is directed under sub-paragraph (*c*) of this rule, be treated as if it did not contain the application in respect of which the notice was served;
    (*b*) the proper officer shall, when he sends copies of the document to the respondents under any provision of these rules, attach a copy of the notice under rule 10.24(1) and a notice informing the respondents of the effect of sub-paragraph (*a*) of this paragraph; and
    (*c*) if it is determined, under rule 10.24, that the court would not be prevented, by section 8 or 9 of the Act of 1991, from making the order sought by the application, the court shall direct that the document shall be treated as if it contained the application, and it may give such directions as it considers appropriate for the conduct of the proceedings in consequence of that direction.

10.26 Human Rights Act 1998

(1) In this rule –

"originating document" means a petition, application, originating application, originating summons or other originating process;

"answer" means an answer or other document filed or served by a party in reply to an originating document (but not an acknowledgement of service);

"Convention right" has the same meaning as in the Human Rights Act 1998;

"declaration of incompatibility" means a declaration of incompatibility under section 4 of the Human Rights Act 1998.

(2) A party who seeks to rely on any provision of or right arising under the Human Rights Act 1998 or seeks a remedy available under that Act –

(*a*) shall state that fact in his originating document or (as the case may be) answer; and

(*b*) shall in his originating document or (as the case may be) answer:

    (i) give precise details of the Convention right which it is alleged has been infringed and details of the alleged infringement;

    (ii) specify the relief sought;

    (iii) state if the relief sought includes a declaration of incompatibility.

(3) A party who seeks to amend his originating document or (as the case may be) answer to include the matters referred to in paragraph (2) shall, unless the court orders otherwise, do so as soon as possible and in any event not less than 28 days before the hearing.

(4) The court shall not make a declaration of incompatibility unless 21 days' notice, or such other period of notice as the court directs, has been given to the Crown.

(5) Where notice has been given to the Crown a Minister, or other person permitted by the Human Rights Act 1998, shall be joined as a party on giving notice to the court.

(6) Where a party has included in his originating document or (as the case may be) answer:

(*a*) a claim for a declaration of incompatibility, or

(*b*) an issue for the court to decide which may lead to the court considering making a declaration of incompatibility,

then the court may at any time consider whether notice should be given to the Crown as required by the Human Rights Act 1998 and give directions for the content and service of the notice.

(7) In the case of an appeal for which permission to appeal is required, the court shall, unless it decides that it is appropriate to do so at another stage in the proceedings, consider the issues and give the directions referred to in paragraph (6) when deciding whether to give such permission.

(8) If paragraph (7) does not apply, and a hearing for directions would, but for this rule, be held, the court shall, unless it decides that it is appropriate to do so at another stage in the proceedings, consider the issues and give the directions referred to in paragraph (6) at the hearing for directions.

(9) If neither paragraph (7) nor paragraph (8) applies, the court shall consider the issues and give the directions referred to in paragraph (6) when it considers it appropriate to do so, and may fix a hearing for this purpose.

(10) Where a party amends his originating document or (as the case may be) answer to include any matter referred to in paragraph (6)(*a*), then the court will consider whether notice should be given to the Crown and give directions for the content and service of the notice.

(11) In paragraphs (12) to (16), "notice" means the notice given under paragraph (4).

(12) The notice shall be served on the person named in the list published under section 17 of the Crown Proceedings Act 1947.

(13) The notice shall be in the form directed by the court.

(14) Unless the court orders otherwise, the notice shall be accompanied by the directions given by the court and the originating document and any answers in the proceedings.

(15) Copies of the notice shall be served on all the parties.

(16) The court may require the parties to assist in the preparation of the notice.

(17) Unless the court orders otherwise, the Minister or other person permitted by the Human Rights Act 1998 to be joined as a party shall, if he wishes to be joined, give notice of his intention to be joined as a party to the court and every other party, and where the Minister has nominated a person to be joined as a party the notice must be accompanied by the written nomination.

(18) Where a claim is made under section 7(1) of the Human Rights Act 1998 in respect of a judicial act the procedure in paragraphs (6) to (17) shall also apply, but the notice to be given to the Crown:

> (*a*) shall be given to the Lord Chancellor and shall be served on the Treasury Solicitor on his behalf; and
> (*b*) shall also give details of the judicial act which is the subject of the claim and of the court that made it.

(19) Where in any appeal a claim is made under section 7(1) of that Act and section 9(3) and 9(4) applies –

> (*a*) that claim must be set out in the notice of appeal; and
> (*b*) notice must be given to the Crown in accordance with paragraph (18).

(20) The appellant must in a notice of appeal to which paragraph (19)(*a*) applies –

> (*a*) state that a claim is being made under section 7(1) of the Human Rights Act 1998 in respect of a judicial act and section 9(3) of that Act applies; and
> (*b*) give details of –
>> (i) the Convention right which it is alleged has been infringed;
>> (ii) the infringement;
>> (iii) the judicial act complained of; and
>> (iv) the court which made it.

(21) Where paragraph (19) applies and the appropriate person (as defined in section 9(5) of the Human Rights Act 1998) has not applied within 21 days, or such other period as the court directs, after the notice is served to be joined as a party, the court may join the appropriate person as a party.

(22) On any application or appeal concerning –

> (*a*) a committal order;
> (*b*) a refusal to grant habeas corpus; or
> (*c*) a secure accommodation order made under section 25 of the Act of 1989,

if the court ordering the release of the person concludes that his Convention rights have been infringed by the making of the order to which the application or appeal relates, the judgment or order should so state, but if the court does not do so, that failure will not prevent another court from deciding the matter.

Appendix 1

Forms

M1	Statement of Information for a Consent Order
M2	General Heading of Proceedings
M3	Certificate with Regard to Reconciliation
M4	Statement of Arrangements for Children
M5	Notice of Proceedings
M6	Acknowledgement of Service
M7	Affidavit by Petitioner in Support of Petition
M8	Notice of Application for Decree Nisi to be made Absolute
M9	Certificate of Making Decree Nisi Absolute (Divorce)
M10	Certificate of Making Decree Nisi Absolute (Nullity)
M16	Request for Issue of Judgment Summons
M17	Judgment Summons
M19	Originating Application on Ground of Failure to Provide Reasonable Maintenance
M20	Notice of Application Under Rule 3.1 or 3.2
M21	Originating Application for Alteration of Maintenance Agreement during Parties' Lifetime
M22	Originating Application for Alteration of Maintenance Agreement after Death of One of the Parties
M23	Originating Summons Under Section 17 of the Married Women's Property Act 1882 or Section 1 of the Matrimonial Homes Act 1967
M24	Notice to be indorsed on Document Served in Accordance with Rule 9.3
M25	Ex Parte Originating Summons Under Section 13 of the Matrimonial and Family Proceedings Act 1984
M26	Originating Summons Under Section 12 of the Matrimonial and Family Proceedings Act 1984
M27	Originating Summons Under Section 24 of the Matrimonial and Family Proceedings Act 1984
M28	Notice of Proceedings and Acknowledgement of Service
M29	Declaration as to Marital Status Under Section 56(1)(*a*) of the Family Law Act 1986
M30	Declaration as to Parentage Under Section 55A of the Family Law Act 1986
M31	Declaration as to Legitimacy or Legitimation Under Section 56(1)(*b*) and (2) of the Family Law Act 1986
M32	Declaration as to an Adoption Effected Overseas under Section 57 of the Family Law Act 1986
M33	Application for registration of Maintenance Order in a Magistrates' Court
M34	Notice under rule 10.24(1)
C1	Application for an order
C2	Application for an order or directions in existing family proceedings
	Application to be joined as, or cease to be, a party in existing family proceedings
	Application for leave to commence proceedings
C3	Application for an order authorising search for, taking charge of, and delivery of a child
C4	Application for an order for disclosure of a child's whereabouts
C6	Notice of proceedings [Hearing] [Directions Appointment] (*Notice to parties*)

C6A	Notice	of proceedings [Hearing] [Directions Appointment] (*Notice to non-parties*)
C7		Acknowledgement
C8		Confidential Address
C9	Statement	of Service
C10	Supplement	for an application for financial provision for a child or for variation of financial provision for a child
C10A	Statement	of Means
C11	Supplement	for an application for an Emergency Protection Order
C12	Supplement	For an application for a Warrant to assist a person authorised by an Emergency Protection Order
C13	Supplement	for an application for a Care or Supervision Order
C14	Supplement	for an application for authority to refuse contact with a child in care
C15	Supplement	for an application for contact with a child in care
C16	Supplement	for an application for a Child Assessment Order
C17	Supplement	for an application for an Education Supervision Order
C17A	Supplement	for an application for an extension of an Education Supervision Order
C18	Supplement	for an application for a Recovery Order
C19	Supplement	for a Warrant of Assistance
C20	Supplement	for an application for an order to hold a child in Secure Accommodation
C21	Order or direction	Blank
C22	Record	of hearing
C23	Order	Emergency Protection Order
C24	Order	Variation of an Emergency Protection Order Extension of an Emergency Protection Order Discharge of an Emergency Protection Order
C25	Warrant	To assist a person authorised by an Emergency Protection Order
C26	Order	Authority to keep a child in Secure Accommodation
C27	Order	Authority to search for another child
C28	Warrant	To assist a person to gain access to a child or entry to premises
C29	Order	Recovery of a child
C30	Order	To disclose information about the whereabouts of a missing child
C31	Order	Authorising search for, taking charge of, and delivery of a child
C32	Order	Care Order Discharge of a Care Order
C33	Order	Interim Care Order
C34	Order	Contact with a child in care Authority to refuse contact with a child in care
C35	Order	Supervision Order Interim Supervision Order
C36	Order	Substitution of a Supervision Order for a Care Order Discharge of a Supervision Order Variation of a Supervision Order Extension of a Supervision Order
C37	Order	Education Supervision Order
C38	Order	Discharge of an Education Supervision Order Extension of an Education Supervision Order

C39	Order	Child Assessment Order
C40	Direction	To undertake an investigation
C42	Order	Family Assistance Order
C43	Order	Residence Order
		Contact Order
		Specific Issue Order
		Prohibited Steps Order
C44	Order	Leave to change the surname by which a child is known
		Leave to remove a child from the United Kingdom
C45	Order	Parental Responsibility Order
		Termination of a Parental Responsibility Order
C46	Order	Appointment of a guardian
		Termination of the appointment of a guardian
C47	Order	Making or refusing the appointment of a children's guardian
		Termination of the appointment of a children's guardian
C48	Order	Appointment of a solicitor for a child
		Refusal of the appointment of a solicitor for a child
		Termination of the appointment of a solicitor for a child
C49	Order	Transfer of Proceedings to [the High Court] [a county court] [a family proceedings court]
C51		Application for a Parental Order
C52		Acknowledgement of an application for a Parental Order
C53	Order	Parental Order
C54	Notice	of Refusal of a Parental Order

FL401	Application for a non-molestation order/an occupation order
FL402	Notice of Proceedings [Hearing] [Directions Appointment]
FL403	Application to vary, extend or discharge an order in existing proceedings
FL404	Order or Direction
FL405	Record of Hearing
FL406	Power of Arrest
FL407	Application for a Warrant of Arrest
FL408	Warrant of Arrest
FL409	Remand Order
FL410	Recognizance of respondent
FL411	Recognizance of respondent's surety
FL412	Bail Notice
FL413	Hospital Order/Interim Hospital Order
FL414	Guardianship Order
FL415	Statement of Service
FL416	Notice to Mortgagees and Landlords
FL417	Transfer of proceedings to [the High Court] [a county court] [a family proceedings court]

****

Appendix 1A

Form A	Notice of [Intention to Proceed with] an Application for Ancillary Relief
Form B	Notice of an Application under Rule 2.45
Form C	Notice of a First Appointment
Form D	Notice of a Financial Dispute Resolution Appointment
Form E	Financial Statement
Form F	Notice of Allegation in Proceedings for Ancillary Relief
Form G	Notice of Response to First Appointment
Form H	Costs Estimate
Form I	Notice of Request for Periodical Payments Order at same rate as Order for Maintenance Pending Suit

****

Appendix 2

Contents of petition

(unless otherwise directed under rule 2.3)

1

Every petition other than a petition under rules 3.12, 3.13, 3.14 or 3.15 shall state –

- (*a*) the names of the parties to the marriage and the date and place of the marriage;
- (*b*) the last address at which the parties to the marriage have lived together as husband and wife;
- (*bb*) where it is alleged that the court has jurisdiction under the Council Regulation, state the grounds of jurisdiction under Article 2(1) of the Council Regulation.
- (*c*) where it is alleged that the court has jurisdiction, other than under the Council Regulation, based on domicile –
    - (i) the country in which the petitioner is domiciled, and
    - (ii) if that country is not England and Wales, the country in which the respondent is domiciled;
- (*d*) where it is alleged that the court has jurisdiction, other than under the Council Regulation, based on habitual residence –
    - (i) the country in which the petitioner has been habitually resident throughout the period of one year ending with the date of the presentation of the petition, or
    - (ii) if the petitioner has not been habitually resident in England and Wales, the country in which the respondent has been habitually resident during that period, with details in either case, including the addresses of the places of residence and the length of residence at each place;
- (*e*) the occupation and residence of the petitioner and the respondent;
- (*f*) whether there are any living children of the family and, if so –
    - (i) the number of such children and the full names (including surname) of each and his date of birth or (if it be the case) that he is over 18, and

>   (ii) in the case of each minor child over the age of 16, whether he is receiving instruction at an educational establishment or undergoing training for a trade, profession or vocation;
>
> (*g*) whether (to the knowledge of the petitioner in the case of a husband's petition), any other child now living has been born to the wife during the marriage and, if so, the full names (including surname) of the child and his date of birth or, if it be the case, that he is over 18;
>
> (*h*) if it be the case, that there is a dispute whether a living child is a child of the family;
>
> (*i*) whether or not there are or have been any other proceedings in any court in England and Wales or elsewhere with reference to the marriage or to any child of the family or between the petitioner and the respondent with reference to any property of either or both of them and, if so –
>
>>   (i) the nature of the proceedings,
>>   (ii) the date and effect of any decree or order, and
>>   (iii) in the case of proceedings with reference to the marriage, whether there has been any resumption of cohabitation since the making of the decree or order;
>
> (*ia*) whether or not there have been any applications under the Act of 1991 for a maintenance calculation in respect of any child of the family and if so –
>
>>   (i) the date of any such application, and
>>   (ii) details of the calculation made;
>
> (*j*) whether there are any proceedings continuing in any country outside England and Wales which relate to the marriage or are capable of affecting its validity or subsistence and, if so –
>
>>   (i) particulars of the proceedings, including the court in or tribunal or authority before which they were begun,
>>   (ii) the date when they were begun,
>>   (iii) the names of the parties,
>>   (iv) the date or expected date of any trial in the proceedings, and
>>   (v) such other facts as may be relevant to the question whether the proceedings on the petition should be stayed under Schedule 1 to the Domicile and Matrimonial Proceedings Act 1973;
>
>   and such proceedings shall include any which are not instituted in a court of law in that country, if they are instituted before a tribunal or other authority having power under the law having effect there to determine questions of status, and shall be treated as continuing if they have been begun and have not been finally disposed of;
>
> (*k*) where the fact on which the petition is based is five years' separation, whether any, and if so what, agreement or arrangement has been made or is proposed to be made between the parties for the support of the respondent or, as the case may be, the petitioner or any child of the family;
>
> (*l*) in the case of a petition for divorce, that the marriage has broken down irretrievably;
>
> (*m*) the fact alleged by the petitioner for the purposes of section 1(2) of the Act of 1973 or, where the petition is not for divorce or judicial separation, the ground on which relief is sought, together in any case with brief particulars of the individual facts relied on but not the evidence by which they are to be proved;
>
> (*n*) any further or other information required by such of the following paragraphs and by rule 3.11 as may be applicable.

2

A petition for a decree of nullity under section 12(*e*) or (*f*) of the Act 1973 shall state whether the petitioner was at the time of the marriage ignorant of the facts alleged.

3

A petition for a decree of presumption of death and dissolution of marriage shall state –

(*a*) the last place at which the parties to the marriage cohabited;
(*b*) the circumstances in which the parties ceased to cohabit;
(*c*) the date when and the place where the respondent was last seen or heard of; and
(*d*) the steps which have been taken to trace the respondent.

4

Every petition shall conclude with –

(*a*) a prayer setting out particulars of the relief claimed, including any claim for costs and any application for ancillary relief which it is intended to claim;
(*b*) the names and addresses of the persons who are to be served with the petition, indicating if any of them is a person under disability;
(*c*) the petitioner's address for service, which, where the petitioner sues by a solicitor, shall be the solicitor's name or firm and address. Where the petitioner, although suing in person, is receiving legal advice from a solicitor, the solicitor's name or firm and address may be given as the address for service if he agrees. In any other case, the petitioner's address for service shall be the address of any place in England and Wales to which documents for the petitioner may be delivered or sent.

Appendix 3
Notices and respondents

(i)	(ii)	(iii)	(iv)
Provision under which proceedings brought	*Minimum number of days prior to hearing or directions appointment for service under rule 4.4(1)(b)*	*Respondents*	*Persons to whom notice is to be given*
All applications.	See separate entries below	Subject to separate entries below:	Subject to separate entries below:
		every person whom the applicant believes to have parental responsibility for the child;	local authority providing accommodation for the child;
		where the child is the subject of a care order, every person whom the applicant believes to have had parental responsibility immediately prior to the making of the care order;	persons who are caring for the child at the time when the proceedings are commenced;
		in the case of an application to extend, vary or discharge an order, the parties to the proceedings leading to the order which it is sought to have extended, varied or discharged;	in the case of proceedings brought in respect of a child who is alleged to be staying in a refuge which is certificated under section 51(1) or (2), the person who is providing the refuge.
		in the case of specified proceedings, the child.	

(i)	(ii)	(iii)	(iv)
Provision under which proceedings brought	*Minimum number of days prior to hearing or directions appointment for service under rule 4.4(1)(b)*	*Respondents*	*Persons to whom notice is to be given*
Section 4(1)(*a*), 4(3), 5(1), 6(7), 8, 13(1), 16(6), 33(7), Schedule 1, paragraph 19(1) of Schedule 2, or paragraph 11(3) or 16(5) of Schedule 14.	14 days.	As for "all applications" above, and: in the case of proceedings under Schedule 1, those persons whom the applicant believes to be interested in or affected by the proceedings; in the case of an application under paragraph 11(3)(*b*) or 16(5) of Schedule 14, any person, other than the child, named in the order or directions which it is sought to discharge or vary.	As for "all applications" above, and: in the case of an application for a section 8 order, every person whom the applicant believes – (i) to be named in a court order with respect to the same child, which has not ceased to have effect, (ii) to be a party to pending proceedings in respect of the same child, or (iii) to be a person with whom the child has lived for at least 3 years prior to the application, unless, in a case to which (i) or (ii) applies, the applicant believes that the court order or pending proceedings are not relevant to the application;

(i)	(ii)	(iii)	(iv)
Provision under which proceedings brought	*Minimum number of days prior to hearing or directions appointment for service under rule 4.4(1)(b)*	*Respondents*	*Persons to whom notice is to be given*
			in the case of an application under paragraph 19(1) of Schedule 2, the parties to the proceedings leading to the care order; in the case of an application under section 5(1), the father of the child if he does not have parental responsibility.
Section 36(1), 39(1), 39(2), 39(3), 39(4), 43(1), or paragraph 6(3), 15(2) or 17(1) of Schedule 3.	7 days.	As for "all applications" above, and: in the case of an application under section 39(2) or (3), the supervisor; in the case of proceedings under paragraph 17(1) of Schedule 3, the local education authority concerned; in the case of proceedings under section 36 or paragraph 15(2) or 17(1) of Schedule 3, the child.	As for "all applications" above, and: in the case of an application for an order under section 43(1) – (i) every person whom the applicant believes to be a parent of the child, (ii) every person whom the applicant believes to be caring for the child, (iii) every person in whose favour a contact order is in force

(i)	(ii)	(iii)	(iv)
Provision under which proceedings brought	*Minimum number of days prior to hearing or directions appointment for service under rule 4.4(1)(b)*	*Respondents*	*Persons to whom notice is to be given*
			with respect to the child, and (iv) every person who is allowed to have contact with the child by virtue of an order under section 34.
Section 31, 34(2), 34(3), 34(4), 34(9) or 38(8)(*b*).	3 days.	As for "all applications" above, and: in the case of an application under section 34, the person whose contact with the child is the subject of the application.	As for "all applications" above, and: in the case of an application under section 31 – (i) every person whom the applicant believes to be a party to pending relevant proceedings in respect of the same child, and (ii) every person whom the applicant believes to be a parent without parental responsibility for the child.

(i)	(ii)	(iii)	(iv)
Provision under which proceedings brought	*Minimum number of days prior to hearing or directions appointment for service under rule 4.4(1)(b)*	*Respondents*	*Persons to whom notice is to be given*
Section 43(12).	2 days.	As for "all applications" above.	Those of the persons referred to in section 43(11)(*a*) to (*e*) who were not party to the application for the order which it is sought to have varied or discharged.
Section 25, 44(1), 44(9)(*b*), 45(4), 45(8), 46(7), 48(9), 50(1), or 102(1).	1 day.	As for 'all applications' above, and: in the case of an application under section 44(9)(*b*) – (i) the parties to the application for the order in respect of which it is sought to vary the directions;	Except for applications under section 102(1), as for 'all applications' above, and: in the case of an application under section 44(1), every person whom the applicant believes to be a parent of the child; in the case of an application under section 44(9)(*b*) –

(i)	(ii)	(iii)	(iv)
Provision under which proceedings brought	*Minimum number of days prior to hearing or directions appointment for service under rule 4.4(1)(b)*	*Respondents*	*Persons to whom notice is to be given*
		(ii) any person who was caring for the child prior to the making of the order, and (iii) any person whose contact with the child is affected by the direction which it is sought to have varied; in the case of an application under section 50, the person whom the applicant alleges to have effected or to have been or to be responsible for the taking or keeping of the child.	(i) the local authority in whose area the child is living, and (ii) any person whom the applicant believes to be affected by the direction which it is sought to have varied; in the case of an application under section 102(1), the person referred to in section 102(1) and any person preventing or likely to prevent such a person from exercising powers under enactments mentioned in subsection (6) of that section.

(i)	(ii)	(iii)	(iv)
Provision under which proceedings brought	*Minimum number of days prior to hearing or directions appointment for service under rule 4.4(1)(b)*	*Respondents*	*Persons to whom notice is to be given*
Section 30 of the Human Fertilisation and Embryology Act 1990	14 days.	The birth parents (except where the applicants seek to dispense with their agreement under section 30(6) of the Human Fertilisation and Embryology Act 1990) and any other persons or body with parental responsibility for the child at the date of the application.	Any local authority or voluntary organisation that has at any time provided accommodation for the child.

INDEX

References are to paragraph numbers, and Appendix document numbers.